DATE DUE

2 08 90	OCT 2 9 1998		
APR 25 1991	DEC 1 8 1998		
OCT 2 9 1991	DEC 2 1 1998		
DEC 1 1 1991	NOV 2 9 2000		
DEC 0 9 1991	DEC 0 2000		
DEC 1 2 1992	APR - 4 2003		
DEC 1 8 1992	AUG 1 5 2003		
DEC 1 5 1993			
APR 1 8 1994			
DEC 2 1 1995			
DEC 1 9 1995			
DEC 1 9 1996			
DEC 1 8 1997			
NOV 1 3 1998			
GAYLORD			PRINTED IN U.S.A.

HEALING THEIR WOUNDS

HEALING THEIR WOUNDS

Psychotherapy with Holocaust Survivors and Their Families

EDITED BY

PAUL MARCUS

AND

ALAN ROSENBERG

Foreword by
MARTIN S. BERGMANN

PRAEGER

New York
Westport, Connecticut
London

Copyright Acknowledgments

Excerpts reprinted with permission of The Free Press, a Division of Macmillan, Inc. from THE
FAITH AND DOUBT OF HOLOCAUST SURVIVORS by Reeve Robert Brenner. Copyright ©
1980 by Reeve Robert Brenner.

"Mourning the Yiddish Language and Some Implications for Treatment" is reprinted from
"Yankev Glatshteyn: Mourning the Yiddish Language," AMERICAN IMAGO Vol. 45, No. 3,
Fall 1988, by Janet Hadda by permission of Wayne State University Press. Copyright © 1989 by
the Association for Applied Psychoanalysis, Inc.

Excerpts from "The Holocaust Survivors' Faith and Religious Behavior and Some Implications
for Treatment" are reprinted with permission from *Holocaust and Genocide Studies*, Vol. 3, No.
4, copyright 1988, Pergamon Press plc.

Library of Congress Cataloging-in-Publication Data

Healing their wounds : psychotherapy with Holocaust survivors and their families /
   [edited by] Paul Marcus and Alan Rosenberg.
      p. cm.
   Bibliography: p.
   Includes index.
   ISBN 0–275–92948–5 (alk. paper)
     1. Holocaust survivors—Mental health.   2. Holocaust survivors—
Family relationships.   3. Psychotherapy.   I. Marcus, Paul.
II. Rosenberg, Alan, 1939– .
RC451.4.P7P79   1989
616.85'21—dc20   89–8638

Library of Congress Catalog Card Number: 89–8638
ISBN: 0-275-92948-5

First published in 1989

Praeger Publishers, One Madison Avenue, New York, NY 10010
A division of Greenwood Press, Inc.

Printed in the United States of America

The paper used in this book complies with the
Permanent Paper Standard issued by the National
Information Standards Organization (Z39.48–1984).

10 9 8 7 6 5 4 3 2 1

For Freda Wineman, who despite Auschwitz still remained capable of dignified living and loving. And to all survivors in their quest for peace of mind.

Contents

Foreword

MARTIN S. BERGMANN

The editors of this book deserve the thanks of the community of psychotherapists working with survivors, their families and children, for giving us a book that cuts across many modalities of treatment. It is characteristic of our era, that models of treatment have proliferated, and if we are to escape the biblical model of the Tower of Babel and avoid having our language confounded, such books are essential. The writers of different chapters do not address themselves to each other and yet the uncommitted therapist/reader will be able to compare their approaches and draw conclusions. I believe that he or she will obtain something of value from each one of the contributors.

The best I can do in this foreword is to give some personal reactions; my own model, that of classical psychoanalysis, congealed a long time ago and yet I enjoyed and learned a great deal from the self-psychologist Anna Ornstein. I appreciated her observation, "only when new relationships become established can the mourning and healing process begin." But I appreciated no less the way the editors brought out the differences among us, regarding the desirability of evoking that difficult phase in treatment when the therapist must be experienced by the survivor as a Nazi. Dr. Ornstein believes that with empathy on the part of the analyst, such an unconscious identification with the Nazi persecutor can be avoided. We—that is myself and my coworkers—believe that if the unconscious identification with the Nazi perpetrator is not to remain forever lodged in the unconscious of the survivor, it has to be reexperienced in the transference.

Reading Eva Fogelman's chapter evoked in me reflection on another aspect of our times. How the elimination of the natural family, and confinement to the nuclear family, have increased our loneliness. It led me to the realization that our culture found a way of counteracting this loneliness by bringing together, in the form of consciousness raising or group therapy, people who share a problem in common. Whether alcoholism, widowhood, or being the child of survivors, the sharing of a problem that one had previously to endure alone is certainly an important aspect of healing; whether it alone will suffice is a question to ponder.

Surprising and welcome to a secular Jew like myself were the chapters written by the two rabbis and the essay on the religious life of survivors written by the editors. I recalled from my student days that the expulsion of the Jews from Spain in 1492 brought about the mystical revolution associated with the teaching of the kabbalist Luria in Safed. Will another religious genius arise and explain God's silence over the murder of 6 million? These chapters forced me to rethink the whole problem of the concerned and loving God: how the first gods of mankind were the projection of man's aggression and jealousy; how the Greek gods had their human favorites and occasionally sexual partners, but on the whole remained indifferent to the fate of man; how in biblical times the Israelites forced their God to enter into a covenant in which they heard and accepted the morality of the Ten Commandments in return for God's promises never to repeat the flood and never allow his people to be destroyed. It seems that every survivor who remains religious has to work through the problem of God's silence over Auschwitz. In the meantime, I have learned that the inner reestablishment of faith is for many a sign that the process of healing is taking place, for the rabbis tell us that it is not their arguments that convinced the survivor but the deep felt wish on the part of the survivor to return emotionally to the world of the living and participate in the construction of a community. Such wishes can be respected by religious and secular Jews alike or for that matter by people of all faiths.

These were some of the thoughts reading this book evoked in me. In different readers other thoughts and reactions will be generated. The aim of my foreword is only to assure the reader that the journey through this book is worth undertaking.

Preface

The field of psychotherapy with Holocaust survivors and their families is wide-ranging and varied with a number of emergent and competing paradigms. This book offers the mental health professional the opportunity to examine this diversity of viewpoints in the professional literature. There are currently no anthologies available that focus on the psychological treatment of Holocaust survivors and their families and include the multiplicity of theoretical perspectives and therapeutic approaches that psychotherapists use in their work with this population. There have been a few collections that have provided the mental health community with illuminating insights into the nature of the survivor's trauma and symptoms and the alleged transmission of a pathological legacy to the second generation. Henry Krystal's *Massive Psychic Trauma, (1968),*[1] Bergmann and Jucovy's *Generations of the Holocaust (1982)*[2] and Luel and Marcus's *Psychoanalytic Reflections on the Holocaust: Selected Essays (1984)*[3] all provide the interested psychotherapist with a wealth of clinical vignettes, case studies, and astute observations organized and interpreted in a more or less classical psychoanalytic manner. Our anthology, by contrast, includes essays from a broad range of theoretical and therapeutic perspectives. While presenting contributions that are classically psychoanalytic in orientation, we have also incorporated articles written from self-psychological, group, family, pastoral, empirical-research and eclectic viewpoints. Finally, although some of the more prominent and senior clinicians in the field appear in this volume, we have tried to solicit articles from some of the younger workers whose views and therapeutic techniques are less well-known and often diverge in interesting ways from the more established approaches. The fact that all these materials are now available for the first time in one volume we hope will be convenient and helpful to the practicing clinician.

By organizing the chapters around broadly defined differing theoretical perspectives we hope to help the psychotherapist become more aware of areas of conceptual convergence and divergence among the experts as well as the variety of therapeutic techniques being used with this population. In this sense we are trying to promote dialogue among various therapeutic communities. In addition, by including some essays on subjects that are not usually part of the mainstream therapeutic discourse on survivors and their families we hope to sensitize mental health professionals to issues that we feel are often relevant but often largely unnoticed by therapists. The pastoral section of this volume, for instance, is likely to generate some new ideas in the therapist about the survivor's religious conflicts and post-Holocaust adjustment in the community. Finally, although this book is aimed at clinicians working with this specific population we have tried to organize the volume so that it is accessible to other clinicians who may not have first-hand experience with this population or familiarity with the main issues in the field.

Part I, "Background," orients the reader to the central issues that have evolved over the last 40 years in the literature as well as the clinical findings and current status of different therapeutic approaches. George Kren's essay gives an historical overview of how the survivor has been conceptualized in psychoanalysis and by other mental health professionals. Kren primarily uses the clinical findings on survivors as an historical source and shows how clinical perceptions have been modified as a result of changes in views about the Holocaust as an historical event. Arlene Steinberg's review of the clinical literature on survivors and their children emphasizes the very different ways psychotherapists over the years have conceptualized the survivors' symptoms and clinical intervention. She particularly stresses the fact that the earlier literature tended to focus on the psychopathology of survivors and their children while more current publications emphasize the adaptive potential and strengths of survivors and their families.

Part II, "Classical Approaches," presents two essays in the Freudian tradition. Milton Jucovy discusses the way in which the classical definition of *trauma* had to be revised in the light of subsequent observations on the effect of massive and cumulative trauma on the human organism. He then focuses on some of the major issues that can impede the therapeutic process, such as the manner in which family secrets about the Holocaust impact on treatment of survivors and their children, the special requirements of the correct timing and dosage of interpretations to this vulnerable population, and the role of metaphor in formulating interpretations of major themes. Judith Kestenberg has clarified her major concept of transposition primarily as it applies to children of survivors but also to child survivors and children of Nazis. Transposition involves simultaneously living in one's own present and in the past of one's survivor parent. In their fantasies, these patients live during the Holocaust and transpose the present into the past. Kestenberg believes that this transposition into the world of the past is an extremely important mechanism of adaption to reality for children of survivors and others, and that it is vital for therapists to be aware of this.

Part III, "Self-Psychological Views," begins with Joan Freyberg's chapter on the emerging self in the survivor family. She describes the impact of the Holocaust on the psychodynamics of its direct and indirect victims and discusses the connection between these dynamics and the special impediments faced by the second generation victims in developing individuality and autonomy. Freyberg presents, in process form, a detailed case history of a female analytic patient, illustrating the clinical techniques that were effective in achieving a distinct autonomous self in the place of a profound archaic tie to a deeply wounded mother. An interview with Anna Ornstein gives the reader an opportunity to see how a psychoanalytic self-psychologist conceptualizes such issues as the nature of the survivor's trauma, survivor guilt, incomplete mourning, and recovery, as well as issues relevant to the treatment of the second generation. We tried where appropriate to encourage Dr. Ornstein to contrast her views with the more mainstream psychoanalytic, usually Freudian, formulations as reflected in the work of Krystal, Bergmann and Jucovy, and Kestenberg.

Part IV, "Group and Family Approaches," includes a paper by Eva Fogelman who has advocated the use of traditional and innovative groups for survivors, children of survivors, generations of the Holocaust, and most recently child survivors. She shows in her chapter how, in groups for second generation and those with intergenerational composition, a group experience can be helpful in working through such delicate issues as communication about the Holocaust between survivors and their children, incomplete mourning, and conflicts about Jewish identity. Participants in these groups report a decrease in isolation and alienation and an increase in hope and a sense of community. Ester Perel and Jack Saul's chapter on family therapy with Holocaust survivor families stresses that the central theme in the formation of survivor families is the restoration of the lost family and readaptation to life. They point out that as a result of experiences of trauma, multiple losses, and the circumstances of their formation, survivor families often display a high degree of cohesion, overinvolvement among members, and enmeshment. Combining structural approaches to improve current family functioning with multigenerational approaches, they show how survivor families can be helped to come to terms with their past.

Part V, "Pastoral Perspectives," consists of two chapters by congregational rabbis who have had extensive experience with survivors in their communities within a pastoral counseling context. Gerald Skolnik's chapter focuses on how survivors' status as "survivor" impacts on them as members of the synagogue community and on those responsible for providing them with pastoral services. He discusses some of the paradoxes involved in the decision of a survivor to identify as a member of a synagogue community, such as the problem of acceptance of a rabbi as a legitimate authority figure (since he symbolizes God/faith/synagogue), all of which failed during the Holocaust. Skolnick offers a variety of practical strategies for rabbis and community leaders to implement if they are to minister to this special group within such a complex organization as the synagogue adequately. Martin Cohen suggests that the role of the rabbi is to help the survivor via immersion into the world of traditional Jewish learning to achieve in a limited and tentative way an interior sense of the demonic. He shows how through using a kabbalistic narrative the rabbi can help provide the survivor with internal imagery that can render the Holocaust experience, and its attendant admixture of grotesqueness and absurdity, more intelligible and perhaps even meaningful.

Part VI, "Empirical Studies," offers two papers that are based on research with control groups done on survivors and their offspring. Moshe Almagor and Gloria Leon, using family systems theory and data from research done in 1978–79, found that survivors as a group and their children do not manifest significant psychological disturbance. Their findings are in opposition to the received view (as personified in the psychoanalytic literature) which suggests that all, or almost all, survivors have been traumatized and psychologically scarred by their Holocaust experience. Almagor and Leon also claim that the family transmission of psychopathology in survivor families is not the universal phenomenon previously assumed and they emphasize the high degree of strength and coping ability of the families assessed. Boaz Kahana, Zev Harel, and Eva Kahana studied a large group of elderly survivors and a comparison group. They found significantly greater symptomatology among survivors than controls. Their findings are in conflict with Almagor and Leon's above-mentioned article and suggest that perhaps as survivors get older they are more vulnerable to psychological problems. However, Kahana et al. also found that survivor's social functioning was at a higher level than that of the comparison group and that many survivors had adjusted well as individuals and made substantial contributions as productive citizens in their new world. Both of these studies suggest that the psychotherapist needs to respect the heterogeneiety of the survivor and children of survivor patient population as well as cultivate a greater appreciation for the positive resources and capacity for adaptation of these populations.

Part VII, "Special Problems," is composed of several novel chapters on diverse themes, themes that have not generally received adequate scholarly attention in the psychological literature on Holocaust survivors. Robert Krell points out that the mental health community had great difficulty treating survivors as no one had witnessed such degrees of torment. Without an adequate psychological vocabulary to describe such suffering as well as a priori assumptions made by therapists that did not address the problems of survivors realistically and perhaps precluded careful listening, survivors were viewed as nearly impossible to treat. Viewing the survivor's rage as the central problematic Krell offers techniques such as memoir writing, Holocaust education, and the preparation of audiovisual testimonies to help survivors find creative expression for their rage. Paul Marcus and Alan Rosenberg, drawing from the work of Ernest Becker, discuss the problems that religious survivors face in light of the Nazi assault on their faith and religious world of meaning. They argue that psychotherapy with the survivor must more fully appreciate the deleterious psychological consequences of survivors' inability to maintain themselves as the "locus of primary value in a world of meaning." They offer a reconceptualization of the symptoms embodied in the "survivor syndrome" and suggest how psychotherapists can facilitate the religious survivor coming to terms with the partial or complete loss of God and his or her world. Janet Hadda shows that Yiddish, the language of many Holocaust victims, could be as deeply and powerfully mourned by a survivor as a parent, spouse, or child. She uses as a case study the works of a Yiddish poet— Yankev Glatshteyn—who observed the events of World War II from the safety of the United States. She chronicles the changing subjective reactions to the loss of an important means of self-identification and processing of meaning and offers some clinical implications for psychotherapists working with Holocaust survivors and their families. Margrit Wreschner Rustow's essay deals with the impact of cumulative trauma on children who during the Holocaust were separated from their parents and found sanctuary in Catholic institutions. She focuses on the difficulties that these children had in returning to their original families and to Judaism. Identity conflicts, loyalty issues, and self-esteem problems were some of the common themes of these children's post-Holocaust adaptation. Whether it is the rupturing of one's faith, the forfeiture of one's mother tongue or the dispossession of one's home world, all of the above mentioned chapters put into sharp focus the survivor's problem of reckoning with the deep and pervasive significance of losing one's world.

We hope that our anthology serves three purposes for the readership: first, that this volume with its wide range of theoretical perspectives and therapeutic approaches will serve as a resource for the practicing clinician working with Holocaust survivors and their families. Although not specifically addressed here, we think that many of the findings and approaches offered have relevance to other persecuted and traumatized populations and to patients suffering from post-traumatic stress syndrome. Victims of state-sponsored torture, victims of terrorism, Vietnam veterans, and survivors of natural disasters are some of the populations whose problems and treatment could be further illuminated by the therapist knowledgeable in psychotherapeutic literature on Holocaust survivors. Second, we hope that the reader will get a good sense of how a discipline, namely psychotherapy, has struggled and evolved over the years in trying to understand the impact of an historical event on its victims. This evolution is best seen in the varying therapeutic approaches that reflect the fact that there have been, and still are, competing and widely divergent ways of conceptualizing both survivors' and their offspring's symptoms and clinical intervention. Third, it is our fervent hope that this volume be understood as a form of historical record of the unprecedented evil of the Holocaust. In a profound sense, the private pain, symptoms, and struggles of survivors, their offspring, and their families is stark testimony and incontrovertible evidence to the horrors inflicted by the Nazis on their victims.

NOTES

1. Henry Krystal (Ed.), *Massive Psychic Trauma* (New York: International Universities Press, 1968).

2. Martin S. Bergmann and Milton E. Jucovy, *Generations of the Holocaust* (New York: Basic Books, 1982).

3. Steven A. Luel and Paul Marcus, *Psychoanalytic Reflections on the Holocaust: Selected Essays* (New York: University of Denver and KTAV, 1984).

Acknowledgments

Both editors would like to thank Dr. William L. Shulman, the Director of the Holocaust Resource Center and Archives of Queensborough Community College for his help in locating survivors who were willing to be interviewed in preparation for this project. Mr. Alfred Lipson, an Auschwitz survivor, was particularly helpful in his gracious willingness to be reinterviewed many times as questions about survivorship came up. They would also like to express their appreciation to Martin S. Bergmann for his thoughtful and supportive foreword.

Dr. Marcus wishes to thank his excellent clinical supervisors Dr. Milton E. Jucovy of the New York Psychoanalytic Institute, and Erwin Lawrence Antinoph of the National Psychological Association for Psychoanalysis (NPAP) for providing considerable help in overseeing much of his psychotherapeutic work with survivors and children of survivors. Dr. Philip M. Stone, also of the NPAP, has been helpful in this regard and has been especially supportive when the going got tough, as it almost always does whenever one is editing a book. Dr. Marcus's membership in the Group for the Psychoanalytic Study of the Effects of the Holocaust in the Second Generation (co-chairpersons, Martin S. Bergmann, Milton E. Jucovy, and Judith S. Kestenberg) has been an especially illuminating professional association for which he is appreciative. He also wishes to express his gratitude to his wife, Irene Wineman-Marcus, of the New York Freudian Society, for her invaluable editorial suggestions and consistent encouragement throughout the project. Finally, his gratefulness reaches out to his young children, Raphael and Gabriela, who have continued to delightfully transform his life even though they have had a father who was sometimes distracted by book matters.

Alan Rosenberg would like to thank Queens College (City University of New York) for granting him a sabbatical so that he had time to complete his project. His gratitude extends to his colleagues in the Department of Philosophy for their moral and intellectual support. Professors Eugene Fontinell, Peter T. Manicas, R. W. Sleeper, and Edith Wyschogrod have been especially helpful. Thanks go to his friend and colleague Professor George Kren, who has sharpened his sense of the historical development of psychotherapy with survivors; to Joan Lesnoy, Gladys Passoa, and Barbara Pauker for their invaluable secretarial assistance throughout this project, and to his dear friend Morris Rabinowitz, Branch Librarian, Dedham Public Library, who has always been a sound critic and enthusiastic supporter of his work on the Holocaust.

I

Background

1

The Holocaust Survivor and Psychoanalysis

GEORGE M. KREN

Fascism, the Nazi experience, and World War II changed not only history, but also language. Words and phrases such as "collaboration," "resistance," "partisan," "concentration camp," and "survivor" not only acquired new meanings, but also became loaded with special feelings and values. The word survivor gained currency as former prisoners recounted in interviews, articles, and books what had happened to them and as still and newsreel photographs portrayed a barely believable reality. The war crimes trials provided detailed evidence of what had taken place by eliciting statements—provided with amazing frankness—from perpetrators, while simultaneously making public the documents that permitted a reconstruction of what was done and how it was done. Rudolf Hoess, the commandant of Auschwitz even wrote a detailed and frank autobiography.[1] The word survivor came to be surrounded by an almost mystical aura which designated someone who had looked into the abyss, and had not been destroyed by it.

Survivor refers to those targeted by Nazism for destruction. Yet the experiences of those who survived were by no means identical. A few lived in the special "family camp" at Theresienstadt, selected because of their "prominence" or because the Nazis wished (usually temporarily) for some reason to save them.[2] Some were in the old German concentration camps, which continued throughout the war—others were temporarily engaged in forced labor. Auschwitz was not only an extermination camp but also a labor camp. Some (very few) survived such "pure" death camps as Sobibor and Treblinka. A few were able to escape from the camps or ghettoes and join partisans.

Early writings focused on the old concentration camps located in Germany, such as Buchenwald, Dachau, and Sachsenhausen, not on the extermination camps which only came into being during the war. Concentration camp survivors were portrayed as heroic figures who, more than others, could comprehend the true nature of Nazism and fascism.

In Anna Seghers' novel *The Seventh Cross,* an escaped concentration camp prisoner is the hero. The work is a brilliant antifascist manifesto. André Malraux's *Days of Wrath* only suggests that the survivor (Malraux does not use this term) is more open to a sense of community with those opposed to Nazism, and that his sufferings as a prisoner strengthen his resolve to oppose Nazism. None of the early antifascist works in which the camps play a role suggest in any way that they produced personality changes in inmates, or could leave permanent physical and psychic scars. These works of the 1930s and 1940s generally lack psychological dimensions. They view the sadism in the camps as a direct consequence of fascism and Nazism, perceiving it as a logical consequence of fascist ideology.

Accounts by those who survived Nazi concentration or death camps make it a point to state that the experience was of such a nature that what really happened cannot be communicated to anyone who was not there. Only those who had lived through it could know what it was really like. David Rousset, in one of the earliest accounts, spoke of the camps as belonging to a radically different universe:

Ordinary human beings do not know that everything is possible. Even when the weight of evidence forces their mind to admit this, they do not really believe in their bones. . . . Death dwelt among the internees at every hour of their existence. Death showed them her every aspect. . . . They are separated from other people by an experience which it is impossible to communicate.[3]

As U.S., British, and Russian armies liberated the camps, the immediate concern was with providing the necessary medical care. Most survivors of the camps also could not or did not wish to go back to what had been their country before the war. Many of them were housed in DP (Displaced Persons) camps. The largest number eventually went to Israel or the United States, where problems of adjustment to new environments, finding housing, employment, and so on, were primary. At first little or no attention was given to any psychological problem; some of these only surfaced at a later time.

The early accounts emphasized the brutality and sadism of the guards, but there was a striking absence of any analysis of how the camp experience had affected the prisoners psychologically. Though the early camps were not death camps, the death rate was high. Eugen Kogon[4] provides figures for the camps he was in and suggests that had the camps not been replenished with new prisoners regularly, they would soon have become empty. The annual death rate between 1933 and 1937 was 10 and 20 percent, respectively, for 1938 and 1939 *before* any death camps were established.

The concentration camp universe was anarchic. The early camps, such as Dachau, were at first primarily concerned with political prisoners—socialists, communists, and individuals with strong religious convictions. Mass roundups of Jews followed *Kristallnacht* when, following the killing of a German embassy official in Paris by a Jew, mass arrests of Jews took place. Many of those were released if they could demonstrate that they had entry permits to other countries. Death camps were developed only after the invasion of the Soviet Union in June of 1941.[5] In contrast to the German concentration camps, which sought to intimidate potential opponents, the primary aim of the death camps was the rationalized mass killings of Jews, Gypsies, Poles, and others. The creation of death became industrialized. All who came through the concentration camp universe experienced a trauma of unimaginable proportions; no one was left unchanged by it, and for many it caused deep physical and psychic wounds. Much time passed before the psychic damage of the camps to its victims was recognized.

One of the earliest instances is found in the novel and film *The Pawnbroker,*[6] which broke new ground with its convincing portrayal of a survivor of the Nazi camps; it developed a sophisticated analysis of what later writers would label as "survivor syndrome." Both the film and the book showed the impact of the camps on the personality of one survivor, who lacked the ability to trust, who was unable to experience feelings, a person emotionally isolated and distanced, unable and unwilling to forge any emotional connectedness.[7] This work dramatically showed the protagonist as emotionally damaged by the camp experience.

In scholarship frequently one work or idea may acquire such status that further advances take the form of a critique of the accepted authority. In Renaissance studies, Jacob Burckhardt's *The Civilization of the Renaissance in Italy* defined the concept of renaissance, and generations of scholarship took the form of attacking, modifying, or reinterpreting what came to be known as the "Burckhardt thesis." Studies of the relationship between economic and religious life begin by examining the question within the framework provided by Max Weber's *The Protestant Ethic and the Spirit of Capitalism.* In many ways the agenda for a study of Holocaust victims was set neither by a novel, a film, nor even a memoir, but by Bruno Bettelheim's "Behavior in Extreme Situation" (1943), an article which Bettelheim published in 1943 in a psychological journal.[8] This article has been central to defining issues of the psychological impact of the camps and questions of "survivorship." Not only is it frequently cited, but it serves as a point of departure for the expression of basic positions. Among psychoanalysts some consensus about the impact of the Holocaust has developed; the general conclusion of those who have treated survivors is that the camp experience has almost always produced permanent, long-range damaging effects, which at times manifest themselves only after a period of latency. Opposition to this view usually takes the form of rejecting the legitimacy of psychoanalytic modes of understanding, or arguing that psychoanalysis is not appropriate for examining the camp experience.

After the publication of "Behavior in Extreme Situations" in the *Journal of Abnormal and Social Psychology,* Dwight Macdonald, editor of *Politics,* a radically left "little magazine" with a small circulation, printed a condensed version of this essay, making it available to others outside the psychoanalytic community. Though the readership of *Politics* was small, it included leading left-wing intellectuals. Bettelheim, in a revised version of the article, noted that the article had been rejected several times:[9]

I met disbelief and criticism when I spoke of the German concentration camps as serving important purposes for the Nazis. The notion of ascribing purposes or intelligent planning to the SS, of taking them seriously was considered both unwise and unsafe. It was put down to a natural loss of perspective after imprisonment in a concentration camp.[10]

The article received little attention at first but as a result of the war crimes trials increasing interest in the Holocaust developed. In the 1960s the psychoanalytic community developed an interest in Holocaust survivors, trying to understand the psychological consequences of massive trauma. Bruno Bettelheim then emerged as the authoritative interpreter of the survivor, the Nazi regime, and above all of the behavior of the concentration camp inmate.[11] He used his concentration camp insight—that external events can indeed change personality—to develop therapies for psychotic children by creating a supportive environment for them. Bettelheim soon became a center of controversies which developed in the 1960s over Jewish conduct during the Nazi period, so much so that few dealt with his work on its own merits.

In "Behavior in Extreme Situations," Bettelheim had argued that one aspect of the adjustment process of most prisoners was the development of a

personality structure willing and able to accept SS values and behavior as its own. Old prisoners were sometimes instrumental in getting rid of so-called unfit new prisoners, thus patterning their own behavior after Gestapo ideology. . . . This was one of many situations in which old prisoners showed toughness, and molded their way of treating prisoners on examples set by the SS.[12]

The concept of "identification with the aggressor" was developed by Anna Freud and has been part of psychoanalytic theory for several decades. Hilde Bluhm's analysis of published survivor accounts explained the brutal behavior of some privileged prisoners to be the result of identification with the aggressor.[13] Bettelheim had, without using that specific terminology, argued the same thing. Some have viewed any critique of concentration camp prisoners as both offensive and immoral—an interpretation of prisoner behavior that showed respects in which the prisoner identified with the SS appeared not only as a psychoanalytic judgment, but as an abhorrent moral one.

Bettelheim had argued that the SS was successful in its attempts to infantilize prisoners. Much of this infantilization centered on the use of latrines: "It was," he wrote, "as if every effort were being made to reduce prisoners to the level they were at before they had achieved toilet training."[14] He then cited numerous ways in which the SS humiliated prisoners by forcing them to soil themselves, to request permission to relieve themselves. Hilde Bluhm arrived at a very similar conclusion, and documented what she labeled as the SS's "anal sadistic practices." In a discussion similar to Bettelheim's, she described

a manifest return to childhood reactions [so that] manifest symptoms of regression occurred. . . . In calling these reactions regressive we are well aware that people who live under extraordinary conditions . . . are able to give up their habitual stands of cleanliness without a deeper disturbance. . . . Neglect . . . means return to the instinctual behavior of early childhood.[15]

Similar views appear throughout the literature, but it was Bettelheim more than any one else who came under virulent attack for having tarnished the image of the heroic prisoner. In an article based upon studying Holocaust survivors who were held in a British detention facility in Cyprus, Paul Friedman had arrived (without any attendant controversy) at a similar conclusion: "Many of the survivors," he wrote, "even after liberation showed strong evidence of complete infantile dependency."[16] In the same article he also used the term survivor guilt, long before this achieved currency.[17]

Robert Jay Lifton documented survivor guilt in his analysis of the victims of Hiroshima.[18] Lifton has been one of the very few to generalize the term survivor guilt—a later essay deals with the Nazi death camps, Hiroshima, and the survivors of the Buffalo Creek disaster (which killed 125 people).[19] Lifton equates survivor guilt with "death guilt." Not only is the guilt a response to the question "Why did I survive, while others died?" but a

part of the survivors' sense of horror is the memory of their own inactivation—helplessness—within the death imagery, of their inability to act in a way they would ordinarily have thought appropriate (save people, resist the victimizers, etc.) or even to feel the appropriate emotions. . . . Death guilt begins, then, in the gap between that physical and psychic inactivation and what one feels called upon to do and feel. That is one reason why the imagery keeps recurring, in dreams and in waking life.

Lifton cites the moving passage in Elie Wiesel's autobiographical novel *Night*, where Wiesel wished to be rid of responsibility for his father, and the sense of freedom he felt when his father died, to argue that a guilt feeling may be a powerful impetus for responsibility. Freud, Lifton noted, had seen in *Civilization and its Discontents* the dangers of guilt, which he connected to aggression. Lifton argued that at the present "the loss of the capacity for guilt . . . may be the greater human threat."[20] It is ironic that survivors are burdened by a sense of guilt for not having died, while the evidence is overwhelming that a sense of guilt, or even an admission of wrongdoing, is a rarity among the perpetrators who do not show any evidence of psychic damage such as may be found in survivors.

Throughout the 1940s and 1950s Bettelheim's article lay almost dormant. It gained some recognition when Stanley Elkins, in a study of American slavery,

attempted to parallel the regression of concentration camp prisoners to the behavior of African blacks brought to the United States as slaves. These, he
maintained, exhibited childlike behavior.[21] Bettelheim's article, as well as his
other writings on the camps and on Jewish behavior during the Nazi period,
became controversial during the 1960s, when the issue of Jewish conduct during
the Holocaust increasingly came to be the subject of bitter polemics and controversies.[22] Certainly one reason for this was that the Eichmann trial focused
attention on Jewish behavior during the Nazi period. Hannah Arendt attended
the Eichmann trial and addressed some of these issues in a series of articles in
The New Yorker.[23] Arendt critically examined the action of the leaders of the
Jewish communities, who cooperated with the Germans, as well as the lack of
Jewish resistance. The work aroused wide and bitter controversy.[24] An eminent
Jewish leader, Jacob Robinson, wrote a book which sought to refute her.[25]
Clearly, more than an academic issue was involved.

Raul Hilberg, in *The Destruction of the European Jews*,[26] argued that Diaspora
Jews had lost their capacity to resist and instead depended upon pleading, bribery,
and other forms of accommodation as means of defense. These proved to be
useless against the Nazis, who had committed themselves to a program of massive
Jewish destruction. For his part Bettelheim gave little comfort to those who
wished to make the victims of the Holocaust into heroes. His collection of essays[27]
contains a critique of the behavior of the family of Anne Frank for assuming
that "life could be carried on as before," (an attitude which) may well have led
to their destruction.[28] Many of the criticisms of Bettelheim avoided addressing
the specific issues he had raised, substituting outrage for analysis.[29] In a bitter
article which contrasts an early Bettelheim who is contemptuous of the victims
with a latter one who is empathetic,[30] Stanley Rosenman defines Bettelheim as

a key spokesperson for that extensive group of Jews who reacted to the victims with
derision, meanwhile defining the malevolence that animated them as bland, banal, au-
tomated, or as simply not heroically good. This view was generally accompanied by
considerable self-promotion. The posture of disparagement of the victims and disavowal
of the evil extant in the victimizer, promised facile resolution of the chief psychological
problems stressing post-Holocaust Jews.[31]

In contrast to these writers, Viktor Frankl, himself a survivor, concluded that
the camps prove that even under extreme situations human beings can make
moral choices. His *Ein Psycholog erlebt das Konzentrationslager* (A Psychologist
Experiences the Concentration Camp) was published in Germany in 1946. It
was translated into English at first under the title *From Death-Camp to Existen-
tialism* and later, in a revised edition, as *Man's Search for Meaning: An Introduction to Logotherapy*.[32] Unlike other survivors, Frankl found in the camp a
few prisoners who transcended their condition, and used this as evidence for a
positive and even optimistic philosophy.

We who lived in concentration camps can remember the men who walked through the huts comforting others, giving away their last piece of bread. They may have been few in number, but they offer sufficient proof that everything can be taken from a man but one thing: the last of the human freedoms—to choose one's attitude in any given set of circumstances, to choose one's own way.[33]

Just as Bettelheim came to his milieu therapy for the treatment of severely disturbed children via his concentration camp experiences, so Frankl's prisoner experiences led him to found the third Vienna school of psychiatry. (The other two are made up of the followers of Freud and Jung.)[34] Frankl regards the "will to meaning," the endowment of life with meaning, to be the basis of human psychology. Although their theoretical foundations differ radically, Bettelheim had also noted that those who held strong metaphysical beliefs, such as Jehovah's Witnesses or Communists, held up much better in the camps than others, who resented "being treated like common criminals," and who thought that somehow a mistake had been made in their particular case.

Whether it was the Eichmann trial, the controversy over Arendt's book, or the fact that survivors were beginning to publish their accounts, by the late 1960s the Holocaust came to be a serious subject for study. It was in this context that Terrence Des Pres published *The Survivor*.[35] The work reviews published survivor accounts (including accounts by survivors of camps in the Soviet Union) to arrive at a philosophy of the survivor.

Des Pres[36] explicitly rejected the applicability of psychoanalysis as a way of understanding survivors, arguing that the problems Freud sought to deal with were predicated on a normalcy which was taken for granted at the turn of the century but inapplicable to life in the camps:

The psychoanalytic approach is misleading because it is essentially a theory of culture and of man in the civilized state. Its analytic power . . . is maximized when turned upon behavior which is symbolic, mediated and therefore at a sufficient remove from necessity. To be of use, the psychoanalytic methods . . . must be applied to actions which have more than one meaning *on the level of meaning*. But that is not the case with extremity. When men and women must respond directly to necessity—when defilement occurs at gun-point and the most undeniable of needs determines action, or when death itself is the determinant—then behavior has no meaning at all in a symbolic or psychological sense.[37]

Freudian theory holds that the basic determinants of the personality are private acts: toilet training is seen as more important than political issues. In the pre–1914 world, private acts could be the basic determinants of personality because public acts did not normally really touch the individual. The rise of totalitarianism as a new form of government, which developed after 1918, changed all this, and the realm of the private radically diminished; public events directly impinged on the individual personality. Everything from musical taste to religion became a matter of politics and many nonpolitical views or acts could mean one would end up in a camp, be killed, or be tortured. Des Pres' implicit argument is that

Freudian theory presupposes a level of civilized conduct, and that it is only in that context that Freud's conclusions are valid. *The Survivor* concludes by formulating a new view of the meaning of the human condition rooted in socio-biological concepts. Des Pres comes close to seeing the survivor as a new human type with a new relationship to death. "Survivors are those who have escaped the murderous circle of our retreat from death, men and women shoved violently back upon a biological wisdom long unheeded." Des Pres, though recognizing how often chance determined who survived and who did not, nevertheless views the survivor as a special person.[38]

The survivor is the figure of all those who, in Hemingway's words, have had to "accept the rule of death. . . . " [The Survivor] is the first of civilized men to live beyond the compulsions of culture; beyond a fear of death which can only be assuaged by insisting that life itself is worthless. The survivor is evidence that men and women are now strong enough, mature enough, awake enough to face death without mediation, and therefore to embrace life without reserve.[39]

The available knowledge of Holocaust survivors does not suggest that they are now embracing life without reserve. On the contrary! The numerous studies of survivors suggest a general sense of depression, a difficulty enjoying life, a distrust of human relationships, and indeed the term "anhedonia" is used to designate the condition of not being able to experience pleasure. Two important writers and survivors—Primo Levi and Jean Améry have committed suicide, a tragic loss. It is unclear whether the rate of suicide is higher among survivors. Eitinger and Strom observed "an excess mortality from violent death (including suicide) in all the calendar-year periods after 1945 and in all ages over 30 years."[40] In contrast to Victor Frankl, whose existentialist philosophy seeks to find and realize values as a way of giving meaning to existence, Des Pres affirms that "Life, the earth in its silence, is all there is."[41]

The common theme of the works of Bettelheim, Elie Cohen, and Hilde Bluhm (to list only some authors already cited) was an attempt to comprehend the Nazi concentration camp system, to understand the dynamics of both the victim and also the SS. But the issue of the survivor is not only one of theory. Most who survived sought to leave Germany—many settled in Israel, the United States, and other countries; some asked for help and were treated by psychoanalysts.

The professional interest in survivors was furthered by a German law which sought to compensate victims who could prove that imprisonment at the hands of the Nazis has made them unfit to pursue gainful work.[42] This very convoluted law required proof that the survivor had been damaged in the camps so that his or her earning capacity was lessened. Bergmann and Jucovy[43] point out the revealing nature of the language involved: The label *Wiedergutmachung* is used to describe the purpose of the law—literally a making good again, a repairing, as if what had happened could in some way be undone.[44] The implementation of the law did not meet its stated preamble that it be applied "in the spirit of warm-hearted and generous indemnification for the injustices committed, taking into consideration the whole range of possibilities provided by the law."[45] It required attorneys and expert medical testimony, including that of psychiatrists and psychoanalysts. It pitted an organically oriented Krapelian psychology against a psychoanalytic orientation. German psychiatrists had argued that a child who spent the first two or three years of its life in hiding would not remember the details and therefore was not damaged.[46] A German psychiatrist reviewing a case for the German court held that the claim of a feeling of inferiority because of scars was not legitimate since, "I have a [fencing] scar also and I feel very happy, and I am even a professor." He concluded that the man with a scar had a constitutional inferiority.[47] Reading the cases and their resolution by the German courts, one is impressed by the incredible insensitivity both of the courts and their German psychiatric experts. "The psychiatrist consulted by the German consulate declared that the symptoms were not created by the camps but the result of a pre-existing condition—*durch Anlage bedingt*. The court agrees. An appeal finds contradictory expert opinions; the opinion by the (German) court appointed *Obergutachter* usually agrees with that of the earlier court expert." Eissler with justifiable bitterness writes that "The victims about whom expert testimony was to be provided had been exposed to tortures and pains in the last analysis because of their *Anlage*. The key was supposedly based on race. . . . One should expect that society would protect individuals who had to suffer so much . . . from a repetition. For how could those who request compensation view it as anything but a reproach if their pains are now viewed as *anlagebedingt* [i.e., based on their previous condition, not on what was done to them in the camps]." Eissler further is properly incensed and outraged that individuals who had gone through the camps should now be accused of simulating damage.[48] The literature is strangely silent in raising questions about the feelings any German legal or psychiatric expert must have in deciding whether an award should be made to a Jew who had suffered at the hands of the Nazis. What was the expert doing in the 1940s? If he (rarely she, where German experts are involved) had participated in the Nazi movement did confrontation with victims evoke guilt feelings or feelings of resentment?[49] K. R. Eissler speaks of the conflict between U.S. and German psychiatrists. It would be tempting to ask about the image the German courts had of a survivor. There is little to suggest that they (and their experts) ever sympathized or empathized with the survivor, ever made an attempt to feel what it must have been like to have been a camp inmate.

Problems arose because many survivors had lived for a period of years without showing any symptoms, and some German courts held that this invalidated their claims.[50] This delay between trauma and symptoms has also appeared in Vietnam veterans. Kijak and Funtowics write that

After liberation a period of freedom from symptoms, in which is included a 'supernormality' is described by some authors until frustrations having diverse origins, unfold, which are defined as the survivor syndrome. We prefer to believe the opinion that such a normal period would be better described as a period of psychic suffering, maintained in secrecy, until the more manifest symptoms appear.[51]

An unintended consequence of the German restitution law was that it brought about additional contact between survivors and psychoanalysts and psychiatrists. Sometimes these first contacts led to the initiation of therapy. The result has been that the psychiatric community began specifically to address therapeutic issues directly relevant to camp survivors. In 1949 Paul Friedman could write that "we still know comparatively little about the deeper psychodynamics of that handful of people who emerged from the camps after liberation."[52] This is no longer true. Bettelheim's "Individual and Mass Behavior" is the only article in Friedman's bibliography concerned with the camps and their survivors. Since that time there has grown a large psychiatric literature on survivors.[53] A number of psychoanalysts have devoted much of their professional lives to studying and treating Holocaust survivors. Steven Luel and Paul Marcus edited an anthology on psychoanalysis and the Holocaust which provides an overview of the range of material available.[54] Terms such as *survivor guilt, survivor syndrome,* and others, are now part of contemporary psychiatric vocabulary.[55]

Those who survived the concentration and death camps experienced a major, historically unprecedented trauma and have been changed by it. Yet even the act of admitting that the experience caused psychic wounds has become problematical. Yael Danieli observed that some analysts feared that "demonstrating the long-term negative effects of the Holocaust . . . was tantamount to giving Hitler a posthumous victory . . . others feared that demonstrating these individuals' strength was equivalent to saying, 'Since people could stay normal, it couldn't have been such a terrible experience and it is almost synonymous with forgiving the Nazis.' "[56] Survivors also found reasons to avoid discussions of the past. Krell cites the comment of a patient who when asked whether the camps had come up [during a therapy session] remarked "Oh no! The doctor asked me about it once, but I decided to save him from all that."[57] Some survivors refused to participate in the German restitution program, since the law required describing events of the past, an ordeal some did not wish to face. Others stated that "Money can't buy blood."[58]

In an angry article, Isaac Kanter attacked the legitimacy of using Freudian (i.e., psychoanalytic) theory in the treatment of survivors. Referring to a discussion of the symptom-free interval, he rejected psychological explanations by holding that the subsequent appearance of "symptoms" served to support a claim against the German government. "Thus the author tries to establish a causal relation between the exposure to trauma in the extermination camp and the appearance of symptoms in 1965, at the time of the examination. A simple explanation would be that many symptoms are claim-related and disappear when the claim is satisfied." The aim of this polemic is a denial of any symptomatology (particularly survivor guilt, identification with the aggressor, self-hatred, and regression). "What exists," he writes, "is not so much a conspiracy of silence

... but a conspiracy of *exaggeration of symptoms* which are probably further exaggerated by psychoanalytic interpretation.''[59]

Survivors who sought therapy found analysts unprepared. The assumption of a therapeutic relationship is that analysts have mastered their own affective life so that they can adequately deal with the patient. Kijak and Funtowics succinctly observe that

The confrontation with the survivors of the death camps mobilizes among interviewers, therapists and researchers, emotional reactions impossible to control, which put in motion intense anxieties and defenses against them. These reactions will vary according to the degree of the patient's sickness, and the state of the psychic health of the investigator. ... Emotional reactions are prone to appear from the denial of the traumatic events and the actual psychic suffering. ... that lead the interviewer to feel himself destroyed and impotent, and includes the blocking of feelings that simulates a certain objectivity.[60]

Yael Danieli in her discussion of the relationship of the therapist to the survivor began by noting that Freud had at one time addressed the issue of dealing with extreme horror:

No matter how much we may shrink with horror from certain situations—of a galley slave in antiquity, ... of a victim of the Holy Inquisition, of a Jew awaiting a pogrom— *it is nevertheless impossible for us to feel our way into such people*—to divine the changes which original obtuseness of mind, a gradual stupefying process, the cessation of expectations, ... have produced. ... Moreover, in the case of the most extreme possibility of suffering, special mental protective devices are brought into operation. *It seems to me unprofitable to pursue this aspect of the problem any further* [italics added].[61]

A recurring theme throughout Holocaust literature is the resistance and denial evoked. Knowledge of it may be threatening in many ways. Robert Krell[62] cites a case where both sets of grandparents were in camps. Only in the third year of the analysis did the analyst become aware of that and recognize that it was a major issue for the person he was treating. Many find the Holocaust reality so terrible that they consciously avoid hearing or reading about it. Several writers have observed a tendency to hold victims (because of guilt feelings and because the reality creates unbearable anxieties) in contempt. This reaction appears even in those who have been professionally concerned with survivors. Frederick H. Hocking's essay manifests a radically negative attitude: He speaks of the survivors as

sick, filthy and emaciated. ... [They] presented an apathetic and depressed appearance that they could almost invariably be identified among the patients sitting in the waiting room. ... Because ... all of the patients examined were Jewish, their symptoms may have resulted, as least in part, from cultural and/or constitutional factors that are not present in non-Jewish people. ... Patients were claiming compensation from ... Germany. ... The prospect of obtaining compensation might suggest that many of the patients were motivated by gain, and it would be ingenuous not to believe that some, and perhaps many exaggerated their symptoms.[63]

Having earlier described the intensity of persecution, Hocking later seeks to minimize its consequences: "Symptoms may result from an inability to adapt to life in a strange country, rather than from wartime persecution."[64]

In order to relate adequately to survivors the therapist was required to come to terms with the anxieties, guilt feelings, dread, and fears their experiences evoked. Paul Chodoff writes that "One gets the impression that potential therapists are almost overwhelmed by the magnitude and variety of the obstacles to their therapeutic efforts."[65] Danieli, who dealt with counter-transference themes of therapists working with Holocaust survivors, noted that records frequently only contain one sentence about the patients' connection with the Holocaust. She singled out counter-transference themes—the feeling that the survivor was too fragile and would fall apart when facing questions, the guilt feelings (on the part of the therapists) of having had a happy life while "these people suffered so much." She cites one researcher expressing the fear that he would be "drawn into a vortex of such blackness that I may never find clarity and may never recover my own stability so that I may be helpful to this patient."[66] Klaus Hoppe analyzed varying responses by "experts" ranging from complete denial to controlled identification.[67] The treatment of a Holocaust survivor involves therapists in ways for which their training has not prepared them. Clearly speaking from his own personal experience, Emanuel Tanay emphasized that "a session with a concentration-camp survivor is . . . an intensely stressful experience. . . . To be emotionally drained and distressed following a session with a survivor is . . . a natural reaction. . . . "[68]

The difficulties that handling this material creates for the therapists is nothing like the trauma created for most survivors who must dredge up memories of the camps in which most of them lost most or all of their families. Their experience is of a totally different order than that normally encountered in therapy. A basic epistemological premise of therapy is that the communication that takes place leads to the creation of a "therapeutic alliance." A recurring theme of survivor accounts is that what was experienced literally cannot be communicated. For all victims the reality experienced was beyond their or anyone else's imagination. Nothing in previous events could have prepared victims for this new reality. They experienced torture on a scale that would make a Torquemada pale. The production of death became bureaucratized. What the industrial revolution had done for the manufacture of textiles and other materials, Germany did for death. Auschwitz, Treblinka, Sobibor, and the other death camps were literally death factories. Some mystics have attempted to describe their experiences, but their attempts have always fallen short of the reality, which involved altered states of consciousness beyond the reach of ordinary language. The camp world was so distant and remote from the normal that the tools used to describe ordinary life have proven themselves inadequate. Accounts include statements from SS men in the camps who said that even if the prisoners were to get out, no one would believe them. The implications of this are important for a general understanding of the Holocaust and they become particularly significant when survivors engage in therapy which relies on verbal communication to examine memories.

Given the unfavorable setting for therapeutic efforts and the unprecedented trauma experienced, successes approach the miraculous. Throughout the literature, analysts cite cases showing that despite the odds against it, many individuals were helped coming to terms with their traumas, neither repressing them nor letting them define every moment of their lives. The key is found above all in the rare ability of therapists (many of whom had directly or indirectly been victims of Nazism) to combine their professional competence with a dedicated empathy. Not many could master the unique requirements that treating Holocaust survivors demanded. The Holocaust has not altered analytic theory,[69] but the term *survivor syndrome* (coined by William G. Niederland)[70] is included in the 1980 edition of *Diagnostic and Statistical Manual of Mental Disorders* as a recognized category: (309.81 Post-traumatic Stress Disorder).[71] Other related concepts such as survivor guilt or anhedonia are becoming part of the contemporary psychoanalytic vocabulary.

Many therapists have argued that the Holocaust experience produced permanent alterations in the personalities of survivors.[72] Marcus and Rosenberg rendered a major service by their critical survey of the different interpretations of the concept survivor syndrome. They themselves raise serious objections to its legitimacy.[73] They argue that the acceptance of the concept of survivor syndrome has led to viewing the survivor as so damaged that a cure is doubtful or impossible.[74] The camps left an indelible mark on all who passed through them. For most survivors the camp experience represents a central event of their lives; it produced physical and psychic scars. The term ''damaged'' has frequently been used by therapists—it is inappropriate, for while the camp experience clearly did damage, some individuals, by standing up to the circumstances and coping without violating their own values, created a new strength. Almagor and Leon note that ''many survivors did manage to restore and rehabilitate themselves, even though it is very unlikely that they came out of the experience untouched.''[75] Kahana, Harel, and Kahana assert that ''there is an optimistic aspect of studying elderly survivors of extreme trauma. Their triumph in coping . . . bears ultimate witness to the triumph of human endurance.''[76] They report, however, that 92 percent of individuals interviewed reported that the Holocaust adversely affected their emotional well-being.[77] Anna Ornstein speaks of the need to shift from a concern with pathology to the survivors' capacity to resume his interrupted life meaningfully.[78] Therapists rarely see individuals who have made a satisfactory adjustment. Hence the psychiatric literature has minimized those survivors who were successful in coping with the traumas they had experienced.

The issue of the time interval between the event and its consequences is now subsumed under the concept of ''post-traumatic stress,'' which suggests that symptoms may manifest themselves years after the stressful event. The concept appears to have received general acceptance—it is used not only in discussing Holocaust survivors, but also survivors of other massive traumas (such as Vietnam).[79]

Only in a limited way has the experience of treating survivors required a modification of established psychiatric theory; the available paradigms proved themselves elastic enough to provide helpful guidelines for healing those who had survived. Previously acquired practical and theoretical knowledge about the consequences of extreme trauma could be adapted to Holocaust survivors. Much of the relevant literature deals with technical issues of treatment. One senses a community among those committed to helping survivors come to terms with their experiences so that they can master it.[80]

A new current concern is the impact of the Holocaust on survivors' children. Judith and Milton Kestenberg note the difficulties they encountered in finding children of survivors who were being analyzed because "the analysts did not connect the parents' Holocaust experiences with the children's material in analysis."[81] They discuss the founding in 1974 of a group for the "Psychoanalytic Study of the Holocaust." Several chapters in *Generations of the Holocaust,* which includes valuable summaries of case histories, connect the parent's Holocaust experience to their relationship with children; James Herzog addresses the problem of the transmission of the trauma from parent to children, while others focus upon issues of treatment of survivors and their children.[82] In a nontechnical work, Helen Epstein vividly presents a series of interviews which she conducted with children of Holocaust survivors.[83] These illustrate dramatically how the trauma of the Holocaust has already affected the next generation—and indications suggest that this will continue for further generations.

The concept of survivor has become part of our contemporary vocabulary. As many governments torture and kill political opponents, new survivors—those who escape or outlive their persecutors—are becoming part of our world. The treatment of Holocaust survivors has demonstrated and documented the invisible damage that was done to victims to a degree never previously imagined. It also shows the strength of the human spirit which makes recovery possible.

NOTES

I owe a great deal to two colleagues and friends for their critical comments on this chapter and for much more: George Christakes of the City Colleges of Chicago and Leon Rappoport of the Psychology Department of Kansas State University.

1. Rudolf Hoess, *Commandant of Auschwitz: The Autobiography of Rudolf Hoess* (Cleveland and New York: The World Publishing Company, 1959).

2. No exterminations took place at Theresienstadt, but individuals were put on transports to Auschwitz where they were killed.

3. David Rousset, *A World Apart* (orig. *L'Universe Concentrationnaire*) translated by Ramon Guthrie (London: Secker and Warburg, 1951), p. 209.

4. Eugen Kogon, *The Theory and Practice of Hell* (New York: Berkeley, 1980), pp. 247–254.

5. Though camps differed from each other, prisoners and personnel were exchanged and it is appropriate to speak of a camp system. A detailed analysis of the camps may be found in Konnilyn Feig, *Hitler's Death Camps: the Sanity of Madness* (New York: Holmes and Meier, 1979).

6. Edward Lewis Wallant, *The Pawnbroker* (New York: McFadden-Bartell Books, 1962).

7. Compare the sensitive and perceptive discussion by Anna Ornstein, "Survival and Recovery," *Psychoanalytic Inquiry* 5, no. 1 (1985): 99–130.

8. Bruno Bettelheim, "Behavior in Extreme Situations," *Journal of Abnormal and Social Psychology* 38 (1943): 417–451.

9. Bettelheim reprinted revised and expanded versions of this essay in Bruno Bettelheim, *The Informed Heart: Autonomy in a Mass Age* (New York: Avon Books, 1971), and in Bettelheim, *Surviving and Other Essays* (New York: Alfred A. Knopf, 1979). Page citations refer to *The Informed Heart*.

10. Bruno Bettelheim, *The Informed Heart: Autonomy in a Mass Age* (New York: Avon Books, 1971), p. 119.

11. Paul Marcus and Irene Wineman, "Psychoanalysis Encountering the Holocaust," *Psychoanalytic Inquiry* 5, no. 1 (1985): 88–89.

12. *The Informed Heart*, pp. 169–170.

13. Hilde O. Bluhm, "How Did They Survive: Mechanisms of Defense in Nazi Concentration Camps," *American Journal of Psychotherapy* (1954): 23–24. Anna Freud proposed the term in 1936. Compare the discussion by Robert Krell, "Holocaust Survivors and Their Children: Comments on Psychiatric Consequences and Psychiatric Terminology," *Comprehensive Psychiatry* 25, no. 5 (September/October 1984): 523.

14. *The Informed Heart*, p. 132.

15. Hilde O. Bluhm, "How Did They Survive," p. 17.

16. Paul Friedman, "Some Aspects of Concentration Camp Psychology," *The American Journal of Psychiatry* 105, no. 8 (February 1949): 604.

17. "The sense of guilt at having remained alive when so many others had died—so universal among the survivors—seems to have played a not unimportant role in the genesis of the symptoms. Paul Friedman "Some Aspects of Concentration Camp Psychology," *The American Journal of Psychiatry* 105, no. 8 (February 1949): 603.

18. Robert Jay Lifton, *Death in Life: Survivors of Hiroshima* (New York: Simon and Schuster, 1967).

19. "The Concept of the Survivor" in Joel Dimsdale, Ed. *Survivors, Victims and Perpetrators* (New York: Hemisphere Publishing Corporation, 1980).

20. "The Concept of the Survivor", p. 119.

21. Stanley Elkins, *Slavery* (Chicago: University of Chicago Press, 1959).

22. Indeed Bettelheim became something of a cult figure—the "Second City" comedy team received a big laugh in Chicago with reference to a Bettelheim lecture on "Some Positive Aspects of Anti-Semitism."

23. These were later published as a book: Hannah Arendt, *Eichmann in Jerusalem* (New York: Viking, 1963).

24. Some indications about the intensity of emotions aroused by her work are given in the biographical study by Elizabeth Young-Bruehl, *Hannah Arendt, For the Love of the Word* (New Haven, CT: Yale University Press, 1982).

25. Jacob Robinson, *And the Crooked Shall Be Made Straight: The Eichmann Trial, the Jewish Catastrophe, and Hannah Arendt's Narrative* (New York: Macmillan, 1965).

26. Raul Hilberg, *The Destruction of the European Jews,* Chicago: (Quadrangle Press, 1961); a revised edition of this has recently been published: Raul Hilberg, *The Destruction of the European Jews: Revised and Definitive Edition,* 3 vols., 1274 pp. (New York: Holmes and Meier, 1985).

27. Bruno Bettelheim, *Surviving and Other Essays* (New York: Knopf, 1979).

28. Bettelheim, in the introductory section of this controversial article notes that "What concerns me here is not what actually happened to the Frank family, how they tried—and failed—to survive their terrible ordeal. It would be very wrong to take apart so humane and moving a story, which aroused so much well-merited compassion for gentle Anne Frank and her tragic fate. What is at issue is the universal and uncritical response to her diary. . . . I believe that the world-wide acclaim given her story cannot be explained unless we recognize in it our wish to forget the gas chambers, and our effort to do so by glorifying the ability to retreat into an extremely private, gentle, sensitive world." *Surviving,* p. 247.

29. An important exception is Elie A. Cohen, *Human Behavior in the Concentration Camp* (New York: Grosset and Dunlap, 1953), which critically addresses some technical issues of psychoanalytic interpretation, the basic outlook of which, however, is similar to Bettelheim's.

30. I examined the two versions and found a comparison of an early arrogant and a later empathetic Bettelheim unconvincing.

31. "The Psychoanalytic Writer on the Holocaust and Bettelheim," *American Journal of Social Psychiatry* IV, no. 2 (Spring 1984): 65.

32. Viktor Frankl, *Man's Search for Meaning: An Introduction to Logotherapy* (Boston, Beacon Press, 1962).

33. Ibid. p. 65; Hilde Bluhm, "How Did They Survive" also noted that "under the most horrible conditions . . . compassion, friendship and humanness were not completely absent."

34. There is a substantial critical literature about Frankl—the bibliographies appended to his works provide a good introduction. Compare also the article by James Woelfel, "Viktor Frankl on Freedom and Responsibility in the Death Camps: A Critique," *Journal of Social Philosophy* XIII, no. 3 (September 1982): 16–30.

35. Terrence Des Pres, *The Survivor: An Anatomy of the Life in the Death Camps* (New York: Oxford University Press, 1976).

36. A major critique, particularly of Des Pres' socio-biological premises, comes from Leon Rappoport, "Survivors of the Holocaust," *Journal of Psychohistory* 4, no. 3 (Winter 1977): 359–367.

37. Des Pres, *The Survivor,* pp. 155–156.

38. Compare Bettelheim's comments in *Surviving,* p. 95.

39. Des Pres, *The Survivor,* pp. 206–207. I learned just after writing the above that Des Pres committed suicide.

40. Leo Eitinger and Axel Strom, *Mortality and Morbidity after Excessive Stress: A Follow-up Investigation of Norwegian Concentration Camp Survivors* (New York: Humanities Press/Oslo, Universitets Forlaget, 1973), p. 102. In an earlier passage Eitinger and Strom, after noting the absence of a statistically significant higher suicide rate, add that "in the age group 50 years and over there were 11 suicides as against the expected

6.1, and that the excess of suicides only occurred after 1960 (pp. 42–43). Reading various case histories makes one aware of the suicides and attempted suicides of survivors.

41. Des Pres, *The Survivor,* p. 208.

42. An important analysis of the German policy is Milton Kestenberg, "Discriminatory Aspects of the German Indemnification Policy: A Continuation of Persecution," in Martin S. Bergmann and Milton E. Jucovy, Eds., *Generations of the Holocaust* (New York: Basic Books, 1982), pp. 62–79.

43. Bergmann and Jucovy, Eds., *Generations of the Holocaust,* p. 7.

44. However, an important work published in Germany in 1964 by Walter von Bayer, et al., *Psychiatrie der Verfolgten* (Berlin: Springer-Verlag, 1964), examines not only the psychological damage done by those in camps, but also addresses issues of expert testimony in reparation with some empathetic understanding.

45. Bergmann and Jucovy, p. 65.

46. Ibid., p. 69.

47. Henry Krystal, Ed., *Massive Psychic Trauma* (New York: International Universities Press, 1968), p. 85.

48. K. R. Eisler, "Die Ermordung von wievielen seiner Kinder muss ein Mensch symptomfrei ertragen können, um eine normale Konstitution zu haben?" *Psyche* XVII, no. 5 (1963/64): 241, 291.

49. Some of the issues confronting psychotherapists in the Third Reich come up in Geoffrey Cocks, *Psychotherapy in the Third Reich: The Göring Institute* (New York: Oxford University Press, 1985).

50. Compare W. von Bayer, et al., "Zur Frage des 'symptomfreien Intervalles' bei erlebnisreaktiven Störungen Verfolgter" in W. von Bayer, et al., *Psychische Spätschäden nach politischer Verfolgung* (Basel and New York: S. Karger, 1967), p. 188–216.

51. Moises Kijak and Silvio Funtowicz, "The Syndrome of the Survivor of Extreme Situations: Definitions, Difficulties, Hypotheses," *International Review of Psycho-Analysis* 9, no. 25 (1982); 27.

52. Paul Friedman, "Some Aspects of Concentration Camp Psychology," *The American Journal of Psychiatry* 105, no. 8 (February 1949): 601.

53. The extent of the literature is indicated in the definitive bibliography by Leo Eitinger and Robert Krell, *The Psychological and Medical Effects of Concentration Camps and Related Persecution on Survivors of the Holocaust* (Vancouver: University of British Columbia Press, 1985).

54. Steven A. Luel and Paul Marcus, *Reflections on the Holocaust: Selected Essays* (New York: KTAV Publishing House, 1984).

55. A detailed discussion appears in Paul Marcus and Alan Rosenberg, "A Philosophical Critique of the 'Survivor Syndrome' and Some Implications for Treatment." In Randolph L. Braham, ed. *The Psychological Perspectives of the Holocaust and of Its Aftermath.* (Boulder, CO: Social Science Monographs and The Csengeri Institute for Holocaust Studies of the Graduate School and University Center of the City University of New York. Distributed by Columbia University Press, 1988).

56. Yael Danieli, "Psychotherapists' Participation in the Conspiracy of Silence about the Holocaust," *Psychoanalytic Psychology* I, no. 1 (1984): 25.

57. Krell, "Holocaust Survivors and Their Children," p. 525.

58. Frederick H. Hocking, "After the Holocaust: Migrants who Survived Massive Stress Experiences," in Leo Eitinger and David Schwarz, Ed., *Strangers in the World* (Bern: Hans Huber), pp. 213–214.

59. Isaac Kanter, "Social Psychiatry and the Holocaust," *Journal of Psychology and Judaism* I, no. 1 (1976): 55–66.

60. Moises Kijak and Silvio Funtowicz, "The Syndrome of the Survivor of Extreme Situations: Definitions, Difficulties, Hypotheses," *International Review of Psycho-Analysis* 9, no. 25 (1982): 28–29.

61. Danieli, "Psychotherapists' Participation in the Conspiracy of Silence about the Holocaust," p. 23–24.

62. Krell, "Holocaust Survivors and their Children," p. 525.

63. Hocking, "After the Holocaust," pp. 204–214.

64. Ibid. Ernest A. Rappaport also wrote that after his release from a camp he found that "people did not really want me to talk about my experiences and whenever I started they invariably showed their resistance by interrupting me. . . . It is the . . . gloss over attitude which also explains the paucity of psychoanalytic literature on the concentration camp." Rappaport, "Beyond Traumatic Neurosis: A Psychoanalytic Study of Late Reactions to the Concentration Camp Trauma," *The International Journal of Psycho-Analysis* 49 (1968): 720.

65. Paul Chodoff, "Psychotherapy of the Survivor," in Joel Dimsdale, Ed., *Survivors, Victims and Perpetrators* (New York: Hemisphere Publishing Corporation, 1980).

66. Danieli, "Silence about the Holocaust."

67. Klaus Hoppe, "Severed Ties," in Luel and Marcus, Ed., *Psychoanalytic Reflections on the Holocaust* (New York: University of Denver and KTAV), pp. 95–112.

68. Krystal, Ed., *Massive Psychic Trauma,* p. 224.

69. As the Eitinger/Krell bibliography demonstrates, a large literature devoted to methods of therapy with survivors has developed. What is still lacking are adequate analyses of the perpetrators. Attempts to explain SS behavior on the basis of Freudian theory remain unconvincing. The inherited perceptions of human nature that serve as a foundation for most discussions—and then view SS behavior as some kind of deviance—fail to explain. It may be necessary to begin by defining the personality structure of the perpetrators as normal.

70. Bergmann and Jucovy, *Generations,* p. 9; compare Marcus and Rosenberg, "A Philosophical Critique of the 'Survivor Syndrome' and Some Implications for Treatment."

71. Yael Danieli, "The Treatment and Prevention of Long-term Effects and Intergenerational Transmission of Victimization: A Lesson from Holocaust Survivors and Their Children," in Charles R. Figley, Ed., *Trauma and Its Wake: The Study and Treatment of Post-Traumatic Stress Disorder* (New York: Brunner/Mazel, 1985), p. 297.

72. Gustav Bychowski in Krystal, Ed., *Massive Trauma,* p. 76.

73. Marcus and Rosenberg, "A Philosophical Critique of the 'Survivor Syndrome,' " p. 61–62.

74. Marcus and Rosenberg, "A Philosophical Critique," p. 60.

75. Moshe Almagor and Gloria R. Leon, "Transgenerational Effects of the Concentration Camp Experience," this volume.

76. Boaz Kahana, Zev Harel, and Eva Kahana, "Clinical and Gerontological Issues Facing Survivors of the Nazi Holocaust" in this volume.

77. Kahana, p. 15.

78. Anna Ornstein, "Survival and Recovery," p. 116.

79. Compare Charles R. Figley, Ed. *Trauma and Its Wake: The Study and Treatment of Post-traumatic Stress Disorder* (New York: Brunner/Mazel, 1985).

80. I believe the biggest failure of psychoanalytic theory is found not in the analysis of survivors, but in its inability to explain satisfactorily the psychology of the perpetrator. The attempts to explain SS behavior on the basis of Freudian theory remain unconvincing, largely because they have largely ignored the power of institutions in shaping individual conduct. Henry Dicks's *Licensed Mass Murder: A Socio-psychological Study of Some SS Killers* (New York: Basic Books, 1972) analyzed several perpetrators; it is clear that they would not have committed the crimes for which they were sentenced if they had acted only as private individuals. Compare George M. Kren, "Psychohistory and the Holocaust," *Journal of Psychohistory* VI, no. 3 (Winter 1979): 407–417.

81. See Bergmann and Jucovy, *Generations of the Holocaust*, p. 36. This work also contains a valuable bibliography.

82. The work is unique in also dealing (in a section titled "The Persecutors' Children") with the children whose parents were enthusiastic supporters of Hitler.

83. Helen Epstein, *Children of the Holocaust: Conversations with Sons and Daughters of Survivors* (New York: Putnam, 1979).

2

Holocaust Survivors and Their Children: A Review of the Clinical Literature

ARLENE STEINBERG

HOLOCAUST SURVIVORS

The effects of Holocaust traumatization were first documented in 1948;[1] however, it was not until the 1960s that numerous psychological studies on survivors were published. For the most part, the initial investigative efforts were derived from psychiatric or psychological evaluations of survivors' eligibility to receive compensation from the German government for psychological damage.[2] The emphasis on pathology in the early literature may have been an artifact of this focus on problems. Later studies also included observations of patients in treatment. This chapter will survey different clinical perspectives on Holocaust survivors and their children. The use of varied treatment modalities and some technical considerations in treatment will also be discussed.

Early investigators studying Holocaust survivors faced difficulties, as there were contradictions among the available definitions of trauma and traumatic neurosis, and no clear theory for viewing the survivor seemed to exist. Freud's views conflicted with other contemporary nonpsychoanalytic views of the traumatic neurosis. Some writers attributed the traumatic neurosis to the experience of a threat to self-preservation. However, Freud[3] considered the traumatic neurosis as influenced by the individuals' pretraumatic experiences, deeper levels of pre-existing psychic structure, and the libidinal coloring of the traumatic experience. Freud said that "the unconscious seems to contain nothing that could give any content to our concept of the annihilation of life . . . and was inclined to adhere to the view that the fear of death should be regarded as analogous to the fear of castration."[4] While emphasis on sexual factors has diminished in the literature, the role of pretraumatic experience has remained both relevant and controversial. Authors writing since Freud have attributed the posttraumatic illness solely to the trauma itself. It is only more recently that writers have begun to view the survivors' post-Holocaust adaptation as influenced by experiences during their entire lifespan (including pretraumatic experiences), with the Holocaust viewed as a significant event within the lifespan.[5, 6, 7]

Freud also described the individual as equipped with a stimulus barrier (the part of the psychic apparatus which protects the ego from excessive stimulation that is directed against both internal and external stimuli). He defined any experience that achieves a breaking down of this barrier as traumatic. Trauma was, for the most part, considered a temporary situation from which one recovers to a relatively stable, nonthreatening state. This definition did not seem to encompass the long-term situation of oppression experienced by most survivors.

The noted discrepant views on the nature and the etiology of the trauma seemed to have contributed to conflicting conceptualizations of survivors' post-Holocaust adaptation, and the effectiveness of psychotherapy. Early psychoanalytic writers concluded that survivor psychotherapy was a condition that was completely determined by Holocaust experiences, with the survivor profoundly affected by the massive psychic trauma experienced and thus developing these symptoms. More contemporary views, as has been mentioned, have begun to consider the role of the patient's pretraumatic and posttraumatic experiences as well as the strengths they bring to bear in their later adaptation. These differing conceptualizations of the traumatic element with their varying implications for the treatment of survivors will be discussed.

Early Perspectives on the Survivor

Early psychological conceptualizations of the survivor described the defenses used by survivors against the stresses of life during the Holocaust.[2, 8, 9, 10, 11] Bruno Bettelheim[8] wrote one of the earliest descriptions of survival, which served as one of the main depictions of the survival experience in the psychiatric literature. The central goal of the concentration camp, according to Bettelheim, was to break inmates' resistance and autonomy, and mold them into more "useful subjects of the Nazi State." A major defense mechanism described by him was identification with the aggressor, in which the inmates assumed Nazi values. This identification was considered necessary for their survival. They were also viewed as isolated individuals who did not appear concerned about their fellow prisoners, nor were they able to resist the surrounding tyranny. Their primary mode of adaptation to the camp consisted of infantile preoccupation and regression. Bettelehim viewed inmates as having been forced to modify drastically their methods of coping, as they were no longer able to use pre-Holocaust coping strategies, and this contributed to basic changes in their personality.

Bettelheim's pessimistic conceptualization of the survivor had been accepted by many of the earlier writers. However, critics of his view noted that he was himself a survivor of the Dachau concentration camp, and was liberated before

1939. In addition, he did not live through the camps when they were in their most fully developed state.[12, 13] Observing his fellow inmates and camp life was his way of coping with the stresses he was forced to endure rather than an objective picture of survival experience. While Bettelheim's view had been the accepted paradigm for many years, his views were challenged in a landmark book by Des Pres,[14] who questioned whether Bettelheim's position was sufficiently objective, was generalizable to other survivors, and applied psychoanalytic concepts where they were indeed applicable.

Niederland,[9] among other authors,[10, 11] has studied the defenses used by survivors during the Holocaust, as well as the psychiatric symptoms observed among survivors after the war. Predominant defenses (besides those mentioned by Bettelheim) included by Niederland were denial, isolation, and somatization. During the Holocaust these defenses seemed to protect the victims against their own overwhelming emotions in reaction to the horrors they witnessed and experienced. Individuals who were unable to cope successfully with camp life became "walking corpses" or *Musselmänner* (the German word used by their fellow inmates) and eventually died. While the defenses utilized may have enabled victims to survive, their primitive nature presented survivors with difficulties during their postwar adjustment. They began to then develop symptoms after a latency period of several years. As has been mentioned, these symptoms were, for the most part, observed by mental health professionals evaluating survivors for eligibility to receive reparations. The context of their being evaluated for damage rather than in treatment to receive help and the possibility of compensation may also have encouraged greater pathology. It was in this context that survivors' symptomatology was first noticed and described.

As a constellation of symptoms was observed that could not be understood through the available psychiatric categories, the "concentration camp survivor syndrome"[15] or "survivor syndrome"[16] (Niederland) was named. The creation of this diagnostic term also served to facilitate easier compensation by the German government for survivors' psychological difficulties. Symptoms mentioned were cognitive and memory disturbances (e.g., hypermnesia of the traumatic experiences), motor unrest, psychosomatic symptoms, feelings of anxiety (including fear of renewed persecution and phobias), guilt, depression, insomnia, nightmares of specific persecutory experiences, and alterations in the sense of identity (e.g., body image, and sense of space and time).[2, 9, 17, 18, 19, 20] Survivors were described as having pervasive, irreversible psychological difficulties as a result of their Holocaust experiences.

Krystal and Niederland considered survivor guilt a major pathogenic force in the large number of cases they observed.[2, 9, 21, 22] They viewed it as a form of pathological mourning, in which the individual felt guilty for aggressive feelings toward the lost object—which feelings were repressed. The proposed death wishes became linked with the actual destruction of the object (possibly as a result of the survivors "identification with the aggressor," according to this view), and the wishes assumed greater significance as a result of this. Niederland later expanded his earlier view and explained survivor guilt as a reaction to survival itself.[23] While still considering it a major pathogenic force, he no longer attributed primary significance to the death wishes toward the lost object.

Several authors[17, 24] have also elaborated on survivors' depressive symptoms, which have included feelings of emptiness, loss, fatigue, sleep disturbance, nightmares, and social withdrawal. Depression has been regarded as a consequence of unresolved mourning, as well as guilt about one's conduct during incarceration. Hoppe, differentiating two groups, distinguished depressed survivors from aggressive ones. Survivors experiencing chronic reactive depression have experienced helplessness and hopelessness, and survivors with chronic reactive aggression have clung to feelings of anger and "hate addiction". The survivors' feelings of anger were directed at representations of their negative conscience projected onto the environment, rather than purely and directly reacting to environmental stimuli. He referred to the externalization process as the "master-slave-seesaw relationship".[24, 25]

Krystal has also described the difficulties that survivors have observing, describing, and utilizing their feelings and fantasies, which he called "alexithymia".[26] A related process has been described by Lifton and others, which they called "psychic closing off" or "psychic numbing," in which the survivor has shut down his or her own emotional reactivity, given the overwhelming nature of the stimulation during the traumatic period. Survivors' emotional numbing has been described as an identification with the dead or with death.[17, 22, 23, 27]

Krystal has further described the prevalent psychosomatic symptoms in this population as the result of a regressive resomatization of affects due to survivors' difficulties with affective verbalization.[17, 28] Those unable to verbalize their feelings return to an earlier somatic stage of affective expression. While several writers agree that psychosomatic symptoms are manifestations of regression,[19, 20, 28, 29] these symptoms have also been viewed as masked depressive states.[23]

Holocaust survivors were also described as having undergone permanent changes of personality,[9, 30] as the extreme stresses they encountered precluded their using prior traits and resulted in the adaptive emergence of new personality traits to cope with the traumatic situation.[2, 9, 19, 31, 32, 33] (The emphasis, initiated by Bettelheim,[8] on the survivor's identification with the aggressor during the Holocaust exemplifies this.) DeWind stressed the significance of these changes in his statement that "massive trauma is capable of causing changes in the personality structure as that which we have previously known to happen in the preoedipal phase of development."[34]

While most authors agree on the array of symptoms present in the survivor syndrome, the etiology of this disorder remains controversial. The Freudian view, as already mentioned, explained the trauma experienced by the survivor in terms of the breaching of the stimulus barrier as well as castration anxiety. Other writers, who disagreed with the castration anxiety hypothesis, considered the danger to self-preservation as a sufficient cause of neurosis.

Leo Eitinger, moving away from the psychological explanations of the trauma and survivors' symptoms predominating the literature, considered a physiological basis for their symptomatology. He explained their symptoms as a result of organic brain changes, due to the experiences of starvation, weight loss, exhaustion, head injuries, and disease (e.g., encephalitis and typhus) in the concentration camp. He found some degree of encephalopathy in 80 percent of the survivors he observed. He also viewed the survivor syndrome as both positively correlated with the severity of imprisonment, and appearing regardless of the individual's pre- or post-Holocaust experiences.[35] Hoppe has disagreed with this explanation, as his patients have experienced severe camp treatment without concomitant brain damage.[25]

Within clinical circles, the survivor syndrome became the accepted paradigm for viewing survivors. Although this model was mostly based on observations from psychiatric evaluations for compensation from the German government, it was applied in order to understand the behavior of Holocaust survivors in treatment—a very different setting. The limited power of this model to explain the behavior of Holocaust survivors in treatment did not appear to inhibit its use. The survivor was often too readily diagnosed as having the syndrome, and other characteristics not readily consonant with the survivor syndrome were ignored.

Proponents of the survivor syndrome presented a pessimistic prognosis for survivors in psychoanalytic psychotherapy, as their personalities were considered irreversibly changed by their Holocaust experiences.[36, 37, 38] According to this model, survivors were viewed as "historyless" with their personalities entirely shaped by the traumatic period. It is therefore not surprising that the application of psychoanalytic theory, with its focus on earlier experiences, would be problematic with this population. Neglect of the survivors' strengths, including their ability to recover, also contributed to the negative prognosis. In addition, certain characteristics described in the survivor syndrome, which include alexithymia (inability to identify and express one's feelings and fantasies), depression, "hate addiction," and difficulty trusting also contributed to the negative prognosis, as these are traits that do not favor successful results in psychotherapy.

Concerns over whether survivors are able to withstand treatment have been expressed by Hoppe[25] and others.[33, 39] They felt that survivors, having undergone traumatic regression during the Holocaust, would experience difficulty and extreme pain undergoing therapeutic regression in their psychoanalytic treatment. Klein recommended that long-term psychoanalytic psychotherapy be conducted in a hospital setting in order to contain the extreme regressions of these patients.[39] Other writers have attempted to circumvent these difficulties by offering alternatives to psychoanalytic treatment aproaches, and have suggested short-term approaches, for example, supportive or limited-objective psychotherapy.[38, 40]

Given the pessimistic prognosis noted in the treatment literature, it is not surprising that survivors have been reluctant to request psychotherapy. In addition, their personality characteristics described above may have also contributed to their reluctance. Survivors' hesitancy has been attributed both to the survivors themselves, as well as their reactions to perceived therapist resistances. Psychotherapy is viewed as both threatening survivors' denial of their pain,[2, 39] and their feelings of specialness at having survived. Lifton has described therapists' own denial of death, which can be threatened by the survivor's recounting of his/her close encounters with death during the Holocaust.[22] It has also been suggested that lack of information about available resources and suitable treatment aproaches may have also contributed to the reluctance of survivors.[41]

More Recent Views of the Survivor

Alternate views of the survivor have been more recently considered, given the limitations and problems with the earlier conceptualization of the survivor. Difficulties have included observations of heterogeneity among survivors not accounted for in the earlier picture, the pessimistic prognosis for treatment with this population, and questions about the relevance of this syndrome to survivors in treatment. These newer views have conceptualized the trauma experienced by survivors in a different way than previously assumed. They emphasized the influence of survivors' pre-Holocaust and post-Holocaust experiences on their later adaptation, as well as stressing the importance of acknowledging the heterogeneity among survivors. Some authors have also presented alternate perspectives on some of the basic assumptions of the survivor syndrome, for example, the extent to which guilt is a major pathogenic force for survivors. These more recent positions maintain more optimistic prognoses for survivors in treatment, and suggest certain technical modifications in the treatment of these patients.

Marcus and Rosenberg, in their review of the literature, summarize what they have called the "alternative narrative" of survivors' behavior during the Holocaust.[42] The writings of Des Pres, Ornstein, Eitinger, Klein, and Luchterhand [5, 12, 14, 35, 43, 44] describe survivors' strengths as they had actively pursued meaningful relationships during the Holocaust, based on their pre-existing values, a very different perspective from Bettelheim's earlier depiction of an isolated individual who survived by accepting Nazi values as his own. Inmates survived the traumatic period through their participation in these relationships, and in an evolving social organization in the camp. Group affiliation provided them with greater opportunities to express pre-Holocaust modes of conduct. This interpersonal dimension mitigated to some extent the destructive impact of the traumatic experiences. These strengths both enabled them to cope during the Holocaust and facilitated their recovery after the war. Other strengths included the ability to resist actively during the Holocaust, and the preservation of pre-Holocaust values (viewed as an aspect of this resistance). Overall, in the "alternative narrative" survivors are depicted in less pathological terms than portrayed in the earlier perspective, and are viewed as more amenable to the help of treatment.

The posttraumatic symptoms, according to this view, were influenced by the survivors' pre- and post-Holocaust experiences as well as genetic endowment. They were not solely the result of the Holocaust trauma as was described in the earlier view. Chodoff[6] included among post-Holocaust experiences, countries immigrated to after the war and extent of familial and financial losses. Terry[7] additionally described the immigrant survivors' painful experience after the war confronting the discomfort and lack of understanding among nonsurvivor relatives.

The variability among survivors was also influenced by the developmental phase of the survivor during the Holocaust. Fink,[45] Danto,[46] and others[47] described those who survived the war as children as prone to experiencing abandonment fears, given their loss of parents and siblings, while those who survived as adults feared losing their newly formed families, given their already having lost spouses and children. Koenig[48] also described experiences of "chronic identity diffusion" among adolescent survivors. He related these difficulties to the experience of having been cut off from parental values during the developmental phase which would have been characterized by identification with those values.

Proponents of the alternative view do not appear to disagree with the array of symptoms included in the survivor syndrome, although their notions of the role of symptoms and specific definitions may vary. The relative importance attributed to some symptoms described in the earlier views have also recently been questioned.

Ornstein,[5] coming from a self-psychological perspective, has viewed survivor symptomatology as having an adaptive purpose, instead of the pathological way it had been depicted. She described its role helping survivors maintain self-cohesion. She specifically explained the function of survivor anger as preventing helplessness rather than as an expression of pathology.

Although earlier writers described guilt as the major pathogenic force in most survivors' lives, more recent writers have found that guilt plays less of a role in the lives of the survivors they observed.[27, 49, 50, 51] Definitions of guilt have also varied from those earlier formulations. While guilt had been considered in purely pathological terms, more recent definitions have stressed its adaptive aspects. Guilt was no longer viewed in terms of repressed hostility toward the love object, and distinctions in the new definitions between various types of guilt were made. Carmelly[52] distinguished passive carriers, who felt guilty about their survival (a definition consonant with Niederland's more recent views), from those who felt guilty about actual immoral acts committed. Lifton[53] differentiated between moral and psychological guilt, and considered classical writings as describing the latter. He viewed moral guilt as an adaptive experience that helps individuals see their shortcomings, but when not worked through can lead to pathology. Klein[43] has also discussed the healthy aspects of guilt which can link survivors and their children to the past, to those who died, and to a sense of belonging to the Jewish people.

Recent empirical studies have also raised questions about the early formulation of survivor symptomatology. Solkoff[41] has criticized the extent to which descriptions of the survivor syndrome have been based on clinical observations rather than systematic study. Recent methodological studies have found survivor guilt[51] and psychosomatic symptoms[54] not to be as pervasive as had been depicted, although some symptoms, for example, the observed experience of diffusion of the time perspective,[55] have been supported by empirical findings.

The more optimistic portrayal of the survivor captured in the more recent views has contributed to more hopeful prognoses for survivors in treatment. Their pre-existing strengths, which may have facilitated their survival, could also play a major role in their post-Holocaust recovery.

Therapeutic Implications of the More Recent Views

While most early psychoanalytic writers were pessimistic about the effectiveness of psychotherapy with survivors, there were also those who came from an analytic tradition, and felt that survivors could be helped in psychotherapy.[56, 57, 58] Freud and Dann,[56] and Gyomroi[58] discussed successful analytic treatment with child survivors. Freud and Dann worked with children at a residential facility in England immediately after World War II. Peergroup cohesiveness seemed to support their adaptation in the concentration camp and to facilitate the children's postwar adjustment. This characteristic was incorporated into the rehabilitation program Freud and Dann provided. Their early work highlighted the importance of interpersonal relationships for the survivors' Holocaust and subsequent adjustment, which was later ignored by proponents of the survivor syndrome. Gyomroi[58] described the successful analysis of a female child survivor during her adolescence. Analysis helped her undergo missed developmental phases, and achieve better personality integration.

DeWind,[13, 31, 59] another early writer, recommended the use of parameters of technique in the treatment of survivors, and attributed the difficulties of classical analysts working with this population to their rigid adherence to classical technique. He included as a parameter the therapist's demonstration of caring for the patient. He also recommended a period of preparatory analytic work in order to strengthen the survivor patient's ego, so that he/she can withstand the later emotional re-experiencing of camp traumata. DeWind considered treatment capable of improving survivors' functioning and relieving their symptoms, although not able to free them completely from their painful memories.

More recently, Klein,[44] Ornstein,[5] and Frankl[60] have also expressed encouraging views of the psychotherapeutic treatment of survivors. Both Klein and Ornstein consider the main task of psychotherapy to be the re-establishment of continuity between survivors' past and present, given the significant disruption of their lives during the Holocaust. Klein felt that survivors can recapture through treatment their prewar levels of ego functioning. Ornstein[5] described recovery as the reestablishment of continuity between survivors pre-Holocaust, Holocaust, and post-Holocaust self-perceptions, given the changes in self-perceptions wrought by Holocaust experiences. Both writers perceive the survivor as having retained pre-Holocaust values both during and after the Holocaust, with psychotherapy focusing on mitigating the damage to this value system inflicted during the traumatic period, when survivors were cut off from family and community.

Frankl[60] described survivors' search for the meaning of their "senseless" suffering. This search can help them restore the human dimension to their experiences of the inhumane, as their quest for meaning is a human endeavor. From this existentialist position, he has developed a form of treatment, called logotherapy, to aid the survivor in this search. As the survivor patient finds meaning, his symptoms are alleviated, for they are viewed as a maladaptive way to give meaning when more adaptive ways are not available. Marcus and Rosenberg[61] have stressed the rupturing of the survivor's symbolic world and consequent inability to sustain his "locus of primary value in a world of meaning." They too view the focus of psychotherapy on the rebuilding of viable human meaning formations in the survivors' lives.

There are also differing conceptualizations of the aging survivor in the literature. Krystal[26] considered the major task of old age to be an integrative one, that is, the coming to terms with and acceptance of one's past. He stressed the importance of accepting shameful, guilt-ridden, and helpless feelings, and renouncing one's rage at others for past victimization experiences. He considered this task difficult for the survivor patient for several reasons. He attributed their difficulty to their need to cling to a justification for their survival, namely, "to be angry witnesses to the outrage of the Holocaust," and considered the quantity and quality of survivors' losses as exceeding that for which human beings are capable of mourning. Survivors experience chronic depression and constriction of their emotional and fantasy life as a result of their mourning difficulty. Krystal felt that their troubles were not successfully treatable in exploratory therapy, and instead recommended supportive therapy to help them acknowledge and accept their painful emotions. Krystal's pessimistic outlook is reflective of earlier conceptualizations of the survivor, although he has found a way to offer them help. While Krystal has focused on the intrapsychic process, Danieli[62] and others[63] have addressed intrafamilial issues among aging survivors and their children, although all stress the important role of integration. Danieli has described the exacerbation of unresolved difficulties between parents and their children as survivor parents age. She and others have recommended family therapy to foster communication between these aging survivor parents and their offspring, and facilitate the integration of parental Holocaust experiences.

The tensions between earlier and more recent perspectives in the general literature of survivors are paralleled in the literature on aging survivors. While the earlier studies seemed to stress survivor pathology, there now appear to be studies also stressing the adaptation of aging survivors.[64] More observations and investigations are needed in this area, particularly as the time left to conduct these studies is rapidly diminishing.

The early investigations seemed to struggle with understanding the survivor via pre-existing theories. Survivors were, in a sense, fit into the theories, but the fit, as critics have pointed out, was not quite right. Aspects of the survival experience that many survivors themselves had described were not acknowledged by those earlier viewpoints. While some continue to uphold views reminiscent of the earlier outlook, recent approaches have attempted to understand more fully the experience of survivors, and have been more attuned to the heterogeneity of the survivor community. In addition, newer orientations and modalities have arisen that seem better suited than the earlier views to explain recent observations and to offer them help. Self-psychology, as well as family and group therapeutic modalities, are among the newer approaches. The usefulness of these newer modalities will be discussed in greater detail in the section on survivors' children, below.

CHILDREN OF SURVIVORS

Many of the problems with and criticisms of the early literature on survivors have continued to reverberate through the psychological literature on survivors' children. There are still tendencies to "syndromize" and label the second generation as was true with their parents. However, these trends have weakened as survivors' children were observed at a later historical period than their parents, and these studies were based on children of survivors in treatment, a different setting than that of the earlier survivor studies. The historical pressures on clinicians to find pathology among the Holocaust survivors they examined for eligibility to receive compensation from the German government did not similarly constrain the later observers of survivors' children. In addition, the development of new treatment approaches has enabled survivors' children to be observed from different perspectives, and also has facilitated the use of various therapeutic techniques and modalities with this population not previously attempted.

Children of Survivors: The Clinical Profile

Survivors' children have presented symptoms resembling those of their parents. These have included depression, anxiety, phobias, guilt, and separation problems.[15] Children of survivors have also manifested similar dream imagery, phobic phenomena, and environmental misperception.[65] Particular fears of separation have been noted. Before further discussion of these symptoms, examination of the way these difficulties were transmitted to survivors' children is warranted.

Trossman,[66] Phillips,[67] Roden and Roden,[68] among others,[69, 70] have attributed transmission to certain characteristics of survivor parenting. Survivors are described as overprotective, warning their children excessively of danger. The concerns of these parents about potential danger in the environment stem from their own past perilous confrontations during the Holocaust. Their children are described as heeding their warnings, believing them, yet also perhaps by way of protecting survivor parents from further pain if they were to confront the dangers. Given this atmosphere of imagined danger and survivors' excessive anxiety about their children's well-being, it is not surprising that these offspring have developed a variety of phobias.

Survivors have also been portrayed as possessing high expectations for their children. These children may be perceived by their parents as replacements for the numerous losses,[49, 69, 71] and may also be expected to give meaning to their parents' lives. Many children of survivors have also been expected to serve as links between their parents and the outside world. However, they are in a bind as their parents have also presented them with the conflicting attitude of suspicion toward the outside world,[66] based on their parents' prior traumatization.

Differing expectations among survivor parents have been related to the age of the survivor parent at the time of traumatization. Older survivors are described as more overinvested in their children, related to their own past losses of spouse and children,[49] while younger survivors are more concerned about abandonment issues related to their losses of families of origin. Sonnenberg[69] and Krell[63] have also described the particular parenting difficulties of adolescent survivors with their teenage children, given their own loss of a normal existence during adolescence.

Separation problems[66, 72, 73] are among the most prevalent clinical features described for survivors' children. The characteristics of the survivor parent-child relationship may contribute to the appearance of these symptoms, as children of survivors are overprotected by their parents, encourged to view the world as a dangerous place and the family as the only shield from those dangers. They are also perceived as possible replacements for the family's lost relatives and world. The child reared in this environment may experience difficulty functioning independently, or at least their awareness of parental suffering may result in submission to parents rather than to cause the latter more pain or incite parental anger. Within this observed context, separation problems develop. Clinical observations of survivors' children have revealed a whole range of problems with separation-individuation from neurotic difficulties to extremely symbiotic attachments.

Separation difficulties have also manifested themselves among survivors' children in the clinical situation as described by Freyberg.[74] They have experienced blurring of their boundaries when confronted with experiences that are reminiscent of their parents' Holocaust experience. In addition, when angered with their therapist, according to Freyberg, they disavowed their anger and instead assumed the feelings and opinions of their therapist, perhaps as a way to ward off their own angry feelings. Freyberg attributed these moments of loss of separateness to deficiencies in the rapprochement subphase of separation-individuation. This phase is characterized by the child's need for parental encouragement and approval for his early individuation attempts. The survivor parent is described as unable to provide the child this necessary support, given the arousal of their own anxieties by the child's independent undertakings.

Children of survivors have also been described as possessing conflicting feelings of pride and humiliation about their Jewish identities. These different feelings seem to be associated with their image of how their parents survived the Holocaust. Feelings of pride may be related to their viewing their parents as Jewish heroes, while humiliation may be associated with considering them helpless victims.[68, 75]

Trossman[66] commented on another characteristic symptom of this population, that is, the depressive reactions of survivors' children. He explained these symptoms as reactions to survivor parents' communications about their victimization during the Holocaust. Cahn[76] has reported that parents' difficulty acknowledging and communicating the details of their Holocaust experiences may contribute to increased depression and other difficulties among survivors' children. This may be related to a preoccupation on the part of the child with fantasies about what parents experienced. Survivors' children have been described as experiencing difficulty expressing anger directly, possibly having been reared in a home environment where the outward expression of aggression was discouraged. They appear instead to focus their anger inward, towards the self, which can also lead to depressive symptoms.[77]

The symptoms and difficulties of survivors' children have led to their experiencing themselves as "scarred or different" from other American children.[78] Helen Epstein has poignantly portrayed those feelings through her interviews with survivors' children in North America. Her popular book helped many grown children of survivors experience themselves as part of a greater legacy, and not so different after all.[79]

Studies of survivors' children in Israel demonstrated their sharing some features, but also differing from their U.S. counterparts.[63, 68, 71] They are described as more closely attached to their families, and more anxious and withdrawn in the face of open aggression or the dangers of war than other Israeli children. However, they seem to feel less "scarred or different" than the American group.[78] Life in Israel, particularly among survivor families living on the kibbutz, seemed to foster feelings of belonging in survivor families. Their survival struggles could be placed in the context of the national struggle and group survival, and their angry feelings could be directed against a common external enemy. Opportunities for collective mourning allowed Israeli survivors to not have to serve as "a living memorial to their lost families. This function has been taken over and institutionalized by the State."[80]

Systematic studies have recently been conducted to assess the actual presence of the observed clinical features with the larger population of survivors' children. Several recent empirical studies have examined both the characteristics of survivors' children and of their relationships with their parents. Many of these studies focused on nonclinical samples. Although survivors' children did not appear any less well adjusted than nonsurvivors' children in Rose and Garske's systematic study, they did perceive their families as discouraging their independence and assertiveness.[81] These perceptions are consistent with the clinical observations of separation difficulties described above. These families were described in the empirical literature as more closely engaged with one another than

American families, with engagement characterized by less extreme involvement than enmeshment.[82, 83] However, the clinical impressions of enmeshment in these families have not been supported.[84] Also, findings of children of survivors with strong motivation to achieve and to help others altruistically have also been reported. Strong achievement motivation has been associated with the high expectations of survivor parents for their children.[83]

The number of empirical investigations of survivors' children has been increasing; however, there are still many clinical observations that are accepted and yet have not been methodologically tested. The important need for these investigations is underscored by the presence of empirical results that have not supported accepted clinical assumptions.

While most writers have, more or less, agreed on many of the features of the clinical picture of the survivor's child, their clinical understanding and approaches to treatment seem to differ.

Psychoanalytic Treatment

Psychoanalytic observers noted symptomatology among survivors' children, and felt that the traumatic impact of the Holocaust was transmitted to survivors' children; they then sought to investigate the mechanisms of the transmission of trauma. Bergman and Jucovy have noted several ways the Holocaust may be transmitted, many of which seem to overlap.[85] Some survivor parents continue to live in the shadow of their Holocaust experiences, comparing their children to those who were murdered during that period, with the children not only forming an identity in the present, but identifying with those deceased relatives, as well. Other children may be identified with the persecutor, based on parental projections; and yet others may be sought after for parenting, given parents having been deprived of their own parenting when it was desperately needed during their victimization. Some survivors have transformed the Holocaust into a personal myth based on fantasies that were passed on to the children, while other children of survivors have created their own personal myth about the Holocaust (in families where Holocaust experiences may not have been discussed) based on their own fantasies. These authors have considered the Holocaust as an extreme trauma that serves as a significant factor around which children's other life experiences and developmental conflicts can organize. The strong effects of trauma on other life events seem to be associated with limitations in the human capacity to respond to trauma, contributing to the generalization of posttraumatic reactions to other aspects of one's life.

Although psychoanalytic investigators describe common features of survivors' children, there appears to be a trend away from the overgeneralizing among the early psychoanalytic studies of survivors. Kestenberg[86] felt it would not be accurate to label their common difficulties in terms of a ''survivors' child syndrome,'' comparable to the survivor syndrome described for their parents, given the existence of differences among the children, as well. She described a ''child of survivor complex,'' which not only included individual differences, but their common strengths rather than just pathology. While she seemed to acknowledge the heterogeneity of this group, a complex or constellation of features in most, if not all, survivors' children is still described. The tendency among psychoanalytic authors to generalize commonalities in a population based on a few cases, continued to exist, albeit in a more cautious manner.

Herzog[87] and Kestenberg[86] have described survivors' children as living a simultaneous double existence, both in their current and in the parental Holocaust world, or the "World Beyond Metaphor", as Herzog described. Kestenberg termed the latter transposition into the past, a process that goes beyond that of identification. In this process, the child's normal developmental affects and conflicts assume greater saliency at certain stages that become associated with the specific traumatic experiences of the parents. For example, the oral phases of the child's development may stir up memories of the parents' experiences with starvation, and may result in an excessively anxious focus on the child's eating behavior, distorting the normal development tasks of this stage.

Kestenberg and Oliner[88] have stressed the remarkable ego strength and capacity for sublimation of survivors' children. This emphasis on the strength of survivors' children and their capacities for adaptation seems to be part of a new trend in the literature which emphasizes strengths. It is also consistent with some of the more recent empirical literature that has described survivors' children as healthier than earlier clinical descriptions.

Maria Bergmann,[89] Ilsa Grubrich-Simitis,[90] among other authors,[91] have described the tendency of survivors' children to project the dangers of their Holocaust-related fantasies onto the environment as do their parents. Enactments in the lives of survivors' children resembling their parents' experiences are an expression of this. The process of projecting and enacting Holocaust fantasies rather than verbalizing them has been referred to as concretization. Maria Bergmann[89] has described how concretization may interfere with working through familial losses through mourning. She suggested that by therapists' encouraging greater awareness of the unconscious meaning of actions, symbol formation, internalization, and psychic representation are facilitated. The process of mourning seems simultaneously to occur.

Extreme cases of concretization, in which survivors' children appeared delusional during their enactments, have been noted. Link, Victor, and Binder[92] described two patients whose delusions resembled their parents' experiences during the Holocaust. Kestenberg[93] specifically described the case of a young adolescent who appeared psychotic, and yet was cured by psychoanalysis in a relatively brief period. Axelrod, Schnipper, and Rau[94] observed another feature of the delusional episodes in a sample of hospitalized children of survivors. They noticed that the age of hospitalization coincided with the age of their parents' incarceration, and considered these episodes as "anniversary reactions." Oliner[88] described these delusions in terms of dissociative/hysterical phenomena rather than derived from schizophrenic-like fragmentation. The remarkable ego strength of survivors' children alongside delusional material supports this view, which can also explain the quick cure of Kestenberg's patient.

Martin Bergmann[91] described the enactments of survivors' children in their treatment, which may include their abandoning and returning to treatment. He encouraged therapists' tolerance of this behavior, as it may be part of their patients' working through of Holocaust material. The meaning of this behavior may only become clearer at a later point. Kestenberg[86] among others has discussed the importance of assuming a caring, nurturing role with children of survivor patients. This role differs from the neutral posture of the classical Freudians, and suggests a modification in treatment style and technique among psychoanalysts working with survivors and their children. Bergmann and Jucovy[85] also discuss analysts' difficulties adhering to a neutral stance of merely reflecting back what the patient says, given the strong emotions evoked in the analyst in reaction to Holocaust material. Other authors also discussed the importance of the analysts' real reactions in providing relief for survivors' children by confirming for them the reality of the Holocaust in an emotional way.[90]

Criticisms of the psychoanalytic position have been expressed by Roden and Roden,[68] Solkoff,[95] and Schwaber.[96] While psychoanalytic writings are rich in case presentations, they have been criticized for their tendency to make generalizations about a population based on a few clinical cases. They have also been criticized for their emphasis on psychopathology, without sufficient consideration of the positive adaptation of survivors' children. Solkoff stated in his review of the literature that empirical studies suggest that "being a child of survivors is not necessarily a significant predisposing condition for the development of psychopathology . . . and that those children may become less psychologically vulnerable, more competent and more creative as a result of their intrafamilial experiences."[97]

Analysts have become more sensitive to the strengths of survivors' children, and have tried to veer away from syndromizing this population. They still seem, however, somewhat unsure of the extent of pathology present in this population. This appears to be an area of controversy that requires more research. While Kestenberg stressed that it would not be accurate to label a "survivors' child syndrome," Bergmann and Jucovy felt that it "is not possible for a child to grow up without becoming scarred, in a world where the Holocaust is the dominant psychic reality."[98] They apologize for their pessimism, and yet it is still unclear whether they feel there are survivors who can provide a home life in which the Holocaust is not the dominant reality, and rear children who are unscathed. As already mentioned, empirical studies[81] have found no differences in adjustment between children of survivors and children of nonsurvivor parents. These findings are not consistent with Bergmann and Jucovy's pessimistic conclusions.

Other unanswered questions have in the past and continue to face analysts exploring this area. The nature of the trauma experienced by survivors' children and the mechanisms of transmission are areas in need of further exploration.

Analytic writers have also struggled with how similar survivors' children are to children of other traumatized populations. More observation and research are needed to gain a clearer understanding of posttraumatic effects, and to refine psychoanalytic theorizing.

Family Approaches

Lack of successful outcome with analytic treatment has led to the effective development and use of other modalities with this population. Several authors have recommended family therapy, given the transmission of Holocaust impact, the resultant close attachments within survivor families, their separation difficulties, and the resistance to individual intervention documented in the literature.

Krell[63, 99] felt that the "transmission of Holocaust experience is inevitable," and stressed the importance of understanding the connection between parental experiences and the child's symptoms. He considered this information more readily available in family than in individual treatment. He also warned that survivors' children seldom present for treatment with difficulties related to their parents' Holocaust experiences, and many therapists may be tempted to accept their presentation and ignore the impact of their parents' Holocaust background. He attributed the noted therapeutic failures of individual treatment to this likely scenario, and felt that in family treatment the survivor parents' history will more likely be confronted. Although Krell has pointed out some important benefits of the family approach to treatment, he may overemphasize the tendency of individual treatment to fail, as successful cases have also been noted.

Family therapists have stressed the heterogeneity among survivors and their families, as opposed to the emphasis among traditional theorists on homogeneity. Danieli[100] has described four different types of survivor families: victim families, fighter families, numb families, and families of "those who made it." She considered survivors also to vary within these categories.

The home atmosphere of victim families was characterized by depression, worry, fear of the outside world, and overprotectiveness. Family members seemed to cling to one another, and guilt was the mechanism whereby children were kept from becoming angry, and also from questioning their parents about war experiences. Guilt also served as a defense against helplessness and an expression of loyalty to the lost family members. In addition, these parents, not having had opportunities to express and work through their own anger after the war, had difficulties providing their children with constructive channels for their aggression and found it hard to discipline their children. As a result of this, the children seemed to inhibit their own anger, assertiveness, and creativity.

The home atmosphere of fighter families was filled with an intense need to build and achieve. Feelings of dependency and weakness were not tolerated. While these families were also characterized by overprotectiveness, they were not necessarily fearful, and aggression against and defiance of others was permitted. These children often sought dangerous situations.

In numb families, both parents were described as sole survivors of their families, having lost their own spouses and children during the Holocaust. This group of survivors experienced severe constriction of their emotional expressiveness, spontaneity, and fantasy life, leading to a similar adaptation on the part of their children. These children were described as deprived of the parenting they needed, and some may have sought parenting elsewhere.

"Families of those who made it" were described as very motivated to achieve, and more assimilated into American life then were other survivors. While these survivors may be actively involved in commemorating the Holocaust, the psychological effects of the Holocaust experiences on themselves and their children were often denied.

Danieli's model provides us with an understanding of a range of postwar adaptation among survivors and their families. She has herself asserted that these categories are not meant to be mutually exclusive types. They were instead intended to alert mental health professionals to the different reactions of survivor families, and to emphasize the need to match therapeutic interventions to these various reactions. She too focuses primarily on the pathological aspect of their adaptation.

Family therapists have also discussed at length the importance of survivor parents openly discussing their Holocaust experiences with their children. When parents avoid discussing their experiences, these are still transmitted to the children in ways that are more difficult to integrate, and may lead to symptom formation. Jucovy,[101] coming from an analytic framework, also described the inadvertent transmission of Holocaust material despite the parents' belief "that the past was guarded by their silence." The children were then compelled to act out a scenario, of which they had no knowledge regarding its familial historical significance within their family. Krell,[63, 99] Rustin,[49] and Danieli,[100] have emphasized the importance of open communication, which can provide the family with a unifying experience. Family therapy can facilitate the sharing of Holocaust experiences between survivor parents and their offspring.

In general, family therapists have stressed the influence of the familial Holocaust history upon the child's choice of symptoms, and family treatment as a forum for discovering the meaning of symptoms in terms of the Holocaust past. This modality can also provide a place for open communication between the generations to prevent intergenerational transmission of Holocaust sequelae. However, there is also some evidence that it is, in fact, not always the treatment of choice. Trossman[66] felt this modality was contraindicated for adolescent survivors' children, given their needs to individuate from their families, as is well-known with adolescents in general. Russell[102] also has presented a guarded prognosis for survivor families, as 19 of the 36 families he observed remained unchanged in family treatment. He also found no difference in efficacy between different types of family therapy (e.g., Ackerman/Epsteinian, Gestalt, Transactional, and Behavioral).

While family treatment may be a beneficial approach for survivor families, given certain of their characteristics, the effectiveness of family treatment in relation to other modalities, and the relative efficacy of different types of family therapy have not yet been sufficiently addressed. In addition, the literature has not clearly indicated when this modality would be the treatment of choice, although some reference has been made to the age of the survivors' child as an important variable to be considered. More outcome and follow-up investigation is needed to gain a clearer understanding of its effectiveness with survivor families.

Group Approaches

Group therapy has become very popular among survivors' children. Until the mid to late 1970s, survivors' children rarely, if ever, discussed their Holocaust-derived feelings, fantasies, and confusions amongst themselves. There had been little recognition of the possible effects of their parents' Holocaust experiences on them. However, as survivors' children became adults, they began to communicate among themselves, and seemed to discover that they had similar feelings and fantasies. The need of adult survivors' children to communicate with one another led to the formation of therapeutic awareness groups. Yalom,[103] in his well-known book on group therapy, comments on two curative factors which these groups seem to provide, namely, the powerfulness of the group in providing hope as well as the relief that others may share similar feelings. The main therapeutic benefit of this approach is derived from the sharing of experiences, rather than the working through of deeper intrapsychic or intrafamilial issues as in analytic or family treatment.

Fogelman and Savran[78, 104] have described common issues and themes expressed by survivors' children in the therapeutic awareness groups they lead. Some of the reactions to parents' war experiences expressed include "feeling scarred, special or different, and fearing another Holocaust." They also reported feelings of guilt, anger, and difficulty communicating with their parents. While they experienced compassion for their survivor parents, they also felt burdened at having to serve as a replacement for the many lost family members. They also experienced difficulty with mourning and separation. Fogelman and Savran portrayed these groups as successfully encouraging the expression of feelings and frightening fantasies about their parents' Holocaust experience.

Danieli[100] also viewed group treatment as providing opportunities to rebuild extended families and for collective mourning. While using a variety of modalities, Danieli has particularly emphasized group approaches. Her approach has extended children of survivor groups to also include their families and communities. The emphasis of this program seems to be on the development of a new social network of support to replace the original network lost as a result of the Holocaust.

Group approaches have offered survivors' children opportunities for support and affiliation. They seem to be the most popular modality among this population. Unfortunately, there have not been follow-up studies of the efficacy of group treatment approaches in the short and long run. It is also unclear whether the positive effects of group—particularly its supportive qualities—continue to be felt after the group is disbanded.

Counter-transference Issues

While authors differ on the types of treatment they offer survivors and their children, they all seem to agree on the emotionally demanding nature of the work with these populations. Kestenberg[105] observed that many therapists tended to deny a relationship between children's symptoms and their parents' Holocaust experiences. This denial may have been the therapists' defense against their own strong reactions to Holocaust material. As a result of more recent awareness among mental health professionals to face their own feelings and reactions in this area, some have even modified their therapeutic technique in a way that decreases the extent to which counter-transference impedes their work. For example many psychoanalysts working with the second generation have felt that they cannot maintain the therapeutic stance of neutrality given the arousal of their own strong reactions,[85] and may be more supportive and accepting of their patients' acting out behavior.[91]

A variety of counter-transference reactions have been described. Hoppe[106] described the counter-transference (if it can be called that) of experts, evaluating survivors for compensation. While this is a different relationship from the therapist-patient one, some of the issues he mentions seem relevant to other clinicians, as well. Hoppe says that best-intentioned clinicians may relate to survivors through denial, reaction formation, rationalization, and isolation, but the danger of overidentification was an even more likely reaction for all clinicians. Overidentification includes feeling overwhelmed by pity and one's own guilt feelings. He considered controlled identification, which he described as the ability to understand the survivor's suffering empathically, without concomitant guilt feelings as the healthiest reaction. Hoppe seems to stress the need for the expert to function in a "conflict-free sphere." This seems to be an ideal that most clinicians find difficult to achieve. The literature has suggested that most therapists find it hard to work with this population.

Danieli[107] has studied and described 49 counter-transference reactions, which appear to fit into 13 major themes. These include bystanders' guilt, rage, dread, shame, viewing the survivor as victim or as hero, considering oneself also a survivor, conflicts over Jewish identity, stressing the death rather than the murder of lost relatives, and feeling like a privileged voyeur, among others. Danieli has considered these feelings as reactions to the Holocaust which are displaced onto survivors and their children, rather than being direct reactions to these populations.

Marcus[108] has elaborated on the difficulties some therapists have helping their patients confront issues of Jewish identity, given that they have not adequately dealt with these issues in their own lives. Issues of Jewish identity, faith in God, involvement in organized religion, intermarriage, and other issues of self-definition after the Holocaust are particularly painful for the survivor or a child of a survivor patient to work through, when the therapists themselves have their own unresolved conflicts and blind spots about their own Jewish identity.

CONCLUSION

The psychological literature on survivors and their children has evolved over the past 25 years. There has been a decreased tendency to generalize and greater acknowledgement of the heterogeneity and strengths of these populations. There has also been modification of therapeutic technique to suit the needs of these populations as well as the greater use of a variety of treatment modalities. Psychotherapists have begun to acknowledge the emotionally demanding nature of this work, which can lead to difficult counter-transference reactions interfering with their treatment. In addition, more empirical studies have been conducted to assess the generalizability of clinical impressions to these populations.

However, continued change is still needed. The literature on survivors and their children remains in an evolutionary state, what one review of the literature has described as "conceptual disarray." There still appears to be a lack of consensus among experts about basic concepts and therapeutic strategies. Differing views on the definition and etiology of trauma, mechanisms of transmission, extent of pathology within these groups, and the efficacy of various treatment modalities are still expressed. The emotionally draining and difficult nature of clinical work and research in this area may have contributed to the conflicting views among clinicians and other investigators. However, their developing ability to confront these difficult emotions, and not just let them interfere with their work, has fostered many of the more recent positive changes reflected in the literature, and helped to deepen and clarify our understanding of the effects of traumatization.

Some of the problems noted may also be related to the fact that the massive destruction of the Holocaust had never been encountered previously, and therefore was a phenomenon that called into question many previously held theories. The evolutionary stage of the literature may be a transitional phase as a new level of understanding is achieved.

NOTES

1. Paul Friedman, "The Road Back for the D.P.'s," *Commentary* 6 (1948): 502–510.

2. Henry Krystal, Ed., *Massive Psychic Trauma* (New York: International Universities Press, 1968).

3. Sigmund Freud, *Inhibitions, Symptoms and Anxiety* (New York: W. W. Norton, 1926; ibid., *Beyond the Pleasure Principle* (New York: W. W. Norton, 1933).

4. Ibid., *Inhibitions, Symptoms and Anxiety*, pp. 55–56.

5. Anna Ornstein, "Survival and Recovery," *Psychoanalytic Inquiry* 5 (1985): 99–130.

6. Paul Chodoff, "Late Effects of the Concentration Camp Syndrome," *Archives of General Psychiatry* 8 (1963): 323–333.

7. Jack Terry, "The Damaging Effects of the 'Survivor Syndrome,' " in *Psychoanalytic Reflections on the Holocaust: Selected Essays,* S. Luel and P. Marcus, Eds. (New York, KTAV Publishing House, 1984).

8. Bruno Bettleheim, "Individual and Mass Behavior in Extreme Situations," *Journal of Abnormal Social Psychology* 38 (1943): 417–452.

9. William G. Niederland, "Clinical Observations on the 'Survivor Syndrome,' " *International Journal of Psychoanalysis* 49 (1968): 313–315.

10. Gustav Bychowski, "Permanent Character Changes as an Aftereffect of Persecution," in *Massive Psychic Trauma,* Henry Krystal, Ed. (New York: International Universities Press, 1968), pp. 75–86.

11. Joel Dimsdale, "The Coping Behavior of Nazi Concentration Camp Survivors," *American Journal of Psychiatry* 131, no. 7 (1974): 792–797.

12. Leo Eitinger, "Concentration Camp Survivors in the Postwar World," *American Journal of Orthopsychiatry* 32 (1962): 367–375.

13. Emmanuel DeWind, "The Confrontation with Death," *International Journal of Psychoanalysis* 49 (1968): 302.

14. Terence Des Pres, *The Survivor* (New York: Oxford University Press, 1976).

15. Harvey Barocas, "Children of Purgatory: Reflections on the Concentration Camp Survival Syndrome," *International Journal of Social Psychiatry* 21 (1975): 87–92.

16. William G. Niederland, "The Problem of the Survivor," *Journal of the Hillside Hospital* 10 (1961): 233–247.

17. Henry Krystal, "Trauma and Affects," *Psychoanalytic Study of the Child* 33 (1978): 81–116.

18. Paul Chodoff, "Depression and Guilt among Concentration Camp Survivors," *Existential Psychiatry* 7 (1969): 19–20.

19. Erich Simenauer, "Late Psychic Sequelae of Man-Made Disasters," *International Journal of Psychoanalysis* 49 (1968): 306–309.

20. P. Matussek, "Late Symptomatology among Former Concentration Camp Inmates," in *The World Biennial of Psychiatry and Psychotherapy* (New York: Basic Books, 1970).

21. Klaus D. Hoppe, "Psychotherapy with Concentration Camp Survivors," in *Massive Psychic Trauma,* Henry Krystal, Ed. (New York: International Universities Press, 1968), pp. 204–208.

22. Robert Jay Lifton, "Observation on Hiroshima Survivors, *Massive Psychic Trauma,* Henry Krystal, Ed. (New York: International Universities Press, 1968), pp. 168–188.

23. William G. Niederland, "The Survivor Syndrome: Further Observations and Dimensions," *Journal of the American Psychoanalytic Association* 29, no. 2 (1981): 413–425.

24. Klaus D. Hoppe, "Persecution, Depression and Aggression," *Bulletin of the Menninger Clinic* 26 (1962): 195–203.

25. Klaus D. Hoppe, "Persecution, Depression and Aggression; The Psychodynamics of Concentration Camp Victims," *Psychoanalytic Forum* (1966): 76–85; ibid., "Chronic

Reactive Aggression in Survivors of Severe Persecution,'' *Comprehensive Psychiatry* 12 (1971): 230–235.

26. Henry Krystal, *Integration and Self-Healing: Affect, Trauma and Alexithymia* (New Jersey: The Analytic Press, 1988); ibid., ''Integration and Self-Healing in Post-traumatic States,'' in *Psychoanalytic Reflections on the Holocaust, Selected Essays,* S. Luel and P. Marcus, Eds., (New York: KTAV Publishing House, 1984), pp. 113–134.

27. Werner Tuteur, ''One Hundred Concentration Camp Survivors: Twenty Years Later,'' *Israel Annals of Psychiatry and Related Disciplines* 4, no. 1 (1966): 78–90.

28. Klaus D. Hoppe, ''Re-Somatization of Affects in Survivors of Persecution,'' *International Journal of Psychoanalysis* 49 (1968): 324–326.

29. J. Shannon, ''Psychosomatic Skin Disorders in Survivors of Nazi Concentration Camps,'' *Psychosomatics* II, no. 2 (1970): 95–98.

30. H. Zvi Winnik, ''Contribution to Symposium on Psychic Traumatization Through Social Catastrophe,'' *International Journal of Psychoanalysis* 49 (1968): 298–301.

31. Emmanuel DeWind, ''Psychotherapy After Traumatization Caused by Persecution,'' *International Psychiatry Clinics* 8 (1971).

32. Joost A. M. Meerloo, ''Delayed Mourning in Victims of Extermination Camps,'' *Massive Psychic Trauma,* Henry Krystal, Ed. (New York: International Universities Press, 1968), pp. 72–75.

33. E. Koranyi, ''A Theoretical Review of the Survivor Syndrome,'' *Disasters of the Nervous System* 30, no. 2 (1969): 115–118.

34. Eddy DeWind, ''Psychotherapy After Traumatization Caused by Persecution,'' *International Psychiatry Clinics* 8 (1971): 112.

35. Leo Eitinger, ''Pathology of the Concentration Camp Syndrome,'' *Archives of General Psychiatry* 5 (October 1961): 371–379.

36. Kurt Eissler, ''Perverted Psychiatry,'' *American Journal of Psychiatry* 123 (1967): 1352–1358.

37. E. Trautman, ''Violence and Victims in Nazi Concentration Camps and the Psychopathology of Survivors,'' *International Psychiatry Clinics* 8 (1971): 115–133.

38. Henry Krystal and William G. Niederland, *Psychic Traumatization: Aftereffects in Individuals and Communities* (Boston: Little Brown, 1971).

39. Hillel Klein, ''Problems in the Psychotherapeutic Treatment of Israeli Survivors of the Holocaust,'' *Massive Psychic Trauma,* Henry Krystal, Ed. (New York: International Universities Press, 1968), pp. 233–248.

40. Emanuel Tanay, ''Initiation of Psychotherapy with Survivors of Nazi Persecution,'' *Massive Psychic Trauma,* Henry Krystal, Ed. (New York: International Universities Press, 1968), pp. 219–233.

41. Norman Solkoff, ''Survivors of the Holocaust: A Critical Review of the Literature,'' preprint. Available in *Catalogue of Selected Documents in Psychology* 12, no. 4 (1982): 5.

42. Cited in Paul Marcus and Alan Rosenberg, ''A Philosophical Critique of the 'Survivor Syndrome' and Some Implications for Treatment,'' in *The Psychological Perspective of the Holocaust and of Its Aftermath,* R. L. Braham, Ed. (Boulder: Social Science Monographs, 1988), pp. 53–78 (distributed by Columbia University Press).

43. Hillel Klein, ''The Survivors' Search For Meaning and Identity,'' cited in Marcus and Rosenberg, ''A Philosophical Critique of the 'Survivor Syndrome' and Some Implications for Treatment.''

44. Elmer Luchterhand, ''Social Behavior of Concentration Camp Prisoners, Con-

tinuities and Discontinuities with Pre- and Post-Camp Life,'' in *Survivors, Victims and Perpetrators*, Joel Dimsdale, Ed. (Washington: Hemisphere Publishing, 1980), pp. 259–283.

45. Hans Fink, "Developmental Arrest as a Result of Nazi Persecution During Adolescence," *International Journal of Psychoanalysis* 49 (1968): 327–329.

46. Bruce L. Danto, "The Role of 'Missed Adolescence' in the Etiology of the Concentration Camp Survivor Syndrome," *Massive Psychic Trauma*, Henry Krystal, Ed. (New York: International Universities Press, 1968), pp. 233–247.

47. Stanley Rustin and F. Lipsig, "Psychotherapy with Adolescent Children of Concentration Camp Survivors," *Journal of Contemporary Psychiatry* 4 (1972): 94–98.

48. Werner Koenig, "Chronic or Persisting Identity Diffusion," *American Journal of Psychiatry* 120, no. 11 (1964): 1981–1084.

49. Stanley Rustin, "The Legacy Is Loss," *Journal of Contemporary Psychotherapy* II, no. 1 (1980): 32–43.

50. Leo Eitinger, "Acute and Chronic Psychiatric and Psychosomatic Reactions in Concentration Camp Survivors," in *Society, Stress and Disease*, L. Levin, Ed. (New York: New York University Press, 1971).

51. Gloria Leon, J. Butcher, M. Kleinman, A. Goldberg, and M. Almagor, "Survivors of the Holocaust and Their Children: Current Status and Adjustment," *Journal of Personality and Society Psychology* 4 (1981): 503–516.

52. Felicia Carmelly, "Guilt Feelings in Concentration Camp Survivors: Comments of a Survivor," *Journal of Jewish Communal Service* 52, no. 2 (1975): 139–144.

53. Robert Jay Lifton, *The Broken Connection* (New York: Simon and Schuster, 1979); ibid., "The Concept of the Survivor," cited in Paul Marcus and Alan Rosenberg, "A Philosophical Critique of the 'The Survivor Syndrome' and Some Implications for Treatment."

54. D. Carmil and R. Carel, "Emotional Distress and Satisfaction in Life Among Holocaust Survivors—A Community Study of Survivors and Controls," *Psychological Medicine* 16, no. 1 (1986): 141–149.

55. Jacob Lomranz, Dov Shmotkin, Amnon Zechovoy, and Eliot Rosenberg, "Time Orientation in Nazi Concentration Camp Survivors: Forty Years After," *American Journal of Orthopsychiatry* 55, no. 2 (1985): 230–236.

56. Anna Freud and Sophie Dann, "An Experiment in Group Upbringing," *Psychoanalytic Study of the Child* 6 (1951): 127–169.

57. Editha Sterba, "The Effect of Persecution on Adolescents," *Massive Psychic Trauma*, Henry Krystal, Ed. (New York: International Universities Press, 1968), pp. 51–60.

58. Edith Ludowyk Gyomroi, "The Analysis of a Young Concentration Camp Victim," *Psychoanalytic Study of the Child* 18 (1963): 484–510.

59. Emmanuel DeWind, "Psychotherapy After Traumatization Caused by Persecution; Emmanuel DeWind, Persecution, Aggression and Therapy," *International Journal of Psychoanalysis* 53 (1972): 173–177.

60. Viktor Frankl, *Man's Search for Meaning* (New York, Pocketbooks, 1973).

61. See Paul Marcus and Alan Rosenberg in this volume. Paul Marcus and Alan Rosenberg, "Survivors of Man-Made Mass Death and Some Treatment Implications," in Lorraine Sherr, *Death and Bereavement: Practical Coping Strategies for Staff* (London, Blackwell Publishing). In Press.

62. Yael Danieli, "The Aging Survivors of the Holocaust, Discussion: On the

Achievement of Integration in Aging Survivors of the Nazi Holocaust," *Journal of Geriatric Psychiatry* 14, no. 2 (1981): 191–210.

63. Robert Krell, "Family Therapy with Children of Concentration Camp Survivors," *American Journal of Psychotherapy* 36 (1982): 513–522; ibid., "Holocaust Survivors and Their Children," *Comprehensive Psychiatry*, 25, no. 5 (September/October, 1984).

64. See Boaz Kahana, Zev Harel, and Eva Kahana, "Clinical and Gerontological Issues Facing Survivors of the Nazi Holocaust," in this volume.

65. Arthur W. Epstein, "Mental Phenomena Across Generations: The Holocaust," *Journal of the American Academy of Psychoanalysis* 10, no. 4 (1982): 565–570.

66. Bernard Trossman, "Adolescent Children of Concentration Camp Survivors," *Canadian Psychiatric Association Journal* 12 (1968): 121–123.

67. Russell E. Phillips, "Impact of Nazi Holocaust on Children of Survivors," *Americn Journal of Psychotherapy* 32 (1978): 370–377.

68. Rudolph G. Roden and Michelle M. Roden, "Children of Holocaust Survivors," *Adolescent Psychiatry* 10 (1982): 66–72.

69. Stephen M. Sonnenberg, "Children of Survivors," *Journal of the American Psychoanalytic Association* 22 (1974): 200–204.

70. Harvey Barocas and Carol Barocas, "Manifestations of Concentration Camp Effects on the Second Generation," *American Journal of Psychiatry* 130, no. 7 (1973): 820–821.

71. Hillel Klein, "Children of the Holocaust: Mourning and Bereavement," in *The Child in His Family*, Anthony and Koupernick, Eds. (New York: John Wiley, 1973), pp. 393–409.

72. Harvey Barocas and Carol Barocas, "Separation Individuation Conflict in Children of Holocaust Survivors," *Journal of Contemporary Psychotherapy* 11, no. 1 (1980): 6–14.

73. Hillel Klein, "Families of Holocaust Survivors in the Kibbutz: Psychological Studies," *International Psychiatry Clinics* 8, no. 1 (1971): 67–91.

74. Joan Freyberg, "Difficulties in Separation-Individuation as Experienced by Offspring of Nazi Holocaust Survivors," *American Journal of Orthopsychiatry* 50, no. 1 (1980): 87–95.

75. Paul Marcus, "Jewish Identity and Religious Conflicts in Children of Survivors," presented at 95th Annual Convention of the American Psychological Association in August 1987.

76. Arlene Cahn, "The Capacity to Acknowledge Experience in Holocaust Survivors and Their Children" (Doctoral dissertation: Adelphi University, June 1987).

77. Arie Nadler, Sophie Kav-Venaki, and Beny Gleitman, "Transgenerational Effects of the Holocaust: Externalization of Aggression Second Generation of Holocaust Survivors," *Journal of Consulting and Clinical Psychology* 53, no. 3 (1985): 365–369.

78. Eva Fogelman and Bella Savran, "Therapeutic Groups for Children of Holocaust Survivors," *International Journal of Group Psychotherapy* 29 (1979): 211–235.

79. Helen Epstein, *Children of the Holocaust* (New York: G. P. Putnam's, 1979).

80. Dov Aleksandrowicz, "Children of Concentration Camp Survivors," in *The Child in This Family*, Anthony and Koupernick, Eds., pp. 385–392.

81. Susan Rose and John Garske, "Family Environment, Adjustment and Coping Among Children of Holocaust Survivors: A Comparative Investigation," *American Journal of Orthopsychiatry* 57, no. 3 (1987): 332–344.

82. Lenore Podietz, Herman Belmont, Marion Shapiro, Israel Zwerling, Ilda Ficher,

Talia Eisenstein, and Myra Levick, "Engagement in Families of Holocaust Survivors," *Journal of Mental and Family Therapy* 10, no. 1 (1984): 43–57.

83. Axel Russell, Donna Plotkin, and Nelson Heapy, "Adaptive Abilities in Non-clinical Second Generation Holocaust Survivors and Controls: A Comparison," *American Journal of Psychotherapy* 39, no. 4 (1985): 564–579.

84. Zoltan Zlotogorski, "Offspring of Concentration Camp Survivors: The Relationship of Perceptions of Family Cohesion and Adaptability to Levels of Ego Functioning," *Comprehensive Psychiatry* 24 (1983): 345–354.

85. Martin Bergmann and Milton Jucovy, "Epilogue," *Generations of the Holocaust*, Bergmann and Jucovy, Eds. (New York, Basic Books, Inc., 1982).

86. Judith S. Kestenberg, "Psychoanalyses of Children of Survivors from the Holocaust: Case Presentations and Assessment, 1980; A Metapsychological Assessment Based on an Analysis of a Survivors' Child in *Generation of the Holocaust*, 1982" Bergmann and Jucovy, Eds., pp. 137–158.

87. James Herzog, "World Beyond Metaphor: Thoughts on the Transmission of Trauma" in *Generations of the Holocaust*, Bergmann and Jucovy, Eds., pp. 103–119.

88. Marion M. Oliner, "Hysterical Features among Children of Survivors," in *Generations of the Holocaust*, Bergmann and Jucovy, Eds., pp. 267–286.

89. Maria Bergmann, "Thoughts on Superego Pathology of Survivors and Their Children," in *Generations of the Holocaust*, Bergmann and Jucovy, Eds., pp. 287–309.

90. Ilse Grubrich-Simitis, "From Concretism to Metaphor: Thoughts on Some Theoretical and Technical Aspects of the Psychoanalytic Work with Children of Holocaust Survivors," *Psychoanalytic Study of the Child* 39 (1984): 301–319.

91. Martin S. Bergmann, "Recurrent Problems in the Treatment of Survivors and Their Children," in *Generations of the Holocaust*, Bergmann and Jucovy, Eds., pp. 247–266.

92. Nan Link, Bruce Victor, Renee L. Binder, "Psychosis in Children of Holocaust Survivors: Influence of the Holocaust in the Choice of Themes in their Psychosis." *The Journal of Nervous and Mental Disease* 173, no. 2 (1985): 115–117.

93. Judith Kestenberg, "Introductory Remarks: Children of the Holocaust," in *The Child in His Family*, Anthony and Koupernick, Eds., pp. 359–361.

94. Sylvia Axelrod, Ofelia I. Schnipper, and John H. Rau, "Hospitalized Offspring of Holocaust Survivors," *Bulletin of the Meninger Clinic* 44 (1986): 1–14.

95. Norman Solkoff, "Children of Survivors of the Nazi Holocaust: A Critical Review of the Literature," *American Journal of Orthopsychiatry* 51, no. 1 (1981): 29–41.

96. Evelyne Schwaber, "Some Reflections in Response to: 'A Psychoanalytic Overview On Children of Survivors' by Judith Kestenberg," presented at Symposium on 'The Psychology of the Jewish Experience: The Holocaust; Psychological Effects on Survivors and their Children' in Boston, May 21, 1978.

97. Norman Solkoff, "Children of Survivors of the Nazi Holocaust," *American Journal of Orthopsychiatry*, 51, no. 1 (1981): 35.

98. Martin Bergmann and Milton Jucovy, "Epilogue," *Generations of the Holocaust*, Bergmann and Jucovy, Ed., p. 312.

99. Robert Krell, "Holocaust Families: The Survivors and Their Children," *Comprehensive Psychiatry* 20, no. 6 (1979): 560–568.

100. Yael Danieli, "Differing Adaptational Styles in Families of Survivors of the Nazi Holocaust: Some Implications for Treatment," *Children Today* 10, no. 5 (1981): 6–10, 34–35; ibid., "The Treatment and Prevention of Long-term Effects and Intergenerational

Transmission of Victimization: A Lesson from Holocaust Survivors and Their Children,'' *Trauma and Its Wake,* Vol. 1, Charles Figley, Ed. (New York: Brunner Mazel, 1985).

101. See Milton Jucovy, "Therapeutic Work with Survivors and Their Children: Recurrent Themes and Problems," in this volume.

102. A. Russell, "Late Psychosocial Consequences in Concentration Camp Survivor Families," *American Journal of Orthopsychiatry* 44, no. 4 (1974): 611–619.

103. Irvin D. Yalom, *The Theory and Practice of Group Psychotherapy* (New York, Basic Books, 1975).

104. Eva Fogelman and Bella Savran, "Brief Group Therapy with Offspring of Holocaust Survivors: Leaders' Reactions," *American Journal of Orthopsychiatry* 50, no. 1 (1980): 96–108.

105. Judith S. Kestenberg, "Psychoanalytic Contributions to the Problems of Children of Survivors of Nazi Persecution," *The Israel Annals of Psychiatry and Related Disciplines* 10, no. 4 (1972): 311–323.

106. Klaus D. Hoppe, "Severed Ties," in *Psychoanalytic Reflections on the Holocaust,* Steven Luel and Paul Marcus, Eds. (New York: KTAV Publishing House, 1984).

107. Yael Danieli, "Countertransference in the Treatment and Study of Nazi Holocaust Survivors and Their Children," *Victimology: An International Journal* 5 (1980): pp. 355–367; ibid., "Psychotherapists' Participation in the Conspiracy of Silence about the Holocaust," *Psychoanalytic Psychology* 1, no. 1 (1984): 23–42.

108. Paul Marcus, "Jewish Consciousness After the Holocaust," in *Psychoanalytic Reflections on the Holocaust,* Luel and Marcus, Eds. (New York: KTAV Publishing House, 1984).

II

Classical Theory

3

Therapeutic Work with Survivors and Their Children: Recurrent Themes and Problems

MILTON E. JUCOVY

INTRODUCTION

In a world characterized by Adorno's statement, "No poetry after Auschwitz,"[1] it would seem appropriate to heed Elie Wiesel's warning that it was well-nigh impossible to penetrate the cursed and spellbound universe of the survivor when he asked: "How do you tell children, big and small, that society could lose its mind and start murdering its own soul? How do you unveil horrors without offering at the same time some measure of hope?"[2] History has enabled us to recognize that the concept adopted in devising the "final solution" was primarily directed toward the Jewish people as a fulfillment of an ideology of hate and an apocalyptic end in itself. The death of 6 million victims and the agony of so many others transcends all previous ordeals that marked the Jewish historical experience. The sophisticated technology applied to the organized and relentless destruction of a people consumed one-half of the Jews living in Eastern Europe and erased an entire civilization. Sigmund Freud, who was hardly an optimist in the last decade of his life, expressed a hope in "Why War?" that the evolution of culture might enable the human race to govern its instinctual life and help to modulate aggressive drives.[3] He was writing at a time of relative enlightenment, but this period ended in mounds of ashes and skeletons and the disappearance of the rich and lively culture of European Jewish life.

The victory of the Allied military forces ended a long night of terror. At last the death camps were liberated and those who remained alive made their way to some semblance of safety. Partisans emerged from the forests and those who were hidden by "Righteous Gentiles" came out of their sanctuaries. It may seem unfair and arbitrary to construct a hierarchy of survivorship. However, this has sometimes been done for the purposes of study, because it seems to have made some difference in subsequent adaptation to have undergone one set of experiences rather than another. However disrupting, those who were able to leave the European continent and find a haven before the persecutions escalated were not exposed to the massive and continuous trauma experienced by survivors of death camps. Some who were liberated attempted to return to their original homes from which they had been deported, only to find desolation and even hostile reception. Large numbers of the stateless and impoverished were cared for temporarily in displaced persons camps, waiting for visas to more hospitable places. Those who tried to emigrate to Palestine before 1948 were often intercepted and returned to camps in Cyprus. A group of survivors was able to make contact with family members in the United States, Canada, and South America and emigrate to these shores.

During the first years after the war, the energies of survivors were absorbed in finding a way back to some approximation of conventional life. Most had to learn a new language, some had to acquire new skills and they all had to meet challenges posed by living in a foreign land. Many families clung together, hoping to recreate their original communities. This was particularly true when they felt surrounded by an alien culture that regarded them at best with a mixture of awe and mistrust, the very embodiment of a past the survivors wished to forget. It was relatively rare for a family to have survived intact. New marital partners, frequently fellow survivors, were found and new families established. While life was certainly safer and more bearable, adaptation was by no means easy.

The shock and drama of liberation and the need to deal with the plight of the victims of Nazi persecution helped to mobilize action and keep survivors in the eyes and conscience of the world for a time. Then, for powerful reasons, a curtain of silence descended. For close to a decade after liberation, intense individual and collective defenses functioned to ward off preoccupation with the past. The Jewish people, enjoined to remember common trauma, was still not prepared to confront the ultimate horror of the Nazi plan for genocide. Another reason for the silence, apart from the need of the victims to forget, was the need of the world to forget. People did not listen, understand, or share and there was a division between those who had endured and those who had only read about the atrocities. The gap was too wide to bridge and a period of latency had to be traversed before the chasm was narrowed.

Mental health professionals were no exception to the general tendency, minimizing or ignoring psychological problems presented by survivors, when plans for rehabilitation of those who had been traumatized were formulated. The process of bridging temporal and emotional distance was facilitated by the passage in the early 1950s, by the German Federal Republic, of legislation designed to provide restitution to victims of the Nazis for damage to health as well as other hardships. The legislation was complicated and created essentially a new legal specialty among attorneys representing clients who made claims. Because medical and psychiatric examinations were necessary to provide a link between previous persecutions and current symptoms or maladaptation, a large number of psychiatrists were able to collect a volume of case histories based on interviews with survivors who sought indemnification. Data collected from treatment sessions rather than from interviews were meager at the time, as there was a natural reluctance for survivors to seek treatment for psychological reasons. This was based in large part on the need for denial and repression of traumatic memories and on a conviction that not even a therapist who was a survivor could readily understand the experiences of his patient.

Many of the psychiatric clinicians who examined survivors for the reparations program were classically Freudian in orientation with respect to their view of the definition of psychic trauma. Their theoretical position did not appear to be sufficient to explain the bewildering array of late sequelae presented by the claimants they examined. Sigmund Freud had originally proposed an explanation, essentially economic in nature, which stressed a breaching of the stimulus barrier, which implied that a response to a trauma was bound to be temporary and that a normal state would ensue following the state of shock and disorganization caused by overstimulation. When the traumatic neuroses were observed during World War I, psychiatrists who disgreed with Freud cited their findings as proof that danger to self-preservation can be a cause of neuroses and that the concept of the sexual etiology of neurotic symptoms was a mistaken notion. Freud's contention had been based on his belief that it was highly unlikely that a neurosis could develop without the participation of deeper levels of the psychic apparatus. He pointed out that there was nothing in unconscious mental life that could correspond with the idea of the complete annihilation of life, so that the fear of death could more likely be regarded as analogous to the fear of castration.[4] These views, although later amended to include other pathogenic factors, rather than sexual ones alone, were difficult to reconcile with the observations of those who were grappling to understand, within the framework of psychoanalytic theory, the continuing symptoms and the late sequelae seen in Holocaust survivors. It is now felt that some previous views of how trauma could affect the human organism could not encompass the experience of those who were victims of persecution involving daily confrontations with degradation and death for months and years. For the persecuted, a new reality existed which was the polar opposite of what had been regarded as customary in acceptable social values. A current view, proposed by Ilse Grubrich-Simitis, suggests that extreme trauma can become cumulative trauma and thus cause permanent rather than only temporary changes in the psychic structure.[5] She has pointed out that the threat of narcissistic depletion was due not only to extended periods of deprivation of external narcissistic supplies, but also to changes in the superego as a result of massive assaults on the victim's psyche. These alterations consisted of regression to more archaic forms of superego functioning and led especially to grave changes in the ego ideal. The devalued image propagated by the persecutors insidiously established itself in the ideal self of the victims. Paradoxically and tragically, this lent an additional dimension to the defense mechanism of identification with the aggressor, originally utilized unconsciously by the victims to try to undo their sense of helplessness and to check the process of narcissistic depletion. A particularly dramatic and poignant example of how the perpetuation of this pattern of defense can affect the future was noted in the case of a young man who was hospitalized during a psychotic episode. When his condition improved and he developed trust in his therapist, he told how, during his childhood, when he misbehaved his mother would place his head in the kitchen oven and warn him that this was what the Nazis did to Jews in the camps.

Children of Survivors

Because there was sufficient evidence of continued generational reverberation as a result of the persecutions during the Holocaust, Judith Kestenberg had, for a number of years, been interested in examining psychoanalytically the effects of the Holocaust on the children of survivors, the second generation. In 1970, she devised and sent questionnaires to colleagues in a number of countries. This effort had been partially stimulated by analytic work with a young patient who had behaved in a bizarre way and had treated his analyst as a hostile persecutor. Dr. Kestenberg asked her colleagues if they had analyzed any children of survivor families and if such analyses had revealed any special or unusual features. The responses seemed to indicate that only a few such offspring had been analyzed and it was also evident that many analysts who had received the inquiry showed an unexpected indifference to the entire question. A number were startled, as it had never occurred to them to link their patients' problems to the history of their parents' persecutions during the Holocaust. It was largely because of Dr. Kestenberg's inspiration and initiative that a study group was organized to pursue an investigation from a psychoanalytic point of view of the effects of the Holocaust on the second generation, and to study the original victims as well when opportunity presented itself. Some of the material described in this chapter is derived from the work of the study group, which was reported in a volume edited by M. Bergmann and M. E. Jucovy.[6]

The study group has met regularly since 1974, each meeting devoted to a detailed discussion of a patient who has been treated by a member of the group or by an invited guest. In order to maintain a spirit of scientific objectivity, a discussion of the general problems presented precedes a shift of focus to the relevance of the Holocaust for a more precise understanding of the psychopathology encountered in the patient and of the patient's general functioning and adaptive capacities. After considerable study of a large volume of clinical material, the group reached a consensus that survivor parents can indeed influence the development of their children as a result of parental trauma incurred during the Holocaust. The forms and mechanisms of this transmission have been reported elsewhere by M. Bergmann and M. E. Jucovy.[7] Grappling with the problem of specificity has been a difficult task. Investigation is constantly faced with the complex and interwoven strands of what can be called a patient's "private pathology'' and what is related to the traumatic effects of the Holocaust, a paradigm of the attribution of pathogenesis common to all methodological problems in scientific investigation. The clinical pictures encountered showed a wide variation and would be difficult to distinguish from those found in offspring of other traumatized groups or even from a population considered average in our culture. The child of a Holocaust survivor is exposed to traumatic impact as filtered through the experience of his/her parents. Although diluted, this exposure can still serve as a significant organizing experience for subsequent developmental conflicts in the child. Although observation indicates that symptoms and conflicts seen in children of the second generation are neither unique nor exclusive, when they are seen as a conglomerate they form a total picture that is palpable and recognizable.

General Considerations Involved in Treatment of Members of Survivor Families

In addressing some issues that should be especially considered in the treatment of members of survivor families, there is no intention whatsoever of suggesting that all or even a majority of these families have one or more members who may require treatment because of psychological impairment. On the contrary, many survivors have shown an unusual degree of psychic strength in the recovery from their ordeals and have adapted to the renewal of their lives with great vitality. Many have achieved remarkable success, and because of their commitment to ideals of continuity and the affirmation of life, have inspired their children to be energetic and dedicated to values involving responsibility and service.

In contrast to our current experience, when survivors first came to the attention of mental health professionals, there was considerable pessimism that psychological intervention had much to offer such a traumatized population. With increasing experience, we have learned that the changes for a more favorable outcome in conducting therapy with members of survivor families is much more likely. Various authors have emphasized some of the basic issues to be kept in mind, so that the skills and sensitivity of a therapist might be enhanced. Martin Bergmann has commented on the extraordinary demands made on a therapist who treats a member of a survivor family.[8] He has singled out a number of counterproductive attitudes encountered in therapists who are themselves survivors as well as in many younger colleagues who have suffered no persecution or haven't lost any family member in the Holocaust. These attitudes include loss of interest and manifestations of anxiety, which can lead to premature closure or too early theorizing about clinical material. Also noted were polarized tendencies to emphasize persistently the role of the Holocust in a patient's problems, or to ignore the importance of Holocaust-derived material. Ilse Grubrich-Simitis has also made similar technical comments and suggestions.[9]

The role of empathy is an axiomatic concept which has been universally accepted as a basic tool in the armamentarium of any therapist in treating patients. The particular skills and sensitivity that facilitate an empathic response in a therapist who works with a member of a traumatized group should be self-evident. Klaus Hoppe has used his findings as an examiner for the reparations program to describe the emotional stupor and alexithymia seen in victims of persecution.[10] Hoppe emphasizes the importance of "matchings" between examiner and applicant or therapist and patient in helping to achieve the optimum degree of empathic exchange in the development of trust and candor in a therapeutic alliance. It should be emphasized that there is an important difference between a therapist's empathic response and the understandable temptation of some therapists to act as saviors for patients who have suffered greatly. This attitude may undermine the treatment process as it can hamper the development of certain significant negative transference responses, in which, for example, the therapist may be seen and experienced as a Nazi persecutor. The mobilization and working through of such transference feelings and fantasies can be extremely important and even essential in the successful outcome of treatment. Although it may be tempting for a therapist to make treatment easier and more serene for both patient and therapist, a phase of the treatment necessary for further progress can be circumvented by a therapist's rescue fantasies when dealing with members of survivor families suffering from the effects of unbearable victimization.

An important issue to be considered in the treatment of survivors and their children is one involving the anonymity of the therapist, often breached in the interests of creating a less cold and formal atmosphere. Bergmann has emphasized that in his papers on technique, Sigmund Freud proposed a cardinal rule that personal data from the life of the analyst should not be allowed to enter the therapeutic work, lest any knowledge of such facts might interfere with the flowering and full development of a transference neurosis based on the fantasies of the patient.[11] Judith Kestenberg has provided a dramatic example of problems involving the anonymity of the therapist in her description of a young patient, who interrupted treatment when he joined a guru's group after he felt alienated by the failure of his analyst to supply him with astrological data related to her birth.[12] Hillel Klein, reporting about his experiences in Israel, noted that when his patients learned that their therapist had also been a victim paranoid projections were diminished.[13] It's not altogether clear how the interference with the projection can be understood. While it is true that anonymity can indeed encourage projection, it is important to note that the emergence of a projection gives a patient the opportunity to work the projection out. This example can highlight yet another technical problem, involving the value of preserving anonymity in instances where projection is found to play a relatively major role, as Bergmann has pointed out.[14] Additional subjects for consideration in therapy with Holocaust survivors and their children have been mentioned by various authors. Henry Krystal has been particularly interested in integration and self-healing in post-traumatic states. He emphasized how an aging survivor might be helped to relinquish anger and outrage and thus facilitate a self-healing process.[15] This might seem very difficult to achieve, as a large number of survivors would feel that this might grant the persecutors an ultimate victory. Some efforts in therapy that can help survivors to achieve serenity through the effective completion of adequate mourning, denied them during the period of persecution, are also underlined. Paul Marcus has considered such matters as Jewish authenticity, the fate of Jewish identity in the Diaspora, and the questions confronting a people, many of whom have felt abandoned by their God.[16] Marcus recommends that questions about Jewish identity, which he feels have been generally ignored in therapy, should be taken up with patients where it might be appropriate to do so. He also expresses the sanguine hope that successful treatment should lead to a flowering of ideals of justice and social responsibility, a laudable goal, but often difficult to attain.

Many of these questions have been considered in some depth in the ever-expanding literature about the Holocaust. It would appear appropriate now to turn to some particular ones in greater detail and to present clinical examples and further discussion which might be of help to mental health professionals in the refinement of their skills when they are working with patients who have been members of a traumatized and therefore vulnerable population.

Family Secrets and the "Conspiracy of Silence"

During the course of our work in psychotherapy or psychoanalysis, we are continually working with secrets, the revelation of which we hope will bring about dynamic, structural, and economic changes in psychic structure consistent with the attainment of greater adaptational capacities. Although encounters with secrets are ubiquitous in our work, it is also noteworthy that their presence and impact are more apparent in members of certain vulnerable groups. The study of survivors and their children, with particular emphasis on communication between the generations, has taught us that certain features of a child's development may be influenced by parental withholding of information, and that even well-intentioned revelations of parental experiences may be shrouded in uncertainty, distortion, or mystery. Despite determination to maintain a secret, inadvertent disclosure may occur, prompting a child to act out a scenario of which there was no apparent knowledge and which belongs to the history of a family member who survived the Holocaust. This scenario may be repeated in the transference responses of patients who engage their therapist in a "conspiracy of silence" during treatment. The latter is then confronted with the withholding of information and even with the appearance of symptoms in members of survivor families, which are rooted in the family secret.

Yolanda Gampel presented us with a dramatic account of the case report of a pretty seven-year-old girl, Michal, who arrived for a consultation with her mother.[17] Michal was the third child in the family and had recently developed disturbances of memory, cognition, amnesia, and "absences." The latter occurred mostly at her school, and also at home. She would appear to wake from these absences in a lost state, according to her mother. In the child's presence, the mother provided details of the family history. She told of the father who came to Israel as a young child and of her own emigration to Israel shortly before her marriage. During this discussion, which lasted for about one hour, Michal looked serious, but not frightened or depressed. The mother was then asked to leave the child alone with the examiner, who attempted to establish a relationship with Michal by playing games, drawing, and talking. Toward the end of this period, in response to a question, the child answered that she would not want to be "an electric fence in the Warsaw Ghetto, because they put the soldiers' children there and if they touch the fence, they will electrocute themselves and die." The analyst was troubled by the child's response, which suggested something so very frightening that the little girl preferred being "absent" rather than aware of her thoughts and surroundings.

The analyst decided to check the family history once more and the next session was held with Michal's mother. The father was invited, but chose not to attend. The mother was asked if there was any story circulating in the family about the Holocaust. The answer was that the father's entire family had been killed, but that this was never discussed at home. The analyst then cited Michal's statement from the first session and asked for help in understanding it. The other paled, appeared to be in shock, and said: "My husband was in the Warsaw Ghetto as a child and later in a concentration camp, but we have never spoken about this with the children. How could she know? My husband always says he arrived in Israel as a child and there are never any further questions about his background." In the course of several further sessions, Michal, her mother, and the analyst worked through the connection between Michal's absences and her father's personal history. The father chose not to join in these sessions, but he allowed his wife to tell Michal all she herself knew, and the symptoms in the child disappeared in due course.

The example cited may illustrate how, despite the belief of parents that the past was guarded by their silence, some aspect of family discourse was communicated to the child, whose decompensation occurred, probably in combination with other pathogenic factors, at a crucial point in her development. One may question whether Michal's symptoms could be sufficiently understood in terms of Oedipal fantasies and the guilt aroused by them, and whether it is necessary to invoke the Holocaust experiences of her father, which involve a family secret, as an explanatory concept. In a communication about the issue of "knowing" about details of the Holocaust, Jucovy asserted that while the usual vicissitudes encountered in development are certainly important, Holocaust material can become a crucial organizing factor in pathogenesis and the secrets about the parents' past are an important consideration in the treatment of a patient.[18] Others have commented on the importance of family secrets as they affect analytic work. Theodore Jacobs pointed out that the word *secret* comes from the same root as "secretion" and suggested that the idea of a secret may be associated with the private secretions of the body.[19] Secrets may thus be associated with issues of control and power linked to sphincter control and also be involved with precursors of superego development. The harboring of secrets may also promote additional guilt as a result of overstimulation of the drives, both libidinal and aggressive. In this context, family secrets about the Holocaust may be experienced in terms of the child's secrets, thus augmenting a connection between universal developmental conflicts and problems derived more specifically from Holocaust-related issues. Excessive drive stimulation may involve sexual and aggressive fantasies and the masturbatory practices associated with such fantasies. It is certainly not unreasonable to suspect that knowing or not knowing about the details of a secret that is suspected to exist may provide additional impetus to scopophilic impulses, particularly those connected with primal scene fantasies. The use of words such as "to know," when interpreted in a concrete, archaic, and "biblical" sense can suggest the possibility of a special coloring to phallic and Oedipal fantasies in some instances. Guilt can thus be increased and pose additional problems for the adequate resolution of the Oedipus complex and the further maturation of a stable superego, freed from its more primitive and tyrannical element.

When one is either excluded from a secret or made partner to it, a burden is created. An increased tolerance for deceit and subterfuge may result when a child is exposed to a collusion or deception. This pattern may result in a survivor family where a pact of silence is maintained or where communication about the Holocaust is excessively colored by a personal myth or distortion. A young man described how his mother, who had been incarcerated at Auschwitz, consistently romanticized her memories. Colleagues who have conducted interviews with survivors in gathering material for archival projects of Holocaust testimony have noted that concentration camp prisoners often sustained themselves by the elaboration of halcyon fantasies that included liberation, reunion with a beloved family member, and a future free of pain and torture. It is quite probable that the energy and imagination required to construct such fantasies can serve an important adaptive function in warding off feelings of helplessness and despair in times of extremity. However, when these fantasies or similar ones are sustained through the years distorting historical truth, and are told to a growing son as if they represented a reality of frolicking with friends in an idyllic setting at a vacation resort, considerable confusion can be mobilized in a child and potentiate later problems in reality testing.

These clinical vignettes have been reported and emphasized to illustrate the importance of the pitfalls that may be avoided in therapy with a Holocaust survivor or a member of the second generation if the therapist is alert to the way in which family secrets about the events of the Holocust can be intertwined with other developmental experiences and thus create a traumatic impact. The therapist must also be sensitive to the effects on the therapy of the "conspiracy of silence" begun in a family setting and later becoming a part of the transference setting so that valuable information may be concealed. The possible effect, both in life and in therapy, of a distortion or family myth about Holocaust experiences should also be considered, as it may pose some problems about assessment of the patient, diagnosis, and treatment.

The Timing of Interpretations

There is universal agreement that the appropriate timing of a therapist's interpretations is of the utmost importance in work with a patient. It can often be particularly crucial in instances where a patient has suffered some severe emotional trauma superimposed on an already vulnerable personality. The following example is that of a man in his early forties who had been a concentration camp prisoner during his early teens. It may serve to illustrate the necessity of paying careful attention to the most scrupulous and delicate timing and dosage of interpretations during the therapeutic process. The patient was referred by a colleague, who had seen the patient and his wife together for various family problems. When the patient indicated that he wished to see someone for individual therapy, he was referred for analysis and immediately indicated the urgent reason for his request. He was increasingly overwhelmed by an inordinate and consuming jealousy which was focused on the relationship his wife once had with a young man years before her marriage to the patient. What triggered his distress was a book inscribed to his wife by her former friend. From first sight, he was constantly preoccupied by thoughts about their relationship and florid fantasies about the sexual activities he was convinced they had shared.

The patient, a trim, good-looking man, described his suffering and his background in a serious, well organized and thoughtful manner. He was born in an Eastern European shtetl; many of the inhabitants belonged to an ultra-orthodox Hassidic sect, led by a rigid and authoritarian rabbi. The patient described what he regarded as the fanaticism and narrow-mindedness of his childhood neighbors with considerable animosity. However, he seemed moderately aware that his attitudes might have been inflamed by the events of his childhood. His father had been ill for a number of years with a pulmonary condition that had limited his ability to work. When Moshe was 12, his father died. For months after the funeral, the patient was troubled by dreams peopled by demonic figures that he had some difficulty describing. In an attempt to help the patient define these figures, I used the term "Angel of Death," employing the Hebrew phrase for the definition. This evoked what appeared to be a grateful smile of recognition. Moshe went on to describe the poverty of his remaining family, which required his being sent, according to custom, to the homes of various neighbors for meals. He reported feeling that he was treated as a degraded beggar and given dregs to eat. A short time after his father died, his younger sister took ill and died of an undefined acute infectious illness.

The Nazis had, at this time, overrun the area where his family lived. When he was 13, he and his mother were captured, herded into a box car, and sent to Auschwitz. Mother and son were separated during the selection process, which took place at the entrance to the camp, and he never saw his mother again. For several days after, he cried incessantly. When he described life in the camp, he tended to gloss over the brutalization and dehumanization that he suffered. He tended, instead, to focus his antagonism on many of his fellow prisoners and his mistrust as well; they seemed concerned only for themselves. He claimed to have admired those with leftist political affiliations because they had a strong sense of discipline. Later he was transferred from Auschwitz to a labor camp, where he said he was treated with a degree of leniency by the commandant. The therapist was puzzled by the seeming discrepancy between his descriptions of his fellow townspeople and his fellow inmates at the concentration camp and his relatively tolerant attitude toward his Nazi persecutors. One could not help but wonder if the thrust of his hostility was defensively employed to salvage his self-esteem to avoid total degradation, or whether his early childhood and the ambience of his native village was really as deprived as he described it.

When the patient was liberated after the war was over, he joined a radical Zionist group and made his way to Israel, where he worked on a Kibbutz for several years before emigrating to the United States in his early twenties. He studied, entered a business, married a young American woman, and embarked on his new life with energy and enthusiasm. However, there remained a lingering bitterness about the past, sometimes directed more fiercely against life in the shtetl of his birth than against the Nazis. His generalized wariness and suspicion erupted acutely and became more sharply focused when he discovered the book his wife's former friend had given her.

In treatment, it did not take long for his mistrust to crystallize in a rather formidable and unyielding resistance. He had some knowledge of psychoanalytic procedure, but expressed grave doubts about using the couch and was eager to prolong face-to-face contact. He told of having seen several consultants before starting his current treatment, something he had not mentioned on his first visit. He expressed the gravest of reservations about each consultant, and criticized their intellectual capacities severely. He also noted that a woman analyst he saw sat in her chair in a most seductive fashion. He verbalized sharply polarized opinions about me. On the one hand, he commended me for being reasonably intelligent, articulate, caring, and humane. But he also wondered if my skills and intellect were sufficient to deal with his problems. His objections also focused on his perception of me as being too "Jewish." He felt that there were far too many books and pictures in my waiting and consulting rooms that dealt with Jewish themes. He acknowledged that the items he saw might have reminded him of his childhood community, where he felt treated with such contempt after he was orphaned. He also wondered if psychological treatment was really what he required and he wanted more time to think before he committed himself to being analyzed. At one point he developed severe tearing of his eyes and a running nose, which he attributed to allergies. He insisted it was truly impossible to use the couch under these circumstances. Because he had told me just two days earlier of his separation from his mother and his disconsolate crying which followed, I asked if he felt it might be possible that some aspect of his symptoms might be connected with the memory he had described. Whereas he had previously told me that I listened too much and said too little, he now rebuked me for jumping to premature conclusions. On the day after he arrived and with dry mucous membranes, he smiled and sarcastically commented that the pollen count must have dropped precipitously. He then told of a recent dream in which he is standing on a rock in a barren place. The landscape around him is bleak and forbidding. Off to one side he notices buildings that look like a concentration camp. He knows somehow that there are Nazis nearby who are rounding up Jews and he has to escape lest he be captured. However the area is so threatening that he feels it may almost be better to allow himself to be taken prisoner. He was perplexed by the dream and not able to associate productively. The analyst commented that his difficulty in committing himself to analytic work might be similar to the feelings of impasse from the past and that allowing himself to be captured might reflect a desire for reunion with his mother. He promised to consider what I had said, returned the next day and told me that the dream he had reported was not a recent one. He had reported the same dream to the psychiatrist who had referred him to me, and had been given a much more sensible interpretation, although he could not remember it. When I asked the patient what came to his mind about this need to plan and execute such a test, he became very angry, reproached me for calling him a liar and decided to terminate his treatment.

The foundering of this treatment process was probably dependent on several issues, although the clinical vignette was chosen to illustrate problems in the timing of interpretations. The patient's symptoms and behavior patterns suggested serious character pathology, a propensity for projection and more than just a moderate degree of paranoia. We are faced here with a situation where it presents more than an average challenge to assess the contribution of so-called "private pathology" and pathology induced by Holocaust experiences to determine the final outcome. It has been suggested that victims who were persecuted during the period of puberty and adolescence have in general shown a greater degree of vulnerability and a propensity to suffer from later emotional sequelae than those victimized as adults. Although there was no opportunity to explore with this man the possibility that he was perhaps exposed to homosexual seduction during his imprisonment, this is a possibility and might well have been a factor in rekindling earlier deprivations and conflicts. On reflection, it seems quite clear that the patient had a need, based on fears of penetration and intrusion, not to be understood too quickly. Premature efforts to establish an alliance by making some clarifying remark about the "Angel of Death" and later comments about his coryzal symptoms were probably counterproductive. The example can alert us to the seemingly paradoxical effect of an interpretation that was probably correct, but made prematurely, when the patient was not prepared to be receptive.

Metaphor and Therapeutic Technique

The value of understanding the use of metaphor in the communication between patient and therapist has a special relevance in the treatment of Holocaust survivors and their children, perhaps even more in the second generation. It has been said of survivors themselves, by James Herzog, that during the Holocaust they lived in a world beyond, or even before metaphor.[20] Terence Des Pres has written movingly of a life in extremity, where behavior has no meaning in a symbolic or even a primitive psychological sense.[21] It might be suggested that one task of a survivor's child may be to seek some symbolic realization of a parent's experience, and that the child's symptoms, when present, may express metaphoric attempts at a recreation and restitution of the parents' symbolic processes. The following clinical account may illustrate how this concept may be used in therapy.

A young, married, professional man sought treatment for an unusual symptom. He had suffered from myopia since childhood, a condition that may frequently be associated with a degenerative process in the vitreous humor of the eyes and the development of so-called "floaters." Most people affected in this way adapt to the presence of floaters, although they may occasionally be distracting. Despite the assurance of ophthalmologists that he suffered from no ocular disease that would impair his visual acuity, the patient was in a great state of anxiety and depression, and despaired that his promising career might suffer severely. Although he regarded his plight as a response to a reality situation, he was sufficiently aware that the intensity of his emotional state was inappropriate and might yield to a better understanding of himself through engagement in psychological therapy.

John was the elder of two children; his sister was several years younger. His mother had died of malignancy while he was in his final year of professional training. He mentioned, almost in passing, that his father had been born in Poland and had been incarcerated in a concentration camp during the Holocaust. His father's brother was the only other survivor of the paternal side of the patient's family. The rest had perished in the death camps. The father rarely spoke of his experiences and the son asked no questions. The patient saw his father as a man who regarded the world as an inimical place, where it was preferable to "keep a low profile." In contrast, the father of the patient's wife was an energetic and optimistic man to whom John turned for support and advice when he felt particularly cast down and pessimistic.

The patient appeared to be pleasant and responsive and quickly formed a firm positive transference with passive and dependent features. It was decided at this point to initiate, as the treatment of choice, psychoanalytically oriented exploratory psychotherapy. He continued to complain that he felt imprisoned by his symptoms and that nothing but a bleak future of despair faced him. Gradually it appeared that the theme of his lamentations was similar to the continued mourning of his father for the latter's murdered family. The patient's diatribes against the floating bodies in his eyes seemed to possess the ring of metaphor. Treatment continued, but there were few references to the Holocaust that might lend themselves to useful interpretation. Despite transient improvement in his symptoms, the degree of progress was little.

After about one year of treatment, he reported the first of a series of dreams in which the content focused on concentration camps. Other material suggested a more available preoccupation with the Holocaust. After some initial preparation, the therapist indicated that the patient appeared to be responding to his floaters as if he had incorporated the persecutors of his father and murderers of his father's family. The patient was initially startled and incredulous, but the change in the clinical picture was dramatic. His eyes no longer troubled him as before, although the floaters were still visible. We spent the next two months in consolidating his awareness of the organizing impact of the Holocaust in influencing the initial response to his ocular symptoms. The patient's career continued to be successful; he and his wife were discussing the idea of having a child, and it proved possible to consider a termination of treatment in the very near future.

Jacob Arlow's attention to the role of metaphor as a derivative of basic, persistent, unconscious fantasy life has been useful in conceptualizing the core technical interventions considered important in the treatment of this patient.[22] Large segments of an analysis may center on the understanding of leading metaphors, and the variations of themes clustering around a metaphor can lead to the discovery of an unconscious fantasy that may be connected with traumatic event. Although there has been some controversy and wariness about the use of metaphor as an explanatory idea in psychoanalysis, it is possible that metaphor can constitute a unique way by which what was previously unknown may be reorganized in a novel fashion. This concept is applicable in all analytic work, but may be especially helpful with patients whose lives have been influenced by overwhelming experiences such as the Holocaust. It might also be mentioned that Arlow, in a brief communication, observed that a persecutor can be unconsciously equated with the subject's feces in the rectum.[23] Anal sensations may then be projected onto an object in the outside world and transformed into feelings of persecution. It would be tempting to speculate that the process may be reversed, also for defensive reasons, and that real persecutors may be treated as introjects, in this case lodged in an eye, commonly identified as an incorporative organ, which has already been rendered vulnerable by a minor alteration of its physical state.

Summary and Conclusion

A brief historical review has been presented to serve as background for the revival of interest in the psychological plight of victims of the Nazis during the Holocaust. A period of latency had to be bridged before it became apparent that late sequelae demanded to be confronted. Initial impressions of the mental health community were rather pessimistic about the efficacy of psychotherapy and analysis in such cases. It also became evident that the traumatic impact of the Holocaust would not disappear with the passing of the first generation of survivors. The urgent need for attention required by both generations, seeking treatment for a variety of reasons, enabled therapists to overcome many of their original negative feelings about prognosis as they worked with their patients.

This presentation has considered some of the problems experienced by therapists who have had to deal with emotions and content rarely experienced in other instances. Apart from some of the general and recurrent themes encountered, the major part of this contribution is addressed to some issues that have engaged special attention. These, considered in some greater detail with clinical examples, included the way in which family secrets about the Holocaust may affect treatment, the special requirement of the correct timing and dosage of interpretations in this vulnerable population, and the role of metaphor in formulating interpretations of seminal themes. Special attention to these issues can be of help in alerting therapists to aspects of treatment that can refine skill.

Larger dimensions of the meaning of the Holocaust have to be minimized or neglected in a contribution that deals with clinical issues. In the wake of coping with the late sequelae of traumatization that occurred during the persecutions, we are inevitably curious about the meaning of this tragic event to the victims, the bereaved, and the rest of the world. In the midst of an explosion of interest in the Holocaust, after a period of latency and silence, we are now facing a controversy involving remembering and forgetting. Some, understandably and with benign intent, feel that an excessive preoccupation with the Holocaust may have a stultifying effect on the desire and ability to get on with one's life and could encourage perpetual mourning. On the other hand, many feel inextricably bound to the Jewish credo which enjoins one to remember, not to forgive easily or forget. The accumulation of archival testimony and dramatic educational programs are used to achieve this goal. This can be accomplished without transmitting a traumatic potential. The commemoration owed to the dead need not be a pathological burden.

NOTES

1. Theodore Adorno, "After Auschwitz," in *Negative Dialectics* (New York: Seabury, 1973), pp. 366–367.

2. Elie Wiesel, "The Holocaust: Three Views," *ADL Bulletin* (November 1977): 3.

3. Sigmund Freud, "Why War?" *Standard Edition*, Vol. 22 (London: Hogarth Press, 1932), pp. 197–215.

4. Ibid., "Inhibitions, Symptoms and Anxiety," *Standard Edition*, Vol. 20 (London: Hogarth Press, 1926), pp. 77–174.

5. Ilse Grubrich-Simitis, "Extreme Traumatization as Cumulative Trauma," in *Psychoanalytic Study of the Child* 36 (1981): 415–460.

6. Martin Bergmann and Milton E. Jucovy, Eds., *Generations of the Holocaust* (New York: Basic Books, 1982).

7. Ibid.

8. Martin Bergmann, "Recurrent Problems in the Treatment of Survivors and Their Children," in *Generations of the Holocaust* (New York: Basic Books, 1982), pp. 247–266.

9. Grubrich-Simitis, "Extreme Traumatization."

10. Klaus D. Hoppe. "Severed Ties," in *Psychoanalytic Reflections on the Holocaust: Selected Essays,* S. Luel and P. Marcus, Eds. (New York: Ktav, 1984), pp. 95–111.

11. Bergmann, "Recurrent Problems."

12. Judith S. Kestenberg, "Survivor Parents and Their Children," in *Generations of the Holocaust* (New York: Basic Books, 1982), pp. 83–102.

13. Hillel Klein, "Problems in the Psychotherapeutic Treatment of Israeli Survivors of the Holocaust," in *Massive Psychic Trauma,* Henry Krystal, Ed. (New York: International Universities Press, 1968), pp. 233–248.

14. Bergmann, "Recurrent Problems."

15. Henry Krystal, "Integration and Self-healing in Posttraumatic States," in *Psychoanalytic Reflections on the Holocaust: Selected Essays,* S. Luel and P. Marcus, Eds. (New York: Ktav, 1984), pp. 113–133.

16. Paul Marcus, "Jewish Consciousness After the Holocaust," in *Psychoanalytic Reflections on the Holocaust: Selected Essays,* S. Luel and P. Marcus, Eds. (New York: KTAV, 1984), pp. 179–195.

17. Yoland Gampel, "A Daughter of Silence," in *Generations of the Holocaust,* M. Bergmann and M. E. Jucovy, Ed. (New York: Basic Books, 1982), pp. 120–136.

18. Milton E. Jucovy, "Telling the Holocaust Story: A Link Between the Generations," *Psychoanalytic Inquiry* 5 (1985): 31–49.

19. Theodore J. Jacobs, "Secrets, Alliances and Family Fictions: Some Psychoanalytic Observations," *Journal of the American Psychoanalytic Association* 28 (1980): 21–42.

20. James Herzog, "World Beyond Metaphor: Thoughts on the Transmission of Trauma," in *Generations of the Holocaust,* M. Bergmann and M. E. Jucovy, Eds. (New York: Basic Books, 1982), pp. 103–120.

21. Terence Des Pres, *The Survivor* (New York: Oxford University Press, 1976).

22. Jacob A. Arlow, "Metaphor and the Psychoanalytic Situation," *Psychoanalytic Quarterly* 48 (1979): 363–385.

23. Jacob A. Arlow, "Anal Sensations and Feelings of Persecution," *Psychoanalytic Quarterly* 18 (1949): 79–84.

4

Transposition Revisited: Clinical, Therapeutic, and Developmental Considerations

JUDITH S. KESTENBERG

The concept of *transposition* has been constructed to define the most important aspect of the psychology of children of survivors.[1] It refers to phenomena already described by Barocas and Barocas, who said:

The children of survivors show symptoms which would be expected if they actually lived through the Holocaust. . . . The children come to feel that the Holocaust is the single most critical event that has affected their lives although it occurred before they were born.[2]

In describing a patient whose father was a survivor, I wrote that she lived simultaneously in the present and in her father's past.[3] However, one could not speak simply of an identification with the father as a victim or with her mother as a rescuer. The patient transposed herself into the father's past via a mechanism similar to, but not identical with, the spiritualist's journey into the world of the dead. It was akin to mourning for the people her father lost, but instead of accepting their death, it revived them in fantasy. Eickhoff,[4] with the help of concepts of Cornut, referred to a similar mechanism in a child of a Nazi as "a quasi melancholic identification for the restitution of the ideal function of the object." Faimberg[5] discovered an identical mechanism in a grandchild of Nazi victims. In analysis, he acted as if he were empty, not present, dead. In his acting out, he behaved as if he lived in his father's past, a time when he no longer could reach his relatives in Poland, to whom he used to send money. Faimberg's patient acted not only as if he were his depressed father, but also played the role of the father's parents who died. Faimberg coined this constellation a "telescoping of generations." Survivors' children identify with the grieving parent who lost his original family members in the Holocaust. The depressed parent is often experienced as dead.[6] To revive the ''dead'' parents, many child survivors feel obligated to restore the lost objects to them.

Rachel, the patient whose long analysis I recounted in ''Psychoanalyses of Children of Survivors from the Holocaust'' and ''Survivor Parents and Their Children,'' not only enacted the role of her father, not only the roles of his relatives, but also the roles of all the Jews under Nazi occupation. In her acting out and her symptoms, she seemed to bring order into the chaos of the Holocaust. She was starving and feeding people. In fantasy, she was putting them into the confinement of her body, holding and releasing them, killing and resurrecting them. She seemed to play all the roles in the historical drama, representing the attackers and the victims in ghettos, in camps, in woods, and in hiding. Integrating all these roles and combining them with her present life, she equated the *unknown* past with the unknown inside of her body. Gampel[7] recognized that transposition is, in some measure, a normal developmental phenomenon when she said that all children ''act out a scenario that is not theirs, but belonging to their family history.''[8] Her patient Liora also used her body to enact the Holocaust drama. She vomitted, had headaches, and spoke in a hoarse voice. She felt an uncontrolled, frightening thing within herself; she wanted to empty herself and was afraid to go mad. When she was in the process of recovery she said, ''Those things don't belong to me, they are theirs, they should keep them in their museum.'' My patient Rachel said wistfully, ''Sometimes I feel like I have memories I should not talk about . . . it's not me, it's him.''

Listening to reports of analyses of children of survivors, we realized that an analysis can be ''completed'' without any consideration of the Holocaust. The analyst may not recognize references to the Holocaust in dreams and behavior or he may feel that discussing the Holocaust will retraumatize the patient and he will consciously avoid the topic. Quite a few symptoms can disappear while the silence about the secret of the Holocaust is preserved in the analysis.[9] The analyst's behavior constitutes a message that the parents' past is their own and should not be invaded. On the strength of this indirect suggestion, the patient may give up his symptoms and begin to look at his parents as if they never had been persecuted. The patient acquires a ''false self'' and the cure is false as well. However, it is equally injurious to concentrate exclusively on the patient's feelings about the Holocaust, disregarding individual pathogenic influence and conflicts or the present day reality. All acting-out symptoms and fantasies have to be analyzed on two levels: one on the personal past and present-day level and the other on the Holocaust level.

An example of how complex, how overdetermined the patient's acting out can be is Rachel's provocation of her teacher, which induced him to lose his temper. She could do to the teacher what she wanted to do to her father but couldn't because she thought of him as vulnerable. Her anger at her father was connected with her frustration that he kept her out of his secret Holocaust life, but it was also fed by two wishes: One wish was to arouse him into being alive rather than numb and indifferent, the other was to defeat him within the framework of a negative Oedipus complex. All these factors and others had to be analyzed to do justice to the complexity of her motivation. While, at first, each of them was analyzed separately, eventually the network that held her acting out in place had to be presented to her so that she might see how many threads were intertwined. When she let go of one thread, several others compensated for its loss.

The desire to enter her father's secret life and to rescue him from the psychic death of continuous, unresolved mourning was played out inside Rachel's body and externalized to the outside. There were complex goings on in her body when she emptied it of food and filled it with feces she would not relinquish. As will be exemplified below, these transactions camouflaged inner genital yearnings for a baby that was in danger of dying. Sexual fantasies about the teacher were filled with a need to control him by giving him a gift of a genuine creative production (a genital baby) and to quickly undo the generous act by dropping brushes and messing up the studio (the fecal, dead baby). The time tunnel into which Rachel descended to change the past and rewrite history had its source in the abdominal cavity, with the mouth or anus as the entrace to the tunnel and the past played out inside the body, and externalized as well. Both Rachel and four-year-old John[10] looked upon their feces as recreations of dead grandparents. Feces also represented dead, discarded children, while the imaginary children, created inside the genital, had the positive connotation of survival in the living offspring. Through their creation in fantasy, dead children were resurrected.

Because the Nazi persecutions had a special effect of debilitating the body and impinging upon body functions, usually taken for granted, survivor-parents transmitted many of their traumatic body experiences to their infants, who required body care. The parents' own acting out of what they had experienced in their body, when they were starved, covered with dirt and boils, ridden by lice, hidden in the ground, and gravely ill, gained an added significance at a time when parents are generally concerned with the baby's body functions. Those who, like John's father, reacted to separation by wetting the bed, unconsciously anticipated that their children would suffer the same way and gave them clues to do so. Eickhoff[11] speaks in a case of a Nazi child, of "borrowed guilt." Here we can speak of borrowed symptoms, with the lending parent an active participant in this process.

It is important to distinguish between adult survivors, child survivors, and children of survivors. A vivid transposition into the past world of parents, never experienced by the child, applies only to children of survivors. In contrast, adult and child survivors continue to live in the past, not on the basis of fantasies alone, but on the basis of memories, verbal and nonverbal. The difference becomes hazy for those who are both survivors and children of survivors. Those who were very young during persecution have to depend on their parents to tell them what happened. They too use transposition to supplement what meager body memories they may have.

Children who were persecuted themselves suffer both from loss of memory and hypermnesia[12] for the events of the Holocaust, events they witnessed. More often than adult survivors, they respond to such triggers as the sight of a uniform or a smell of gas or soup, with unbearable and intrusive recollections from which they want to escape. Many adult survivors associated with other survivors and had an outlet in reminiscing together. Groups of adolescent survivors who emigrated to Palestine together also exchanged memories, yet their minds were turned to the future. Adult survivors were frequently demoted in their social status and liked to talk about their pre-Holocaust past. Child survivors who were looking forward to education and new careers placed a moratorium on remembering the past and put their whole self into the service of building new lives. They went to school and acquired new friends whom they emulated in order to achieve a feeling of belonging.[13] Many of those who survived with their parents were encouraged not to remember and those who were adopted were practically forbidden to remember. There were elements of transposition not only in the very young survivors, but also in those who had been separated from their parents and did not know what the parents did during separation.

METAPSYCHOLOGICAL CONSIDERATIONS

The question has arisen of how to characterize transposition metapsychologically. Having given this question much thought, I came to the conclusion that transposition is an organization of the self in relation to time and space. It is an intrinsic factor in the transmission of cultural heritage and in the changes occurring transgenerationally within it. Through transposition of a mild rather than pathological kind, the parents' culture is elaborated by the children and modified. Transposition must not be confused with a dual personality. It is rather a mechanism, used by a person living in the present and in the past. It is based on identification with one or both parents who are working through their past traumatic experiences in today's reality. However, it transcends identification, as it serves the perpetuation of the influence of major historical events through generations.[14]

All psychic agencies participate in transposition. The wish to intrude into the parents' secret past is often coupled with a competition with the victimized parent regarding who is more of a victim or who is more heroic.

Varied in its details, transposition encompasses the basic conflict between the wish to kill and the wish to save one's parents, one's children, and beyond this the whole ethnic group or the world. Identification with the aggressor vies with the identification with the victim. A number of these identifications are used as defenses against sexual and aggressive wishes. Transposition contains traces of family romance,[15] with belonging to the Nazi elite substituting for a wish to be a king, queen, prince, or princess. Mixed with Oedipal fantasies and defenses are pregenital fantasies of saving oneself by stealing or hoarding food or by becoming immune to the threat of starvation, of being sullied and degraded or cleansing oneself and others. A common theme is the rescue fantasy and the reenacting of rebirth through descending in the time tunnel and coming out. This symbolizes not only one's own rebirth, but also the rebirth of the whole nation. All this may be condensed in the wish for children to continue the family line and to triumph over Hitler. The conflict between dying and surviving remains in the center of the survival complex; it develops alongside the death wishes toward parents and children.

The superego of survivor-parents is elected as a judge whether their survival was justified. "Why me and not so many others?" asks the survivor and he transmits this question to his children. The parents' present and past are scrutinized by the children to see whether their conduct has made them worthy of surviving. If the parent did not deserve to be chosen to live, this casts a doubt on the childrens' right to be alive. They say, "If they (the parents) had not survived, I would not be here." By being themselves worthwhile, they justify their parents' survival. The right to live assumes great proportions. When affirmed, it increases narcissism; when in question, it increases narcissistic vulnerability. The ego ideal, which dictates many aspects of transposition, especially saving others, is built on the wish to redeem parents and their relatives. Messianic in its nature, transposition not only rescues dead Jews, but the whole suffering mankind. The aims are to defeat the Nazis, strengthen the resistance of the victims, and devise ingenious means of survival. When Rachel was 12 years old, she did not want to live in the city. She wanted to be a hermit in the woods where she would subsist on berries. No one knew what became of her father's lost relatives. She hoped to find them in the forest. Implied was the reproach to her father because he never went back to look for them since he heard that they had all perished. Rachel wished to undo his sin and join the lost relatives in their presumed hiding place. When she grew up, Rachel wanted to rescue people by inventing new cures for diseases.

Transposition is an organizing agency which arises from the survival complex of generations.[16] This complex is a normal phenomenon, comparable to, but more basic than, the Oedipus complex. Only under extreme stress and danger of death does the survival complex become manifest. Otherwise it is as silent as wanting to live, which is inherent biologically in all living tissue and taken for granted. Intake of food, breathing, and expelling waste are all adaptive instinctual components of living. Lack of nourishment, overcrowding, interference with normal waste expulsion, lack of hygiene and a continuous assault on body integrity evoke drastic survival mechanisms which may persist beyond the time of danger. Where they fail, the wish to die and be left in peace becomes conscious. A few who survived were rescued when they were about to give up, but many died even after liberation, which came too late to resuscitate them. Acting out the stresses of the past, and each time coming out alive, has a healing effect upon the survivor.

The children of survivors did not experience the profound physical deterioration of ghettos and camps and the stressful conditions in hiding. In survivors, the hormonal and metabolic transformation of the body was interrelated with anxiety and the numbness of masked depression. Children of survivors somatize their anxieties and depressions when they go down into the time tunnel of their parents' and grandparents' existence. On the basis of this somatization, they construct fantasies that may or may not be fed by what they have heard about the Holocaust. A starving child of survivors experiences the physical feelings that go with it without knowing that she reenacts the hunger of her parents or relatives. Even when parents observe the silence of a mourning that never ends, children's fantasies based on somatizations can come close to the actual experiences of body changes during the Holocaust. As noted before, selection of somatic symptoms is most probably transmitted during early body care.

TRANSPOSITION IN CHILDREN OF NAZIS

The question has arisen whether children of Nazis also suffer from transposition. The silence imposed by Nazis who tried to destroy the evidence of their crimes, lest they be severely punished, may be incorporated into the superego of their children and grandchildren who are not supposed to discredit their parents. However, the unraveling of parental secrets plays an important role in many accounts of the second generation in Germany.[17]

As in the case of survivors, we have to distinguish between the adult participants in the Nazi world and their children. I shall refer to those who were children, born before the end of the war, as the young first generation of Germans, and to those who were born after the war, as the second generation. A representative of the young first generation is Dietrich, described by Eckstaedt.[18] She wrote that, at least in part, Dietrich lived in a world of delusion. In this delusion, he denied that Germany lost the war; he refused to admit that the war had ended in defeat, and his father's failure. He lived two lives, with one part of the ego "consciously reanimating the past."[19] For him, defeat meant inglorious death and victory meant life. When the analyst became "victorious," he literally lost his mind.

Dietrich was almost six years old when the war ended, but the family continued to live in a narcissistic splendor. Trying to elevate himself into a position which he did not deserve was in keeping with the family tradition that he did not have to deserve anything to get it. It was coming to him. For him, the elementary question of survival presented itself as "kill or being killed." His superego perpetuated Nazi ideology. In contrast, the child-survivors grappled with the problem, "To survive or die." Killing rather than surviving and being killed rather than dying is crucial in the lives of fathers and children who succumbed to Nazism.[20]

We have come a long way since I posed the question of whether the Nazis wanted to kill their own children and diverted these wishes to Jewish children.[21] We have collected more and more evidence for this view. Nazi youth was imbued with the glory of dying for the fatherland. Victory and German *Lebensraum* (life space) were more important than their lives. If they won and were killed (but were victorious), they expected to consort with other Germanic heros in Valhalla. It hardly occurred to them that they could die and lose the war. Being killed in defeat was shameful, but dying for the glory of their fathers was a source of pride, even for the bereaved mothers.

A generation of Germans who grew up without fathers was encouraged to vindicate their defeat in World War I and to bring glory to them at the expense of their own and their children's lives.[22] Dietrich's struggle between killing for the sake of his father or being killed was represented in a fairy tale he read as a child, called "Witzenspitzel." A young nobleman served the king and for his sake, to please him, he plundered and killed others.

In contrast to Dietrich, who acted out mainly his own childhood beliefs and fantasies, which were part of Nazi ideology, five patients born after 1945 and described by Hardtmann[23] became part of their parents' past. They were irritable and depressive; their concentration was disturbed and they lived in constant fear. They experienced themselves as "their parents' Jews," as "strangers in their own house." They felt in body and soul like "skin and shells," without a nucleus of the self, and they suffered from psychosomatic disorders. Like the survivors' children, they lived in their parents' past and tried to intrude into the secret lives of their fathers. However, their parents' past was quite different from that of survivor parents. The secret of the Nazi past, not only of the active SS man, a party member, but also of the silent nonprotestor, is fraught with the aura of child murder. Inmates of camps were reduced to the status of helpless children, dependent on their cruel "caretakers." They ate what was given to them; they were told when they could defecate and were confined to camp like small children who cannot go out without an adult. No matter how the Nazi generation tried to deflect their filicidal impulses upon aliens, it started and ended their villainous activities with killing German children. Their own children, after the war, felt their hatred, their coldness and what von Westenhagen called her mother's "deadly clinging" to her.[24] These Nazi parents still lived in the past when defective or sick children were gassed or injected with phenol. Woe unto the children of Germany—a sickness might end their young lives! When these children reached adolescence, they were sent to the front to combat seasoned allied troops. Innocently they trusted their idol Hitler, and died believing in Germany's victory.

A child's death is a central theme among survivors and Nazis, but their content differs. A survivor parent may feel guilty that his young son died at the hands of the Nazis, but the child born after the war survived. A survivor mother feels terrible that her mother is dead and she has become a mother herself. Does she deserve to have a live child, since her little sister died? The problem of children is fraught with guilt. In contrast, Nazi parents still aspire to have an ideal child to fit into Hitler's ideal German youth, who all belonged to him. Imperfection in the child is paramount to a death sentence because defective children must be eliminated from the German race.

If we look at the material produced in the analyses of the young German first generation, we often find the theme of child killing. Miss T.[25] dreamt that she was in a room with a homicidal man. This reminded her of a man who had been committed to a state hospital for trying to kill his family in a gas oven. The analyst pointed out the similarity to the gas chambers in which Jews were killed. It did not occur to him that German children, who were "useless consumers," were gassed by the Nazis long before the Jews. As a matter of fact, the early gassing was a prelude and a preparation for the later wholesale gassing in camps. This might explain the other dream Miss T. recalled, about a fish tank in which nothing was alive. Repeatedly, dreams dealt with fish tanks in some of which dead fish were littered on the bottom. The analyst understood that the tanks were representations of the vagina and uterus, but the fish, as dead children whom the patient wanted to resuscitate, were not mentioned. There is a similarity to Rachel, who killed and resuscitated the children of Israel in her abdomen. She played the role of attacker and victim. However, in the Nazi child, the dread of being one of the dead fish in the tank and bearing dead children herself, in identification with the Nazi child murders, is in the forefront of conflicts. Her hands feel bloody.

For the children of Nazis born before, during or after the war, the problem of child killing was in the forefront of their concerns. This had its roots in the German culture, which led to Nazism, in the murderous acts of Nazis, which revealed their wishes to kill their own children. Hardtmann[26] prefaced her chapter on analyses of children of Nazis born after the war with an excerpt from Hoffmannsthal and Strauss' *Woman without a Shadow* (*Die Frau ohne Schatten*). In it, the Dyer's Wife gives her husband roast fish to eat, which symbolizes unborn children. Hardtmann quotes Hoffmannsthal's comment about it to the effect that "These unborn children are the improved mirror images of their parents. Parents gain their self-realization by gaining their children." Despite this need for narcissistic aggrandizement through their children, Nazi parents "expand at the expense of their children and cause their destruction."[27] In researching their parents' Nazi past, children of Nazis are compelled to transpose themselves into the whole Nazi culture. At the same time, their understanding of their parents' murderous souls is based on their own experience as well. One of Hardtmann's[28] second generation patients was told by a feminist friend she should put up her newborn child for adoption because he was a boy. That night, she dreamt that members of the National Socialist Women's Federation turned a child over to the Gestapo. The child in the dream represented her son, but also represented herself. Another of Hardtmann's patients, Miss B., realized in her analysis how much she hated her mother. When she aborted a child, she experienced it as aborting her mother.

In treating survivors or first generation Germans, we have to be aware of their personal experiences during the Nazi reign. In treating members of the second generation, who are more apt to use transposition in their acting out, we have to be aware of the history of the era and location they are trying to live in. Rachel, for instance, not only lived in the region where her father was born and where he was persecuted, but she was a part of ghettos, concentration camps, and hiding places. Thus, she attempted to redeem all the Jews of her father's native country. In other cases, there is more focus on a smaller area confined to a certain time of persecution. In Rachel's analysis, we had to search for the sources of information upon which her symptoms and acting out were based. This must be done in the treatment of second generation Germans as well. Universal themes, such as killing of Jews and Gypsies, may obscure more personal experiences of their parents, whose neighbors disappeared never to return. The parents' silence, carried over from Nazi times when silence was imposed under threats of being sent to a concentration camp, became proof of their condoning what had been done, not only to Jews, but to Poles, Russians, Greeks, and German nationals themselves. The second generation, on hearing where their fathers served, consults textbooks and archives, and draws on confidential information from relatives to help their transposition into Nazi times. Some families lived in areas where it was known that gas wagons were used to kill the infirm and the sick, among them many children. It became known that a retarded or disturbed child must be kept at home to avert his or her murder in a state institution. Still, in other locations, Nazis insisted on abolishing religious education and substituting for it the heathen Nazi indoctrination. Much of this was ignored or repressed. It comes back in dreams and fantasies of people who had been children during the war and also in their children and grandchildren, who transpose themselves into the past of their parents. Through the study of the history of the area where German parents lived and the location where fathers and brothers served in the armed forces or in the SS, one can connect dreams and fantasies with what has been transmitted to children directly and indirectly. As Hardtmann[29] and Simenauer[30] pointed out, Nazi ideology intrudes upon the psyche of children of Nazis. Hardtmann speaks of parents of today's children in Germany who commit "soul murder" of their children. Narcissistic mothers who happily sacrificed the lives of their children during the war, mothers who found fulfillment in National Socialism, continued after the war to live still in the Nazi system where "might was right." Their children only had value if they were perfect and eligible to die for Hitler.

There is imminent danger that the second generation, despite their best intentions and liberal views, will be tempted to sacrifice their children as well on the altar of their ideals. A striking example is that of von Westernhagen,[31] who assiduously pursued the past of her Nazi father. In the midst of unravelling her relationship to her father, she became aware of the wish to harm her nursling baby. In analyzing children and grandchildren of people who had been imbued with Nazi propaganda, we have to distinguish between what they hear about the past and what kind of hostility they actually suffer at the hands of their parents. Children of survivors who use transposition into the past to study Holocaust history and to become active in averting another Holocaust, can help parents and the entire Jewish community to mourn after their dead. Can children of Nazis do the same for their parents and help them mourn after the many dead who were killed in camps and in the war? Can they help the older generation to mourn not only the loss of people in World Wars I and II, but also the loss of humanity, which is not easy to restore? The German analyst, who himself mourns the death of more than 6 million Germans, can help his patients to mourn[32] and accept their parents' way of mourning, or facilitate it. The Jewish analyst who treats survivors and children of survivors, must overcome his own guilt and must be able to face his own losses when so many of his brethren died and a whole shtetl culture was destroyed.[33]

DEVELOPMENTAL CONTEXT

In treating people who transpose themselves into their ancestors' past, we have learned a great deal about an aspect of development that had hitherto escaped our attention. In my own case, despite the fact that a great deal of my research focused on the inner-genital phase,[34] despite the fact that I knew that this was the time when continuity was established between the past and the present, as well as the future, despite the fact that I knew how the exploration of the inside, invisible and unknown, is externalized to the outside, it took me years to connect transposition with the task of the inner-genital integration phase.

No doubt, some basic kinesthetic and sensory memories of the first year influence and connect the happenings of the second and third year to the first. These early experiences are sifted out, played out, and reorganized in the third and fourth year of life in the inner-genital phase. This phase has also been called the phase of integration, because more than other preOedipal phases, does it reintegrate diverse drives, their derivatives, the sense of self and objects, affects, and ego functions. In this manner, relations can be built from their early rudiments. This is accomplished during the process of the child's transformation from a baby to a preschooler who can take over many maternal functions to care for himself and for his imaginary babies in a new way, often unlike the way it was done in his infancy. For instance, a depression after weaning may be revived and a new solution is found for it. Rebelling against toilet training may be exacerbated and resolved in a new way. A feeling that parents hated the child can be now clearly expressed. All previous images of the baby as good or bad and having a bad or a good mother, become transposed upon each other and reorganized in a unified image, under the influence of inner-genital feminine sexuality and its sublimatory outlet in maternality.

Toward the latter part of the fourth year, the child becomes preoccupied with death. His or her understanding of being alive or dead is predicated on the repeated experiences of inner-genital excitement which comes to life and departs in rising and falling waves. When they leave, there is a feeling of emptiness inside. The image of the baby which has become unified, becomes hazy when the excitement dies down. To succeed in this transition between babyhood and childhood, the child needs the guidance of his mother. She must help him understand what is going on inside of him and how it fits in with the outside.

When his mother leaves, that too makes him feel empty, as he connects the inner and outer events. Soon, he becomes afraid that his mother will never return, that she will die, and he himself will die and not come back to life again. The live baby which she had equated with the mysterious inner excitement appears strange now. The child wishes to expel the baby that gives him so much trouble and he develops the idea that his mother wants to get rid of him. Expelling the baby also destroys the baby he once was. The child is afraid of losing this aspect of himself.

The continuity of existence is of utmost importance to the three year old. He begins to ask about his ancestry. He wants to know who was his mother and father's mommy and who were her mommy and daddy. A three-and-a-half-old girl drew a series of pictures which ended in a portrait of herself. Having created a pictorial representation of her origins, she became uneasy and asked me, "Where was I before I was born?" I answered, "Inside Mommy." She asked, "And where was I before that?" I answered, "In Mommy's egg." She asked, "And where was Mommy's egg before she was born?" I answered, "In her Mommy's egg." This conversation was continued through several generations and the child's presence established since time immemorial.[35] Another conversation of this kind, with another child, ended with the mother's saying that the child descends from Adam and Eve. The fear of nonexistence, of being inanimate or dead, gives children sleepless nights. When someone they know dies, they have no peace until they can see their new abode, their grave. At the same time, children like to look at family albums and to identify relatives and themselves when they were babies. This journey into the past is enriched by anecdotes mother and father tell from their own childhood and the child's babyhood. The child achieves what might be called retroactive immortality, matched by immortality in the future, which transcends into the phallic narcissistic phase that follows the inner-genital.

The journey of the second generation of the Holocaust in the time tunnel originates in the third and fourth year of life, when children ask about their grandparents and begin to make up stories about their origin. Ground has been laid for somatization in pregenital phases. Bodily sensations and nonverbal representations of parental responses to body needs become imbedded in the unified self-representation of the toddler and reorganized in new fantasies and beliefs. On the basis of these images and their reinforcement by parents, the journey of the second generation of the Holocaust in the time tunnel has been prepared and can begin in the third and fourth year of life, when children ask about their grandparents and make up stories about their origin.

The family romance allows the phallic and Oedipal child to enter into another world,[36] a world of the past when kings and queens reared princes and princesses, and tyrants enslaved people and heroes liberated them. They learn from stories, especially those parents tell and read to them. In their investigations of the parents' and grandparents' and ancestors' pasts and of the culture in which they lived, children establish a continuity of the family that gives them a feeling of belonging and a corresponding identity, based on the question: "To whom do I belong?" In their fantasies, they change the past to suit themselves, whereby they seek control over a past which is not really theirs.

The three year old may start on the exploration of the past, but this is just a beginning. The curiosity about the prenatal, fetal, and infantile history may remain latent and is reinvoked in prepuberty when physical maturation is expected and experienced.[37] The hormonal reorganization in adolescence is accompanied by a psychological reorganization in which the representations of the inside and the outside of the body are transformed into an adult body image. This new development requires a new continuity, a continuity of change, and an expectation of the future in which the wish for a child is realized. During pregnancy and child rearing, the question of life and death of parents and baby are revived. Attempts are made to improve on the way one has been reared by one's own parents. The close connections between the body and the psyche at those times increase primary narcissism[38] and works overtime to assure survival. This then is the developmental background of transposition that occurs full blast in a telescopic manner[39] when the survival of one's family line has been threatened and has to be reestablished.

SUMMARY AND CONCLUSIONS

Children of survivors have a tendency to go back in time and explore their parents' past. In their fantasies, they live during the Holocaust and transpose the present into the past. I called this phenomenon transposition.

Transposition is akin to mourning, except that the lost objects are not the mourner's own, and their death is never accepted. Instead, there is a continuous attempt to revive them. This constitutes a restitution of the lost objects to the bereaved parent.

From the metapsychological point of view, one can define transposition as an organization of the self in relation to time and space. All psychic agencies participate in it. Wishes, adaptations, and defenses, as well as value systems, are organized in a unique way to fit into the double life of the children of survivors. Transposition is part and parcel of the survival complex of generations, a normal phenomenon, which becomes exaggerated and highly visible when there is a threat to the survival of generations.

From the developmental point of view, it appears that transposition is a phenomenon that begins when toddlers grown out of their babyhood and want to take the place of their mothers. They want to know where they came from and explore it transgenerationally. They wish to live in the parents' and grandparents' past and never die. The imaginary baby, created in this phase, is a recurrent fantasy, which eventually ends with its "death." The creation, the death, and resurrection of babies, are a theme of this phase that becomes prominent in ongoing fantasies of children of survivors.

Children of Nazis also show evidence of transposition. Many seem to live in the Nazi past, in the era when their parents might have been persecutors. They, too, play the role of persecutors and victims. However, a striking contrast between children of survivors and the children of Nazis is that the former struggle with the conflict "to survive or to die," while the latter think of "killing or being killed" as the main theme.

The transmission of survivor-parents' feelings about their persecution to their children seems to occur especially during child care. This may lead to somatization, from which, at a later date, fantasies arise about such conditions as being starved or tortured by Nazi persecutors. The central issue conveyed to the children, whether one should live or should have died with the others, stems from a very real confrontation with death during the Holocaust. Many German parents were not able to resolve the conflict between child killing and child saving, to the advantage of their children. Thus, their children feel endangered from the start.

It is necessary to distinguish between children of survivors, who live in the world of their parents, and the survivors themselves. Both older and younger generation survivors had been persecuted themselves and tend to live in their own past together with the acknowledgment of the present. One must also distinguish between children of Nazis born after the war, who transpose the present into the past, and those born before or during the war, who act out their own childhood experiences during the Nazi era.

Transposition should not be confused with the identification with one's parents. Children of survivors, who descend into the time tunnel of their parent's past, may play different roles (of the parent, various relatives, or the persecutors), but are able to integrate this fantasized past with the present and with fantasies arising from present-day conflicts and their own past. In treating them, one must analyze both these aspects of their lives. The somatic symptoms must be understood by the therapist as arising from early infantile experiences and reinforced by later fantasies about being persecuted. Sensations not only give rise to fantasies such as the revival of dead relatives in one's own body, but also reinforce them, creating a vicious circle.

Quite a few German children, who had been treated cruelly by their parents, somatize as well and their fantasies also frequently arise from the soma. They often pull toward death and need help in overcoming it.

Therapists of children of survivors must understand what happened in the Holocaust and come to grips with their own grief. Therapists of children of Nazis must familiarize themselves with the Nazi side of the Holocaust and must overcome their own resistance in order to help their patients confront their country's past.

Treatment of the second generation of the persecuted and the persecutors must of necessity focus on the conflict between ceasing to exist and survival, which first becomes articulated in the inner-genital, pre-Oedipal phase.

NOTES

1. Judith S. Kestenberg, "Psychoanalyses of Children of Survivors from the Holocaust," *J Amer Psychoanal Assoc* 28 (1980): 775–804; "A Metapsychological Assessment Based on an Analysis of a Survivor's Child," in *Generations of the Holocaust*, Martin S. Bergmann and Milton E. Jucovy, Eds. (New York: Basic Books, 1982), pp. 137–158.

2. Harvey Barocas and Carol Barocas, "Wounds of the Fathers: The Next Generation of Holocaust Victims," *Int Review Psychoanal* (1979): 331.

3. Kestenberg, "Psychoanalyses of Children of Survivors from the Holocaust," p. 778.

4. Frederick W. Eickhoff, "On the Borrowed Unconscious Sense of Guilt and the Palimpsestic Structure of a Symptom—Afterthoughts on the Hamburg Congress of the IPA," paper presented at the *NPAP Meeting*, May 1, 1988.

5. Haydee Faimberg, "The Telescoping of Generations," *Contemporary Psychoanalysis* 24, no. 1 (1988): 99–118.

6. Andre Green, "The Dead Mother," in *On Private Madness* (Madison CT: International Universities Press, 1986), pp. 142–173.

7. Yolanda Gampel, "A Daughter of Silence," in *Generations of the Holocaust,* Bergmann and Jucovy, Eds. (New York: Basic Books, 1982), pp. 120–157.

8. Ibid., p. 120.

9. Milton E. Jucovy, "Telling the Holocaust Story," *Psychoanal. Inquiry* 5 (1985): 31–49; Faimberg, "The Telescoping of Generations."

10. Judith S. Kestenberg, "Survivor-Parents and Their Children," in *Generations of the Holocaust*, Bergmann and Jucovy, Eds. (New York: Basic Books, 1982), pp. 137–158.

11. Frederick W. Eickhoff, "Identification and Its Vicissitudes in the Context of the Nazi Phenomenon," in *J Psychoanal* 67 (1986): 33–44; ibid., "On the Borrowed Unconscious Sense of Guilt and the Palimpsestic Structure of a Symptom—Afterthoughts on the Hamburg Congress of the IPA."

12. Wanda Poltawska, Andrej Jakubik, Jozek Sarnecki, and Julian Gatarski, "Wyniki badan psychiatrycznych osob urodzonych lub wiezionych w dziecinstwie w hitlerowskich obozach koncentracyjnych" (Results of psychiatric examinations of persons, born or incarcerated in their childhood in Hitler's concentration camps, *Przeglad Lekarski* 1 (1966): 21–36.

13. Judith S. Kestenberg and Milton Kestenberg, "The Sense of Belonging and Altruism in Children Who Survived the Holocaust," *Psychoanalytic Review* 75, no. 4, winter 1988, 533–560.

14. Faimberg, "The Telescoping of Generations"; Paulette Wilgowicz, "Après le Shoah" (After the Shoah), paper presented at the *Paris Psychoanal. Society* in June, 1988.

15. Monique Taub, "Fantasme l'origine des mythes et romans de la filiation *D.E.S.S. de Psychologie Clinique Université Paris* (1987–88).

16. Kestenberg, "A Metapsychological Assessment Based on an Analysis of a Survivor's Child."

17. Doerte von Westernhagen, *Die Kinder der Taeter* (The children of the perpetrators) (Munich: Kosel-Verlag, 1987).

18. Anita Eckstaedt, "A Victim of the Other Side," in *Generations of the Holocaust,* Bergmann and Jucovy, Eds. (New York: Basic Books, 1982), pp. 197–227.

19. Eckstaedt, "A Victim of the Other Side," p. 212.

20. Judith S. Kestenberg, Milton Kestenberg, and Janet Amighi, "The Nazis' Quest for Death and the Jewish Quest for Life," in *The Psychological Perspectives of the Holocaust and Its Aftermath,* Randolph C. Braham, Ed. (New York: Social Science Monographs, 1988), pp. 13–44.

21. Judith S. Kestenberg, "The Psychological Consequences of Punitive Institutions," in *Humanizing America,*: A Post-Holocaust Imperative (Proceedings of the Philadelphia Conference on the Holocaust) Josephine Knopp, Ed. (Philadelphia: Institute of the Holocaust, Temple University, 1977), pp. 113–29. Reprinted in a modified form in *Israel Annals of Psychiatry and Related Disciplines* 18, no. 1 (1981): 15–30.

22. Judith S. Kestenberg, "The Development of the Ego-Ideal, Its Structure in Nazi Youth and Persecuted Jewish Children," *Issues in Ego Psychology* 10, no. 2 (1987): 22–34.

23. Gertrud Hardtmann, "The Shadows of the Past" in *Generations of the Holocaust,* Bergmann and Jucovy, Eds. (New York: Basic Books, 1982), pp. 230–246.

24. von Westernhagen, *Die Kinder der Taeter,* p. 217.

25. Anonymous, "Child of Persecutors," in *Generations of the Holocaust,* Bergmann and Jucovy, Eds. (New York: Basic Books, 1982), pp. 183–196.

26. Hardtmann, "The Shadows of the Past," p. 228.

27. Ibid., p. 229.

28. Ibid., p. 230.

29. Ibid., p. 244.

30. Erich Simenauer, "The Return of the Persecutor," in *Generations of the Holocaust,* Bergmann and Jucovy, Eds. (New York: Basic Books, 1982), pp. 167–175.

31. von Westernhagen, *Die Kinder der Taeter,* pp. 117, 171.

32. Eckstaedt, "A Victim of the Other Side"; Alexander Mitscherlich and Margarete Mitscherlich, *Die Unfähigkeit zu trauern* (Munich: R. Piper & Coverlag, 1970); Eickhoff, "On the Borrowed Unconscious Sense of Guilt and the Palimpsestic Structure of a Symptom—Afterthoughts on the Hamburg Congress of the IPA."

33. Paul Marcus, "Jewish Consciousness After the Holocaust," in *Psychoanalytic Reflections on the Holocaust: Selected Essays,* Steven Leul and Paul Marcus, Eds. (New York: KTAV, 1984), pp. 179–196.

34. In 1956, I described a phase which precedes the phallic and Oedipal phases, but is no longer pregenital. I referred to it as "early maternal phase," because at that time the wish for the baby is predominant. After collecting more material from observations and analyses, I realized in 1968 that this phase occurs in both sexes, but is essentially feminine, that is, it is based on inner-genital zones from which the need for a child arises. Tying up his lost babyhood with his/her early maternal strivings, the child integrates pregenital and inner-genital drives and prepares him- herself for future motherhood. In conformity with the terminology used for libidinal phases of development, I named this phase "inner-genital." The imaginary inner-genital baby in this phase is a successor of pregenital baby creations. Because of the 'rise and ebb' nature of inner-genital sensations, the child, especially the girl, fluctuates between feeling full and empty. Feeling "alive" and feeling "dead" is then connected with early representations of life and death. Disappointed because the live baby is not forthcoming, the child turns to the outer-genital

for consolation and enters the phallic phase of development. The earlier externalization
of inner-genital sensations upon the "baby" now focuses on the penis or clitoris instead.

For further elucidations of the inner-genital integration phase, see text and the following
references: Judith S. Kestenberg, *On the Development of Maternal Feelings in Early
Childhood: The Psychoanalytic Study of the Child* (New York: International Univ. Press,
1956), pp. 257–290; ibid., "Outside and Inside, Male and Female," *J. Amer. Psychoanal. Assoc.* 16 (1968); 457–520; ibid., "The Inner-Genital Phase, Pre-Phallic, Pre-
Oedipal," in Dale Mendell, Ed., *Early Feminine Development: Contemporary Psychoanalytic Views* (New York: Spectrum Publications, 1980), pp. 81–125.

35. Kestenberg, The Inner-Genital Phase, Pre-Phallic, Pre-Oedipal, p. 109–117.

36. Taub, "Fantasme l'origine des mythes et romans de la filiation *D.E.S.S. de Psychologie Clinique Université Paris,* pp. 109–117.

37. Judith S. Kestenberg, *Parents and Children* (New York: Aronson, 1975).

38. Judith S. Kestenberg and Ira Brenner, "Narcissism in the Service of Survival,"
presented at the Vulnerable Child Workshop of the Amer. Psychoanal. Meeting, Chicago
(1987) and to the *Review française de psychanalyse* in June, 1988.

39. Faimberg, "The Telescoping of Generations."

III

Self-Psychology

5

The Emerging Self in the Survivor Family

JOAN T. FREYBERG

It is of increasing interest to those of us in the mental health community that the effects of the Nazi Holocaust resulted, not only in sustained and severely traumatic psychological sequelae to its direct victims, but also continued on to the next generation. Violence casts a long shadow and has profound consequences for many who have not been its immediate targets. The focus of this chapter will be on the offspring of concentration camp survivors and their struggle for emotional individuation and autonomy. The data are drawn from the patients of the author who are or have been in analysis or analytically oriented psychotherapy, clinical interviews conducted by the author with nonpatients, and many group experiences with the offspring of concentration camp survivors.

Thousands of offspring were born to the concentration camp survivors in the two to five years after the war, as the victims hastened to replace their devastating losses by creating their own families. These parents were countryless, homeless, jobless, and in poor health as they brought their offspring into the world, a world that to them was hostile, inhospitable, and had betrayed the Jews. As they faced the enormous task of rebuilding their lives, these parents were in shock and deep grief, suffering from the newly defined "Post Traumatic Stress Syndrome," in which psychic numbness, lack of affect, depression, fear, suspiciousness, and deeply buried anger predominate.[1] The survivors began leaving Europe and settling in Israel, the United States, Canada, Australia, and South America, for the most part, in tightly knit refugee neighborhoods and tightly knit families. To survive against the terrible odds of relocation, reeducation, poverty, poor health, and emotional scarring, the survivor family had to band together, often feeling isolated from non-Jews and even from American Jews who were perceived to have emerged unscathed from the war. Survival dictated repression of all anger and conflict within the family and placed first priority on the control of behavior. Emphasis on conformity and achievement, as ways of remaining safe in the new world, was powerful and pervasive. It was essential that the offspring child excel in school and strive for a secure and prestigious vocation, often in the professions. Female children were expected to cater to their fathers and brothers, marry early to successful Jewish partners, and bear children. Survivor parents were understandably demanding and controlling. As Krystal,[2] Hoppe,[3] Niederland,[4] Rustin and Lipsig,[5] and Rakoff[6] pointed out, the survivor parents tended to regard their children as possessions meant to compensate them for what they had lost. Thus, the stage was set for strong bonds of interdependency in the survivor family.

The insufficient resolution of the separation-individuation conflict for the child of the survivor family stems in great part from the extraordinarily difficult circumstances of family adjustment following catastrophe. Consequently, there are some consistently seen intrapsychic difficulties of the offspring related to handicaps in child-rearing on the part of the survivor parents. There is, of course, considerable variation in severity and quality, depending upon such factors as prewar personality adjustment of the parents, length of time in the camps, age at time of internment, degree of suffering, quality of the marriage, degree of success in adjusting to their new lives, and other such factors. Most mental health experts who have treated this population have found common basic reactions to the Holocaust experience on the part of the survivor parents: death anxiety with its unforgettable and surreal images; death guilt, the memory of one's own helplessness to help loved ones; psychic numbing in which the ability to feel is diminished and is mourned, resulting in withdrawal, apathy, depression, and despair; suspicion of counterfeit nurturance and alienation from the world; and the struggle for restitution. Many psychotherapists who have written on the subject[6, 7, 8, 9, 10] have found that survivor's children experienced their parents as controlling, unemotional, demanding, unrelated, and self-absorbed. These children felt like highly valued possessions of the parents to be utilized to make restitution in the world. Parents were overprotective and obsessed with fears of loss. Born into a grieving, fear-ridden home, it is not difficult to imagine the dangers to the development of a separate sense of self for the child. He is rewarded when he is conforming and submissive to the fearfulness and controllingness of the parents. He is good when he makes his parents feel good, when he conforms to the family's heavy emphasis on achievement, family solidarity, repression of feeling (especially anger), and submission to authority. When he transgresses, he feels he is the cause of their deep disquiet and fearfulness. Guilt and a sense of heavy responsibility for the parents' well-being develops very early. The child's experience of the parents as fragile or brittle constitutes a heavy burden on the child's shoulders, but he feels loved and relieved of anxiety when carrying the mantle of parental well-being. One can see that spontaneous, self-initiating, or creative behaviors would be discouraged by this state of affairs. His individuality causes pain and fear to himself and to his parents. His merging with the emotional needs of the parents brings surcease of tension and guilt. The survivor parents tend to experience the child's wish to individuate as a loss, an unbearable reliving for them of what happened in the death camps. To cling to life, the parent must cling to the child.

The offspring is also motivated to please and merge with the parents' wishes and needs in a never-ending quest for relatedness, expression of affection, and warmth, emotions that do not come easily for the survivor parents. The grieving parents experience difficulty in communicating and expressing feeling and hence the children try to please, ingratiate, and nurture their parents in often vain attempts to gain emotional responsiveness from them. Such children frequently form deep identification and closeness with the depressed mother as a way of being with her, and loving her, and as a way of obtaining her relatedness, affection, and admiration. In this fashion, the stage is set for boundary blurring, incomplete individuation, and an imprecise sense of self. The identification with the victimized, depressed, "self-despised" mother (parents) results in feelings of shame, depression, sadness, and worthlessness in the child that often baffles him and is puzzling in light of his academic and vocational successes and usually high level of functioning in the world.

Mahler[11] related boundary blurring to the critical rapprochement subphase of the separation-individuation process occurring at about 16–24 months of age. At this time, the child has achieved some differentiation from the mother, yet has also identified with her in important ways. The child at this age has not yet established a stable inner representation of himself, as separate and distinct from the inner representation of the mother. This incomplete individuation from the mother implies limitations in self-cohesion, self-continuity, and positive affective estimation.[12] Sixteen to 24 months of age is a critical period for the development of autonomy. It is a developmental period when there are strong strivings in the child for exploration and self-initiated action. Language development and the ability for representational thought are advancing rapidly. During this time the child's capacity for mental representation of self, object, body parts, feelings, and so on, is developing at a fast pace.[13] The child needs the verbal and affectional relatedness and interaction with the mother to strengthen his representations, to label his feelings, to differentiate his feelings from hers. This interactional process aids individuation from the mother and consolidates mental representations of self and mother, resulting in enhanced object constancy and toleration of separation from the actual mother. The psychic numbing, withdrawal and uncommunicativeness of the survivor mother often resulted in a paucity of verbal interactions between mother and child, thus interfering with important developmental strides.

At this time, the child's impulses toward autonomy conflict with the need for control, conformity, and concern over object loss on the part of the parent. There is constant concern about mother's approval and disapproval at this developmental juncture, her disapproval often evoking a depressive mood state in the child. It is at this critical phase that the mourning, grieving, affect-lame, guilty, and overwhelmed survivor-mother has difficulty gratifying her child's need for emotional responsiveness, admiration, and availability. Maternal withdrawal arouses the child's fears of abandonment, destruction, and annihilation, resulting in panic and rage. Thus he clings in the hope of gaining emotional gratification, often at the expense of his autonomous strivings. He internalizes the depressed, anxiety-ridden maternal object which will, in varying degrees, complicate his future development. Of course, it must be remembered that development is subject to a wide variety of influences that may aggravate or ameliorate the affects of the separation-individuation irresolution.[14]

Every child needs the emotional support and encouragement of his mother as he tries out his autonomous urges. The survivor-mother, because of her own fears and losses, has a much harder time lending her support to the child's developing individuality and may even withdraw and become emotionally unavailable at such times. Further, the tremendous sense of loss creates in all family members a need to forge a strong family interdependency and lack of separateness. The wishes of the differentiated self must be repressed because they threaten the solidarity of the family, a strong unit against a hostile world. Because of the lack of clear boundaries of separation, the child acutely experiences the parents' panics and terror about annihilation.

As Kohut[15] explicates this state of affairs, a child who experiences a loss of relatedness and empathy from the actual mother revives an archaic connection to her in order to restore his inner state of well-being. Accordingly, in response to the maternal emotional withdrawal, the Holocaust offspring attempts to revive his old bond with the mother as a restorative action. He attempts to retain the external, actual selfobject functions of the mother. This archaic tie to the actual person of the mother is needed to maintain self-cohesion, self-esteem, and narcissistic equilibrium. In normal development, there is a gradual internalization by the child of the self-selfobject matrix which allows for the autonomy from the actual mother and family. This internalization of the self-selfobject matrix is interfered with for the Holocaust offspring by the difficulties the survivor mother experiences in relating empathically to her child, in admiring and mirroring him and interacting verbally and emotionally with him, especially at the time of the emergence of his autonomous strivings.

IMPACT OF SURVIVOR-PARENTING ON THE DEVELOPMENT OF SENSE OF SELF

From what has already been discussed, it appears that in these Holocaust offspring there is blurring of ego boundaries; confusion of the me and the not-me; narcissistically restorative identification with the mother (and later with significant others); incompletion of the individuation process; feelings of emptiness, loneliness, depression; lack of clarity about feeling states and difficulties in distinquishing one's own feelings from those of significant others. There is often coexistence of feelings of worthlessness and inadequacy and compensatory feelings of special entitlement.

Holocaust offspring come to treatment with a wide variety of symptoms and

complaints. Often they are vague feelings of anxiety and depression, dissatis-
faction with their lives without the ability to change, moderate to severe difficulties in their love and interpersonal relationships, phobias, psychosomatic
disorders (most often colitis), and sexual dysfunction. They are often confused
about who they are and what they really want out of life.

Sooner or later, these patients begin to describe the overprotectiveness and
demandingness of their parents, the lack of privacy in their lives growing up.
(One patient reported that no doors in the house could ever be closed, not even
in the bathroom). There is an atmosphere, that most speak of, of fear and
suspiciousness about the world and the need to be close and for the family to
stick together. Sooner or later most patients describe their mothers as removed,
unrelated, unexpressive, and unaffectionate. In an attempt to protect the children,
most patients report, their parents very seldom spoke of their wartime experiences, which facilitated the development of bizarre fantasies. Frequently the
children were named after relatives slaughtered in the camps and several patients
have told poignant stories to this author about how this experience affected their
relationships with their mothers. One female patient named for her mother's
dead sister reported that her mother coerced her into the study of the piano
although she had no talent. Her namesake had been an outstanding pianist. The
patient was plain looking and had dark, uncurly, unremarkable hair. Her mother
frequently extolled her beauty, especially her beautiful curly hair. The patient
was confused—angered that the mother could not see her as she was and yet
anxious not to take away what gave obvious satisfaction to her mother. She said
nothing because the only time her mother appeared happy was during these times
of merging sister and daughter. Holocaust offspring unfailingly report that their
parents demand assertion and high achievement in the outside world in order to
achieve security, but severely discourage assertion and aggression within the
family. Even as the offspring grow up and have their own busy lives and families,
the parents demand attention, help, frequent visits, and usually daily phone calls.

As the treatment of the offspring patient develops, it becomes clearer and
clearer that there is identity confusion. Underneath the varied symptomatology
there is deep confusion—Are they angry or guilty? Do they want to become the
professional person the parents hope for or to become an artist? Do they want
to marry someone approved by the parents, or remain single, marry out of the
faith, or to someone who lives out of town or out of the country, or in some
cases to live openly as the homosexuals they are? Do they hate their parents for
their controllingness or do they feel it is their mission in life to compensate the
parents for all that they have suffered? Are they worthless, inadequate creatures
who are filled with angry, rageful feelings who can never make the parents
happy, or are they very special (as they have been told all their lives by the
parents, more as a push to achievement than as a compliment)? An illuminating
clinical example of this lack of sense of self and confusion was a patient who
asked to tape record our sessions because she could never remember what we
talked about. It was near the beginning of treatment and she said she found it

helpful to hear the tapes at night. Most of her sessions consisted of vacillations of feeling toward her mother who kept a very tight rein on her, phoning her several times a day at her place of business and demanding that she do all her errands and take care of all the family business affairs. The patient was annoyed and complaining and reported that she had been short with her mother lately. This was invariably followed by anxiety, expressions of guilt, and a recital of all the mother's sufferings. One session the patient was unusually upset with her mother because she had tried to talk to her about a problem at work that she was very troubled about. The mother replied, "Please don't tell me about it. I have enough of my own problems. I would only stay up all night worrying about it." The patient began to weep in the session and expressed anger that her mother had never been there for her emotionally. She felt her mother was selfish. This session was also being tape-recorded. However, the next time the patient came, she reported that she had "inadvertently" erased that tape, the tape on which she had most clearly been very angry with her mother. The interpretation that she could not bear to be angry at her mother or see her shortcomings brought about intense feelings of anxiety and guilt in the patient, as well as fury at the analyst for "trying to put a rift between me and my mother." Finally, however, the patient was able to allow that she does realize she is angry at her mother sometimes, although she feels very guilty about admitting it.

A very troublesome problem for the Holocaust offspring, related to the lack of self-cohesion and clear sense of self, is his rage, a rage resulting from insufficient emotional interaction and relatedness, the need to perform a restitution mission for his parents instead of fulfilling his own destiny, and the often suffocating overprotectiveness, overconcern, controllingness, and demandingness of the parents. Their pervasive guilt leads to rage and feelings of unworthiness. This intense rage must be suppressed at all costs as it threatens everyone's survival. The rage is particularly intense because of its archaic, untamed, and primitive quality. How the child deals with this intense rage has enormous portents for his future development.

Ironically, the strong rage draws the child into greater dependency on the parents. The rageful, frightened child tends to cling tenaciously to his mother as a superego support, that is to help him control the explosion of his feelings. He joins in the family consensus to avoid overt anger at all costs, as such destructive emotions threaten already beleaguered people and are reminiscent of the parents' Nazi persecutors. Reviving the archaic self-object tie to the mother who controls behavior is restorative to the child.

In the place of overt anger, offspring patients report parents and siblings who are sarcastic, ridiculing, subtly belittling, siding with the "enemy," teasing, bickering, and giving the silent treatment, to name just a few. Additionally reported in this population are high incidences of panic disorders, phobias, sexual dysfunction, and psychosomatic ailments. Despite the fact that the family is often experienced as tense, unhappy, demanding, and critical, it nevertheless is seen as a haven or bulwark against the massive outpouring of rage on the part of the parents and children. This need constitutes a strong family bond. Thus, identification with the aggressor and narcissistically restorative identification with the mother are employed to control anger. This unresolved anger and rage form harsh punitive components in the adult superego of the offspring. There is identification with the parents' shameful feelings of impotent rage and the humiliation of victimhood. Frequently, there is a compensatory identification (on the part of the parents as well as the offspring) with the overt aggressor, the Nazi persecutors. Many offspring patients report, for example, that their parents reprimanded them in tones and words reminiscent of the Nazi persecutors. For example, several male offspring reported that their fathers would call them "swine" when they were angry. This was a taunt frequently employed by the Nazi guards at the concentration camps. This identification with the aggressor tends to establish a familial paradigm of persecutor and victim between the parents and between parents and children, a system of scapegoating that impedes the emergence of the child's own sense of self and positive self-worth. In a more adaptive vein, strong identification with the parents' intense need for their children to excel in this world usually has helped these offspring succeed in their vocational aspirations and therein find some important and suitable outlets for their assertion and aggression.

TREATMENT IMPLICATIONS

How does the clinician proceed to help develop and strengthen the unique sense of self of these offspring patients in the face of so many impediments? The wide range of presenting symptomatology has been discussed above and it is very important to note the considerable variation in success of life adaption, reflective awareness, psychological-mindedness, insight, and awareness of the connection of their difficulties with the Holocaust experience of the parents in this population. There is usually no history of adolescent delinquency, no marked psychopathy (although there are usually strong needs to control and manipulate), no antisocial acting out, nor any bizarre projections onto the analyst.

It is the experience of this author that in this patient population, most have not been able to tolerate the loss of the analyst that they experience in using the couch. It made them feel alone, unconnected, and abandoned. There is nearly always a deep concern for the mother (and transferentially the analyst) whom they see as troubled, depressed, fearful, uncommunicative, and emotionally detached. (Some mothers are described as superficially warm and friendly, but withdrawn in the face of the child's demands for emotional relatedness.) Criticism of the mother always arouses intense anxiety and guilt, followed by rationalizations, undoing, and denial.

As the transference develops, there is an intense concern and sense of responsibility for the analyst. There is a strong need for approval and relatedness. There is a hyperalertness to the analyst (as there must have been to the mother) in other words, no change in the analyst's office, personal appearance, facial expression, or tone of voice goes unnoticed nor fails to cause anxiety. They frequently express concern that they are not interesting patients, do not work hard enough in treatment, are suspicious of the analyst's wish to help ("What do you get out of this?"), inability to let in narcissistic supplies, as well as frequent jealously of other patients (wishing to be special or the favorite). A very common early dream of offspring patients is arriving for a session only to find the analyst missing, busy with other patients, or allowing other patients to interrupt their sessions. Considerable anxiety is expressed by these patients (and the nonpatients who were in groups or who came for interviews) about displeasing or disagreeing with the analyst. Fear was expressed that some shortcoming of theirs would terminate the analysis, the interview or their participation in the group. There is strong concern and responsibility for the welfare of the analyst. When the analyst once had an upper respiratory infection, nearly all the offspring patients felt it was in some way their fault. The expressions of transference clearly illustrate the poorly delineated self, low self-esteem, blurred ego boundaries, and narcissistically restorative identification with the external mother.

An illuminating clinical example of boundary blurring was the female patient who fretted continously that she was boring and not saying anything worthwhile in a session that actually seemed quite productive. Inquiry brought forth that, at first, she felt she was talking about something useful, but completely lost that feeling when she looked at the analyst's face. The analyst was not nodding, or responding overtly at the time, and the patient also thought (incorrectly) that the analyst had glanced at the clock. The patient concluded the analyst was bored and that, as a direct consequence and for that alone, she *was* uninteresting. The patient could not conceive that she could be working in a useful way if she believed that the analyst was not "entertained" at that time. This constitutes significant boundary blurring.

With some regularity, these patients (and some of the nonpatients) reported experiencing affect states corresponding to their perceptions (often incorrect) of the analyst's feelings (pleasure, boredom, excitement, annoyance, anxiety, contempt, calm, anger, etc.). There are frequent requests for feedback about whether the analyst liked or cared about them; questions about how many patients the analyst sees; does she like them all, does she like them equally, what would she do if she did not like a patient (or a group member)? There is a real dread of anger, indifference, or disagreement (even minor) with or from the analyst. Frequent dreams of oral, tactile, or general emotional gratification from a maternal figure, as well as nightmares of abandonment and retribution, support the hypothesis that these offspring intensely yearn for gratification and validation and are clinging to the significant other toward that end, at a great cost to their own sense of self and the internalization of the self-selfobject matrix. Causing displeasure to the maternal figure creates so much anxiety that the child must give in to what the mother wants, no matter how much violence this does to his sense of rightness or fairness. In his search for relatedness and validation from the mother, he follows her into her depression (identifies with her) and internalizes her depression, anxiety, and low self-esteem. As mentioned before, these feelings of low self-worth are sometimes defended against by grandiose feelings of entitlement.

For example, a patient who frequently complained of feeling worthless and not deserving the analyst's time or interest would also, with great frequency, make requests for appointment changes, fee reduction, and other special considerations to which he felt entitled. Denial of such special requests would lead to significant lowering of self-esteem, increased anxiety and depression, and sometimes overt expression of annoyance or anger at the analyst. No request was denied without empathic exploring of the wishes and their connection to depriving experiences in the past. The vicissitudes of analysis and the transference in particular highlight the difficulty the offspring patient has in integrating the angry and loving aspects of themselves and others.

An example of regressive inability to be clear and cohesive about the needs of the self and to separate them from those of significant others is the case of Carl. Carl, four years before, had fallen in love with a half-Jewish, nonreligious woman whose family and career were in California. After a torturous period of indecision, he married her and moved to California. He felt so much guilt that he called his parents every day and came to visit them every other weekend. He had found a good position in his field in California and loved his wife, but when she began to make demands about having children, Carl panicked. He felt he had a mild "nervous breakdown" and had to come back to New York to be near his parents whom he felt were becoming older and needed him. His unhappiness about leaving his wife led him to treatment. His parents were pressuring him to stay in New York and his wife wanted him back with her. He felt completely confused and did not know what *he* wanted to do. Sometimes he could express some anger at his parents for interfering, but then he would find himself overwhelmed by anxiety. His anger toward his parents created a strong fear of abandonment, so that each outburst of anger was followed by intense anxiety and regressive giving up of the self (feeling that *he* really wanted to stay in New York). The identification with his parents' wishes and obliteration of his own feelings quelled his anxiety and also represented a bid for his mother's love and regard.

DISTINGUISHING FEATURES OF TREATMENT OF HOLOCAUST OFFSPRING

There is no attempt here to make a case for exclusivity or specificity for the psychodynamics of the Holocaust offspring population. There are indeed commonly found psychodynamics, such as poorly developed sense of self, low self-esteem, boundary blurring, difficulties in handling aggression and in establishing an autonomous adult life; however, there are certainly other patient populations who suffer these difficulties.

What then may be some distinguishing features? For one thing, the enormous

strength of the bond, the archaic tie to the actual mother (and family) that results
not only from the early mother-child interaction, but from the perceived and real
needs of people who have had their lives destroyed in a uniquely catastrophic
manner by fellow human beings and who have had to try to rebuild a sense of
belonging, security, and safety. That the bond is so strong and implacable implies
a long, slow, often torturous treatment process in which the analyst's attempts
to help the patient separate are experienced as attacks upon the family. The
analyst becomes the enemy, the Nazi, who tries to break up the family, the only
security these betrayed persons can rely upon. The converse also occurs, when
the analyst, perhaps a bit too sympathetic to the horrors experienced directly by
the parents, is perceived by the patient as allying with his parents against him.
There are frequent discouraging stalemates in which the patient induces in the
analyst the deep frustration of what seems to be a hopeless impasse, a feeling
the patient has always had and always expects to endure.

Another distinguishing feature of this population is that for them the cruel and
sadistic fantasies most human beings only imagine and think about have been
real for their immediate families—nightmares come true. Grandmothers, aunts,
uncles, cousins, and others, were tortured and killed without their families being
able to bury and mourn them. Survivors were beaten, starved, raped, degraded
in every possible manner, and experimented on by Nazi "doctors." There were
the numbers on their parents' arms, lest they try to forget. While most Holocaust
offspring were not told the details of their suffering directly by the parents, the
children nearly always overheard their parents talking to each other or to survivor
friends about it. These patients heard their parents' nocturnal screams and violent
words, as they relived their concentration camp experiences in nightmares.

These fragments of real-life horror stories were often woven together in distorted fantasies by the offspring, in the absence of solid, cohesive information.
These sadistic fantasies commonly combined with and were confused with sexual
aims. Some offspring patients, for instance, reported finding fantasies of Nazis
invading their homes, not only frightening, but sexually stimulating. Others,
especially women, that fantasies of the Nazi "doctors" and their experiments
were sexually arousing, as well as terrifying. This condensation of sexual and
sadistic fantasies, of terror and arousal, and the fact that they were based in
good part on real events of extraordinary and degrading human cruelty, seems
quite unique. The knowledge these patients have that catastrophic and grotesque
nightmares do come true and may come true again results in a kind of terror not
commonly found in other patient populations.

Another unusual and probably unique aspect of the psychological life of the
Holocaust offspring is that his whole existence is living someone else's life,
someone else's history. He was in no way a direct victim of persecution and
cruelty as were his parents and, of course, other populations. However, because
of the devastation of the survivors and the sense of isolation of the survivor
family and its need for close solidarity in order to survive, because of the strong
identification of the child with the mother and family (and the frequent need of

the child to revive the archaic tie to the mother) these offspring do not psychologically inhabit their own world, but the world of their parents, even though it is experienced in a fragmented and often distorted way. As an example, there seems no other way to understand the real and instinctive fear of Holocaust offspring of "authority figures" (salespersons, post office clerks, clerks in government offices or hospitals, to say nothing of policemen) except for the realization that these patients lived their lives "as if" they had experienced cruelty at the hands of German officials as did their parents.

Finally, a distinguishing feature of treatment of this population is an issue of countertransference. There are very often feelings of guilt on the part of the analyst (Where were we or our parents when Hitler was torturing and killing the Jews?) and stark horror at facing in this concentrated manner man's inhumanity to man, thus inducing terror, despair, and sometimes immobilization. Many analysts working intensively with this population have been obliged to seek treatment for themselves in order to deal with their difficulties in facing their inner terror when they listen to the gruesome story about when Hansel and Gretel were really pushed into the oven.

CASE HISTORY

A case history will now be presented, providing the significant details of the process of the treatment and the techniques employed to aid the emergence of the self, its cohesion and a sense of positive self-worth. Hopefully, this case history will illustrate points in the previous discussion.

Clara was born in a displaced persons' camp in Europe less than two years after her parents' liberation from Dachau. Her parents had not known each other before the war and married hastily following liberation, before really getting to know each other. They emigrated to the United States after almost two years in a displaced persons' camp in France. They had no money, no prospects for jobs, and were not able to speak English. In the beginning, they shared a very small apartment with another survivor family and endured poverty because of the father's ill health and his difficulties in finding and keeping employment. When Clara began school, her mother went to work in a hat factory where she did well and was promoted frequently. She eventually started her own small hat business that was the prime support of the family. The father continued to be sickly and was irascible and demanding. Clara was terrified of him. The mother never became proficient in English, so that Clara was obliged to write letters for her and take care of some business matters for her from a young age. Clara had little time to play with other children because there were always things her mother needed her to do. She felt resentful, but that caused much guilt because her mother was often tired, sad, not feeling well, and felt mistreated by her husband with whom she bickered continuously. When Clara was ten, a baby brother was born and was named after the father's father. He quickly became the father's favorite. Clara felt she had lost her father and that the only thing that mattered to him was her brother. She also had to take care of the brother when the mother was busy with her work. By now the family had its own apartment. The father was authoritarian and rigid and yelled loudly when things were not done his way. He never managed to make much of a living and was resentful and felt belittled by his wife's greater success. The patient was never allowed to be angry at anyone, inside or outside the family. She was expected to comply with all her parents' extensive demands cheerfully and to do very well in school. She remembers resenting all the pressures and demands, and yet feeling so guilty and anxious when she heard her mother and father bickering and her mother crying and having nightmares at night. The mother had lost all her relatives and Clara always felt she had to make up to her for all those losses. She would conform, do well in school, help her mother and then maybe sometime she would see a smile on her mother's face instead of the constant worried frown or the blank stare. As she grew older, Clara vacillated and was confused about her feelings toward her parents to whom she had never been able to turn for emotional support; who would not tolerate anger, aggression, or disagreement; and to whom she felt she could not communicate anything real. It was all superficial, an "as-if" existence.

Clara worked her way through college taking jobs during summers and after school. The parents were saving money to send her brother to a "good" school. She finally attained a degree in accounting. She had done fairly well in college, but suffered extreme anxiety over her adequacy, and could never write research papers. It took her almost a year to find a full-time job because she was immobilized by her fear of interviewers. (She had extreme fear of all authority figures.) She was sure she would not know how to answer their questions about what she wanted to do or what she was good at. Finally, through a friend of the family, she obtained a low-paying position, worked a great deal of overtime and spent all her free time helping her mother with business matters and personal errands. Clara's mother also wanted to take a summer trip with Clara, just the two of them, to another city to visit some people who had been family friends in Germany. The mother and father were not on good terms and the brother aligned himself with the father. Clara did not want to go on the trip with her mother to visit these friends and she felt guilty about leaving her father behind when he was in poor health. She went around "in a fog," not knowing which way to turn. It was resolved by the father's having a stroke and needing to be hospitalized.

Clara had made a few friends in college, but never dated. Her friends were getting their own apartments and Clara thought "What a wonderful way to get away from the bickering and belittlement in the family." The parents objected strenuously, saying she was needed now and that she was being selfish. A studio apartment became available two blocks away from the parents' apartment and Clara impulsively took it, but then was so anxiety-ridden she could not go to work. At this point, she came for treatment. She was trembling, stuttering, stammering and totally immobilized. She was completely confused about whether she had done the right thing in taking the apartment. She felt dizzy and foggy and sometimes the street seemed to come up to meet her face. She felt alienated, disconnected, not belonging, outside of everything. Whenever an attempt was made to explore her feelings more specifically, she would reply, "I really don't know what I feel. I am confused, unhappy. I wish I could cry, but I'm really empty inside. I have no feelings, but I know something is terribly wrong." She needed others to tell her what she felt, what she was like, and what she should do.

Treatment got under way by helping her to understand that she was looking to others to know what she wanted and felt and that we would have to find those answers *in her*. She felt inadequate to the task and tried to turn the full responsibility for finding her real feelings onto the analyst. In discussing her apartment, which represented her first autonomous move, she occasionally sounded pleased and proud about it. This was noted, and differentiated from the anger she had begun to express about her parents' controllingness, and her guilt and close identification with her mother's suffering. We began to explore the different feeling states and name them and differentiate them from the diffuse mass of inner turmoil. It was a very slow process taking the better part of a year before she could feel the difference between fear, anger, sadness, guilt, and so on. She was able to return to work after a month of treatment, but then began to have bouts of fairly mild colitis. She still could not express feelings to others and still spent much of her time at her parents' apartment. She did occasionally go to a movie with a girlfriend.

THE PROGESS OF TREATMENT

In the transference, Clara needed a selfobject to help identify her feeling states, validate her experiences, and give importance to her inner life, as her mother had not. This was provided without yet interpreting it. Clara complained about her inadequacy at work, as well as about her lack of advancement. Grandiosity began to emerge (as a defense against her intense feelings of inadequacy). She asked for a reduced fee, the right to change the times of her appointments from week to week, the right to telephone whenever she felt "upset," and she wanted to postpone indefinitely payment of fees when she was "short of cash." These requests were always interpreted as her need to feel special and important, to have her special needs recognized, as they had not been in childhood.

There were frequent contemptuous complaints about the progress of the analysis, negative comparisons with how other friends were faring in treatment with other therapists, and criticism that she was not given specific advice. Her disappointment was accepted and acknowledged and gradually she could express her anger at the analyst more openly and assertively and with less (but still persistent) fear of abandonment and retaliation. After a long period of listening and acceptance, her needs for special treatment were related to her underlying feelings of worthlessness and emptiness, her feeling that her brother had been the most special in the family and that in the family everything and everyone was more important than she.

Clara was feeling better about herself and asked for and received a raise at work. She continued to feel, however, that she was in a dead-end job. She believed that she needed some graduate training to advance any further in her career and was resentful that her parents would not help her with that financially. It reinforced her contention that the parents gave her brother everything. As she expressed this anger and resentment more frequently, she began to report frightening dreams of abandonment. (There was a dreadfully frightening dream about crying at her mother's grave.)

Clara's enormous rage toward men and their power and privileges were explored extensively. She was jealous and yet very frightened of them. She reported sadomasochistic sexual dreams and fantasies. Mistreatment by men (as well as fantasies of being physically harmed by Nazis) was arousing and frightening at the same time. She began to date inappropriate, tyrannical men of lower-class background who either disappointed her, physically mistreated her, demeaned her, or abandoned her. It was helpful to Clara to see the connection between choosing tyrannical, demeaning men and being like her mother and recreating her homelife with her parents. The directing of her anger against herself (tolerating the men's mistreatment and blaming herself for that) instead of at the man was related to the prohibitions against overt anger toward anyone by the family. We spoke also of retaining her deep tie to her mother by picking inappropriate men whom she would never marry. Still unreliable, demeaning, and inappropriate men (married, jobless, very emotionally unstable) were attractive to Clara for a very long time. She was sexually aroused by the idea that they would physically harm her and had elaborate fantasies of torture by Nazi soldiers. She had also needed to control these frightening men, so that she never allowed them to arouse her enough sexually to achieve orgasm.

DISCUSSION

In this material we can see the identification and merging with the depressed, unhappily married, beleaguered mother who was often demeaned and disappointed by the irascible, emotionally unstable father. We can see that in her male choices she could cling to her mother forever, as man after man abandoned her. We can also see her primitive rage, its confusion and condensation with genital aims, and the prominent sadomasochistic trends. Further exploration elucidated a central concern. She felt profoundly defective, inadequate, unlovable and in constant fear of disintegration. She had little sense of her own continuity over a period of time. Only through merging with a significant external other and pleasing that person at any cost would she enjoy a sense of worth and adequacy.

Treatment progressed slowly. She was most at peace pleasing her mother, but she could no longer obliterate and deny her anger. She was moody and short with her mother and furious with the analyst for letting her get angry at her mother—who was, after all, all that she had in life. The analyst was an enemy, exposing her to harm, she felt. Expressions of anger toward the mother in response to her demandingness were always followed by a restorative identification with her mother and boundary blurring. She did not know what she felt, other than extreme anxiety and guilt. No other feelings were discernible. This confusion was usually followed by giving in to the mother's latest demands, no matter how farfetched they became (to go shopping with her every Saturday; to go on trips with her without the father; to let her sleep over in Clara's apartment whenever she had a fight with the father, and so on).

The accession to all of the mother's wishes clearly reflected the unresolved attachment to the maternal figure and the instability of Clara's individuation. The self-selfobject matrix had never been internalized. Clara also attempted to discern the analysts's wishes and conform to them in an effort to reduce anxiety about disintegration. There was lengthy exploration of her need to give up her sense of self and her own feelings to feel whole, loved, and validated. It was a strange new notion for Clara that she could be separate, different, disagree, and to refuse—and be able to hold on to her own values, feelings, and needs. To love and to be loved had meant merging with another person and giving up the self. She realized her feelings and opinions were not real or valid until discussed with her mother and now with her analyst. Her need for a selfobject to validate her experience, acknowledge her experience, acknowledge her feelings, and regulate her self-esteem flowered in the transference. Very little interpretation of this seemed to be necessary or desirable. After about one year, there were real signs that she had experienced acceptance and validation and that she could withstand differences and disagreements with significant others much more often than previously.

There were still times when grandiose material emerged, even though there was more cohesion of the self. She felt entitled to special privileges at work, with friends, with the analyst. At the same time, she lost a significant amount of weight, began dressing very fashionably, and felt that she was one of the most beautiful women she knew. She felt entitled to special male attentions socially and at work. Her grandiosity and feelings of special beauty were also very frightening to Clara. She believed others would hate her for it and abandon her, especially her mother who was becoming more crippled with arthritis now. She was terrified of jealously. Her own intense jealousy of her brother had been dealt with with extreme harshness by the family. Could she dare to appreciate her own beauty without expectation of retaliation?

Empathic understanding and exploration of her grandiosity in response to her experiences of maternal unrelatedness and nonacceptance and the father's remoteness and preference for his son resulted gradually in improved self-cohesion and awareness of her own feelings. She seemed more self-confident and began taking some accounting courses at night to advance her career. She made more female friends and took some vacations with them. Her self-esteem, however, remained heavily dependent on how others reacted to her. Any significant slight or rejection caused her to become confused, depressed, and feel unworthy. When the archaic tie to the mother was pointed out interpretively, she was able more and more to pull herself out of the slump and get in touch with her inchoate good feelings about herself. She began to have the feeling that she could be more in control of her life and select people who generally treated her as a separate person, with respect, admiration, and caring. She was able to go to some parties even though she would become depressed if she did not meet more suitable men who could treat her more respectfully and reliably.

Clara's sense of self was still vulnerable, but it would bounce back more quickly than in the past. Gradually, she began to date more suitable men. However, her fears of sexual intercourse were still troublesome. Sexual urges were still confused and mingled with aggression (and fantasies of abuse at the hands of the Nazis) and she both feared being harmed and fantasized harming the man. During one session, she remembered overhearing her mother talking to someone when she was a child about the sexual abuse done to Jewish women by the Nazis. She suddenly thought she now understood her mother's aloofness and lack of affection or sensuality. She realized that she had identified with her mother's sexual fears and hatred of the male power (phallus). She recognized and became aware of wishes to cut off the hated phallus, to bring men down to size, to make them feel as impotent as she always had.

Empathic exploration of her use of the transferential object (the analyst) to supply her with self-cohesion (and to connect her current problems and her, (now better understood, childhood experiences) resulted in enhanced ego strength. The self-representation, however, remained vulnerable to identification with the maternal object when she felt out of control, helpless, or did not get her way. The need to be in control became an important issue in treatment. Whoever was in control decided how things would be. She felt entitled to that, entitled to run things to suit her needs. She became manipulative in every area of her life, including treatment. Graudally, through some empathic confronting and exploring, Clara came to understand that she needed to manipulate, as her mother did, because she felt (as her mother felt) that no one would willingly do things for her or that her own straightforward efforts would never succeed.

Clara reported that she felt better understood, and not judged, by these explorations and interpretations and even felt them to be uplifting. Her understanding that control and manipulation had seemed necessary because overt assertion and anger were not acceptable sustained her self-esteem.

Clara's relationship with Barry, a coworker, began to be more important to her and their meetings more frequent. He treated her well and was highly reliable. Still she feared and hated his power and could not achieve orgasm with him. Clara's mother objected to Barry because he was ten years older than she and he did not make enough money. The mother needed to hold on to Clara because her relationship with her husband was almost nonexistent. Clara began to see her mother's enormous fear of abandonment. Her mother's tearful demands that she stop seeing Barry still precipitated confusion and anxiety and significant boundary blurring. She would merge with her mother's need to keep her to herself. She felt she owed her life to her mother. Clara still needed the analyst to bolster her right to be separate and to regain self-cohesion. Her confusion took the form of gaining a considerable amount of weight. She also developed fantasies of owning a penis and thereby gaining power and control. She claimed that she felt most in control when she had intercourse and could fantasize that the penis inside her was her own. This merging with the idealized phallus, as a symbol of power, provided more self-esteem and self-cohesion and served to create more sense of separation from her mother.

In the fifth year of treatment after more internalization of the self-selfobject matrix, more object-oriented phallic issues emerged, such as competition with and hatred of men, envy of their authority over themselves and others, fear of the penis, but at the same time, strong wishes to have a man as a protector. The self-oriented disturbances were strongly disruptive in trying to work out the object-oriented conflicts. Feelings of disintegration, panic, and identification with the mother accompanied hurts and failures in the phallic and Oedipal areas. The same psychological phenomena served at times to elevate self-esteem and consolidate the self-representation, but at other times they served as defenses against the competitive and Oedipal strivings (for instance, the weight gain). Filling the self with food or a penis counteracted her empty, uncohesive self and, at the same time, the overeating reinforced her deep feelings of unattractiveness and unworthiness. If she felt unattractive to men, she did not have to deal with sexual fears or fears of women's jealousy. For a long time, both the selfhood issues and the phallic and Oedipal conflicts were prevalent in the clinical material. It was the difficult task of the analyst to determine whether, at any given moment, she was afraid of the archaic tie to her mother and loss of self, or afraid of competition with others (men and women), so that appropriate empathic or uncovering approaches would be employed. For a long period, Clara fantasized owning a penis and this was interpreted as her wish for admiration and her way of differentiating herself from her mother and from the analyst. Both the admiration of the penis and the hatred and fear of it had to be worked through— the former by empathic understanding of her need to be esteemed and to differentiate from her mother; the latter by confronting her rage at her father and brother. Facing the rage was always highly anxiety-provoking and it frequently caused a giving up of the self.

The transference, for about five years, most resembled the selfobject transference in which the analyst was utilized to provide the self with cohesion, continuity, and positive regard. There were grandiosities to be admired, as well as idealizations, devaluations, and rages (the latter mostly in the fifth year) at empathic failures. With the beginning of the sixth year (and greater internalization of the self-selfobject matrix) came jealously and rivalry with women, a frightening prospect because being abandoned by the woman or being harmed by her was an awesome fear. In the transference, Clara's idealizations of the analyst took on a new feel and were interpreted as a way of not dealing with her anger, jealousy, and rivalry with the analyst. She was able to express her feelings of superior attractiveness to the analyst and subsequently regain her sense of self after a period of anxiety and confusion in which she expected abandonment or retaliation. The lack of completion of the individuation process and dependence on an external selfobject made the resolution of competition with the mother particularly traumatic. The strong early identification with the mother's needs and affective states created extraordinary anxiety in the patient, often resulting in serious setbacks in her striving for autonomy. During such times, uncovering work became secondary to interpretations about her difficulties in mastering and regulating her own emotional states.

Toward the end of the sixth year, Clara was enjoying a closer, more intimate relationship with Barry and enjoying their sexual relationship more. She no longer needed sadomasochistic fantasies to arouse her, but she still could not allow herself to relinquish control and achieve orgasm. Barry asked her if they could live together and she agreed to the arrangement. She had been increasingly able to tolerate uncovering work that revealed her deep love and yearning for her father and the desire for his admiration and affection as a woman. The focus of attention in treatment was on her difficulty in loving a man because it required her to relinquish the old tie to her mother.

Unfortunately, at that point in treatment, the husband of the analyst died suddenly and Clara learned about it. When the analyst returned to work, Clara told her that Barry had proposed marriage to her, but that she had declined. In fact, she said she was not sure she wanted to live with him anymore. This was quite shocking because the relationship had become increasingly tender and close in recent months. Clara was also very puzzled by her feelings. Much exploration for about a month's time revealed her deep feelings that she could not have a husband if the analyst did not have one. She could not bear the guilt and fear of jealousy. Years of analytic work seemed down the drain, as this notion persisted for many months. It was the old archaic tie with mother—that she could not be separate and must share the mother's fate. There was an Oedipal component in this development: How could she compete with a significant woman who had had such a tragedy befall her. Her guilt was intense. A lengthy period of empathic exploration of her need to stay tied to a mother she saw as unhappy, unloved, and lonely and her conviction that she must give up everything for people she cared about gradually helped Clara to accept the fact that her analyst and mother could be happy for her and want her to have her own life even if there were sadnesses and problems in their own lives. Further uncovering work continued for two more years on the Oedipal conflict which was enormously complicated by a breakdown in self-cohesion around anger, anxiety, and fear of abandonment. Archaic identification with her mother in order to regain cohesion was easily precipitated by uncovering her love for her father, her love for Barry, and her wish to be truly separate from her mother. After two more years of alternating empathic and uncovering approaches to the degree the patient could tolerate, Clara was able to marry Barry, gain a graduate degree and a well-paying job. She had sufficiently individuated from her mother at long last, so that she was able to form a true love bond with her husband and to build their lives together on the basis of their own needs, feelings, and wishes, while loving and feeling compassion for a separate and different mother.

CONCLUSION

This clinical vignette has been offered as a way of illustrating the techniques of empathic acceptance and understanding of the patient's narcissistic wounds, techniques essential to the building of a stronger sense of self- and enhanced self-esteem. The interweaving of empathic techniques and uncovering approaches, as illustrated, is essential to full consolidation of self-cohesion and the ability to relate to significant others in an autonomous and mutually respecting manner. Interpretation of rage and the establishment of appropriate sublimatory channels is viewed as essential to the development of self-cohesion and the ability to love another separate person. Identification with the selfobject (analyst), no longer seen as a selfobject, but as a separate person, enhances ego and superego functioning. Identification with the selfobject (analyst) formed the basis for the internalization of her own self-regulatory and self-esteem functioning. The old tie to the depressed, needful mother is largely undone, thus providing the opportunity for identification with a whole and separate person with whom anger, disagreement, separateness, and affection may be exchanged without threatening the ego integrity of either person.

We are beginning to understand more and more about the impact of the Nazi Holocaust on the psychodynamics of its victims. As it is, the passsage from the earliest inchoate state at birth to the achievement of a distinct, autonomous self is fraught with tribulation in all human development. It is now very clear, however, that there were special impediments faced by the second generation victims in the development of self-cohesion and self-esteem. The unspeakable horrors of the Holocaust, as well as the isolation and alienation of its victims from the rest of the human community resulted inevitably, though in varying degrees, in long-term psychological wounds. These wounds proved to be handicaps to the survivor generation in every aspect of living. Afraid, grief-stricken, overwhelmed with seemingly insurmountable tasks of rehabilitation, the survivors' wounds inevitably played a substantial role in the psychodynamics of the family and offspring. Sheer survival, the myriad problems of integration into a new society, as well as the psychological wounds of grief, shock, and terror conspired to place special burdens on the offspring in developing a separate sense of self essential for successful functioning in love and work. The courage of these offspring in facing and overcoming their special impediments in therapy, analysis, support groups, and individual efforts is remarkable and deserving of the highest respect.

NOTES

1. William Niederland, "The Problem of the Survivor," in *Massive Psychic Trauma,* H. Krystal, Ed. (New York: International Universities Press, 1968), Henry Krystal, *Massive Psychic Trauma* (New York: International Universities Press, 1968), Robert J. Lifton, "Witnessing Survival," *Transactions* (March-April 1978): 40–44.

2. Henry Krystal, *Massive Psychic Trauma* (New York: International Universities Press, 1968).

3. Klaus Hoppe, "Persecution, Depression, Aggression," *Bulletin of the Menninger Clinic* 26 (1962): 195–203.

4. William Niedlerland, "The Problem of the Survivor," in *Massive Psychic Trauma,* H. Krystal, Ed. (New York: International Universities Press, 1968).

5. Stanley Rustin and Florence Lipsig, "Psychotherapy with the Adolescent Children of Concentration Camp Survivors," *Journal of Contemporary Psychotherapy,* 4 (1972): 87–94.

6. Vivian Rakoff, "Long-term Effects of the Concentration Camp Experience," *Viewpoints* (March 1966).

7. Stanley Rustin and Florence Lipsig, "Psychotherapy with the Adolescent Children of Concentration Camp Survivors," *Journal of Contemporary Psychotherapy* 4 (1972): 87–94.

8. Bernard Trossman, "Adolescent Children of Concentration Camp Survivors," *Canadian Psychiatric Association Journal,* 13 (1968): 121–123.

9. Marvin H. Lipkowitz, "The Child of Two Survivors: A Report of an Unsuccessful Therapy," *Israel Annals of Psychiatry* 11 (1973): 141–155.

10. Harvey Barocas, "Manifestations of Concentration Camp Effects on the Second Generation," *American Journal of Psychiatry* 130 (1971): 820–821.

11. Margaret Mahler, "On the Three Subphases of the Separation-Individuation Process," *International Journal of Psycho-Analysis* 53 (1972): 333–338.; Margaret Mahler, Fred Pine, and Anni Bergman, *The Psychological Birth of the Human Infant* (New York: Basic Books, 1975).

12. Joan T. Freyberg, "Difficulties in Separation-Individuation as Experienced by Offspring of Nazi Holocaust Survivors," *American Journal of Orthopsychiatry* 50, no. 1 (1980): 87–95.

13. Robert D. Stolorow and Frank M. Lachmann, *Psychoanalysis of Developmental Arrests: Theory and Treatment.* (New York: International Universities Press, 1980).

14. Jean Piaget and Bärbel Inhelder, *The Psychology of the Child,* H. Weaver, Trans. (New York: Basic Books, 1969).

15. Heinz Kohut, *How Psychoanalysis Cures* (Chicago: University of Chicago Press, 1984).

6

Treatment Issues with Survivors and Their Offspring: An Interview with Anna Ornstein

PAUL MARCUS AND ALAN ROSENBERG

Marcus and Rosenberg: Bruno Bettelheim and Terrence Des Pres, among others, have very different portraits of the survivor. How do you as a self-psychologist view survivorship?

Anna Ornstein: You are asking your question regarding my views of survivorship by referring to the difference between Terrence Des Pres and Bruno Bettelheim. By so doing you are suggesting that one of these authors is closer in his views to those of a self-psychologist than is the other. In this, you are correct. I had found that in his book *The Survivor*,[1] Des Pres was able to establish, and to maintain, an empathic position in relation to the survivors he had interviewed. I did not find this to be true in the writings of Bettelheim.[2] I found Des Pres to be remarkably open to the survivors' subjective experiences as they, in his presence, appeared to immerse themselves freely in their painful memories of the past. In contrast, Bettelheim appeared to have listened with a set of theoretical preconceptions that may have prevented him from getting in touch with what it was really like to have lived through those horrifying experiences. The best example of this difference in listening perspective was the way Des Pres "heard" the survivors' description of what it was like to have to defecate into one's pants and live with the stench of one's own excrement, while Bettelheim reduced these experiences to "anal regression." Des Pres gave a description of the sense of humiliation as this was being experienced by people whose overall level of psychological maturity was not reduced to the lowest common denominator. Bettelheim, on the other hand, by "explaining" the same situation with the concept of "anal regression," created the impression that survivors had become children or savages in this process. Should the latter have been the case, their actual suffering might have been greatly reduced.

The question could be raised whether or not it is possible to listen to anything atheoretically. I would say, we all have theories and preconceived ideas in our hands as we listen and make our observations. However, there is a difference between using a theory to enhance one's *understanding* versus using the theory to explain a mental state and disregard the subjective experiences of the other.

What I am emphasizing here is not a difference in theory, but a difference in the mode of listening. In this respect Des Pres had a definite advantage: Not being a psychoanalyst, he did not have to deal with theoretical preconceptions, he did not feel compelled to "explain" the survivors' experiences before he understood them. This way he was free to immerse himself empathically in the subjective experiences of the survivors. It is of importance to note here that Des Pres did not encounter the kind of "resistances" that others who interviewed survivors had. Feeling understood rather than "diagnosed," they appeared to have been eager to share some of their most painful memories with him.

M.& R.: How do you conceptualize the survivors' trauma and symptoms? How do you differ from the more classical views of Krystal and Niederland and Bergman and Jucovy, especially in terms of treatment implications?

A.O.: This question regarding the conceptualization of the survivors' trauma, and the manner in which this affects our view of symptom formation, is of particular importance.

I view the nature of the Holocaust trauma as falling, by and large, under the heading of "adult traumatization." My view regarding adult traumatization does not differ from that of Dr. Krystal. In my paper "Survival and Recovery,"[3] I had referred to the very useful distinction Krystal made between the consequences of adult traumatization, and the consequences that tramatization in infancy or childhood may have for the later development of psychopathology. The adult, by virtue of the structure of the adult psyche, has the capacity to block emotions and constrict cognition, in other words, to call on defensive operations in response to "trauma signal." The capacity to call upon defenses prevents the adult psyche from life-threatening regressions that are the likely outcome of significant (i.e., frequent and severe) childhood traumatization.[4] However, and this is crucial to Krystal's thesis and the point at which our views do differ, he maintains that massive psychic trauma, as this occurred to Holocaust survivors, had similar consequences to those that follow significant childhood traumatization.[5]

Since most survivors were adults or in their late adolescence at the time of these catastrophic events, the symptoms that survivors presented with had developed in relation to adult traumatization. On theoretical grounds, therefore, they would have to be considered closer in nature to a traumatic neurosis than to a psychoneurotic condition.

What are the treatment implications of such a distinction between conceptualizing the symptoms of the survivors as a traumatic neurosis rather than as a psychoneurosis? The answer to this question is made complex by Mardi Horowitz's finding that "as the traumatic neurosis is studied in a given person, it seems to lose its connection with the immediate stress event and gain connection to conflicts and character traits present before the event."[6]

While Horowitz's finding thus makes things more complicated, it also helps us recognize the implications for treatment when we have to consider this kind of complexity in the pathogenesis of an illness. Specifically, we have to consider the significance of the preexisting conflicts and character traits in the assessment of the Holocaust survivor, and we cannot—as Krystal does—dismiss these because of the massive nature of the trauma.

The opinions regarding the connection between the nature of the trauma (how massive or relatively insignificant it may have been), on the one hand, and their possible pathological consequences on the other, vary among psychoanalysts. This question was recently taken up in detail in a panel discussion by a number of well known analysts and published in a monograph of the American Psychoanalytic Association: "The Reconstruction of Trauma; Its Significance in Clinical Work."[7]

The differences of opinions were well summarized by the editor, A. Rothstein: A. Cooper and G. Pollock distinguished *psychic trauma*, as the term is usually used, from *massive psychic trauma*, that is, those events that disrupt the ego's capacities for defense and coping. In other words, in the opinion of these two authors, beyond certain clearly defined limits, the integrity of the organism is compromised; therefore certain events are traumatic for all individuals. In this, these two authors appear to be in agreement with Krystal. In contrast, S. Abend, C. Brenner, S. Dowling, and I defined trauma from what could be thought of as an exclusively psychological or hermeneutic perspective. From this perspective, trauma is not defined by its immediate descriptive characteristics, but by its uniquely individual meaning and long-term consequences to the individual.

M.& R: Incomplete mourning of murdered loved ones has been viewed as the central obstacle for the survivors' adaptation. How do you understand this problem and how do you help survivors work it through in treatment?

A.O.: In response to this question, I would have to ask: What does a clinician view as "incomplete mourning"? At the time survivors were examined in large numbers for the purposes of monetary compensation by the German government, their mourning must have been incomplete, indeed. But could this have been otherwise? I believe their mourning was termed "incomplete" because of an assumption—strictly on theoretical grounds—that mourning ought to precede the establishment of new relationships, or rather, that the establishment of new relationships is not possible unless the cathexis to the old ones is first given up.

The theory of the self would dictate an entirely different sequence here, a sequence that is in keeping with my clinical as well as with my personal experiences. Rather than assuming that old cathexes have to be given up prior to the establishment of new relationships, our observations would indicate that only when new relationships become established, can mourning and the healing process begin. Only a self that is helped to regain its cohesion through a meaningful selfobject tie can face the arduous psychological work of adequate mourning. In the case of Holocaust survivors, such selfobject ties did not necessarily become established with a mental health professional but with those in their environment who were eager to understand the special nature of their suffering and who responded to the efforts they have made to recover with enthusiasm, even when these efforts did not correspond to an expected hypothetical norm.

You may be familiar with Weiss and Sampson's work; they conceptualize the process of recovery essentially in the same way: "Unless he [the patient] is under considerable pressure . . . he does not face his central unconscious conflicts until he has acquired the strength and the confidence in the analyst to deal with them safely."[8]

The meaning of this observation for the treatment of Holocaust survivors is that this ought not differ in its essential elements from the treatment of any other patient who walks into a therapist's office. The survivor, as all other of our patients, needs acceptance and understanding of the uniqueness of his or her experiences, a uniqueness that was as much determined by infancy and childhood experiences as it was by the uniqueness of Holocaust experiences. Feeling understood by the therapist fosters the development of one of the self-object transferences which, in turn, is essential in rehabilitating a weakened self. Only when such a rehabilitation of the self has occurred, can the process of mourning begin.

The intermingling of the consequences of the trauma of the Holocaust with character traits that have become established in relationship to pre-Holocaust experiences had led me to the conclusion that as long as the therapist is aware of the difficulties she may experience in her effort to make empathic contact with someone whose experiences have been beyond the ordinary, and as long as she is aware of the countertransference possibilities, her approach to the Holocaust survivor ought not be in any way different from her approach to any one of her patients. All patients demand of us acceptance, understanding and explanation—the hallmarks of a well conducted psychoanalytic treatment process.

M.&R.: "Survivor guilt" has been viewed as a primary problem in survivors. You have written that "the frequently cited guilt of survivors is related less to having survived while others have died (which has been related to the survivors' death wishes toward their family members) than to the survivors' difficulty in reconciling the alternation in their behavior and moral conduct during the Holocaust and their conduct and behavior under civilized conditions." Can you explain this point and say how this view differs from the earlier formulations put forth in psychoanalytic and psychiatric literature?

A.O.: I had not come across the particular explanation regarding "survivor guilt" that I am here postulating, which does not mean that such an explanation has not been offered before. My understanding of the explanation that classical psychoanalytic theory had offered of "survivor guilt" is contained in the quote you have cited, namely, that it is related to death wishes that had been fulfilled. Classical psychoanalytic theory maintains that the creation of neurotic guilt is related to the fulfillment, or feared fulfillment, of instinctual impulses or infantile unconscious wishes. I, on the other hand, had emphasized the impact that the drastically different circumstances between living in "extreme conditions" and under "civilized" ones had on the conduct of survivors.

Based on my clinical and personal experiences, I had found that survivors themselves had a hard time placing themselves back into the conditions under which they lived in the camps. Once they had plenty to eat and were able to protect themselves from the elements, they tended to disregard the conditions under which they had to make fateful decisions. They experienced guilt for behavior they would not engage in under ordinary circumstances. Obviously, there were many situations in which a survivor may have had good reason to feel guilty about omissions or commissions of certain actions that may have contributed to the death of someone. This, however, is not neurotic guilt but an expectable response that has to be responded to accordingly.

M.& R.: How does recovery occur with survivors in self-psychologically oriented psychotherapy and what is its relationship to adaptation?

A.O.: I believe that to some extent I have already answered this question in relation to your second and third questions. I shall summarize my answer here in two points: (1.) A more strictly psychological or rather hermeneutic approach to the meaning of the Holocaust trauma helps to put the experience into the context of the survivor's total life experiences. This, in turn, protects the therapist from using the Holocaust as if it were a giant magnet that draws to itself everything that may be problematic in the survivor's current adjustment and is then used as an explanation for all these problems. Taking this more "balanced" view regarding the place that the Holocaust plays in the formation of a given symptom and/or personality trait, survivors can be expected to benefit from psychoanalysis and psychotherapy the same way as any other of our patients do. (2.) The second point is related to the question you asked about "incomplete mourning." Recovery of the survivors, as is true of all traumatized patients, has to begin with the strengthening of the traumatized and weakened self. A therapist familiar with the various forms of selfobject transference will welcome their establishment as they promote self-cohesion and with this, signify the first step in the process of recovery. These selfobject transferences and their working through are essential in firming up the self so that mourning can take place. In many survivors this process took place spontaneously as they were fortunate in finding new objects in the postwar years who, unbeknown to themselves, fulfilled vital selfobject functions for the survivors.

As to the second part of your question, I do not consider recovery and adaptation to be identical psychological processes. Ideally, recovery means that the self has attained the capacity to fulfill its basic inner design, that ideals and ambitions work in "harmony," that is, in keeping with the person's basic skills and talents. Adaptation, on the other hand, may require that the individual make internal compromises in order to live in "harmony" with the environment. I believe this distinction between recovery and adaptation has to be made in relation to survivors as much as in relation to other individuals.

Adaptation to a socially and culturally new environment may have required considerable internal compromises in many cases from the survivors. However, I believe that these new and different environments had also provided many survivors with expanded opportunities for the fulfillment of the basic design of their nuclear self. I am making this statement on the basis of the frequently noted observation that Holocaust survivors have not been less successful in living creatively in their new environments than were immigrants of previous generations.

M.& R.: How does empathy as distinct from interpretation enable the survivor-patient to experience and work through painful affects?

A.O.: This question indicates a common misconception regarding the way a self-psychologically oriented psychoanalyst works. It has been assumed that empathy is something akin to tact, kindness, and consideration and as such it replaces interpretations. Empathy, as I am sure you know, is a mode of observation. Psychotherapists with a self-psychological orientation place emphasis on the empathic immersion in the inner life of the other because they offer their interpretations from within the patient's perspective, that is empathically. Such interpretations have three essential elements: acceptance, understanding, and explanation.

As I mentioned in connection with your question regarding the difference between Bettelheim and Des Pres, we place special emphasis on understanding, and on conveying understanding in the interpretive mode, before offering a comprehensive explanation in relation to the patient's problems.

You are asking me whether this mode of working would not be true for "all good therapists." Very likely it would be. However, I had found that when the empathic method is supported by a theory, such as psychoanalytic self-psychology, then method (empathy) and technique (interpretations) mutually support each other, making the work of the clinician smoother and more affective.

I assume that you are making the distinction between empathy and interpretations because, in the past, we had failed to distinguish between interpretations offered from an empathic vantage point and confrontations, as these may be offered from the point of view of the external observer. When interpretations are offered from within the patient's perspective, and in the interpretive mode, they become part and parcel of a dialogue in which therapist and patient jointly endeavor to articulate thoughts and feelings that have heretofore been frightening and confusing to the patient. Most importantly, such communications are not likely to increase resistances and deepen the therapeutic process in a natural way.[9]

M.&R.: Some psychotherapists have found that some survivors are unable to use psychotherapy because they fear emotions, are suffering from alexithymia or are unable or unwilling to give up their anger. How do you approach these therapeutic obstacles when they arise?

A.O.: The position you are articulating here is familiar to me from Krystal's work. Survivors, not different from other patients in psychotherapy, have to be helped first to experience and then to express painful affects. (See my response to your question regarding mourning.) I see danger in the generalization you are making in this question. A psychotherapist, with her conscious and unconscious attitude and the manner of her responses—as well as with her silences—affects the content of the patient's associations: psychotherapy is a dyadic process. Should, in the course of treatment, hopelessness and helplessness emerge in the therapeutic dialogue, the therapist would not have to deal with these affects differently than she would with any other affect: She first has to accept them rather than question their presence; she then has to be able to resonate with them to the best of her ability, that is, she has to make an effort to identify these leading affects through vicarious introspection. Only after the therapist had been successful in making meaningful contact with the patient's subjective experiences in the present, or what the patient may have experienced in the past, and after therapist and patient have been successful in articulating these subjective experiences, can the therapist proceed with an attempted explanation as to the genetic and traumatic roots of these subjective experiences. With these attitudes and approach to interpretations, the therapist is less likely to encounter alexithymia and/or an ''unwillingness to give up anger.''

M.&R.: Bergmann and Jucovy have claimed that it is necessary for the survivor to develop a transference neurosis that includes the equation therapist = Nazi. They argue that if this dimension of treatment is avoided, then a phase of negative transference essential for future cure is bypassed. Do you agree or disagree? More generally, do you understand the problem of the transference of survivors differently than working from a classical analytic framework?

A.O.: I believe that what I had described so far makes it fairly clear that there are indeed important differences in the way in which the therapeutic process is conceptualized when the therapist (fairly consistently) maintains an empathic position and offers her interpretations from that listening perspective, rather than when she anticipates what ought to emerge in the transference. However, I believe, here you are asking me to say something specific about the transference that a self-psychologically informed analyst would recognize in a well conducted treatment process.

As you probably know, Kohut described three forms of selfobject transference: the idealizing, the mirror, and the twinship transference. In this context however, it is more important to emphasize the fact that selfobject transferences are different in nature from the transference that Freud described in *The Interpretation of Dreams* than to elaborate on the various forms of selfobject transference. In contrast to the traditional view of transference, selfobject transferences are not considered to be only repetitions from the past, nor are they considered to be simply displacements. Rather, as Kohut had put it, they are to be considered as the "continuation of early reality." Rather than viewing transference as being primarily the expression of a compulsion to repeat, as my observation would indicate that the patient dreads the repetition of the past, both as this may occur on his part, or on the part of the analyst.[10]

This does not mean, however, that repetitions of the past do not occur. Rather, when they do occur, when the therapist does respond to the patient's transference in a manner similar to the way in which important people in the patient's past had responded, a disruption of one of the selfobject transferences takes place. The reconstructive interpretations of these disruptions, both in the transference and genetically, constitute some of the most important aspects of the working through process, since such interpretations make important contributions to the patient's efforts to establish a sense of psychic continuity.

I believe that what you mean by "negative transference" is hostility experienced in the transference. And hostility, as well as other affects in the transference, may have—and usually do have—varied sources. One frequent source of hostility in the transference is in the patient's experiencing the therapist as having his or her own agenda and not being open or eager to comprehend the patient's own unique, and at times hard to communicate, subjective experiences; or, as I had just mentioned, when the analyst inadvertently, and in some innocuous way, had repeated the original trauma. My patients did not have to experience me as a Nazi in the transference in order to achieve their "cure." This may have been related to the general ambience of the treatment situation in which I had tried to maintain fairly consistently an empathic position and offer my interpretations from that vantage point. Also, my survivor-patients were aware of my being a survivor myself who had, I believe, made them confident that I listened to the description of their experiences with considerable understanding.

M.&R.: It is generally assumed that the treatment of survivors and their children makes extraordinary demands on the therapist. What are the kinds of countertransference that therapists need to be sensitive to and does self-psychology add anything new to our understanding of this process?

A.O.: Regarding the question of therapists' reactions to survivor patients, we may have to distinguish between transference that many therapists appear to have toward their survivor-patients, and countertransference in the strictest sense of the word, namely, reactions to the patients' transference. I am familiar with some outstanding forms of transference reactions toward survivors: In one, survivors are viewed as being extremely vulnerable; in another, survivors are viewed with awe, as if they were supermen or women, towards whom the therapist feels inadequate. Then there is guilt, a common reaction by Jewish therapists, well documented by Y. Danieli.[11] These therapists feel that either they or their parents should have done something to prevent the tragedy of European Jewry. I believe that it is in these instances that the concept of the "survivor guilt" truly applies. The treatment of survivors is frequently experienced as making greater than usual demands on therapists because the extraordinary nature of the Holocaust survivors' experiences make empathic attunement very difficult; the therapist is not readily able to use vicarious introspection to assess the patient's mental state. In order to achieve a modicum of empathy, the therapist has to become familiar with aspects of the reality in which the survivors had to live. I have found that the survivor-patient is usually able (and in many instances eager) to supply these details, as long as the therapist is able and willing to listen.

What a self-psychologically oriented therapist would emphasize in this respect would be that the therapist's own subjective experiences in relation to the patient pay a very important role in the therapeutic process. The therapist's responses, her wording and phrasing of interpretations, as well as her silences shape, and to a great extent determine, what the patient feels free to experience and to communicate. However, what the specific content of the therapist's reactions may be will vary from one therapist-patient pair to another.

M.&R.: How do you understand the manner in which the traumatic impact of the Holocaust on the survivor can be transmitted to their offspring?

A.O.: As you know in my previous work,[12] I had questioned whether or not such a transmission of trauma actually occurs. The frequent references we find regarding the transmission of the trauma of the Holocaust from one generation to the other may well be related to a phenomenon not infrequent in the psychoanalytic literature, namely, someone with authority makes a statement that is then referred to as if it were a proven fact. Eventually, the children of survivors themselves, who became members of the mental health profession, began to study this issue and had raised some relevant questions regarding the validity of these earlier studies. I refer you to the work of N. Solkoff,[13] Leon and his collaborators[14] and the studies of Z. Zlotogorsky (1983)[15]—none of whom could find significant differences in psychopathology between the children of survivors and their control groups. I am not maintaining that the parents' Holocaust past does not effect their children's development in many ways. I do question, however, the findings that maintain that this occurs only in relationship to the transmission of psychopathology.

In this respect it is of interest that I had received a letter from Dr. J. J. Sigal of Montreal, telling me that he had recently repeated his earlier studies with children of survivors and their grandchildren and found that my objection to his earlier findings in which he had emphasized the transmission of psychopathology only, has been corroborated in these recent studies. He is now impressed with the many positive aspects of these young peoples' personalities. I am sure these new studies will be of interest to all of us.

M.&R.: Judith Kestenberg, among others, has observed that in some children of survivors every phase of psychosexual development can become invaded by the Holocaust memories of the parents. Given that there can be this kind of pathology in some children of survivors, how do you assess the contributions made by the Holocaust experience of the parents, as distinct from other incidental or personal sources? What are the implications for treatment?

A.O.: My response to your previous question, concerning the transmission of the Holocaust trauma to the next generation, answers the question regarding Dr. Kestenberg's findings.

However, distinguishing the contribution that the parents' Holocaust past makes to their children's development from other ''personal and incidental sources'' is still relevant. Children of survivors do experience themselves as being different from their contemporaries because of the special nature of their parents' past. In my professional and personal life I had come across two very different kinds of reactions with equal frequency: one, in which the second generation had accepted this unique heritage and derived from it a measure of wisdom regarding both the precariousness and the preciousness of life; and another, in which this heritage was experienced as a burden by the offspring, with only negative consequences on their lives.

It may be of interest to you that in the more recent past I had received letters from the now grown children of survivors who were describing a change in their attitudes. As adolescents, they resented their parents for having burdened them with their traumatic past, but more recently, as they were growing older, they had developed a greater acceptance and a greater degree of empathy toward their parents. This, in turn, had favorably affected their own self-acceptance and their own self-esteem.

The implication for treatment is that, in each individual instance, the therapist has to be able to ascertain the meaning that the parents' past has for the given child, rather than listen with a set of preconceived ideas to what this particular heritage must mean to them.

M.&R.: What can self-psychologists uniquely offer children of survivors and the community at large in their attempt to develop ways of remembering the Holocaust without transmitting its traumatic potential?

A.O.: I believe all psychoanalysts would agree that the capacity to remember and the capacity to integrate painful memories is an essential aspect of relatively good mental health. Having facilitated group discussions for children of survivors for many years, I had found that these children learned to judge their parents' own comfort with their memories in keeping with the parents' ability to tell their children not only of their experiences during the Holocaust, but also about their lives prior to that. More than anything, these children wanted to know about the family members of their parents; what kind of people their grandparents were, how many and what kind of siblings they had, and so on.

I understand this kind of interest to be related to a need to establish psychic continuity, a need all human beings share. A sense of psychic continuity includes generational continuity. Any ritual that is being established, such as the observance of Yom Ha'Shoah, and any opportunity that survivors and their children may have to reflect on these events, promotes remembering and, with that, the firming up of their sense of psychic continuity. For the children of survivors this had become a particularly important process: not having any material possessions, such as photographs, a piece of clothing or furniture—memories, as these can be transmitted orally or through literature and art, have become the sole carriers of the past. For survivors and their children, memories had attained symbolic significance and they appear to have a great need for their preservation.

I believe this need to remember in order to assure a personal and generational sense of continuity may explain why more and more communities around the world where Jews live find it necessary to erect memorials or build museums. To me, this is ample evidence that there is a deeply felt need not only in the survivors but in their children as well for these events to remain in the consciousness of future generations.

I cannot quite see how such efforts to preserve the memory of the Holocaust and all that preceded it in the form of Jewish life in Europe could be "transmitting a traumatic potential" That assumption would be contrary to what psychoanalysis maintains in relation to the theory of recovery and what I think is a readily observable phenomenon in terms of the interest that human beings express in relation to their more recent, as well as the more distant, past.

NOTES

1. Terrence Des Pres, *The Survivor; The Anatomy of Life in the Death Camps* (New York: Oxford University Press, 1976).
2. Bruno Bettelheim, *The Informed Heart*. (Glencoe, Il: Free Press of Glencoe, 1960).
3. Anna Ornstein, "Survival and Recovery," *Psychoanalytic Inquiry*, D. Laub and N. Auerhahn, Eds. (Hillsdale, NJ: The Analytic Press, 1985), pp. 99–130.
4. Henry Krystal, "Trauma and Affects," *The Psychoanalytic Study of the Child*, Vol. 33 (New Haven, CT: Yale University Press, 1978), pp. 81–116.
5. Ibid.
6. Mardi Horowitz, *Stress Response Syndrome*. (New York; Jason Aronson, 1976).
7. Arnold Rothstein, *The Reconstruction of Trauma; Its Significance in Clinical Work* (Madison, CT: International University Press, 1986).

8. Joseph Weiss and Harold Sampson, *The Psychoanalytic Process* (New York: The Guilford Press, 1986).

9. Paul Ornstein and Anna Ornstein, "Clinical Understanding and Explaining: The Empathic Vantage Point," *Progress in Self Psychology,* Vol. 1, A. Goldberg, Ed. (New York: Guilford Press, 1985), pp. 43–61.

10. Anna Ornstein, "The Dread to Repeat and the New Beginning: A Contribution to the Psychoanalysis of the Narcissistic Personality Disorders," *The Annual of Psychoanalysis,* Vol. 2 (New York: International University Press, 1974), pp. 231–248.

11. Yael Danieli, "Countertransference in the Treatment and Study of Nazi Holocaust Survivors and Their Children," *Victimology* 5 (1981):45–53.

12. Anna Ornstein, "Survival and Recovery," *Psychoanalytic Inquiry* Vol. 5, D. Laub and N. Auerhahn, Eds. (Hillsdale, NJ: The Analytic Press, 1985), pp. 99–130.

13. Norman Solkoff, "Children of the Survivors of the Nazi Holocaust: A Critical Review of the Literature," *American Journal Orthopsychiatry* 51 (1979):29–42.

14. G. Leon, J. Butcher, et al. "Survivors of the Holocaust and Their Children: Current Status and Adjustment," *Journal of Personality & Social Psychology* 41 (1981):503–516.

15. Zoltan Zlotogorski, "Offspring of Concentration Camp Survivors: The Relationship of Perception of Family Cohesion and Adaptability to Levels of Ego Functioning," *Comprehensive Psychiatry* 24 (1983):345–544.

IV

Group and Family Approaches

7

Group Treatment as a Therapeutic Modality for Generations of the Holocaust

EVA FOGELMAN

In 1976, Bella Savran and I formed the first in a series of short-term therapy groups for children of Holocaust survivors at the Hillel Foundation of Boston University. Bella and I, ourselves children of survivors, proceeded on the assumption that children of survivors had had little opportunity to discuss their feelings and concerns related to their parents' traumatic experiences. Research revealed that an estimated quarter of a million children of survivors were living in the United States. And yet, the "second generation," as we discovered, had lived alone with troubling Holocaust-related fantasies, secrets, and confusions; had highly individualized and yet collective difficulties communicating with their parents and others about the past; and shared a deep longing for community, and a desire to repair a shattered world.

Since 1976, I have continuously run therapeutic groups for the second generation. In 1977, I undertook a new form of group which for therapeutic reasons is a mixture of second generation and child survivors of the Holocaust. My 12 years of work with survivors and their children has brought me to several conclusions. For one thing, the second generation is generally a highly motivated and resilient population that does not display any significant incidence of pathological disorders. Those individuals who sought out therapeutic intervention were not suffering from symptoms of personality disorder, but rather, were engaged in a painful struggle with issues related to: (1) communication; (2) identity (most specifically Jewish identity); and (3) incomplete mourning.

Group therapy is an ideal setting to work through these struggles for several important reasons: (1) family dynamics and transference can be reexperienced in group process; (2) the "work of mourning," both collective and individual, is facilitated by the sense of community; (3) the group provides an opportunity to work through identity conflicts over "sameness" and "difference," as well as Jewish identity conflicts, both of which are specifically related to the shared background of this population.

BACKGROUND

Therapy and self-help groups for Holocaust survivors and their children have proliferated over the past 12 years.[1] The therapeutic process has enabled members of this population to overcome the lingering scars of Nazi persecutions, such as difficulty in forming attachments, a sense of rootlessness, identity conflicts, and personal loss. Group involvement enables members to validate emotions, master new methods of intergenerational communication within and outside of the family, develop a constructive Jewish identity; mourn multiple personal losses; and channel intense reactions in constructive ways. Indeed, the feelings of hope and cohesiveness that develop as a result of these groups account for some of their "curative factors."[2]

Groups for Holocaust survivors and their children have utilized many different models. To date there have been short-term therapy groups; long-term therapy groups; and leaderless groups that utilize a self-help model. In addition, organizations, such as the Bergen-Belsen association; social events designed for or by Holocaust survivors or their children; intergenerational dialogue meetings; Holocaust conferences; commemorations; and reunions, have provided participants from a wide range of backgrounds with supportive environments in which to exchange Holocaust-related memories, feelings, and attitudes. From a coping strategy perspective, such nontherapeutically oriented groups have provided a way to sublimate intense feelings of anger, rage, guilt, revenge, depression, or helplessness into constructive action, and have helped participants to reduce feelings of isolation, anomie, and alienation. Most of all, theme-oriented group settings create supportive environments for lifting the taboo against expressing painful memories.

This chapter will consider therapeutic short-term awareness groups for offspring of survivors—the second generation—and short-term intergenerational groups in which both the second generation and child survivors of the Holocaust were participants. The participants in these groups were all functioning well; the work of Axelrod and Blumenthal,[3] who have worked with hospitalized children of survivors and in multiple family groups, should be consulted to gain an understanding of therapeutic methods for a more severely traumatized segment of this population.

SECOND GENERATION SHORT-TERM AWARENESS GROUPS

The second generation groups from which clinical data will be discussed in this chapter were composed of approximately eight members each, with men and women equally represented. The groups met for eight to twelve sessions.

Participants were highly educated professionals or students engaged in career preparation. Group members represented a range of marital status, ranging from single and married to separated or divorced. Their Jewish backgrounds were very diverse, ranging from Hasidic to atheist.

Most participants shared the goal of finding a forum in which their experiences in relation to the Holocaust could be expressed in a supportive environment. As one person put it, "I am looking forward to talking to people with whom I can share, whom I feel will really be able to understand and accept me." Other goals (which were, of course, never uniform) included: (1) understanding the extent to which the Holocaust influenced personality and social development; (2) resolving existing conflicts between themselves and their parents; (3) identifying the ways in which their experience as children of survivors was likely to affect their relationships with their own children; (4) learning ways to attain and to transmit to future generations a positive sense of Jewish identity without obscuring the tragic family and Jewish history.

Each prospective group member underwent a clinical intake interview. In addition to routine clinical evaluation, the therapist assisted the interviewee in constructing a three-generational family history of life before, during, and after Nazi persecution and in assessing family and individual Jewish identity.

MEMBERSHIP

Group discussion began with the group leader asking each person to introduce him- or herself and to speak about personal goals in the group. In round-robin fashion, members then highlight a range of experience.

Suffering becomes the first criterion for cohesion and membership in second generation groups. Those whose parents suffered deeply react spontaneously to being part of the group. Offspring of survivors whose parents suffered some persecution but managed to escape while other family members were killed feel they perhaps don't belong.

Suffering is, of course, an ambiguous criterion. It is measured and evaluated differently depending on each person's perspective, and the definition of "an acceptable level of suffering" must be negotiated by each group.

Inevitably, the criterion for group membership underwent a transformation. Over time, group members began to react to current feeling, that is, the open sharing of painful and intense personal feelings and experience, rather than past suffering. Current feeling then became the criterion for belonging. This validation of feeling contributed to each member's sense of worthiness. Validation and worthiness contributed to increased self-esteem.

To summarize, during Phase I the severity of family Holocaust trauma is the first membership criterion. Acceptance and credence of emotions reassure each individual of belonging. Worthiness and cohesion become manifest as initial feelings of mistrust, ambivalence, and outsider status dissipate. The group fosters free sharing of intimate feelings and problems, and a sense of group belonging increases self-esteem.

COMMUNICATION

Offspring of survivors, the second generation, tend to learn about their parents' Holocaust experience through bits and pieces of information, and intense, non-verbal messages. This pattern of intergenerational communication renders the second generation unable to understand fully what their parents suffered, how they survived, and what the implications of their parents' experiences might be for them. Second generation survivors have a great need to master and express their feelings about the Holocaust and to mourn or memorialize deceased family members whose names, faces, and characteristics they never knew. For the second generation, participation in groups opens up a relationship to the past, especially to their parents' past.

The initial intake interview for second generation groups is a crucial part of the therapeutic experience. As part of this initial assessment, prospective group members were assisted in constructing a family tree or genogram. This exercise makes the subject's inability to specify the extent to which the prewar family was affected painfully clear. This interview initiated the process of confronting death and denial of the past. Many patients reveal embarrassment regarding their ignorance of family history, a subject their parents had either refused to speak about or had only discussed in sketchy detail. A family atmosphere of mourning pervades these households, yet there is rarely direct discussion about actual losses. When survivor parents did speak of loss, it was often too close or detailed for comfort, or was used for manipulation. Survivors' children, frequently named for lost loved ones, feel, even as children, that they have been born to replace profound losses. Often, after several intensive group sessions, survivor children begin to reveal their (sometimes well-founded) suspicions that their parents had had children during the war, whose death they preferred to keep secret. The group helped facilitate and ease the process of encountering survivor parents, and also served to alleviate a common second generation fear and fantasy—that close questioning of survivor parents, whom they perceive as fragile, might trigger a parental "breakdown," or even "kill them," should the past prove too overwhelming to reenter. Participants who had successfully encountered their parents offered support to others who had not, and even shared techniques that might aid one in an open discussion of traumatic events. Over time, members began to feel exhilarated by the transmission of family treasures, such as songs, customs, tales, that had lain dormant for years.

JEWISH IDENTITY

Children of survivors often have difficulties in developing a positive sense of Jewish identity because, in addition to all the other problems of Jewishness, they associate being Jewish with being slaughtered.

Most second generation participants described themselves as feeling isolated and alienated from the Jewish community. Only 20 percent felt part of Jewish life, either through a strong connection to the State of Israel, to Jewish ritual, or to Jewish culture and intellectual tradition. As members worked through their ambivalence about their personal Jewish identity, they began to feel more integrated into the many aspects of Jewish life. After the group experience, many began to reconnect personally to Judaism, either by studying Jewish history, Judaica, language, or by joining a synagogue or other Jewish organization. Healing, in part, is dependent on overcoming the negative aspects of a Jewish identity the only component of which is suffering or victimization. Dialogue with parents about Jewish life, ritual, and customs before the war trauma helps to alleviate the sense of discontinuity that many children of survivors experience, and fosters a new, more positive relationship to both one's personal and collective past heritage and culture.

In addition, a concern that frequently, if not always, arises in second generation groups is that of one's relationships to non-Jews, particularly as regards dating and intermarriage. Most survivor parents have given their children a very clear message about intermarriage: "You'll kill me, or I'll kill you if you do it." In the groups, members would try to help each other discover their own reasons for wanting to marry either within, or outside of the faith, and to come to terms with the conflict.

MOURNING

The difficulty of mourning overwhelming losses and the fear of breaking down or losing control, should one release feelings of tremendous grief, rage, and guilt, complicates the lives of survivors and their children as well. Second generation survivors must mourn, not a direct loss of loved ones, but rather, a memory of those they have never known. Their parents, as Bergmann has pointed out,

are often too traumatized to mourn their lost loved ones, [and so] engage in a variety of displacement mechanisms that might be called survivor's "substitute-for-mourning" mechanisms. Symbolic displaced actions, lived out with current *real* objects (children), are unconsciously addressed to lost love objects.[4]

For those offspring of survivors who are the only remnant of a once thriving community, the burden of identification is even greater. It is through the process of mourning, best facilitated in a group setting, that people of the second generation can come to identify with those aspects of the deceased that are positive and constructive. Idealization or degradation of either parents or lost family members can lead to problems in adult identity development. Many members of the second generation tend to idealize their parents or the dead as "heroes," or, contrarily, perceive them as victims and victims only. It is therefore crucial to work through each group member's perceptions of his or her survivor parents, as well as perceptions of lost relatives and extended family who are active parts of their own or their parents memories and fantasies.

Second generation individuals are not necessarily aware of their need to mourn relatives they did not personally know. In second generation groups, it is often only close proximity to death—through their own or other group members' recent experiences—that submerged feelings surface that may be related to an identification with strangers who died before they were even born.

A survivor family's response to an immediate loss frequently replicates a coping style that the parents have utilized in the past. If survivor parents engaged in denial after the Holocaust, children of survivors have difficulty confronting death. This is especially problematic for children of survivors who lose a survivor parent. The parent's death may cause the child to feel responsible, guilty that he survived, helpless that he did not save the parent, and angry that he was abandoned. In the absence of mourning, these feelings are repressed only to be acted out unconsciously. "The disease," relates eminent psychiatrist Robert Jay Lifton, "is not grief but its distortion—not mourning but impaired mourning."[5] This "disease" often affects interpersonal relationships and can have detrimental effects on a second generation survivor's self-image. The role of the therapist in second generation survivor groups, therefore, is both to facilitate mourning of current and past death, as well as to make group members aware of the *mourning patterns* in the family, especially as they relate to the traumatic losses of the Holocaust.

In a group situation, one encounters the spectrum of mourners: those who deny they need to remember those strangers who, though they never knew them, are nonetheless significant; those who feel guilty, enraged, and helpless about the suffering their parents endured before their birth; those who identify with the dead, but only as "victims" or "heroes"; and those who wish to exorcise the Holocaust, to "be rid of it, to forget it, and move on once and for all," as one offspring of survivors expressed.

Thus, in second generation groups, the issue of loss is a frequent topic of discussion. Offspring of survivors, now in their thirties and forties, frequently have parents who are ill or who have died. Sometimes this very sense of loss is what motivates them to join the group. In one group, for example, a woman was deeply concerned about her survivor father's deteriorating health and impending death. She had interviewed him about his experiences in a concentration camp, but wanted to know more about his life before the war. She saw her father as a link to the old world—to the values, ideas, and memories that would disappear as the last witness of the family passed away. The natural continuity between generations was nonexistent to her. Nonsurvivor families tend to sustain the loss of elder members without terrible anxiety, simply because society as a whole retains the memory of its past. But this woman, typical of the second generation mourner, felt total despair at the prospect of what she perceived as the disappearance of centuries of Eastern European Jewish civilization which, retained in her father, would with his death be forever obiterated from historical memory.

Survivor children, when faced with the death of a parent, feel an often frightening onus to know everything that must be known about the past, to pose the questions they have been thus far afraid to ask of their survivor parents, and to ensure that the memory of the Holocaust, and the legacy of the family, now their personal responsibility, is *transmittable* to the next generation. As one group participant put it, "If we [the second generation] don't know what happened . . . what will happen to the memory?" Because the Jews have been without a national or political identity for the past two millennia, the importance of memory—personal, as well as collective—has been paramount. Yerushalmi (1982) alerts us to the importance of memory in Jewish history since Biblical times. He states: "The modern effort to reconstruct the Jewish past begins at a time that witnesses a sharp break in the continuity of Jewish living and hence also an ever-growing decay of Jewish group memory."[6] The paradox in the post-Holocaust era is that though there is more need than ever to record Jewish history, the dying survivors take with them the remains of an entire civilization, that of European Jewry. Second generation people feel a special responsibility to provide a healing link in this broken continuity. Memory, therefore, is a constant theme in second generation groups, and as members help each other to find ways to mourn the past, as well as to construct ways to fulfill their second generation survivor mission of bearing witness and transmitting the past, a healing takes place. Through mourning, blocked creativity is manifest.[7] Creative expression such as writing, filmmaking, research, painting, have a healing effect that serves to complete the mourning process, transforming pain constructively, and offering hope for a newly imagined future.

There are cultural as well as psychological barriers to mourning the Holocaust. When, for example, survivors emigrated to the United States after liberation, they were often explicitly discouraged from remembering. "Get on with your life," was the attitude of American friends and relatives who knew nothing of, or worse, preferred to ignore or trivialize the massive trauma survivors had endured. It was not until many years later that society allowed a direct confrontation with Nazi atrocity, and by that time, it was often too late to benefit survivors and their families: Memory had been repressed, mourning had been impaired, and guilt, rage, and grief had found their expression in suffering.

The process of breaking the silence, of confronting the past, can bring intense feelings to the fore. One can observe the healing process as pain, anger, and helplessness are transformed through insight and the experience of trust into creative energy.

In this stage, members begin to really feel and experience guilt, rage, helplessness, and anger. Group members express a sense of being overwhelmed by these new feelings; they share vengeful fantasies of killing Nazis, of confronting bystanders and governments, about their passivity. The verbalization of these feelings is encouraged. Members serve as supportive role models for each other, alleviating the fear of loss of control over anger or grief. Finally, denial is transformed into a constructive commitment to memory. It is most important at this stage to transform loyalty to suffering and pain into a constructive loyalty to each member's individual and cultural heritage. Thus therapy groups begin an ongoing process that helps the participant integrate the images of suffering and pain and loyalty to the dead in a positive way. Rather than identify with suffering and thereby duplicate helplessness and isolation, the group enables people to search out and give memory a place in the *present* that is meaningful and energizing.

The termination of the group brings up feelings of loss and urgency. Members discuss ways to actively utilize the insight they have gained and creatively transform their intense feelings. Some members begin to get involved in politically oriented activities such as bringing Nazis to justice, or fighting for Soviet Jewry. Others seek more personal cultural enrichment by learning Yiddish or Hebrew, or making a trip to Israel. Some formally document their family history through film and cassette. Others began to work artistically with Holocaust-related themes.

The role of the leader in such second generation groups goes beyond the normal facilitative role. One must help each group member, in his or her own way, connect with the Holocaust traumas in their families. The leader must have a good historical background in order to discern discontinuity in related stories or to fill in missing, but perhaps crucial, historical information. He or she must interpret the similarities and differences in each group member's responses to his or her family situation, ultimately helping each person to feel less overwhelmed by the traumatic past.

INTERGENERATIONAL GROUPS

In 1977, I began to treat child survivors, those who lived through the war, perhaps even concentration camps, while they were still young. The experience of child survivors, I was to discover, was often dismissed by adult survivors, largely because they were thought too young to have remembered what happened. Because child survivors suffer from the same anomie and isolation as the second generation, group therapy again seemed appropriate. I began two *intergenerational groups,* which consisted of child survivors and second generation individuals.

Intergenerational groups are unique in that they include those who actually experienced trauma, and those who learned about it secondhand. The advantage to this kind of group is that it replicates a survivor family, that is, the intergenerational dynamics of a survivor family are mirrored in a group of first and second generation survivors. The feeling and interaction which develop among group members enable the generations to understand each other in new ways and in turn change how they behave in their own families. These short-term groups enable both generations to change destructive patterns of communication, to enhance self-esteem, and to experience new coping strategies. As in second generation groups, the group setting facilitates mourning, helps integrate the past, and reduces isolation and alienation, increasing the sense of belonging.[8]

In initial sessions child survivors tend to empathize only with each other. Child survivors who were old enough to remember help fill in imagery and feelings for younger child survivors. Child survivors initially have difficulty engaging with offspring of survivors in the group. Later in group development, child survivors come to understand that offspring of survivors want to know about what happened to their own parents as well as to the child survivors in the group. Communication between the generations becomes the basis for a renewed sense of hope.

Another advantage to intergenerational groups is that a parent-child transference develops between child survivors who are parents and offspring of survivors. When child survivors witness the feelings of suffering and hopelessness of offspring of survivors, they attempt to instill optimism, and later begin to work through conflicts of communication with their own children via their experience with second generation members of the group.

INTERGENERATIONAL COMMUNICATION AND JEWISH IDENTITY

In the middle phase of group development, the intergenerational group replicates the family dynamics of a survivor family. Similar family histories of persecution and migration amplify transferential feelings. Differences in personal experience with trauma within the group echo intergenerational differences.

Child survivors who are now parents feel that their own children, as well as second generation group members, cannot possibly understand what they went through and are thus reluctant to talk. Children of survivors feel that the subject of the Holocaust is taboo, that it will evoke painful memories and feelings that are too intense for their "fragile" survivor parents (and child survivor group members) to handle. These concerns arise in the group. Interventions by the leader enable breakthroughs in communication within the group, breakthroughs that, once experienced, can help members to communicate more freely within their own families. For offspring of survivors, the major insight is that survivors generally are not damaged by discussion of their painful pasts. Child survivors learn that offspring of survivors are in fact profoundly interested in their past. They also realize that at least some of the resistance to communicate with their own children stems from them and not from their children. For child survivors, the group becomes a testing ground for sharing their past and realizing that others can be responsive and caring. As members increase their ability to empathize, their self-esteem grows.

The process of achieving communication is not simple. Inevitably, child survivors accuse others in the group of failing to understand them. The leader's role is to confirm that while some might not understand, one must beware of projection, of blaming one's own inability to comprehend personal suffering, or to justify one's own survival, on others who want to listen and respond.

For offspring of survivors, the opportunity to witness, listen, and ask questions of child survivors as they relate painful memories serves to dispel fantasies and fears of what it might be like to have such a dialogue with their own survivor parents.

During the group meetings, child survivors often begin to interact with their own surviving family members. Between sessions, they make efforts to contact their parents or extended family to discuss the past. Often the group helps them to acknowledge their avoidance of discussing war memories with their families. Child survivors return to the group with reports of what they have learned and share how it feels finally to open up the past. Because some of the group members' families are deceased, the issue of survivor guilt arises. Solutions are explored and some begin to seek out distant relatives or acquaintances who might provide them with relevant information.

As communication improves, so do personal relationships. A new sense of reality emerges, especially regarding suffering. Child survivors begin to understand fears, anxieties, conflicts, and defenses as they relate to their early childhood trauma. They begin to feel closer to their parents and families, more empathetic, and at times, change their old perceptions about them.

Offspring of survivors also began to communicate more with their parents, but with a different agenda. Whereas child survivors try to recapture their own experience, offspring attempt to understand the experiences of their parents. Lacking a coherent family history, offspring often find that their personal identity—namely, the family's involvement in the Holocaust—has been unconscious, rather than conscious.[9] Until the group experience, many of their own behaviors, anxieties, defenses, fears, and attitudes were inexplicable to them. Insight begins with having the courage to speak to their parents, to make explicit what had previously been unspoken aspects of the family history, events, feelings, values, memories, and losses.

Outside the group, encounters with parents and other family members become the new criterion for group membership. Leadership in the group then depends on the stories of successful attempts to find out about the past. Crises develop for those who can't manage to create such exchanges with parents. These members feel jealous and guilty during discussions. Group pressure is exerted upon members who fail to contact their parents during the course of the group's meetings and these members are encouraged to encounter family at a future time.

A unifying concern for children of survivors and child survivors is communication with the next generation. By learning about what interferes with the transmission of the past, group members begin to feel more confident about sharing with their own children. As one child survivor put it,

I realized that when one of my kids tried to ask me a question [about the Holocaust] he immediately withdrew it, saying: I don't want to upset you. But I suddenly understood how he has been trying to protect me by avoiding the subject.

Upon hearing of this, another child survivor shared:

I've been guilty of wanting to protect my kids. And the overwhelming message I'm getting from [the group] is that this is wrong. Perhaps I have not shared enough of what happened to me with my family.

Despite new awareness, conversations about the past are still difficult.

Jewish identity serves as a unifying experience and a bridge which provides continuity between the past, present, and future. Although there were often great differences in religious identification and practice in these groups, religion rarely, if ever, became a subject of conflict or pressure.

As in second generation groups, the identity problem shared by most inter-generational group members was to develop a sense of their Jewishness as positive, given the intense negative associations of the past. Discussion of Jewish identity often aroused feelings of pain and confusion. Although both child survivors and offspring struggle with identity conflicts, the process of Jewish identity development is much more traumatic for child survivors, for whom Jewish identity is linked with victimization and for whom it seems impossible to imagine feeling joy, enrichment, and strength through the experience of being Jewish.

In addition, the basic unconscious motivation for a child to identify with the parents' Jewishness is problematic for child survivors. Ostow describes two components for Jewish identity: the unconscious core developed in early childhood and the manifest identity that varies externally.

The unconscious core of Jewish identity is established by identification of the young child with the parent; his need for generational continuity; his sensitivity to the distinction between family and non-family; his acceptance of group myths; and his use of sensitivity to language, names, dress and ritual as a means of establishing identification with the family and community.[10]

During the Nazi era, danger forced many children to hide external evidence of being Jewish. Internal identification and unconscious early childhood identity was, however, preserved. The continuity and search for ways to identify as Jews is necessary for child survivors to reduce the pain of loss of parents and other family members. A sense of loyalty to the dead, indeed, part of the process of mourning the dead, is linked to an identification with that very element, Jew-ishness, which was responsible for the loss in the first place. Identification with the lost object, however difficult, promotes mourning.

Most child survivors and offspring of survivors have tended to play down their Judaism as young adults. As in second generation groups, most intergen-erational members were not actively involved in synagogues, Jewish organiza-tions, or other groups that met spiritual, cultural, or national needs. Only 20 percent of the overall participants felt that they belonged to some segment of the organized Jewish community. As they matured, they began to feel a desire to come to terms with their Jewish identity. This desire was often precipitated by perceptions of increased anti-Semitism which brought about fears of persecution. In addition, life cycle events, such as marriages and child bearing, raised issues of basic values, priorities, and family customs.

Individuals often came to the group with the specific goal of clarifying their Jewish identity. This desire was sometimes as strong a motivation as the wish to explore and master feelings about being a survivor or child of survivors.

During the middle phase of group development, members began to express a deep need to belong to a Jewish community. Participants also indicated cognitive needs relating to their Judaism. They wanted information about ritual, custom, belief and discussed whether it was possible to be Jewish but not observant, as well as what it meant to believe in God after the Holocaust. They were also troubled about whether and how to transmit Jewish identity to their children. For all group members, the search for meaningful ways to express Jewish identity was important. The following issues were vital to group discussion and personal understanding of Jewishness.

1. *Values*. Many members felt that they possessed "Jewish values," including social/ political concerns, humanitarian feelings, charitable impulses. They felt, however, that their experience or their parents' Holocaust experience had made them privy to another, conflicting set of values including lack of trust in others, disbelief in God, personal survival concerns first.

2. *Practice/Tradition*. Cognitive questions about *how* to practice Judaism, and emotional questions of how much Judaism to practice.

3. *Belief in God*. The conflict over whether one is Jewish in a religious way is related to the difficulty of believing in God after the Holocaust.

4. *Israel*. Members' conceptions about God after the Holocaust were debated, but an even deeper concern, that is, whether a Jewish life was a communal life, emerged in passionate discussion of Israel.

Although group discussion of Jewish identity was for the most part unifying, certain statements led to conflict. The greatest controversy evolved over issues of members' relationships with non-Jews, for example, when an individual would confess that he or she "only dates non-Jews," or only has non-Jewish friends. There was at least one person in each group who made such a comment. Group members often responded to these remarks as if they were personal affronts. Discussion often led to a deeper understanding of negative stereotypes of both Jews and non-Jews, as well as men and women.

Issues of Jewish identity also raised concern over anti-Semitism. Child survivors in general felt especially vulnerable about their Jewishness, or, as one remarked, that one must always "be on guard."

Offspring of survivors, as stated before, often feel that religion presents a conflict for them, and that this conflict is related to parental ambivalence. Jewish identity was discussed in both groups in terms of individual belief and practice, as well as parental belief and practice before, during, and after the Holocaust. As was revealed, some parents maintained or deepened their faith as a result of their Holocaust experience, some continued the family tradition of assimilation or cultural identification, while others who had been deeply religious lost all faith in God.

With regard to the development of Jewish identity, there is a marked psychological difference between second generation and child survivors. People who as children directly experienced persecution associate Jewishness with extinction. Offspring of survivors, though they may have similar associations, do not express extreme, adverse feelings about Jewish identity. Once a child survivor's intense feelings are related to his or her Holocaust experience, a new clarity about this discomfort develops, thus allowing the individual greater control over internal conflict.

Children of survivors and child survivors share a common need for community. This community does not necessarily have to be religious; it simply must serve their needs to associate with people of similar values and moral concerns, and, especially for child survivors, must function to recreate lost family.

CHILD SURVIVORS AND THE MOURNING PROCESS

Facilitating mourning was, of course, a crucial component of my work with child survivors as well. Whereas second generation individuals must mourn strangers, child survivors who have lost their entire family find it profoundly difficult to accept that the loss is real, that no one will ever come back. It is most traumatic to accept the death of a loved one when the death was not actually witnessed. Jacob, for example, had developed an extreme adaptive mechanism so as not to accept his parents' death. In his late forties, Jacob resided in a metropolitan city, but continued to live as if the war was still raging. He never established any roots by setting up a home or a family, and his career was always shifting. His most obvious problem was sleeping: he could not sleep at home. Occasionally, he would stay with friends, but his fantasy was to sleep on the streets, or in railroad stations. His reaction to authority was total acquiescence, regardless of circumstance. When I suggested that he was living as if the war was still going on, the reason for his behavior became very clear. As long as the war was not over, Jacob could still hope that his parents would come back. Helping the individual move beyond the denial of death, whether he be a survivor, child survivor, or child of survivors, is of primary importance.

As eminent psychoanalyst, Judith Kestenberg, has emphasized, "the resolution of the trauma requires not only dealing with the loss of parents but also the loss of one's environment and atmosphere, including mementoes of the past."[11] Denial, Kestenberg adds, also serves to protect child survivors from guilt about their attachments to or loyalty toward surrogate parents who rescued or adopted them after the war, as well as the guilt that they survived and others did not.

Those surviving the death of their own parents and siblings suffer guilt on many levels. As Lifton has observed, "no survival experience . . . can occur without severe guilt." In his elaboration of survivor guilt, Lifton notes, "the survivor's tendency [is] to incorporate within himself an image of the dead, and then to think, feel, and act as he imagines they did or would."[12] This identification with the dead which induces "guilt over what one has done to, or not done for, the dying while oneself surviving," continues to torment child survivors. Often they try to live out, not their own life, but the lives of those who perished. Sharing how relatives were killed, as well as realizing that one may still cling to hidden hope because the death was not witnessed or confirmed, is the beginning of the process of separating the memory of loved ones from the hope that they may still be alive. Like children of survivors, child survivors can transform denial into creative action, identifying with the dead through values, social action, and creativity, rather than identifying with them through guilt or suffering. The denial that afflicts child survivors is related to survivor guilt; second generation denial is qualitatively different, for they rely on fantasies of what might have been, and experience guilt that they did not (as did their parents) directly suffer, or helplessness that they can't undo the Holocaust trauma for their parents or other loved ones.

The intergenerational group setting is ideal to help individuals move through the stages of mourning. Those consumed by rage are encouraged by other group members to move beyond self-immolating behavior. Those half-drowned in guilt and helplessness are encouraged to act. Growth is a collaborative effort. The Holocaust was a collective tragedy, thus collective mourning facilitates the healing process. By having the strength of the community and spirit that comes through group mourning and intergenerational communication in a safe environment, tremendous individual progress can be made.

SUMMARY

Given the short duration of these groups, a high frequency of behavioral changes are reported, both by second generation and child survivors. People often express feeling energized to "do something" constructive or creative with their Holocaust experience, a stark contrast to their previous feeling that the Holocaust "weighed [them] down." One of the outcomes of each of my groups has been a flurry of constructive actions which Kestenberg (1980) has characterized as a result of superego reorganization.[13] Through involvement in social action and education, for example, children of survivors transform their rage and guilt into mature moral action and remembrance.

Because the Holocaust is not just an individual trauma, because it affected a community of people, healing is facilitated by a group setting. Group involvement enables members to validate emotions, master new methods of intergenerational communication within and outside the family; develop a constructive Jewish identity; mourn multiple personal losses; and channel intense reactions and feelings in constructive ways.

NOTES

1. Eva Fogelman and Bella Savran, "Therapeutic Groups for Children of Holocaust Survivors," *International Journal of Group Psychotherapy* 29, no. 2 (1979): 211–235; Eva Fogelman and Bella Savran, "Brief Group Therapy with Offspring of Holocaust Survivors: Leader's Reactions," *American Journal of Orthopsychiatry* 50, no. 1 (1980): 96–108; Marty Trachtenberg and Mia Davis, "Breaking Silence: Serving Children of the Holocaust Survivors," *Journal of Jewish Communal Service* 54 (1978): 294–302; Florabel Kinsler, "Second Generation Effects of the Holocaust: The Effectiveness of Group Therapy in the Resolution of the Transmission of Parental Trauma," *Journal of Psychology and Judaism,* no. 6 (1981): 53–67.

2. Irvin Yalom, *Theory and Practice of Group Psychotherapy* (New York: Basic Books, 1970).

3. Sylvia Axelrod and Norman Blumenthal, "Psychiatric Hospital Treatment of Offspring of Holocaust Survivors," paper presented at the American Group Psychotherapy Association Annual Meeting, New York, February 1985.

4. Martin Bergmann, "Reflections on the Psychological and Social Function of Remembering the Holocaust," *Psychoanalytic Inquiry* 5, no. 1 (1985): 304.

5. Robert Jay Lifton, *Death in Life: Survivors of Hiroshima* (New York: Simon and Schuster, 1967).

6. Y. H. Yerushalmi, *Zakhor: Jewish History and Jewish Memory* (Seattle: University of Washington Press, 1982).

7. George Pollack, "Mourning and Adaptation," *International Journal of Psycho-Analysis*, no. 42 (1961): 341–361; George Pollack, "The Mourning Process and Creative Organizational Change," *Journal of the American Psychoanalytic Association,* no. 25 (1977): 3–34.

8. Eva Fogelman, "Therapeutic Alternatives for Holocaust Survivors and Second Generation," in *Psychological Perspectives of the Holocaust and its Aftermath* (New York: Institute for Holocaust Studies, 1988), pp. 79–108.

9. Robert Prince, "Knowing the Holocaust," *Psychoanalytic Inquiry* 5, no. 1 (1985): 51–62.

10. Mortimer Ostow, "The Psychological Determinants of Jewish Identity," *The Israel Annals of Psychiatry and Related Disciplines,* 15, no. 4 (1977): 313–335.

11. Judith Kestenberg, "Coping with Losses and Survival," in *The Problem of Loss and Mourning: New Psychological Perspectives,* Peter Shabad and David R. Dietrich, Eds. (New York: International Universities Press, 1987).

12. Robert Jay Lifton, *Death in Life,* p. 90.

13. Judith Kestenberg, "Psychoanalytic Contributions to the Problem of Children of Survivors of Nazi Persecution: Case Presentation and Assessment," *Journal of the American Psychoanalytic Association* 28, (1980): 775–804.

8

A Family Therapy Approach to Holocaust Survivor Families

ESTHER PEREL AND JACK SAUL

Much of the psychological literature on the Holocaust refers to the survivors and their children, that is, the second generation. It documents the long-term after-effects of the Holocaust trauma on the survivors as well as on the behavior and problems of their children. A number of clinicians have written about the Holocaust survivor family conceptualizing it as a single unit and stressing the importance of a family approach to understanding and treating such families.[1] While much of the literature and research on these families is based on a psychoanalytic approach, there has been a growing body of observations and conceptualization from a family systems theory perspective.[2]

In this chapter we present a family systems approach to the treatment of Holocaust survivor families as well as a discussion of common family configurations and patterns of transactions. Of course, the clinical population we refer to must not be taken as representative of the entire survivor family population. In fact, despite massive traumatization, many survivor families have adapted successfully, integrated themselves well in their communities, and live a healthy family life, sometimes even drawing upon the parents' Holocaust experience as a source of strength and inspiration. Our conceptualizations and treatment methods are drawn from structural, strategic, and multigenerational family approaches.

FORMATION OF HOLOCAUST SURVIVOR FAMILIES

To Holocaust survivors who had experienced the destruction of their entire world—their families, communities, systems of beliefs, values, and sometimes self-images—marriage represented the reemergence from the *Weltuntergang*. It was a life-affirming act. Marriage was a way of compensating for the losses, countering massive disruptions in their lives, and undoing the dehumanization and loneliness experienced during the war.[3] For many, marriage was a response to an overwhelming sense of loss and inability to mourn. A new family was a symbol of rebirth; it provided a sense of continuity with the past and hope for the future. The family context was the framework for readaptation and for ''the process of renewal after living for so many years as one in an anonymous crowd without privacy, walls, a concept of ownership, or any physical boundaries for intimacy.''[4]

Those who married during the war did so for mutual protection, physical survival, and as an act of defiance. Many of the survivor families were formed in the immediate years following liberation, often in the displaced persons camps. The couples married after a brief courtship with no real choosing and weighing of the qualitities of the spouse, often disregarding the usual prewar criteria for marriage such as education, socioeconomic level, and age.[5] As a result, some of these marriages which were successful in the context of survival, during and just following the war, experienced increased difficulty in the transition to normal life, when the exigencies for survival were no longer present. The need for togetherness and cohesion, so important in the couple's beginnings, dissipated with time and with the alleviation of suffering. The bond of survivorship was often not enough to sustain an intimate relationship with true sexual and emotional attachment.

Of course, the course of the marriage was also influenced by each spouse's personality, prewar life, and how he or she had been affected by particular war experiences. As the marriage deteriorated, the parents' attention shifted even more onto the children as a source of meaning and affection. Nevertheless, when dissatisfied in their marriages, survivors tended to remain together in a hostile stalemate rather than face physical separation again.

Spouses who initially turned to each other for freedom and sheer survival, later saw each other as a haunting reminder of the past and blamed each other for being their mutual wardens in the prison of memory. Mrs. B. met her husband in a labor camp where she admired his hard work and determination to live, feeling that he would make a good husband. They married shortly after liberation and had a child in the first year of their marriage. The couple was seen for consultation because of Mrs. B.'s increased depression and paranoia following the marriage of their only child. Mrs. B. had been unable to be affectionate with her husband for many years because, she claimed, ''he doesn't act like a man, he is still like a prisoner in the camp who works like a slave and waits for someone to tell him what to do.''

Survivors came out of the camps emaciated and physically debilitated. Many feared that their experience had scarred them and would somehow damage their offspring. Yet, many survivors became parents shortly after premature marriages. Having a child was a tangible reaffirmation of life and symbolized the ''replacement'' of the lost loved ones. As a symbol of survival, the child was special and imbued with a mission in life.

Survivors' own deprivation and lack of parenting during important phases of development would create strains in their new families. A particularly difficult issue was separation. Survivors' separation from their own parents often had been sudden, final, and unresolved, forgoing the normal gradual process of leaving home. Given the experiences of trauma, multiple losses, and the circumstances of their formation, survivor families display a high degree of cohesion, overinvolvement between members, and enmeshment. The intensity of unresolved issues of the past continues to haunt these families in the present.

THE STRUCTURE AND ORGANIZATION OF SURVIVOR FAMILIES

External Boundaries

Many survivors immigrated to the United States or Israel after the war. Others returned to their towns and cities in Europe, only to find that the world that they had known and loved had disappeared. Many wandered from country to country searching for family members. All experienced a sense of profound dislocation and displacement that contributed to the establishment of closed boundaries between families and the outside world.

The survivor family faced the usual challenges of immigration, such as a decline of parental authority as a result of their decreased effectiveness and status in the new society, the clashes of values and loyalties, and the rise of the younger generation which was more adaptable to the new society and often became the liaison between the family and the external world.

But the survivor family also had to endure the "conspiracy of silence," or the collusion between the survivor and society not to talk about the Holocaust. This silence further intensified the family's isolation, mistrust, and lack of integration into society. As a result, the external boundaries of the survivor families were rigid, and a strong family cohesiveness warded off a dangerous and hostile external world. The binding message conveyed to the children the security and trust of the home and the unexpected dangers of the world outside. This guardedness served to control the children and strengthen the family bonds.

Boundaries and Hierarchy within the Family

The lines of demarcation that define the various interrelations and functions of the family members are often diffuse in survivor families. As in immigrant families, the child acts as the appointed negotiator with the outside world and the carrier of the language of the new society. As a result there is a reversal of hierarchies in the organization of the family with the children taking on parental roles.

The interdependence between parents and children is strong. Children may act as caretakers or as mediators between quarreling parents. In one family, a mother openly expressed to her children her disappointment in her husband,

saying, "If it weren't for the war, I would have never married your father."
She was sick and depressed but refused her husband's care for her as she complained that he made her even sicker. She would only allow her daughters to attend to her. Since the mother was unavailable, the daughters cooked and cared for the father. The parents' enlisting of their two daughters for emotional and physical support led to a confusion regarding the separate identities of parents and children and made for a blurring of the generational boundaries.

Survivor families frequently present the following constellation.[6] The mother is the parent in charge, domineering, overprotective, and infantilizing. She is the spokesperson of the family. The father provides for the material needs of the family, but remains peripheral. His position in the family is withdrawn and passive, leaving the child rearing to the mother. These roles were common in traditional Jewish families in prewar Eastern Europe. The parents are preoccupied with the past. As a result, they respond inflexibly to the child resulting in an inconsistency of limit setting and assertion of parental authority. They compensate for their dissatisfying marital relationship, and hope to overcome their insurmountable losses by involving the children in enmeshed relationships, sometimes treating them as spouse surrogates. Furthermore, attempts to establish independence and privacy on the part of the children are perceived as a threat to the family's stability.

Members of the survivor families are more closely engaged than members of "American families," their attachments are tighter, and separation is effected with greater difficulty.[7] Several forces are operating to intensify the attachment between parents and children. The parents' past experience of loss and trauma has made them especially concerned that their children may be harmed. They want to protect their children from pain, making sure that they are exaggeratedly healthy and hypernormal. As a result of their parents having suffered massive trauma and manifesting symptoms of the survivor syndrome, the children are concerned about their parents' health, see them as frail and vulnerable, and want to protect them from any further suffering.[8] The mutual overprotectivenes intensifies the enmeshment.

BINDS AND BONDS: LOYALTY IN SURVIVOR FAMILIES

Survivors suffered multiple losses in their families of origin; some also lost spouses and children. The circumstances surrounding these deaths had often remained ambiguous and the survivors had been bereft of the traditional rituals and symbols to help them mourn these deaths. As a consequence, the unresolved issues of the past intruded on the family's present life. For some survivor families, the past is more present than the present, and there is no future.[9]

Loyalty to the dead is an adaptive strategy for dealing with multiple losses, and way of maintaining a connection to the dead. Sometimes, this creates a situation of divided loyalty for the parents, for whom investing in their newly formed families means betraying those who died. Mr. C. was forced to leave his only son behind during the war. He remarried a few years after liberation and named his second son after the son who had perished. Mr. C. could not relinquish the past and live in the present. He continuously compared his son to the dead one whom he idealized. As a consequence, his son felt inadequate; that he could never "win Father's love from the dead over to the living." Mr. C's inability to give up his lost son, his "loyalty," enabled him to keep his dead son alive through his new son. Yet he could never bring his dead son back to life nor did he appreciate what he had in his living one.

Survivor guilt arises from the unconscious or conscious sense that one could or should have done something to prevent the death of a loved one. It may be accompanied by feelings that one is not worthy to live when the others have died. This guilt deeply affects the family's atmosphere, its ability to deal with stress, its development of coping skills, as well as its internal transactions. Guilt operates as a "vehicle of loyalty to the dead. As with chronic hate and rage, grief and suffering, guilt keeps both generations engaged in relationships with those who perished, and it maintains a semblance of familial continuity."[10] This loyalty is carried transgenerationally in the family. The parents' loyalty to their families of origin is succeeded by their own children's loyalty to them.

In the more dysfunctional families, this loyalty carries with it an element of competition in which the children attempt to rival their parents in the extent of their suffering. In his/her suffering, the child sends messages to the parents such as, "I could have survived too," or "Stop making me feel guilty for having a better life." In these families the guilt permeates all family members and the past weighs heavily on the present. There is an atmosphere of prolonged brooding and a general incapacity to enjoy life.

In a different way, guilt is evoked to maintain the family's homeostasis and often undermines its ability to deal with change and separation. Guilt operates as a means of control, a way of regulating emotional distance and closeness, confrontation, and expressions of autonomy and independence. Parents invoke feelings of guilt and appeal to the loyalty of the child by sending the covert message, "We can't survive without you." In turn, children feel guilty about their parents' pain and depression. They cannot rebel against their victim parents nor fight against their unrealistic expectations. As a result they become depressed or resort to aggressive, explosive, or self-destructive behavior. The loyalty and the guilt associated with it can take extreme forms in which the children sacrifice themselves for their parents. The children struggle to reconcile their strivings for independence and autonomy with the strong ties of loyalty to the parents. "My parents had only me, I wanted so much for them to be proud of me," or "How can I leave my parents when they have lost everyone around them?" "How can I be happy when my mother is so sad and besides I have to pay tribute to the dead." Guilt provides a formidable bonding between parent and child.

Perhaps the most powerful dynamic in the Holocaust survivor families revolves around the issue of separation. We have described the various forces that operate in intensifying the overinvolvement between parents and children and making separation especially difficult; the mutual overprotection, the lack of role differentiation, the binding behaviors, the distorted communication, and the undermining of autonomous functioning. The survivor parents, who were not able to mourn adequately the deaths of family members, suffer a deep sense of emotional deprivation, suppressed grief, and delayed mourning. This makes it difficult for them to tolerate the loss created by separation from their own children. Thus stages of the family's development that involve the assertion of autonomy and independence—particularly adolescence, leaving home, and marriage—present transitional crises for these families. In the D. family, the parents were strongly opposed to the marriage of their son. At the wedding, unable to rejoice, Mr. D. repeatedly told his guests, "You know, my son is named after my father who died in Buchenwald. Now I am losing my son."

In its most dramatic form, the bind around separation operates in the following way: Since the child symbolizes "life," without him/her, the parents may die. And if the child leaves, he/she may die, because the world is a dangerous place. Separation thus evokes death and a life and death struggle. They may lead in more intense situations to actual physical violence between family members.[11]

THE MISSION OF THE CHILD

The child in the survivor family is imbued with a special mission: to restore the lost family members and to make up for the parents' unfulfilled lives. This creates a particular bind between parents and their children and keeps the parents overly involved in their children's lives. Statements such as, "I live my life through my children," are not uncommon.

The centrality of the child in providing meaning to the survivor parents and in filling the family void makes him/her the recipient of an inordinate array of expectations. This is sometimes an overwhelming task that even the most compliant and submissive child cannot possibly accomplish. Furthermore, the childrens' pressure to achieve in order to ensure the well-being of their parents creates difficulties for the child in securing his/her own identity and differentiation within the family. Success is often equated with material achievement; children are expected to surpass their parents educationally and professionally. Yet parents also envy their successful children because of their own missed opportunities, and fear losing them since success is often accompanied with autonomy. This leads the children to be confused about what the real expectations are.

In one family the parents placed great demands on their childrens' achievement. They worked very hard, and sacrificed their own comforts so that their son and daughter would be able to attend respectable colleges. But in order to do well in school and in their professions afterward, the children cut themselves off from their parents to avoid confusing messages. Though they were encouraged to surpass their parents, it also meant leaving them behind. At the same time, the children never believed that they could ever really surpass their parents, for life had been so much easier for them. Therefore the children felt that what they had achieved was worth less.

The burden to make up for the missed lives of those who died, for the shattered lives of the parents, as well as to fulfill their own aspirations puts an excessive or undue pressure on the children. In some cases children respond by overfulfilling the expectations and take on a kind of grandiose defiant attitude that they could meet any challenge. As a consequence, any small defeat is experienced as tragic. The overvaluation of the child because of his being "special" often does not take into consideration the child's realistic capacities. In response, some children try to fulfill the excessive demands by what Kreil calls "living on the edge," putting themselves in dangerous situations, leading their lives as a series of successes in avoiding disaster.[12] In other cases, they retaliate for the burden in ways that are self-defeating. Some children overevaluate their parents and see them as heroes whose adversities surmounted, would never be equaled by their own achievements. In more extreme cases, they compete with their parents by inflicting pain on themselves and creating obstacles so that their accomplishments will rival those of their parents.

PATTERNS OF COMMUNICATION AND EMOTIONAL EXPRESSION

Communication about the Past

In some Holocaust survivor families, the parents are able to give a balanced account of their experience to their children, to inform them of their past. In these families the Holocaust becomes an integral part of the family's awareness and a vehicle for the intergenerational transmission of values and worldview.

In troubled families, communication about the Holocaust experience can range from silence and denial, to isolation of affect, to constant preoccupation with the events of the past. Predictably, it effects the family's functioning and more general communication patterns in the home.

Those who chose silence may have wished to bury their past in an effort to establish new lives for themselves. Inevitably one of the family members confronts the silence either directly or through symptomatic behavior. For others, silence is a protective maneuver to shield both parents and children from pain. "What good would it do to tell them about the camps?" one parent asked. "It would only hurt and burden them." The silence around the parents' past may take on an aura of a shameful family secret. The organization of the family around preventing secrets from being revealed may drain the family's energy and block communication in general. Furthermore it may force the members to carry out additional acts of loyalty to the family. When the past is referred to mysteriously and with elusive hints, it leaves the child confused, bewildered, and filled with fantasies. He may feel an unexplained sense of guilt, but is reluctant to ask for clarification.[13] In one family a daughter said, "When I asked my mother why she lit an extra candle every Friday night, she would tell me that it was in memory of her dead parents. Once I asked her how her parents had died and she answered elusively, "They died," and then stared off into space." The mystifying *Lagerblick* (camp gaze) said, "don't ask."

In isolation of affect, the survivor recounts painful experiences without an accompanying emotion. "The words poured out of her like blood, but they no longer seemed connected to anything else she had experienced."[14]

Yet in other families, adult children often use the term *osmosis* to refer to the verbal and nonverbal ways the parents' Holocaust experience was communicated to them and to describe its omnipresence in their family. Some survivors become completely preoccupied with their Holocaust experience, using the Holocaust as a constant point of reference in describing, dealing with, and talking about family life. It becomes a language in itself: "You're worse than the Germans," "Eat, for months I wanted to have a piece of bread," "Don't tell me what to do, the time when I was given orders is over." The language serves as a camouflage to avoid dealing with other emotional processes going on in the family and to avoid taking personal responsibility by labeling and linking them to the Holocaust. This continuous preoccupation with the past and rigidity leads to distorted communication, unclear and double messages, and encumbers the family's capacity to change.

Expression of Anger

During the war the survivors had to contain their rage in order to survive. The enormity of their rage related to the trauma and losses made it difficult for them to deal adequately with their anger later on. A number of rules dictate the expression of anger in these families, usually prohibiting its open and direct expression. Anger threatens the cohesion and stability of the family system. When the rules are violated, so is the loyalty to the family, and fear and guilt may result.

The family engages in various conflict-avoiding maneuvers to maintain its homeostasis. The avoidance of conflict with the parents is associated with the implicit message that because they have suffered enough, they should be spared any further suffering. Statements such as "Your father is weak, don't make him weaker," "Momma is sick, don't scream at her," or "I'm weak, leave me alone," are potent deterrants to any expression of anger. In other instances, parents, while depressed or withdrawn may implicitly encourage a child to express anger and defiance for them, yet be unable to deal with these confrontations when directed toward themselves. The children's difficulty in confronting or rebelling against their victim parents may lead them to turn their aggression inward, becoming depressed, self-destructive, or even violently explosive. Furthermore, in their attempts to protect their parents, the children may attribute their parents' shortcomings to their war experience, thereby minimizing their own anger, and denying their parents' responsibility.

Since there are few direct and normal expressions of anger in survivor families, they may resort to indirect outlets such as somatization and other symptomatic behaviors. The youngest daughter of an orthodox survivor family became severely depressed after taking her first steps toward independence. She had begun college and had taken an apartment of her own. But eventually she decided to return home to live with her parents as they wished, for they did not approve of her living alone. In a treatment session, the family reenacted a typical scene: When the daughter angrily asserted her wish for autonomy, the mother responded by being hurt and withdrawn. The daughter then said, "This is how she punishes me, then I feel guilty because I can't stand causing her any more pain—she's already had such a hard life." The family could not tolerate open confrontation. The expression of anger was defined as unacceptable and was translated into guilt for causing the mother more suffering.

FUNCTION OF SYMPTOMS: SOMATIZATION AND ILLNESS

As in most families, symptoms in Holocaust survivor families serve the function of maintaining the stability of the system, and are used to avoid confrontation, autonomy, and separation. Somatization and illness may provide a focus for many of the family's interactions, and can modulate the relationship between the family and the outside world. The F. family believed that everything had already been taken away from them except their lives. Contact with the outside world had to be limited and people were not to be trusted. The family had organized itself around the illness of the father and had gradually isolated itself, opening the door only for medical doctors who also were not to be trusted.

Caring for an ill member of the family allows for an intimacy that the family might otherwise avoid. The position of the members in these families is one of complementarity: the strong and the weak, the helper and the helped, the savior and the victim. If there is a rule, it is that closeness requires some family members to be weak. In the G. family, illness was a potent signal calling the family to a truce in the midst of their fighting. It carried with it the threat of death. Mr. G., a stern, self-reliant, and hard-working man spent many hours out of the house having little contact with his wife and children. When he was ill, the usual tension that existed in the house would temporarily subside; the screaming would stop because "Papa was sick." On those occasions the family would rally around and nurture him back to health.

Children often carry contradictory and unrealistic views of their parents' health and emotional condition, vacillating between the images of strong heroes and stricken victims. As a result, they feel protective and responsible for their parents. According to Klein,[15] this "myth of illness" also operates when there is no real physical symptom or when there is no real present illness. Illness is invoked to maintain the family homeostasis and to account for an exaggerated guardedness. In the H. family, the parents were able to maintain the facade to others that their son was a normal and healthy child. But at home they treated him as fragile and sick, thereby justifying his not leaving the home to spend time with his peers, or taking on any activity even remotely dangerous. In the I. family, a mother exaggerated her husband's minor heart condition to keep him in the ill role as well as to create distance between him and their children. The mother used the father's illness to undermine confrontation and autonomous actions on the part of the children by making such statements as, ''Don't leave for vacation now, you know father would be worried and his heart is weak.'' The children's attempts to separate from the parents in this binding situation correlate with an exacerbation of the somatic symptoms in the parents.

FAMILY THERAPY WITH HOLOCAUST SURVIVOR FAMILIES

Survivor families come to therapy around a whole range of present-day problems usually having to do with their children (e.g., delinquent behavior, substance abuse, school failure, depression, psychosis, family violence, and problems of separation and leaving home). Adult children, creating their own families and having children of their own, present postpartum reactions, problems of parenting, and difficulties in establishing boundaries between their new families and their families of origin, prompting them to renegotiate their relationship with their parents in order to further differentiate. Rarely do families come to treatment presenting problems explictly related to the parents' Holocaust experience.

Treatment approaches with Holocaust survivor families range from those which deal primarily with the family's present problems and transactions to those which seek to improve family functioning by dealing with the unresolved issues of the family's past. Thus, they differ in the extent to which they highlight the Holocaust and bring it into a sharper focus in the process of family therapy. In our work, we attempt to incorporate both approaches.

Engagement

Survivor parents who have not pursued therapy for themselves are usually reluctant to cooperate in the treatment of their children. The normal fear of being labeled as bad parents and blamed for the problems of the child is compounded by their intense attempt to deny that they may have been harmed interminably, that their ineffectiveness as parents is related to their war experience.[16] The children often collude in this denial in order to protect their parents. The collusion of silence may further extend to the therapist: In seeking a Jewish therapist with similar background or one who is intimately aware of the Holocaust, with the hope that if it is known and understood by all, the subject will not have to be raised. In other instances, families will seek the same such therapist with the implicit or explicit wish that he or she will facilitate communication about the Holocaust.

Joining with survivor families requires the therapist's skillful use of empathy, authority, and power. The family, suspicious of outside authorities, may perceive therapy as an intrusion in their private sphere. The parents' ultimate fear is that the authority will separate them from their children. On the other hand, when the parents are unable to assert their authority in effective ways with their children, that is, by combining caring with limit setting, they attempt to recruit the therapist as an authority to control, punish, or frighten the child.

Most importantly, the therapist must show a tremendous respect and empathy for the parents' Holocaust experience, but must be careful not to be inducted into the family's perpetual mourning. It is essential that he gain their trust, and may obtain it more readily by tracking and observing the transactions instead of challenging them. The therapist may take a position of humility rather than expertise, as in the following statement, "I cannot possibly imagine what it must have been like for you; you have lost so many people beyond what I could ever imagine—You're right, it is beyond understanding."

When providing the family with a new definition, or a reframing of the problem, it is often more effective to define the symptom in interpersonal terms and connect it to the family's historical experience. In this way, the reframing presents a more expanded view of the meaning and function of the symptom. For example, "Your son thinks that he can only equal you and deserve your attention if he suffers as much as you have. Yet how could he ever rival a father who has survived such a horrible experience and suffered so many losses?" Though at this stage, therapy is not aimed at exploring the parents' past, the past will transpire through the sessions and surface in various contexts.

Restructuring the Family: Enmeshment

In the beginning of treatment, when tracking the symptoms in the family, the therapist will hear the historical antecedents, yet may choose to remain focused on dysfunctional interactions in the family that maintain the problem, and intervene at the level of organization, communication, or symptom relief. In certain cases, the family's reality is so centered on and mesmerized by the Holocaust issue, that it will need to be neutralized in order to deal with the interpersonal problems at hand. The following exchange took place in one family session:

Son: My mother doesn't think that I can take care of myself. I am 26 and she needs me to remain her baby.

Therapist: Then teach her how to treat you as an adult.

Son: I can't teach a European woman who knows it all, saw it all, and has been through it all.

Therapist: Your mother is not the Jewish history.

Son: My mother is very strong. She survived the camps, my father's death. . . .
Therapist: If she is so strong, maybe she doesn't need you.[17]

In such a case it was necessary to demystify the parent as a Jewish mythical figure so that parent and child could relate to each other with a wider range of emotional expression. It enabled the son to present himself as a competent adult whose achievements also had meaning.

As with other enmeshed families, structural work with survivor families entails delineating and strengthening individual and subsystem boundaries, realigning cross-generational alliances, and facilitating communication between family members.[18] In working with Hasidic and Orthodox Holocaust survivor families, the strategic techniques of symptom substitution, hypnotic and relaxation maneuvers, faith-healing strategies, and dream induction have been found useful.[19]

In the following case vignette, direct structural approaches were insufficient to deal with the crisis of drug abuse in a survivor family. The therapists had reached an impasse and, as a last resort, used confrontation, paradox, and restraining. The K. family is composed of mother, father, and their only son, Mark, age 30, who has been a drug addict for the past 11 years. The parents' despair over their son's repeated relapses provided the grounds for their engagement in therapy. They were told that their son needed all the help he could get and that the one thing missing in his previous treatments was the opportunity to let his parents help. Parents and son live together in an atmosphere of tension, sadness, and mutual surveillance. The father is detached and peripheral to the family, working long hours away from home. The mother protected him from knowing about Mark's drug problem for years and now they are in conflict over how to handle him. Mark is depressed, unemployed, and socially isolated. His interaction with his father is one of deference and defiance. Both parents are concentration camp survivors; the father is the sole survivor of his family, the mother survived with one brother. Their son, Mark, is literally all they have. Mark was meant to be a symbol of life, an act of courage on the part of the parents in their struggle to affirm life, but now he is destroying himself as if his life were not worth living.

Mark's drug use has kept him in a dependent position and has absolved him of adult responsibilities and of his failure to separate. Concurrently, it has reinforced his parents' feeling of the necessity to take care of him as a helpless child and has legitimized their overinvolvement and enmeshment. The father criticizes his son for his drug use but covertly supports it by leaving money around the house. This time the mother caught Mark stealing again, and as a consequence asked him to move out of the house. For the first time the father did not interfere, but since Mark's departure he has thrown himself even more into his work. He has been depressed and in mourning as if his son had died, despite the fact that Mark is staying with relatives and is in contact with his parents.

The following session, the parents came alone. The father is enraged at the therapists for not only having failed to save his son, but for now supporting his wife in her maintaining a firm stance not to let his son return home unless he resumes treatment. For the father, taking that stance is synonymous with giving up entirely on his son. The focus of the session at this point is to redefine the problem from the son's drug use to the binding dynamics of the family that prevent separation. The addiction is embedded in the family relationships and will continue unless the parental and child subsystems become less fused. The therapists then proceed to make the bind between father and son overt and explicit:

Therapist 1: Your wife will survive because she has her brother, but you may not. If your son destroys himself, he'll destroy you, because he's all that you've got. If your son destroys himself, you won't have anything to live for anymore.

When the father is asked to support his wife and be firm with his son, he vigorously resists:

Father: You don't want me to give him shelter?

Therapist 1: You are to decide if you want to let your son run and destroy your life.

Father: He doesn't destroy my life, he destroys his own.

Therapist 1: But your son is your life. If he destroys himself, he destroys you.

Mother: We have to influence him. We can't continue to indulge him.

Father: That means not to let him in? That's impossible.

Confronting the father was not effective because all he could hear was that he must give up his son; separation for him is synonymous with total loss.

Father: If you've lost everything and this is all you have left, you want to hold on to it.

Therapist 2: I wonder who we are to say to a father to give up on his son. Because I think for people who have lost so many loved ones, beyond what I could ever imagine bearing. . . . Maybe this story should go on as it is.

Father: It can't go on, because then I'm killing him, and I don't want to kill him.

Therapist 2: What choice do you have?

Father: Let him suffer a little bit. When people suffer, they realize there is another way to live.

Therapist 2: You're a man with great experience in suffering.

Father: I was young, only 19.

Therapist 2: That's when Mark started.

Father: I had no choice, don't compare.

Therapist 2: I wonder if Mark knows he has a choice. For you I can only think of three choices. I can't come up with any good one. In any one of them you lose your son. If you take a hard line, and refuse to see him, and have no contact, then you lose your son. If he keeps doing as much drugs as he has been doing, he could die and you'd lose your son. And if he gets well and gets off drugs and moves on with his life, you'll lose your son.

Father: That I don't mind.

Therapist 2: But Mark doesn't know that. He knows you can't bear to lose him, and he doesn't feel he has a choice.

Father: Which way is better? If he goes on his own, his life is better.

Therapist 2: I don't know if you can do that.

Father: I have to. I have to do it, its my only chance.

By increasing the proximity between the son and his parents, the chances for disengagement were increased. The family must develop a more viable structure, one that does not require the child to sacrifice himself. Mark's self-destructive behavior is intimately tied to the unresolved mourning in his family. In this intervention, the therapists joined with the father's dilemma enabling him to distinguish between separation and death; for him, leaving home had been equated with the tragic death of his family. Though the parents did not deliberately conceal their losses, they were unaware of their significance vis-à-vis Mark's behavior. Further therapeutic work would be aimed at helping the parents reinvest in their own lives and in each other.[20]

Facing the Past

An important component of the treatment of Holocaust survivor families involves dealing with unresolved issues of the past, such as survivor guilt, loss, delayed mourning, and life disruption. The sharing of the parents' Holocaust experience with their children, though not in itself the purpose of family therapy, can be a unifying experience for the family and is an important part of the process of mourning. It can reduce the mutual protection between parents and children and help the family out of an atmosphere of secrecy, by demystifying and clarifying important elements of the family's history and its losses. It thus opens up new possibilities for intimacy between family members and can lead to mutually empathetic intergenerational exchanges.[21] However in families in which the survivor parents were extremely traumatized, delving into the Holocaust may be too disorganizing and painful and therefore contraindicated.

Survivor families that have been able to make a successful adaptation maintain loyalty to their lost loved ones by embracing life, by commemorating the dead, by bearing witness to the Holocaust, and by identifying with the dead through values and social action rather than through guilt. Similarly, therapy is aimed at helping the family remain connected with its past in ways that are not detrimental to the family's present functioning. Strategies for mourning include helping the survivors transform their guilt in relation to past loved ones into a sense of responsibility,[22] turning the guilt into action, for example, by doing good deeds for others, carrying out the hopes and wishes of the dead, and attending collective rituals such as survivor gatherings.

Rituals aid the process of mourning, and may be prescribed in treatment to help the family concretize transitions and move on. Through state institutionalized rituals and memorials, survivors have been able to express openly a continuity with their past and feel less isolated. For many survivors, Israel is a symbol of rebirth. In one family, the parents took their children to Israel to commemorate their lost families. The parents were to choose a site to engrave the names of their dead relatives—a genealogical tree on a memorial stone—such as in museums and synagogues. The stone would symbolize the endurance and continuity of the family. From then on, there was a site where the family and its future generations could commemorate their ancestors.

In the following case vignette, helping a single parent mother deal with her Holocaust past was a crucial step in the treatment of mother and daughter. Mrs. M. came to therapy with her 13-year-old daughter complaining about their bitter and sometimes violent quarrels. Mrs. M. had recently separated from her second husband, and now lived alone with her daughter, Joan. Joan was a bright teenager who had begun to fail in school. Mrs. M. was intrusive with her daughter and could not tolerate the normal assertions of autonomy of her teenaged daughter. When she was 13, Mrs. M. had been in a concentration camp where she lost both her parents. She would exclaim during the sessions, "If my mother were alive, I would get down on the ground and kiss her feet." Mrs. M. expected similar respect and gratitude from her daughter, who in turn vehemently rebelled against such excessive expectations. The initial work in treatment dealt with the enmeshment between mother and daughter by establishing clearer boundaries, improving communication, and reinforcing the mother's competence as a parent. The therapist helped them to connect in a different way by supporting their interactions and communications around appropriate mother-daughter issues, rather than their constant bickering. When seen individually, Mrs. M. eventually began speaking about her Holocaust experience. The therapist helped her establish the connection between her own difficulties in being a parent to a teenage daughter and the loss of her mother and subsequent feelings of deprivation during her teenage years in the camps. After exploring her Holocaust past with the therapist, he encouraged her to join a multigenerational discussion group between survivors and their children. This became an important vehicle for opening communication about her own past with her daughter. She was able to make a connection between her experience in the camps and her present demands on her daughter which enabled her daughter to come closer rather than avoid her. The therapy combined structural and multigenerational work with the family to help the mother find more appropriate ways of parenting her teenage daughter.[23]

The grief in survivor families not only afflicts its members with pain, but also leaves the family in a state of confusion and disorganization. Family therapy deals with the rearrangement of transactional patterns, distribution of family functions and roles, as well as improvement of the intergenerational dialogue.

CONCLUSION

The distinctive patterns of transactions in Holocaust survivor families must be seen in light of the dominant family motif—the restoration of the "lost" family and the undoing of the destruction.[24] The high degree of enmeshment in these families is a direct consequence of the powerful events of the past and of the ways in which the past impinges on the family's present life. The child holds a central place in the survivor family as a symbol of life and provider of meaning for the parents. The families are characterized by overinvolvement and over-protectiveness between parents and children making the process of separation difficult at different stages in the family's development.

Family therapy with survivor families requires that the therapist be aware of the ways in which the family's Holocaust past intensifies its enmeshment. Therapy is aimed at helping the family find adaptive ways to maintain family cohesion and loyalty that do not preempt the growth of its individual members. It thus combines structural and strategic work to lessen the family's enmeshment with interventions that help the family members come to terms with their past.

NOTES

The authors would like to express their appreciation to Randy Gerson, Ph.D., Emma Genijovitch, M.A., Olga Silverstein, M.S.W., and Jill Pliskin, M.S.W. for their helpful comments and contributions. This chapter is dedicated to the memory of Hillel Klein, M.D.

1. Hillel Klein, "Families of Holocaust Survivors in the Kibbutz: Psychological Studies." *International Psychiatry Clinics* 8 (1971):67–92; ibid., "Holocaust Survivors in Kibbutzim: Readaptation and Reintegration." *Israel Annals of Psychiatry and Related Disciplines* 10 (1972):78–91; ibid., "Children of the Holocaust: Mourning and Bereavement," in E. J. Anthony and C. Koupernik, Eds., *The Child in His Family* (New York: John Wiley, 1973); John Sigal, "Second Generation Effects of Massive Psychic Trauma," in H. Krystal, Ed., *Psychic Traumatization* (Boston: Little Brown, 1971); Robert Krell, "Holocaust Families: The Survivors and Their Children," *Comprehensive Psychiatry* 20, no. 6 (1979):560–568; ibid., "Family Therapy with Children of Concentration Camp Survivors," *Americal Journal of Psychotherapy* 36, no. 4 (1982):513–522; Yael Danieli, "Families of Survivors of the Nazi Holocaust: Some Short Term and Long Term Effects," in C. D. Spielberger, I. G. Sarason, and N. Milgram, Eds., *Stress and Anxiety*, Vol. 8 *Psychological Stress and Adjustment in Times of War and Peace* (New York: McGraw Hill/Hemisphere, 1981); Shamai Davidson, "The Clinical Effects of Massive Psychic Trauma in Families of Holocaust Survivors," *Journal of Marital and Family Therapy* 6, no. 1 (1980): 11–24; Axel Russell, "Late Psychosocial Consequences of the Holocaust Experience on the Survivor Families: The Second Generation," *International Journal of Family Psychiatry* 3, no. 3 (1982):375–399.

2. Leslie Rabkin, "Countertransference in the Extreme Situation: The Family Therapy of Survivor Families," in L. R. Wolberg and M. L. Aronson, Eds., *Group Therapy* (New York: Stratton International Corporation, 1975); James Framo, Panel Discussion at the Holocaust Survivor Family Symposium, 3rd International Family Therapy Conference, Tel Aviv, Israel, July 1979; Maleta Pilcz, "Understanding the Survivor Family: An Acknowledgement of the Positive Dimensions of the Holocaust Legacy," in L. Y. Steinetz and D. Szonyi, Eds., *Living after the Holocaust* (New York: Block Publishing,

1979); Lloyd Siegel, "Holocaust Survivors in Hasidic and Ultra-Orthodox Jewish Populations," *Journal of Contemporary Psychotherapy* 11, no. 1 (1980):15–31; Z. Zlotogorski, "Offspring of Concentration Camp Survivors: The Relationship of Perception of Family Cohesion and Adaptability to Levels of Ego Functioning," *Comprehensive Psychiatry* 24 (1983):345–354; Israel Zwerling, Lenore Podietz, et al., "Engagement in Families of Holocaust Survivors," *Journal of Marital and Family Therapy* 10, no. 1 (1984):43–51; Sophie Kav Venaki, Arie Nadler, and Hadas Gershoni, "Sharing the Holocaust Experience: Communication Behaviors and Their Consequences in Families of Ex-partisans and Ex-prisoners of Concentration Camps," *Family Process* 24 (1985):272–280; Susan Rose and John Garske, "Family Environment, Adjustment, and Coping among Children of Holocaust Survivors," *American Journal of Orthopsychiatry* 57, no. 3 (1987):332–344.

3. Danieli, "Families of Survivors of the Nazi Holocaust: Some Short Term and Long Term Effects," p. 406.

4. Hillel Klein, *Survival and Revival*, unpublished manuscript.

5. Danieli, "Families of Survivors of the Nazi Holocaust: Some Short Term and Long Term Effects," p. 406.

6. Axel Russell, "Late Psychosocial Consequences in Concentration Camp Survivor Families," *American Journal of Orthopsychiatry* 48, no. 4 (July 1973):611–613; Davidson, "The Clinical Effects of Massive Psychic Trauma in Families of Holocaust Survivors," p. 13.

7. Zwerling, Podietz, et al. "Engagement in Families of Holocaust Survivors," 43–51; Rose and Garske, "Family Environment, Adjustment, and Coping among Children of Holocaust Survivors," pp. 332–344.

8. John Sigal, D. Silver, V. Rakoff, and B. Ellin, "Some Second Generation Effects of Survival of the Nazi Persecution," *American Journal of Orthopsychiatry* 43 (1973):320–327; Zwerling, Podietz, et al., "Engagement in Families of Holocaust Survivors," pp. 43–51; Klein, *Survival and Revival*, unpublished manuscript.

9. Olga Silverstein, personal communication, 1988.

10. Danieli, "Families of Survivors of the Nazi Holocaust: Some Short Term and Long Term Effects," p. 413.

11. Phyllis Cohen, personal communication, 1988.

12. Krell, "Holocaust Families: The Survivors and Their Children," p. 473.

13. Davidson, "The Clinical Effects of Massive Psychic Trauma in Families of Holocaust Survivors"; Krell, "Holocaust Families: The Survivors and Their Children," p. 14.

14. Helen Epstein, *Children of the Holocaust: Conversations with Sons and Daughters of Survivors* (New York: Putnam, 1979), p. 143.

15. Klein, *Survival and Revival*, unpublished manuscript.

16. Russell, "Late Psychosocial Consequences," 1973; Robert Krell, "Family Therapy with Children of Concentration Camp Survivors," *American Journal of Psychotherapy* 36, no. 4 (1982):513–522.

17. Salvador Minuchin, clinical consultation, 1987.

18. Salvador Minuchin, *Families and Family Therapy* (Cambridge, MA: Harvard University Press, 1974).

19. Siegel, "Holocaust Survivors in Hasidic and Ultra-Orthodox Jewish Populations," pp. 15–31.

20. Jill Pliskin, clinical consultation, 1987.
21. Eva Fogelman, personal communication, 1988.
22. Klein, *Survival and Revival*, unpublished manuscript.
23. Ed Ross, clinical consultation, 1988.
24. Klein, "Children of the Holocaust: Mourning and Bereavement," p. 394.

V

Pastoral Perspectives

9

The Holocaust Survivor in the Synagogue Community: Issues and Perspectives on Pastoral Care

RABBI GERALD L. SKOLNIK

INTRODUCTION

Given the staggering amount of historical, clinical, documentary, and even fictional material that has been generated by the Nazi Holocaust of Jews during World War II, the status of the survivor in the postwar synagogue community has thus far remained curiously free from systematic exploration. Even cursorily undertaken, such an endeavor readily yields substantive—even primal—issues which, though in some ways unique to the microcosmic Jewish world called "the synagogue," also touch more generally the very core and essence of the Jewish Holocaust experience. Both psychodynamically and spiritually, the transition from a community in which the "primordial struggle for survival"[1] was the most significant commonality of its members, to one more commonly characterized by a shared faith in God and His redemptive powers, is a treacherous one indeed. To be sure, not all survivors even wished to attempt that transition after their liberation, and of those who did, a significant number ultimately met with frustration and failure.

The purpose of this chapter is to explore, on both theoretical and practical levels, the nature and experience of those survivors who have succeeded, and how their status as survivors continues to impact on them, as members of the synagogue community, and on those charged with providing them with pastoral services, most especially rabbis. My perspective is that of a congregational rabbi who, though sensitive to the psychodynamic issues necessarily a part of such a process, is neither a psychoanalyst nor a therapist. It is not my intention to provide a new insight into the survivor qua survivor, about which much of great value has already been written.[2] It is, rather, to enhance our understanding of the survivor as he/she relates to a clearly defined and limited subgroup of today's

Jewish world, namely the synagogue, and to clarify the unique issues generated by this interaction.

Because of the relative dearth of material on this particular aspect of the survivor experience, this is not so much a research paper—that is to say, the gathering together for scholarly purposes of others' contributions to the issues at hand—as it is the author's own perspectives on the two major issues previously defined: what it means to be a survivor in the synagogue community, and what it means to minister to them. Inasmuch as all synagogues, regardless of how different, share certain essential commonalities and dynamics, it is hoped that this chapter may provide some theoretical and practical guidance to others whose task it is to teach and heal within the context of the synagogue world.

Just as it is possible from an emotionally detached and fundamental perspective to view the Holocaust as "a set of historical events whose record comprises a singular text,"[3] so, too, is it possible for a rabbi to see the Holocaust survivors in his/her[4] synagogue community as one of a number of subgroups in the greater synagogue family. Today's rabbi ministers to a congregation characterized by heterogeneity of previously unknown proportions: young singles, older singles, single parents, young married couples, older married couples, widows and widowers, and many more. Each of these smaller units represents from a systems-analysis perspective, a special interest group with particular concerns and needs, for which it lobbies when it deems fit or necessary. Survivors can be understood as yet another of these special interest groups, contributing to the greater dynamic of synagogue life through the assertion of their own needs and concerns, which may or may not come into conflict with the interests of the other subgroups.

Yet obviously, Holocaust survivors can no more be seriously regarded by the rabbi as "just another group" in the matrix of congregational synagogue life than the Holocaust itself can be regarded as merely a "set of historical events" by the Jew. The sheer enormity of the event, with all of its attendant implications, virtually demands that those who have actually lived through it enjoy some special status within the synagogue world. Were this enhanced status to derive from compassion alone, it would surely be reason enough, but the phenomenon is a far more complex one. It is rooted in the catastrophic nature of the Holocaust itself, and at least partially in the fact that the survivor, regardless of his ability or inclination to share his wartime experiences with others, is a personal witness to that catastrophe. As an interpreter of Jewish history and its meaning, the rabbi has, in the survivor in his congregation, an invaluable primary source, his very own Josephus,[5] whose intimate knowledge of what actually transpired enriches his *own* ability to both understand and teach the most difficult chapter in all of Jewish history.

Ultimately, however, the Holocaust survivor in the synagogue community is of greatest significance because of what he represents symbolically, on a level far beyond mere access to primary historical data. Good—no matter how bruised, battered, or abused in the process—has outlived evil—no matter how strong or demonic. The power of faith—no matter how sorely tested—has proved stronger than death itself. By his very presence at and participation in a synagogue service, the survivor is a powerful symbol of God having survived Auschwitz and not having died there, as philosopher Richard Rubenstein has claimed.[6] Both to the rabbi and to the laity of the synagogue, the survivor represents the ultimate example of what Max Dimont referred to as "the indestructable Jew,"[7] buffeted and even victimized by the vicissitudes of historical experience, yet somehow persevering against all odds. He also represents continuity, on the most primary level, of Jewish existence and history, but, just as significant, also of the ancient covenantal relationship between the Jew and God. If the Holocaust represents the coming to pass of the dire biblical forebodings of Leviticus[8] and Deuteronomy,[9] then the survivor represents God's promise of remembrance after the cataclysm:

Then will I remember my covenant with Jacob; I will remember also my covenant with Isaac, and also my covenant with Abraham; and I will remember the land.[10]

By professing faith after the Holocaust, the survivor in essence legitimizes, validates, and fuels the faith of the other members of the congregation. If the survivor can believe in God, they might reason, so then must we whose faith struggle has been so much less existentially terrifying and challenging.

Yet, given all that the synagogue-affiliated Holocaust survivor represents conceptually, existentially, symbolically, and even pedagogically, his relationship with the synagogue world would be only partially revealed were this study not to focus as well on those factors which mitigate *against* the success of that relationship. They are as fundamentally compelling as any of the theoretically positive dynamics which have previously been discussed, and reflect, from the survivor's perspective, a profound, deeply internalized ambivalence about the nature of his experiences during the war years themselves.

At the heart of these issues—indeed, at their spiritual epicenter—lies the seemingly irresolvable discussion about who can claim the right to call himself a survivor. Many who lived through the war years in Europe somehow avoiding incarceration in the concentration camps exhibit great difficulty in allowing themselves to be categorized as survivors, owing to their own perceptions of "not having lived through the worst." In the organization of a Yom Hashoa[11] program last year in my own synagogue, a letter was sent to the entire congregation soliciting information as to who among our members was a survivor. A very small fraction of the many survivors in the community responded, with a similar result from an attempt to find someone willing to speak about his experiences during the war. Again and again, the question was posed: "Am I really a survivor? I would feel ashamed speaking of my experiences—I didn't suffer enough. Ask 'him,' or 'her'—they had it much worse." How sad it is that even within the synagogue community in which, as previously mentioned, he or she should be an honored member, the survivor can exhibit such terrible difficulty giving expression to a legacy of suffering. It only serves to exacerbate the survivor's suffering and guilt even more. It should, of course, be added that, within the "legitimate" survivor community, there are also those men and women who consciously wish to "lose" their survivor label, or status, in the greater unit of the synagogue family. Their hope is of finding a greater peace of mind outside the often obsessive world inhabited by survivors, whose main social and recreational outlets are, as often as not, each other. Needless to say, this phenomenon serves to complicate the rabbi's task of isolating the survivor group within the synagogue for any constructive purpose, whether programmatic or therapeutic.

In addition to this very fundamental issue of group definition, there exist a number of dynamics that serve as powerful counter-transferrential forces in the relationship between the survivor and the synagogue. The first among them to be considered must be the difficulties involved in accepting the rabbi—any rabbi—as a legitimate authority figure after the Holocaust.

The contemporary rabbinate is, to be sure, an institution in transition in many ways. Some changes are empirically observable, such as the growing numbers of women being ordained, and others are less obvious to the naked eye, such as the slow but steadily increasing emphasis on a pulpit rabbinate which is more pastorally oriented than 10 or 20 years ago. When all is said and done, however, and differences in denomination, style, and nuance have been set aside, the rabbi, as a professional, is unavoidably an official symbol of God and faith— both of which, to the minds of many survivors, failed during the Holocaust.

That a believing Jew might verbalize his anger against God for His perceived impotence, as it were, is not a new phenomenon. More than 1800 years ago, during the period of the Hadrianic persecutions in ancient Palestine following the failed revolt of Bar-Kokhba against the Romans in the years 132–135 BCE, Rabbi Yismael, a scholarly and pious contemporary of Rabbi Akiva and, like him, soon to be martyred,[12] uttered the following scathing indictment of God in a comment on a biblical text:

'Who is like unto Thee among the mighty, O Lord' (Exodus 15:11) . . . who is like unto Thee among the silent ones, O Lord, who is like unto Thee, who though seeing the insult heaped upon Thy children, yet keepest silence . . .[13]

It should be obvious from this rather startling text that personal piety, even to the extent of involvement in the scholarly rabbinic establishment of one's time, has never stood in the way of a Jew communicating his anger and/or frustrations to God in a direct and unmistakable way. Certainly, the literature of Hasidism is replete with stories of angry Masters "taking God to task," as it were, for the plight of the Jewish people.[14]

With the gradual evolution of the modern rabbinate over the course of the past few centuries into its current sociological model, the rabbi has increasingly come to be perceived by his followers as God's representative, if not spokesperson, with the inevitable transferrential results, both for better and for worse. The person who perceives himself to be blessed may wish to reward the rabbi (and through him, the synagogue) for his own good fortune, while the person who perceives himself as the victim of cosmic injustice may displace his anger at God onto His nearest representative—usually the rabbi. To confirm the validity of this latter phenomenon, one need only speak to any rabbi who has helped more than a few families through a period of devastating personal loss. Rare is the rabbi who has not, at one time or another, been lashed out at in a thoroughly inappropriate and undeserved way by the mourner who perceives him as God's "agent," somehow responsible for his—the mourner's—own misfortune.

If this particular dynamic is so often operative in the normal routines of offering pastoral care, then, as the rabbis of old might have said, *Al ahat kammah V'hammah*—how much more so is it the case with regard to the Holocaust survivor. To be sure, the survivor's main "problem" is with God, and not the rabbi. But, as mentioned earlier, the rabbi is by definition a proponent of the power of faith, and what can the rabbi—*particularly* the nonsurvivor rabbi— really say to a survivor about faith and its parameters? Who is whose teacher? Essentially, the rabbi stands at the symbolic head of a larger, symbolic faith construct all of which, even for the most pious, proved largely ineffective as a tool for survival during the Holocaust. The synagogue-affiliated survivor represents a constant reminder of the existential tenuousness of the religious enterprise as a whole.

Related but not identical is the issue of the extended synagogue family. Other than merely seeking a place to pray, the modern Jew seeks in the synagogue a community: a group of people with whom he shares not only a shared history as a Jew, but also a shared destiny. Almost by definition, the Jew who affiliates with a synagogue becomes a member of its extended family, sharing life cycle events with other members, as well as the sociability which is an inevitable result of an active synagogue membership.

Yet, for the survivor, the issue of embracing other synagogue members as part of his extended family can, even if only subliminally, be a difficult concept to accept. As a number of recent books have pointed out,[15] the degree to which the American Jewish community—both individuals and leadership—asserted itself vigorously on behalf of the doomed Jews of Europe is at best a matter of some scholarly contention. It would be neither an exaggeration nor a new insight to characterize the aggressive assertiveness so typical of today's Jewish communal efforts on behalf of Soviet Jewry as owing, at least in some measure, to unresolved guilt over failure to be more assertive during the years of World War II. Accepting the middle-aged American synagogue Jew as a member of his extended family implies, by definition, that the survivor has made his peace with the nonsurvivor members of his Jewish generation, and that simply is not universally the case. Profoundly troubling questions about a recent history which they decidedly do *not* share in common linger stubbornly, not terribly far beneath the surface of many survivors' minds. Who are these people that I would call my family, and why can I/should I trust them? How can I allow myself to become immersed with them in the trivia of today's Jewish life when there are so many other substantial issues that can never be adequately resolved between us? Where do I fit into today's nonsurvivor synagogue world?

How, one might well ask, do these questions get articulated? In what behavior patterns do they find expression? Although a number of answers will be alluded to in the section which follows, it should be understood that the same principle that generally governs how the therapist understands his client is also operative in the realm of rabbinic counseling. The presenting problem is rarely the problem. The vexing issues that lie at the heart of whatever pathology the survivor brings to the synagogue world are rarely, if ever, specifically articulated. The challenge confronting the rabbi in such an instance is like that confronting the therapist. He must see beyond the presenting problems or issues to the larger concerns of the client, in this case the survivor. The rabbi's task is to frame them in an acceptable way, and to address them together with the survivor.

As was discussed at the beginning of this chapter, my perspective as an author is that of a congregational rabbi who, though sensitive to the psychodynamics involved in the interchange between survivor and synagogue is nonetheless not a therapist. At this point, however, having given expression to some of those dynamics which are operative independent of the particular rabbinic personalities involved, it is obviously necessary to discuss the other variable in this complicated relationship: namely, the rabbi himself.

Just as it can be said that in any encounter between two people each contributes in equal measure to the nature of the relationship that develops between them, so too can it be said that the rabbi—both as an individual and as a symbol of the congregation—is an equal partner in the relationship that develops between survivor and synagogue. Certainly the rabbi brings his own counter-transferrential dynamics into that relationship. He may indeed perceive the survivors within his synagogue as a uniquely—and sometimes frustratingly—single-minded interest group. On some occasions, it may manifest itself in an almost manic concern for the security of the State of Israel; on others, in tremendous anxiety about intermarriage and assimilation here in America; on yet others, in a persistently articulated perception that the synagogue is "not doing enough to remember." Perhaps the rabbi himself falls into the category discussed earlier— a nonsurvivor member of the survivors' generation, for whom the presence of survivors in the congregation represents an unremitting guilt-ridden stab of conscience.

Ultimately, however, what I as a rabbi born *after* the Holocaust have found to be the single greatest disadvantage which the rabbi brings to the survivor/ synagogue relationship was articulated more than 10 years ago in a different context by Elie Wiesel. What he said, simply and eloquently, was: "Those who have not lived through the experience will never know; those who have will never tell; not really, not completely."[16]

Fundamentally, like all other Jews, the rabbi, too, is charged with the painful and invariably difficult challenge of remembering that which he himself has not experienced, but has only learned about. Under most circumstances, the average Jew must and does struggle to fulfill this modern command rooted in the ancient biblical precept concerning Amalek.[17] After all, how can one remember that which he can never truly know, and which no one can adequately describe to him?

But for the rabbi, this challenge is made all the more troublesome because his charge is not merely to remember the unknown. Upon him devolves as well the primary responsibility for *transmitting* that unattainable knowledge to other Jews who look to him for guidance. The rabbi's task, as a teacher and interpreter of Jewish history, is to make sense out of the Holocaust. Yet obviously, even with all the objective data that has been gathered together in countless volumes, "making sense" out of the Holocaust is not a feasible or reasonable goal for rabbi or layperson. Essentially, the nonsurvivor rabbi, just like the layperson, will never know, never understand, even though he may teach.

Just how true this last statement is became brutally apparent to me only a year ago when, in the context of a rabbinic trip to Europe and Israel, I had the opportunity to spend three days in Poland. Like most Jews of my age and background, Auschwitz had always been for me a series of horrible mental images generated by black-and-white still pictures and newsreels, and the Holocaust as a whole was, for all that I had read and been taught about it, essentially an abstraction. After all, who among us—survivors included—can really conceptualize what 6 million dead means? "The 6 million" had, in my universe of discourse, always been used interchangably with "the Holocaust," and just as the term Holocaust conjured up a wide variety of graphic images, so, too, did "the 6 million." Auschwitz was, within this abstraction, more an idealized expression of evil than an actual murder factory of mortar and brick.

Being in Poland and visiting the Auschwitz complex itself—walking through its main gate boldly emblazoned with the words "*Arbeit Macht Frei*,"[18] standing on the rubble of the crematoria at Birkenau or in one of its barracks, seeing the huge exhibit cases literally filled with human hair, eyeglasses, toothbrushes, suitcases (with names and addresses on them), and, most personally devastating to me, baby shoes and broken dolls—forever stripped me of my ability to escape the horror of the Holocaust by relating to it as an abstraction—as "the 6 million." To stand on that ground was to intuit, if not to know, one infinitesimal fraction of the horror that was, and to be transformed forever.

Just how radical and traumatic that transformation was became apparent to me the very morning after coming home from the trip. As luck would have it, I was to return on a Friday afternoon, having to deliver a sermon in synagogue the very next morning, so a few hours of the long plane ride home were spent preparing my remarks. Barely five minutes into the sermon, which dealt extensively with my experiences in Poland, I began to cry uncontrollably in front of the entire congregation. I, who had not cried in at least 20 years, and who considered myself in total professional control, found myself virtually mute—

incapable of transmitting my own sense of horror of the place. At the Kiddush[19] following services, though certainly everyone was sympathetic to what obviously had been a difficult experience for me, the embraces of the survivors were the warmest, and the longest. As often as not, not a word was exhanged between us, but the look in their eyes made me begin to understand the true nature of my transformation. I had, for a terrifying moment, been granted a glimmer of insight into what it meant to be one of them. No longer was I "the rabbi born after the Holocaust," incapable virtually by definition of understanding their past and their present. I had, through some vicarious and painfully cathartic process, *become* one of them on that morning. Like them, I had been reduced to silence by the sheer horror of the images that flooded my mind, and my tears had spoken more eloquently than my words ever could. Interestingly, before that trip, a number of the survivors in my synagogue had questioned me somewhat skeptically, even caustically, about why I had any desire to visit Poland. My reply was always the same—I wanted to know what it felt like to stand on the ground of Auschwitz, to match those deeply ingrained black-and-white images with the actual place. Only now—having enabled them to witness the traumatic spectacle of *their own rabbi* being reduced to tears on the Bimah of *their* synagogue, describing *their* indescribable experience—had I finally established a truly significant and meaningful connection with them. Previous Yom Hashoa programs at my synagogue had drawn perhaps 400 or 500 people at most. This past year's program, which featured my own slide presentation about the trip to Poland, drew some 1200 people, with more survivor participation by far than ever before. Something dramatic had happened, to be sure, and the nature of my relationship with the survivor community in my own synagogue would never be the same again.

Regardless of the domain in which it is endeavored, the attempt to draw broad, sweeping conclusions from very specific experiences is always a dangerous one. Particularly with regard to survivors, one must be even more acutely aware of the tenuousness of this process, since no two survivors share exactly the same wartime history, and *each* of their experiences, because of what it represents both Jewishly and universally, is actually deserving of its own set of criteria by which it might be adequately evaluated. For the rabbi, however, as the primary pastoral caregiver to the synagogue-affiliated survivor, there are a number of practical suggestions that merit careful consideration, particularly in light of all the aforementioned forces serving independently to make the relationship a difficult one. None of them, either alone or in concert with the others, guarantee the rabbi a "breakthrough" with his survivor community. They do, however, serve to sensitize him to those issues which are most key in the survivor community.

The first and most important of these guidelines is simply to listen. The agenda is not so much to talk about the Holocaust, but rather to listen carefully and patiently to those who survived it, and to allow one's silence to be interpreted as a respectful expression of solidarity with those people who have suffered so greatly. Though humility is becoming in any human being, and most of us strive for it, it is not a quality universally associated with rabbis. Far too often they are forced, in the context of their work, to be articulate and even outspoken on issues about which they know little. As much as silence or terseness of expression may sometimes serve as a vehicle for conveying the survivor's sense of horror at his own past, it can and should also be the vehicle for rabbinic validation of the survivor's ongoing trauma. When visiting a mourner in his home during the shivah period,[20] one does not speak until spoken to by the mourner. The mourning of the survivor is unlike any other in the Jewish community. It may be 40 or 50 years since his loss, but for so many the horror stubbornly persists as intensely—at least in flashes—as for a mourner during shivah. The best therapy for such a synagogue-affiliated survivor is to feel that his community understands and respects not merely his ongoing trauma, but also its uniqueness. And it is the rabbi who, as the symbolic head of the synagogue community, is uniquely suited to fulfill this function. Find the survivors in your congregation, gather them in a room or meet with them individually and encourage them to share their story and their burden with you—the quiet but ultimate empathic *and* sympathetic listener. There is no suitable rabbinic wisdom to be offered to the person who has been through hell and survived—there is only comfort, and the validation of pain.

The second guideline is closely related to the first, but it stands on its own as well. One might think that it would go without saying, but it does not—at least not to the extent that it is meant here. One of the best and most effective steps a rabbi can take to minister more effectively to the survivors in his community is to learn more about their experience. Learning can take on many forms. It may mean reading books and articles, seeing relevant movies, or, as just mentioned, listening to survivor testimony. What I have discovered, however, as you have read, is that no book, movie, or testimony can substitute for the experience of walking the grounds of Auschwitz, or standing on the rubble of the crematoria in Birkenau, or encountering the grotesquely inappropriate natural beauty of the woods that are today Treblinka. What one can begin to understand of the Holocaust experience in a week's time in today's Poland can *never* be transmitted by the written and spoken word. That beginning of insight is but the tiniest fraction of what there is to know, but it can bring the rabbi—especially the rabbi born after the Holocaust—immeasurably closer to the survivors in his synagogue by sensitizing him more profoundly to their trauma. Spending a week in Poland may not rank high on any rabbinic vacation list, but it should rank near the top of a list of important business trips.

Third is the issue of survivor guilt, and the rabbi's role in easing it. That it is a major—if not the major—component of ongoing survivor trauma has been amply attested to. As a psychoanalyst colleague from within my own synagogue family has written,

Who are we to judge? Are you a survivor if you "only" were confined to life in a ghetto and to forced labor? Or, if you lived through hiding, or going "underground," through arduous journeys from country to country in search of shelter? Are you a survivor if you were not harmed physically, yet you lost your parents, grandparents, brothers and sisters, spouse and children?

The atrocities of the Holocaust cannot be measured in quantities alone. For it is the losses, the human degradation, the denial of our very right to be that affected so many people in so many different ways.[21]

The rabbi *must* take a clear and unequivocal stand to resolve, at least within his own synagogue, the question of "who is a survivor," and that resolution must be an inclusive one. The label of "survivor" cannot, by any justifiable Jewish criteria, be limited within the synagogue world merely to those who emerged alive from one or more concentration camps.

That the rabbi, along with all other Jews, has an ethical responsibility to work to lessen the burden of survivor guilt is certainly true. What is also true, however, is that he is uniquely positioned to be effective in this particular regard. Today's rabbi may, in the name of accessibility to his congregants, downplay the sacramental aspect of the rabbinate. He would usually rather be perceived as a prophet than a priest. Yet it is in precisely this sacramental role that he may be able to do his best work. The priest of old had the power to forgive and grant forgiveness, some of which has found its way into the modern transferrential relationship between rabbi and congregant. The guilty survivor is a person in dire need of forgiveness, merely for being alive. Ideally, that forgiveness must come from those who can no longer give it—those who died while the survivor lived. But because of the priestly authority which the rabbi bears, he may be able to accomplish here what even the therapist might not be able to do.

Fourth, with all of the pressing and eclectic responsibilities and expectations that seem to fall on the shoulders of today's pulpit rabbi, he must, nonetheless, isolate the time necessary to solicit the stories of those survivors who are members of his congregation. That they are anxious to tell their stories is undoubtedly true,[22] even if the process of telling is painful and difficult. It is far better, and more advantageous to the long-term relationship between the two, for the rabbi to err on the side of asking the survivor to do that which he is not yet ready to do (i.e., tell his story), than simply to pretend that he is not there, or to imply that no one in the synagogue cares to hear what he has to share.

Last, but certainly not least, it is essential for the rabbi to involve himself in making sure that the younger generation of Jews in his synagogue learn the essential facts and lessons of the Holocaust. Nothing—with the possible exception of revisionist historians who claim that the Holocaust is a myth perpetrated by the Jews—so vexes and worries the survivor community as does the possibility that when the survivors are no longer alive to tell their stories, Jews themselves will no longer remember what happened. There may someday be enough Holocaust museums for the non-Jewish world, but for the Jewish world, the story, from the survivor's perspective, needs to be told and retold like that of the exodus from Egypt, which ultimately became a deeply internalized facet of the Jewish liturgical consciousness. There can be no late twentieth-century Jewish education without competent and adequate Holocaust education, and the rabbi must serve as the ultimate guarantor of this fact.

Ultimately, the experience of the survivor in today's synagogue community will always be rooted, as is his entire life, in paradox: the need to hold on to his uniquely horrible past on the one hand, and the need to let go of it on the other so that, once again, he can be a totally participating member of a faith community—including believing and trusting in God. As in so many other instances in synagogue life, the unique transference between rabbi and congregant endows the rabbi with the capacity to exert tremendous influence on the lives of those who look to him for leadership, and survivors are no exception to this rule. Their relationship will always, of necessity, be a complex one. Yet, there undeniably exists as well the potential for a relationship between the two that is not only mutually beneficial, but also special. Whatever the risks, there can be no doubt that the potential certainly warrants the effort.

NOTES

1. Primo Levi, *Survival in Auschwitz* (New York: Collier Books, 1961), p. 80.

2. See Bruno Bettelheim, *Surviving and Other Essays* (New York: Alfred A. Knopf, 1979); Terrence Des Pres, *The Survivor: An Anatomy of Life in the Death Camps* (New York: Oxford University Press, 1976); and other works.

3. Helen Fein, "The Holocaust: What It Means and What It Doesn't," *Present Tense* 15, no. 1 (November/December 1987):25.

4. Henceforth, the generic "his" will be used, though the reference is to both male and female rabbis. The same will be true of the use of the generic "his" with regard to survivors.

5. The reference is to Josephus Flavius, a Jewish/Roman historian of the first century of the common era, whose historical works remain to this day a major source of information on the Second Temple period in Jerusalem.

6. Richard Rubenstein, *After Auschwitz: Radical Theology and Contemporary Judaism* (New York: Macmillan, 1966), pp. 128–129.

7. Max Dimont, *The Indestructable Jew* (New York: World, 1971).

8. Leviticus 26:14–41.

9. Deuteronomy 28:15–68.

10. Leviticus 26:42. The translation is from *The Torah: The Five Books of Moses* (Philadelphia: The Jewish Publication Society of America, 1962), p. 234.

11. Holocaust Memorial Day, designated as a national day of mourning by the government of the State of Israel. The date selected was the twenty-seventh day of the Hebrew month of Nisan.

12. Rabbi Yishmael's tragic fate found liturgical expression in "The Martyrdom of the Ten Sages," a prayer recited on Yom Kippur. For the full text of the prayer, see Ben Zion Bokser, *The High Holiday Prayer Book* (New York: Hebrew Publishing Company, 1959), p. 431.

13. Jacob Z. Lauterbach, *Mekilta de-Rabbi Ishmael* Vol. II (Philadelphia: The Jewish Publication Society of America, 1949), p. 60.

14. See, for example, the section on Rabbi Levi Yitzhok of Berditchev in Jacob S. Minkin, *The Romance of Hassidism* (North Hollywood, CA: Wilshire Book Company, 1971), pp. 168–171.

15. See, for example, Haskell Lookstein, *Were We Our Brothers' Keepers?* (New York: KJR Publishers, 1986).

16. Elie Wiesel, "For Some Measure of Humility," *Sh'ma* 5, no. 100 (October 31, 1975): 314.

17. *Deuteronomy* 25:17–19.

18. Literally, "Work makes one free," meant to reinforce the myth that Auschwitz was a work camp, as opposed to a death camp.

19. Hebrew for the social reception which usually accompanies the blessing over wine following Sabbath morning synagogue services.

20. The first seven days following burial.

21. From an unpublished address by Dr. Yudit Jung, a psychoanalyst whose practice has focused on survivor-related issues.

22. Terrence Des Pres, *The Survivor*, Chap. 2.

10

The Rabbi and the Holocaust Survivor

RABBI MARTIN S. COHEN

Of all the persons to whom the Holocaust survivor may turn for succor or for solace, the rabbi generally has to handle the questions that are both the simplest and the least solvable. The questions raised are simple to identify, because, at least in the experience of this author, no matter what the survivor formally presents as his or her ''real'' problem, the very fact that he or she has chosen to present that problem to a rabbi means that the problem is one of faith. The various ways in which the request is made to the rabbi—that he explain how one can believe in God after Auschwitz, that he explain how Israel is to understand its covenant with God after suffering so grievously, that he explain how God can be good when men created in His image can be so bad—are all variations on the single dilemma that lies beneath them all: How can the post-Holocaust Jew believe in a God either so pathetically unable or so perversely unwilling to come to His people's aid when they needed it the most.

The obvious corollaries to this most basic problem bring in the larger picture of continued religious observance and of the need to develop some sort of cogent post-Holocaust theology, but both are developments of a common theme; for observance and faith to have meaning beyond the satisfaction self-induced by ritual performed and dogma faithfully upheld, the question of the role of God during the Holocaust years needs somehow to be dealt with first. In my experience, no survivor that has come to me has ever presented me with a problem, dilemma, or question that does not derive directly from this single crux of theology and theodicy and that would not be at least half-solved were the solution to this more basic problem forthcoming. Yet, for all the appealing simplicity of the question with which he must deal, the rabbi's task in working with survivors is made seriously less simple by the fact that the problem the survivor presents him (veiled or unveiled, implicitly or explicitly, formally or allusively, clearly stated or cleverly distorted) is basically insolvable.

Yet, the counseling relationship between rabbi and survivor is even more unusual than this odd matrix of simplicity and insolvability would suggest—and in two basic areas. First of all, it seems that the survivor who turns to his or her rabbi rarely, if ever, expects a serious answer to the asked or unasked question; no one really expects that there *is* an explanation of divine inactivity during the Nazi period, much less that, of all the rabbis in the world, one has somehow chosen to address oneself to the single savant who actually knows what it is. Put differently, this author has never encountered a survivor who accepts the validity of the problem, but who refuses to accept its insolvability as well. This set of givens presents the rabbi with a certain freedom in helping the survivor to construct a Jewish world in which he or she can accept a role without suffering alienation, discomfort, or feelings of crippling absurdity. The other odd aspect of the dialogue between rabbi and survivor has to do with the (only apparently) more basic issue of faith in God. Despite the importance that the nonbeliever might expect to be connected to this grave theological issue, it seems that the actual existence of God is rarely (in this author's experience, never) a real issue; turning to a rabbi in the first place generally presupposes the existence for the survivor of a web of religious and philosophical dilemmas that depend on belief in God for their justification and definition. To put all this another way, the survivor who comes to a rabbi is rarely if ever seeking proof for the existence of God, and neither is he or she hoping for an easy (if elusive) answer to the question of divine inaction during the debacle. We are therefore left in a highly unenviable situation: The only real question on the table is considered *a priori* and by both parties to be basically insolvable. Yet, for all that, it is to solve that very problem that the survivor has come. He or she has turned to a rabbi precisely because of a deep-seated desire to pursue a life of ritual piety and good works that is being thwarted by the perverse conviction, derived from the survivor's personal experience, that the God served by those rites and deeds is Himself derelict in His own covenantal responsibilities and is, as such, unworthy of such piety and service.

Traditional Jewish theology lays the groundwork for dealing with these grave problems by declaring God to be the author both of good and of evil.[1] This observation often brings on a spirited response from the survivor, especially if it is perceived to suggest that the Nazis were acting as latter-day pharaohs, their hearts hardened by God himself, lest they turn from their evil plans when the author of history decreed otherwise. The survivor often shows himself quite anxious to acquit God, so to speak, of any responsibility for the Holocaust. In the experience of this author, in fact, any suggestion of impropriety on the part of God can be profoundly counterproductive in dealing with the survivor. On the contrary, blaming God for the Holocaust is such an obvious, simple, and potentially satisfying pattern for dealing with the horror, that it can almost be assumed *a priori* that the kind of survivor who turns to his or her rabbi for counseling will have already, either formally or informally, rejected it. Some survivors will put it in terms of blasphemy, while others will speak simply of the idea being false and wrong, but the fact is that, were the survivor prepared to hate God for the Holocaust, there would be no problem in need of a solution. On the contrary, the goal is somehow to bring the survivor to the point at which he realizes that the reality of the Holocaust and the goodness of God are only apparently antagonistic notions and that, in the final analysis, they are not at all mutually exclusive realities.

As my own expertise is in the area of Jewish mystic literature, it is within the corpus of old Jewish mysticism, known loosely as kabbalah, that I generally choose to begin.[2] For the kabbalah, the roots of pain and sadness, and of evil itself, lie within the earliest self-manifestation of God. In a nutshell, the slow elaboration of this single idea and the study of the ancient texts that contribute to its understanding are the work in which rabbi and survivor engage. I will set down below the details of the theory, but perhaps first I should observe that the technique proposed recommends itself for a variety of reasons. First of all, it preserves the traditional role of the rabbi as teacher, specifically of classical Jewish texts. This is often quite important to the survivor, who begins by doubting that the young, naive man seated before him is a "real" rabbi, by which he means a rabbi of the kind he knew before the war in Europe.[3] The discovery that the rabbi intends to deal with the problem at hand by seeking its solution in classical Jewish texts appeals immediately to the kind of survivor inclined to seek out a rabbi in the first place. Second, the atmosphere is created in which the survivor feels himself taking his place in a line of others, as long as Jewish history itself, who have already grappled with the same difficult questions and who were also moved to seek their solutions in the study of classical texts. (If this observation is not forthcoming, I generally take the lead and make it myself.) Finally, the ambience itself—the book-lined study, the tea, the oversized book lying open on the table, the skullcap, the almost atavistically satisfying combination of dark wood and yellow light—is instantly evocative of a mythic, highly idealized Jewish world, the world perceived (either rightly or wrongly) to have been destroyed by the Nazis. The ambience therefore itself speaks directly to the survivor, encouraging hope and providing a sense of living tradition. One survivor who had had a strongly traditional education as a boy remarked to me that the setting reminded him of the comment in *The Ethics of the Fathers* to the effect that when two sit together to study, it is as though they were invited to dine at God's own table.[4] Be that as it may, the fact that the survivor perceives himself to be seeking the solution to his problem within Jewish tradition has its own calming and satisfying aspect.

We begin by presenting a paradox—the same Bible which harps over and over again on God's essential ineffability and unknowableness also insists on describing God with not one but hundreds of various epithets and descriptive terms. Furthermore, the Torah itself commands the pious to love God—this commandment is emphasized above all others in the daily liturgy—and certainly love requires knowledge as its basis. From this matrix of paradoxical ideas, we jump to the medieval theory that all adjectives of qualification and modification are essentially limiting factors and hence that all discussion of God, at least insofar as such discussion involves the assignation of limit and boundary to God, is *ipso facto* hubris and blasphemy. From this jumping-off point, the kabbalah begins to weave its theory about the nature of evil.

There is an aspect of God, the kabbalah teaches, that is unknowable and that is above all human ken or comprehension. This aspect of God, called the *En-Sof* ("The Infinite One") exists above and beyond the concepts of time, space, or quality. Texts are presented (in translation) that speak of the En-Sof as that aspect of God which is undifferentiated, absolutely unknowable, timeless, space-less, nameless, and utterly without quality.[5] Discussion is devoted to these concepts, especially to the notions of spacelessness and timelessness and various models are proposed for understanding them, or at least for beginning to try to fathom their ultimate meaning. In attempting to squeeze meaning from these texts, the ennobling atmosphere of initiation into arcane mysteries is fostered and this, in turn, aids in the establishment of an ambience of purposeful endeavor.

After these ideas are presented, a new notion is suggested and discussed. To create, it turns out, the En-Sof had to bring an aspect of its self into existence, for creation (as distinct from procreation) implies relationship and the En-Sof was far beyond the prerequisites of dialectic and dialogue even to begin to create, much less to love. To love, God needed to create a context in which He might be loved, and to be loved meant being able to be known. The En-Sof, therefore, brought forth from deep within ten universes of quality, nonsubstantive yet existent self-aspects that, by virtue of existing (even without physicality or space) could nevertheless bear quality. This self-emanated aspect of God is the God terrestrials may know and are called, after a traditional kabbalistic term, *Sefirot.*[6] These ten Sefirot are God and are to be taken neither as child nor projection, patina, nor servant of the One God. This is the perceptible God, He to whom the pious pray, who governs the world and who exists primarily and perhaps even solely to be known and adored by His creations. This second set of ideas (the En-Sof and its related concepts of spacelessness and timelessness was the first) is developed freely. Depending on the background of the survivor, more or less time is spent presenting these ideas and connecting them to traditional Jewish practices. For instance, the kabbalists were well-known for explaining all Jewish ritual in terms of the precise interior effect it would somehow have on one or several of the Sefirot. Penultimately, the goal of all religious activity is to bring about a union of the male and female aspects of the godhead and, ultimately, it is to participate actively in that union. But this might be too much for the survivor with no religious background or training. At any rate, the details of the system of the Sefirot cannot take up too much time, because it is the next set of ideas that begins to lay the groundwork for the type of demonologizing that is eventually therapeutic and, with luck, meaningful.

The third set of ideas is the most potent for the survivor and presents the sinister side to all this theosophy: Just as all opportunity entails danger and all potentiality conceals the possibility of failure, so does the possibility exist that human inadequacy can destroy the delicate mechanism. The enormous sacrifice on the part of God and His own absolute nature for the sake of being loved entails the horrible but undeniable possibility that He might not be loved, for forced love is no love at all and love freely given can, by definition, just as freely be withheld.

The emanation of the sefirotic aspect of the godhead was neither accidental nor unneccessary. The act of creation, just like procreation among humans, was an act of love and, indeed, it was to enter into a dialectic of love with humanity that God first brought forth His Sefirot. The point is that it was only by first bringing forth an aspect of His self that could bear quality and, at least, metaphysical existence, that God could create the universe. Creator and creation need at least a certain commonality of aspect to sustain the intimacy of any relationship, and how much the more so if that relationship is destined to transcend its past history and evolve into a mature love relationship. Thus, it was to create the world that God, in His original, quality-less and undifferentiated aspect, first created a sefirotic godhead that could bear relationship and quality and which, created, could create.

The emanation of the Sefirot was, therefore, more than a mere event in the secret life of God; it was the first and only attempt at self-limitation experienced by God. Quality, time, and space are all notions that delimit and confine an existence element of creation—but, by definition, God is the sole existence to which these concepts do not and cannot apply. The emanation of the Sefirot imposed these limits on God—or more precisely, by bringing forth the Sefirot, and God imposed these limits on Himself.

Here the puzzle becomes evident; all subsequent discussion between survivor and rabbi is devoted to solving this apparently insolvable riddle. In the world of God and men, evil is defined as the imposition of limit or boundary on the omnipotent nature of God. Here the situation is odd in that it is God Himself who has limited Himself. The result must be evil—for any limit on God is, by definition, evil—and yet cannot be evil, for God is, by equally hoary and authoritative definition, good and, by undeniable extension, so are His works. The Zohar puts it succinctly: the world was created with *din*, that is, with the rigorous justice untempered with either mercy or compassion that men naively identify as evil in their world.[7] The Zohar takes this as its jumping-off point and it is ours as well in the therapeutic context, for if the world is good and its creator is good, then the roots of evil, of din, of rigor, and of cruelty are nonetheless part of the essential aspect of all created things. The evil generated by existence itself is hidden deep within all things, including, of course, all people, and can either be affirmed or repressed as one develops and learns to love God. The love with which the pious are commanded to love God is therefore rooted in the individual's relationship with and within the celestial world.

The point must be stressed that the notion of evil lurking within the fact of individual existence should not be misinterpreted to suggest that people are basically evil—just the contrary is taught specifically in the Bible and is affirmed repeatedly in kaballistic sources. Rather, the Zohar, for example, chooses to find humanity, and all things, founded on the roots of rigorous din which, should mankind choose to abandon God, can become a deadly swamp of spoiled potential poised to destroy humanity like so much malevolent quicksand.

This notion of deeply interior potential otherness and alienation from the world of the divine is the subject of a great deal of literary and mythological speculation in the kabbalah and it is the investigation of all that speculation that forms the rest of the therapeutic context. The notion is almost endlessly productive and it is possible to find it personified, mythologized, hypostatized, reified, and discussed in an almost dizzying number of metaphoric ranges, symbolic matrices, and literary categories and constructs within a few pages of zoharic text. Just what direction and just how deeply within the textual sources the analysis may proceed will therefore vary from survivor to survivor, but the jumping-off point all approaches will share is that the Holocaust need not be interpreted merely as tragic history, and neither must we posit some tragic lapse of consciousness on the part of an otherwise watchful and loving God to explain the events of the Nazi years. The point is that the Holocaust can bear interpretation within the inner history of God as well as within the political history of men (regardless of whether, by men, we mean aggressor or victim), and the result be seen to demean neither God nor humanity.

The two dangers inherent in the approach outlined above are a tendency to use the notion that evil on earth is the natural concomitant of existence itself to absolve the Nazis of their crimes (a tendency effectively resisted, incidentally, by the very biblical texts that show neither any hesitation in identifying God as the hardener of Pharoah's heart nor in exulting in Pharaoh's defeat as the justified fall of an evil man) and an equally strong tendency to file the dead away as so much grist for the handmills of theosophy. Both tendencies are the normal outgrowths of any attempt to interpret the Holocaust in a way that will preserve the traditional image of God as the master of human history and destiny and as a just judge of human affairs. That both tendencies need to be thwarted goes without saying, yet it is the very impossibility of finding a solution that squares the traditional conception of God with the horrors of the Nazi period that provides the impetus for renewed speculation. In other words, as we said above, the fact that the problem is basically insolvable need not deter the rabbi intent on offering solace and the renewed possibility of meaningful religious activity to the survivor struggling with the reality of his or her private history.

Having determined that the possibility of the Holocaust does not contradict the possibility of there being a God (and a God who exists according to the outlines of Jewish tradition at that!), the next problem that must be encountered is the explanation of why, as passivity was certainly not the *only* plausible divine course of action, God did not prevent the debacle. This opens up much more complicated ground for the survivor. After all, a positive answer to the initial question of whether there could be a God in the first place given the facts of the Holocaust was an *a priori* assumption of the survivor of the kind who turns to a rabbi for support or succor. Certainly, the survivor does not expect the rabbi to flip through the pages of a Talmudic tractate and discover why God allowed the Nazis to perpetrate their ghastly crimes! Yet that is, in a very real manner of speaking, precisely what the rabbi is being asked to do. Recourse to traditional slogans about the ways of God being too august for human comprehension or about the duty of mankind being to obey God rather than to question the propriety or reasonableness of divine policies is hardly a satisfying avenue of approach for the deeply distraught survivor. In this regard, it also needs to be pointed out that the survivor who comes to his or her rabbi today for discussion on these points has undoubtedly been deeply involved with these issues for four decades now and can hardly be bought off with traditional formulary that seems to contradict the survivor's life experience. On the contrary, it is precisely because these traditional formulations have failed to provide adequate solace or comfort for the survivor that the issue remains alive and in need of resolution in the first place. In my experience, I have never been able to think of a single traditional solution to the questions of theodicy or divine inactivity during the Holocaust that comes as news to the survivor and the reality of the situation is that it is almost always the survivor who brings up the traditional formulation so that we may reject it as absurd or preposterous before we begin. Often, the survivor's inability to accept the traditional understanding of God's role in human affairs (which is usually presented by the survivor as "a basic principle of our faith") is the very problem being formally presented to the rabbi. The solution does, perhaps, lie within the problem itself, but throwing the dilemma back into the survivor's face by citing biblical chapter and rabbinic verse is hardly a productive step. What then *is* a reasonable approach?

My own response to the search for a reasonable avenue of approach has to do with the conception of what is called in Hebrew *hastarat panim* (hiding the face). Although the idea is originally biblical and eventually rabbinic, it is in the Kabbalistic guise that I find it the most reasonable to present the concept to the survivor. The key to the concept rests in the prior understanding of two other kabbalistic doctrines, so closely allied so as to be more accurately described as the two sides of a single issue, and they are *ashgehuta* (supervision) and *itaruta* (awakening). It is to these two terms I propose to turn our attention first.

The Zohar describes the dialogue of love between mankind and God in dialectic terms, such that there is a terrestrial consequence for every celestial action and an appropriate heavenly response for every earthly gesture. As such, the sefirotic godhead and the human soul, especially when melted into each other in the communion with God that is the goal of all human religious activity, becomes the background of metaphysicality against which the mystic may become the lover of God. The absolutely undifferentiated, quality-less En-Sof lies without, beyond, and far above the physical constraints of the created universe; humanity, the collective jewel of creation, lies mired and stuck in the material midden of the physical world. As is the case for all lovers, compromise is the key to success. There can be no love without intimacy and no intimacy without context; the potential role in the dialectic of love and dialogue for which all mankind was created in the first place must remain unfulfilled in the absence of possibility. To speak to this problem, the Zohar develops its middle-ground theory: the En-Sof brings forth a metaphysical, less nonexistent realm than itself that is still far enough above the world to merit consideration as part of God. The human counterpart to the sefirotic manifestation of God is the human metaphysical aspect itself. The soul transcends the physical world, just as the Sefirot transcends the absolutely aphysical En-Sof; together they create the context, background, and possibility of love between heaven and earth.

That love is characterized, just like the love between any terrestrial lovers, by gifts from one to the other, gifts intended to represent the giver in his or her absence. The ancient biblical author who used the Hebrew word for "blessing" to mean simply "gift" may have been on the way to understanding this for himself, having correctly perceived that the blessing cements the relationship between the individual and God just as the gift cements the love between earthly lovers.[8] The great gift of God to mankind is, of course, the Torah. Described throughout the Zohar as an act of love, the revelation at Sinai enabled the pious student of sacred Scripture to unravel the secrets of the dialectic between humankind and God and thereby to transcend the limitation of that very humanity when measured against the divinity of the godhead. Like one privileged to read a lover's diary with permission, the Jew can learn from the Torah the correct techniques for perfecting the love relationship for which he or she was created. The counterpart, from the human point of view, is acts of faith, obedience, and love which are the commandments and their willing performance. The Zohar describes in vivid, often erotic, detail the ways in which the performance of the various commandments unites the godhead in the union that parallels sexual, sensual love among humans, thereby creating the context of love, harmony, and union into which the human soul may integrate itself in order to become at once the lover and the beloved of God. This integration, called *Devequt*, is the ultimate goal of all human endeavor.

The Zohar has names for the two sides of the dialectic, conceived here in the metaphoric context of sympathetic behavior and the commonality of thought, deed, and reaction. The terms are *Ashgehuta* and *Itaruta*, meaning respectively "[divine] supervision [of mankind]" and [human] stimulus [of God.]" The two are sides of the same coin; Ashgehuta is the attention God showers on the world, while Itaruta is devotion and the sympathetic effect the world has on God. Just as on earth, the two sides of the dialectic are rarely, if ever, in perfect harmony. Just as mankind falters, falls, and fails to "awaken" the godhead to union (for such is the literal meaning of Itaruta), so does God respond in kind, challenging on occasion the potential permanence of the relationship by purposefully averting his otherwise omniscient eyes. Certainly an omnipotent God is capable of limiting His omniscience and of restraining his customary responsiveness to the deeds of humanity. This, the Zohar calls *Hastarat Panim*, a term borrowed from older rabbinic lore and ultimately deriving from the Bible, but here invested with a new meaning derived from and defined by the nature of love that may exist between the pious below and their God.[9]

Ashgehuta is thus protecting, sustaining love—the type of observation and analysis of others' behavior, far different from the stern care of watchful parents, that characterizes lovers' love. This protective glance, this loving observation of terrestrial behavior is rooted in God's desire to perfect love between the upper and lower realms, between Himself and His other. The supervision of children by their parents derives from the parents' need to instruct and guide. The Ashgehuta that characterizes the love relationship is different in that it is stimulated by the observed, rather than by the observing lover. The desire to cast a net of protecting attention over one's lover is a response to love felt or perceived or longed for, and such is the Ashgehuta that characterizes the love between God and the world. It is solely in response to men's deeds that the supernal world is awakened to dialogue. Whether the results are pleasant or unpleasant is almost a negligible detail determined by the nature of the deed; what counts in the long run is the fact that the Lover above is responsive to the deeds of the beloved below.

The counterpart of Ashgehuta is Itaruta. In kabbalic books, the term has its own specific and technical meaning—it is the name given to the act of stimulating the godhead, of awakening within God the same feelings of love that the divine Ashgehuta inspires within the human breast. Two lovers, as all lovers know, form a universe of two. They are both, both I and Thou, both lover and beloved; in a word, they are each other's equals, for there can be no real love except between equals. Itaruta and Ashgehuta are thus two terms for more or less the same thing, for they are both the stimuli of love. The notion of the world and God united in a type of love akin to (but many times more powerful than) the love that exists between earthly lovers suggests, after all, that such love needs to be "awakened" in each lover's bosom if it is not to be permanently and tragically dormant forever. The Zohar is quite insistent in its claim that there is no action above except such as is reaction to that which transpires below. This is not to say that God is shackled and powerless, like some giant computer capable of far outdoing the puny brains of its own programmers, yet in need of a human hand to be plugged in and switched on. The idea of Zoharic dialecticism is just that—that the Sefirot were emanated in the first place precisely to allow God to allow Himself the luxury of existing in a limited metaphysical state in which He might exist as the formal equal of his terrestrial lovers.

By the time all this is explained and discussed, the survivor has already guessed that we are going to discuss the Holocaust as a horrible rupture in the relationship between God and Israel. How can Israel proclaim itself to be God's lover, when the divine counterpart to that very love—the Ashgehuta—was so tragically suspended for such long and tragic years. To put it another way: Is it possible that Israel can only exist in the context of Ashgehuta and Itaruta dialecticism to the extent that the suspension of the dialectic process results in tragedy of such overwhelming proportions? Can Jewish theology tolerate the notion that the ovens were just the down side of the love between God and Israel?

The Zohar long ago raised the issue of just such a rupture in the relationship. Since God and Israel form a lovers' universe of two, there can be no alternative to the dialectic love we have described. In a relationship founded on such deeply felt dialecticism, there can be no way of separating action from reaction. Both parties are so intimately tied to each other that the outside observer cannot state, in the event of rupture, which side is categorically responsible. Whatever the ultimate cause, the Zohar acknowledges the possibility of God's face becoming hidden from Israel, which is to be explained as a unilateral withdrawal of Ashgehuta in response to a break in terrestrial Itaruta. Of all the biblical authors who provide the background for the Zoharic development of the concept of Hastarat Panim, none is so important as the post-exilic prophet whose sermons and speeches are preserved as the last third of the Book of Isaiah. Although textual study of the various Zoharic passages mentioned above is beyond the average survivor in need of help in maintaining his religious self-definition, the study of the biblical passages is well within the realm of possibility, be that study in translation or in the original. These passages, therefore, should be studied by rabbi and survivor, not merely discussed.

The anonymous prophet (often called, because of the literary setting of his work, Deutero-Isaiah or Second Isaiah) understood the phenomenon of Hastarat Panim not as having been designed to damage the love relationship between mankind and God, but rather to strengthen it, to normalize it and to lend it pathos, passion, and significance. Hastarat Panim is meant to make of that love a love of equals, a love that can bear interpretation as an exalted rather than as a debased form of the love that exists between earthly lovers. The prophet proclaimed, "The Redeemer of Israel says, 'For a short moment, I have abandoned you, but with the greatest compassion shall I bring you back. In a surfeit of anger, I hid My face (Hebrew: *histarti fanai*) from you for a moment, but with eternal mercy I have had mercy upon you.' "[10] The prophet describes the exile as a quarrel between two lovers, and the point must be made that the exile of the Jews to Babylon in the beginning of the sixth century BCE is more or less the only event in Jewish history that can be compared to the Holocaust in terms of the shattering and permanent effect it had on Jewish beliefs and assumptions about God and about the covenant. The point of the prophet is that, when the anger subsides, one lover says to the other, "For a moment, my passions were so intense I mistook love for hatred, but now it is over and my renewed love has been made permanent, even stronger, for having been tested." The anger on the part of God is part of the dialectic; it is the nature of dialogic love that there is never any action that is not essentially reaction. Elsewhere, the prophet sets this forth even more clearly: "God's hand is not too short to save you and neither is He deaf—rather it is your sins that separate the two of you; your sins which hide His face from you, from hearing you. . . . "[11] This is a new expansion of the idea, one that points even more clearly to the notion of Hastarat Panim being part of the love relationship, for here, instead of the regular idea that it is in response to human sin that God turns His face, we have the idea that it is the sins themselves that obscure God's vision. He would love, but He is thwarted, so to speak, by the failings, inadequacies, and flaws of His chosen partners in love. This is the reason the kabbalah is able to adopt this line of thinking with such relish, for the very idea that there is no inherent contradiction between the notion of divine omnipotence and divine self-limitation is at the root of all Zoharic and post-Zoharic kabbalistic thought. All lovers consider themselves the victims of their lovers' inadequacies; the notion that one lover reacts to the other's flawed behavior is far less appealing than the feeling that one is being victimized by one's partner's failings. This is obviously a point of great importance to the survivor grappling with God over the events of the Holocaust.

The point of all this is to bring the survivor to the point at which he or she realizes that it is the case that, just as lovers must occasionally sink back into a state of introspection that precludes (but ultimately secures) his or her being able to focus on the Lover (the Thou, the Other), so must the divine Ashgehuta be occasionally withdrawn to allow God to do battle with the shadow He casts upon Himself in creating the world. These are the times of famine and of suffering on earth, during which Israel has no alternative but to wait for God. The suffering the world must endure during times of Hastarat Panim is truly what the old rabbis called "suffering for the sake of love," here transformed from midrash into dialectic, from unfortunate side effect of existence into unavoidable concomitant of dialogic and mature love.

The lines of thought and therapeutic analysis of Jewish texts set forth above are not meant to suggest that the Holocaust can be explained away as an unfortunate lapse in an otherwise successful covenantal love affair between God and Israel. On the contrary, the Jewish people have not even begun to revise Jewish theology to speak to the events of the last war. In a certain sense, biblical Judaism (as opposed to the earlier cult of the monarchic period) grew out of the ashes of the First Temple, just as rabbinic Judaism can be said to have sprung from the ashes of the Second Temple. What type of Judaism will one day be said to have been born in the ashes of the Holocaust I cannot even begin to imagine, but for the time being, the job of the rabbi in the generation after Auschwitz is to provide the survivor with a Jewish method (i.e, a method rooted in Jewish tradition) of overcoming the sense of crippling pointlessness and covenantal betrayal that are the legacy of the Nazis to the few who escaped with their lives.

The point of our approach is that it offers the survivor an opportunity to develop an inner imagery adequate to render the Holocaust experience (and its attendant admixture of grotesqueness and absurdity) more intelligible and perhaps even more meaningful. The Holocaust was an experience that undermined self-esteem, self-respect, and dignity to such an extent that the survivor is often faced with a loss of individual values and beliefs. The traditional Jewish method being described in this paper offers the survivor an opportunity to develop inner forms and images that are more adequate representations of the self-world relationship in a post-Holocaust world than the standard stuff of political or economic mythology. In particular, it is the senseless death of the closest family members that constitutes the most violently painful aspect of the Holocaust experience for any survivor. The approach we have proposed is designed—at least in a limited, tentative way—to provide the survivor with an interior sense of the demonic that can speak directly to that part of his or her past. The survivor is encouraged to redefine the self, to reorient his or her values and to undertake a new quest for an inner imagery to link mortality with survival. The role of the rabbi therefore is to help the survivor via immersion into the world of traditional Jewish learning as a method of mediating between chaos and meaning, of reconceptualizing the nature of death and of generating within the survivor's imagination a myth designed to confront hopelessness and despair.

NOTES

1. For example, see Isaiah 45:6–7: "So that they shall know from east to west that there is none except Me; I am the Lord, there is none else—He who fashions light and creates darkness, He who makes peace and creates evil. I am the Lord, who does all these things." It is not without interest to note that when the second half of this proclamation (begining with the words, "He who fashions light") was adapted for very prominent liturgical usage, the liturgist felt compelled to give the text as though it read "He who makes peace and creates all." Whether the liturgist had a different text before him (perhaps one that skipped by haplography from the word "creates" to the word "all") or whether he was moved by a desire to delete a reference to God he found vulgar or tasteless, is unclear. The fact that the Dead Sea manuscript of Isaiah gives "good" where the textus receptus reads "peace" suggests that we see an intentionally euphemistic misreading by the liturgist, an observation already found in the Talmud at Berakhot 11b.

2. The reader entirely unfamiliar with the history of Jewish mysticism should begin by reading Gershom Scholem's *Major Trends in Jewish Mysticism* (New York: Schocken, 1941). The secondary literature is immense, but between this volume and the basic secondary works listed in Scholem's bibliography, the beginner will have a clear idea of what is meant by kabbalah and what the various issues are with which kabbalists and kabbalistic authors deal. Moshe Idel's new *Kabballah* (New Haven: Yale University Press, 1988) will serve as the companion volume to Scholem, providing the more sophisticated reader with an update of new trends in kabbalistic research since Scholem's day.

3. The university-trained, professional rabbi is not exactly a North American invention, but this was certainly the exception to the norm in the villages of Eastern Europe from which the majority of survivors I have encountered derive. Naturally, the historical reality has no importance here. The point is that the older survivor generally recalls the rabbis of his youth to have been elderly men of unquestioned piety whose lifework consisted of the story of Talmud and other works of classical Jewish law and thought, not university-trained professionals willing to share their own religious angst with their congregants.

4. It is not without interest that the actual statement in the Mishnah (The Ethics of

the Fathers is actually the mishnaic tractate Avot), is that when three dine at a table together and discuss Torah, it is as though they had eaten at God's table. The remark appears in the beginning of the third chapter of that work in the name of Rabbi Simon.

5. Because it is the high-water-mark of kabbalistic creativity and the classical text of the kabbalah par excellence, we choose our texts almost exclusively from the Zohar. There are three major sources of English translations from the Zohar: The Simon, Sperling, and Levertoff translation of large chunks of the text in five volumes (London: Soncino Press, 1934), Daniel Matt's *Zohar: Book of Enlightenment* (New York: Paulist Press, 1984) and David Goldstein's translation of Tishby and Lachover's Hebrew language Mishnat Hazzohar (Oxford: Oxford University Press, 1986; Hebrew original: Jerusalem: 1957–1961). Most Zoharic texts are unintelligible to the uninitiated, especially in translation, a quality which recommends them for group study.

6. The term *Sefirot* was apparently a neologism coined by the anonymous author of the obscure but pivotal work of ancient Jewish mysticism, the Sefer Yetzirah. In its original context, the term refers to the primal numbers, the contemplation of which can lead the mystic to communion with God.

7. *Zohar*, ed. Mantua, vol. II, p. 238a.

8. The biblical text uses the word *berakhah* (generally "blessing") to mean simply "gift" at Judges 1:15 (Joshua 15:19.)

9. Compare Deuteronomy 31:16–18: "The Lord said to Moses: You are soon to lie with your fathers. This people will thereupon go astray after the alien gods in their midst, in the land that they are about to enter, they will forsake Me and break My covenant that I made with them. Then My anger will flare up against them, and I will abandon them and hide My countenance from them. They shall be ready prey; and many evils and troubles shall befall them. And they shall say on that day, 'Surely it is because our God is not in our midst that these evils have befallen us.' Yet I will keep My countenance hidden on that day, because of all the evil they have done in turning to other gods."

10. Isaiah 54:8.

11. Isaiah 59:2.

VI

Empirical Studies

11

Transgenerational Effects of the Concentration Camp Experience

MOSHE ALMAGOR AND GLORIA R. LEON

The effect of the Holocaust on its survivors and their offspring is an area of continued interest for clinicians and researchers as well as philosophers and the lay public. In the first years after the end of World War II, the clinical focus was on assessing and describing the psychological sequelae of the survivors' extremely traumatic experiences. The concept of a "survivor syndrome" was developed and resulted in extensive study.[1] A number of these investigations were oriented around psychoanalytic interpretations of functioning, and concluded that a significant degree of psychopathology was evident in the survivors. It should be noted, however, that these first studies dealt primarily with survivors who had sought psychiatric help and might not have represented a range of the population of survivors.

Since the late 1960s, professionals and laypersons have expressed interest in the effects of the concentration camp experience on the offspring of survivors. A frequently expressed attitude was that the consequences of such a horrible and prolonged experience were likely to be passed on to the next generation. Initial papers addressing this issue proposed that the survivor offspring were significantly affected by their parents' experience.[2]

INTERGENERATIONAL THEORY

In order to understand the transgenerational effects of the concentration camp experience, it is important to examine the systems approach to the study of families. A system can be defined as an interpersonal unit of at least two persons who are in a contractual and continuous relationship. In addition, theorists have expanded from these particular formulations and extended the notion of the system across generations. The transmission of different roles, expectations, and even psychopathology from one generation to the other would then be the domain of study. The latter perspective is called the intergenerational approach.

Intergenerational theory is closely associated with the work of Bowen, Boszormenyi-Nagy and Framo, and Spark.[3] Although these writers differ in some of the specifics of techniques and formulations, their basic assumption is similar, that is, that unresolved issues between the parents are transmitted to the next generation, in other words, their children. (The mode of transmission may be understood through the processes of modeling and/or identification.) Thus, the quality of the family interactions becomes highly dependent on the function and structure of that particular family.

An understanding of this intergenerational family process requires the use of the concepts of boundaries[4] and differentiation.[5] Boundaries can be defined as "the rule defining who participates and how."[6] Minuchin classified boundaries into three types: enmeshed, clear, and disengaged. Bowen[7] used a similar distinction, although he placed boundaries on a continuum based on the degree of differentiation. Fusion (similar to Minuchin's concept of enmeshed boundaries), is on one end of the continuum, and on the other end, differentiation (similar to Minuchin's clear boundaries). Enmeshed boundaries indicate that no clear boundaries were developed in the family due to a lack of accepted rules and order. For a person in this family system, the result is an interference in the development of a differentiated and integrated sense of self. Disengaged boundaries refer to strong and rigid interpersonal family boundaries in which family rules are applied arbitrarily, irrespective of the particular circumstances. This process is viewed as leading to difficulties in communication within the family and causing problems in the development of a sense of self.

The lack of appropriate boundaries both across and within generations therefore is likely to interfere with the development of a separate, differentiated self-concept of the individual family members. This phenomenon leads to what Ackerman[8] referred to as the interlocking of family pathology as well as its across generational transmission. Menninger[9] similarly observed that parents transmitted unresolved tensions, frustration, and hostilities generated within their own family of origin onto their children. Whitaker[10] argued that the influence of past generations is expressed through the existence of "ghosts" of the parents affecting the current functioning of their children. Further, Boszormenyi-Nagay and Spark[11] discussed the process through which the children are used by their parents to satisfy unmet needs and wishes (parentification). The parents were seen as unconsciously placing the children in a parenting position. This latter point was also made by Epstein,[12] who quotes one of the survivor's children: "It was not as if they were the parents and we were the children. We became the parents sometimes and I didn't like it" (p. 37).

A related useful and important concept is that of "Operational Mourning."[13] An incomplete and unresolved mourning for one's own parents may lead to the activation of defense mechanisms operating to prevent further losses and disappointments. This process can be manifested by the overprotection of one's children, reliving the past through the children's lives, and emotional distancing. Therefore, in families with generally unclear boundaries, the intergenerational boundaries might also be blurred. The children might be seen as extensions of their parents and psychologically undifferentiated from them. However, it is extremely important to emphasize that while pathology might be transmitted in an already pathological system where no gross pathology exists, it seems unlikely that across generational transmission of pathology will occur.

CHARACTERISTICS OF SURVIVORS AND THEIR FAMILIES

The survivor syndrome as presented in the psychological literature is characterized by chronic depression, obsessive rumination of past traumas, chronic anxiety states with accompanying nightmares, and a sense of hopelessness, guilt, and despair.[14] Lifton[15] referred to the concept of "psychic closing off," pointing to the inability to feel and show affection in the way the person had prior to the trauma. The feeling reported by survivors was: "There was always a sense that life was tenuous. Things weren't that secure."[16]

On the basis of his clinical experience, Davidson[17] felt that the initial marital choice of survivors was dictated to some extent by the trauma they had experienced. Survivors might choose another survivor as a spouse because of his or her resemblance to a lost parental figure or spouse, a prewar acquaintance, or because of a shared experience in the concentration camp. Davidson stated, "When the marital relationship was based essentially on the attempt to reconstruct a previously destroyed marriage and family with an inability to accept the destruction of the first family, the memory of the former unmourned partner and children overshadowed the new marriage and prevented the establishment of a satisfactory relationship" (p. 14). Certainly, this process can be applied to the lost parents as well. The mourning becomes unfinished and unresolved with significant effects on the way the children are brought up.

Kestenberg and Aleksandrowicz[18] discussed the survivors as parents. Each emphasized the importance of the parents' expectations and the pressures they exert on their offspring for the continuation of the lost families. Barocas and Barocas and Russell[19] proposed that the parents might expect the children to give meaning to the parents' life and replace all that was lost. This process could also be manifested by the tendency to name the children after the perished grandparents, although this custom of naming after a deceased person has a long history in the Jewish tradition. Further, parents might have exaggerated expectations regarding the child's academic and vocational success. Living under such pressures the children might not be allowed to develop an individual, differentiated identity. Barocas and Barocas theorized that, "Destructive identification is associated with the parent's expectation that the child will become an extension of him rather than a separate person and that he act out that aspect of the neurosis the parent most wishes to deny" (p. 820).

Russell[20] carried out extensive family therapy with the survivors and the children, and described the mothers as having difficulties nurturing their children, bound by fears that the child may get killed or kidnapped, and preoccupied with the child's health. The mothers tended to be overprotective of their children and appeared to be the dominant figure in the family. This observation was shared by Davidson, Fogelman and Savran, and Freyberg.[21] The fathers were described by Russell[22] as being weak, withdrawn and quiet, and passive and ineffectual as parents. Davidson[23] reported that the fathers tended to appear adaptive outside of the home, but emotionally restricted within the family. However, the mother was viewed as the one who manifested the symptoms of the survivor syndrome.

These observations present a picture of the family system of survivors as one in which the boundaries are either extremely rigid or nonexistent. The relationships between the parents are likely to be stressful and heavily loaded with the reminiscences of their traumatic past. Further, parental difficulties, such as symptoms of the survivor's syndrome, unresolved mourning, and stress reactions, are likely to be manifested by parental psychological problems and/or difficulties with their children. Thus, the children's symptoms could serve the function of reducing tension by distracting the family from the more severe parental problems. This formulation is basically Bowen's[24] concept of "triangle". Clearly, a triangular interaction is not conducive to the development of a differentiated sense of self by the children within this family, and may be associated with behavioral difficulties by the offspring.

A number of clinical reports[25] indicated that the parents complained that their children were difficult to control. These children (who were being seen in treatment) were viewed as having difficulties with aggression. Sigal, et al.,[26] found support for their hypothesis that the children's behavioral difficulties would be manifested in the area of impulse control, mainly that of aggression, and by a sense of anomie and alienation. Sigal, et al., concluded, "The parents may unconsciously encourage the children to further displays of aggressive behavior, having the children express what they, the parents, cannot permit themselves to express because of the burden of guilt they carry over the death of their own parents or siblings" (p. 326). This view is similar to that expressed by Barocas and Barocas.[27] This impression may further support the notion of the "triangle" in the child-parental interaction pattern, and the children's role in the pathology of the family system.

The children of survivors may be placed in an extremely difficult position. For example, Trossman[28] worked with adolescent children and found a predominance in this group of identity problems and depressive features. Their awareness and knowledge about their parents' experience, even in cases where the issue was not openly discussed, were seen as likely to cause the children to feel responsibility for their parents and desiring to compensate their parents for their traumas. On the other hand, the offspring may feel the need to assert their own individuality. "I felt they had imposed a burden on me and I had a right to feel a little resentful. . . . I had to be happy in order to make up for everything that happened.''[29] Thus, the child might feel that he or she has been placed in an impossible situation. The child could feel resentment and anger which he or she cannot express, consequently blocking still further the process of differentiation.[30] This potential conflict could then produce behavior problems in areas related to impulse control.

EVALUATION

The process of pathology transmission as described above theoretically could lead to similar pathology among the children of survivors. However, it should be recalled that there is not evidence that all survivors display pathological behavior. Most of the initial survivor data were obtained from persons who had sought psychiatric help, and these persons or families are not necessarily representative of the general survivor population. Epstein[31] pointed out that the clinical impressions developed about survivors tended to ignore their strengths and created an image that was overwhelmingly negative or pathological.

It does not seem justified to conclude that the long-term family effects of the Holocaust trauma are invariably pathological. Bowen[32] implied that the vicious transgenerational transmission process can be broken. He argued that when persons marry others who are at the same level of differentiation, then there may be a change in the pattern. An interesting question arises, therefore, regarding cross-generational effects. What kind of family structure and/or personality pattern would lead to a transgenerational transmission of pathology versus the kind of family and/or personality pattern that would lead to adaptive family functioning? The intuitive answer may be that an already dysfunctional system would tend to maintain itself. Dysfunctional families would be maintained if the children mate with others who are at the same or at a lower level of differentiation.[33] However, one can assume that the heterogeneity of the population would increase the likelihood that some of the survivor children would break the cycle. Over generations, then, the pathological effect would wane.

One should recall our caution regarding the pathological bias in most of the studies discussed above. There is evidence that many survivors did manage to restore and rehabilitate themselves, even though it is very unlikely that they came out of that experience untouched. The issue of the transmission of psychopathology to the children is likely to be quite complicated. For example, high-risk research indicates that not all the children who are at high risk for the development of pathology eventually develop a psychopathological disorder.[34]

SURVIVORS OF THE HOLOCAUST AND THEIR
CHILDREN: CURRENT STATUS AND ADJUSTMENT

Our study of concentration camp and other survivors of World War II and their families[35] was carried out in 1978–1979 and focused on the assessment of current adjustment and attitudes. We were also interested in the general issue of personality adjustment and coping mechanisms in dealing with severe stress, as well as the influence of the Holocaust on the children of survivors. We received the cooperation of Jewish social service agencies in Minneapolis, St. Paul, and Milwaukee, and personnel from those agencies began contacting persons whose names appeared on their agency list identified as World War II refugees.

Our research was different from others in the literature at that time because we tried to study a sample of survivors functioning in the community, that is, persons who had not been identified for study specifically because of visits to hospitals or clinics. We also evaluated the offspring within these same families rather than following the more usual strategy of studying separate groups of children whose source of identification was through clinic or hospital rosters. Further, our findings on the survivors and their families were compared with data obtained from an assessment of a control group of families. The parents of the latter group also were European in origin and of the same general age and religious background.

Our initial strategy was to compare three groups of families: those in which at least one parent had been in a concentration camp, those in which at least one parent had survived World War II in extremely harsh conditions, and families in which at least one parent had emigrated to the United States in the period preceding World War II. However, since the data analyses indicated no statistically significant differences between concentration camp and noncamp survivor samples, these groups were combined to increase the statistical power of subsequent analyses.

The study therefore consisted of a group of 52 concentration camp and other survivors and 47 of their children, compared to a group of 29 persons of similar background and 16 of their children. The study was carried out approximately 33 years after the end of World War II. The mean current age of the survivors was 60.5 years; for the comparison group, 65 years. The mean age of the survivor children was 28 years, and the comparison group children, 36.5 years. All participants completed the Minnesota Multiphasic Personality Inventory (MMPI). In addition, Parent and Children's versions of a Current Life Functioning Form were specially constructed for this study. These instruments elicited information about family interactions, eating patterns, and political attitudes. The Children's version measured the child's perception of the parents' attitudes and behavior. The mental health items developed for the Midtown Manhattan Study (Srole, 1974–1975) were embedded in each version of the questionnaire. The subjects independently completed the inventories in their homes and mailed the forms back to the investigators.

SUBJECT PARTICIPATION

Of the survivors contacted, 52.7 percent agreed to participate and 74.3 percent of this group completed and returned the forms. The participation rate for their children was 74.6 percent. The comparison group parents' participation data were as follows: 64.8 percent agreeing to participate and an 82.9 percent return rate from this group. The comparison groups children's return rate was 48.5 percent.

We also attempted to obtain whatever information we could about the psychological status of the survivors contacted who refused to participate. The interviewers' impressions were that four of the persons contacted who did not send back the forms gave evidence of psychological impairment, and two others were known to the agency staff to have a history of severe psychopathology. However, many of those who refused to participate also were known to agency staff persons and were judged as productive, successful members of the community. Several were involved in planning extended vacations at the time they were contacted and did not want to invest the time necessary to fill out the forms. Eight others indicated that they did not want to arouse painful memories about their wartime experiences, or they had concerns about how the study findings would be used.

PSYCHOLOGICAL ADJUSTMENT

Parents

The MMPI findings indicated that the psychological adjustment of the survivor and comparison parent groups reflected normal range functioning. The group profiles were within normal limits for each of the MMPI validity and clinical scales. The D (Depression) scale mean score was relatively highest of the scale scores for both the mother and father groups (T score mean = 63.6, 60.6, respectively). These scores demonstrate a moderate normal range elevation on the D scale. In addition, a small but statistically significant difference was found for the males on the Ma (Hypomania) and Pd (Psychopathic Deviate) scales, with the survivors scoring higher. The female survivors also demonstrated a significantly higher score than the comparison females on the Pd scale.

The relatively higher normal range scores of the survivor group on the Pd scale suggests a more marked tendency in the survivors to act quickly when circumstances require quick action or greater interpersonal guile. These characteristics would certainly be extremely adaptive for surviving in dangerous and unpredictable circumstances. In addition, the moderate elevation of the D scale score in both groups may reflect a cultural or ethnic characteristic. It should be noted as well that the range of scores on each of the MMPI clinical scales suggests that a small number of persons in *both* the survivor and comparison groups were exhibiting an impairment in some areas of functioning. However, the mean scores for both groups were within the normal range, with few significant scale score differences between groups.

The mental health ratings based on 21 items used in the Midtown Manhattan Study indicated a small but significant difference between the survivor and comparison parent groups for both males and females. A higher proportion of the survivor females endorsed several items expressing suspiciousness about the motives of others. A greater proportion of the survivor males endorsed health-rated items such as problems of dizziness, fainting spells, poor health, and a greater frequency of episodes of restlessness.

Children

Comparisons of the offspring group scores on the MMPI and the mental health rating showed no significant differences between groups. The psychological functioning of both the survivor and comparison group children were within the normal range as measured by these psychological inventories. Thus, there was no evidence that the group of survivor children suffered from psychological impairment. As with the parent analyses, there was a range of scores for each of the MMPI clinical scales, but there were no group differences in adjustment level between the survivor and comparison group offspring.

CURRENT LIFE ATTITUDES

There were few differences between the survivor and comparison groups regarding their attitudes about their present life experiences. Both parent groups tended to report a feeling of comfort and satisfaction with their current life (survivors—89.3%; comparison group—96.4%). However, the survivors reported a greater frequency of continued memories about circumstances they had lived through during the war. A greater proportion of the survivors than the comparison group endorsed items indicating that they still found themselves thinking about their experiences during the war even when they tried not to do so (survivor females—81.8%; survivor males—84.2%), and that wartime experiences had affected their present mood (survivor females—66.6%; survivor males—57.9%). On the other hand, the majority of both survivor and comparison groups indicated that they felt comfortable and secure in their daily life (survivors—89.3%; comparison—96.4%). The majority of both parent groups indicated that they trusted the current government to treat them fairly (survivors—64.5%; comparison—84.5%), but they felt that the world community should share responsibility with Germany for the Holocaust (survivors—90.6%; comparison—70.7%). The majority of both groups felt that the Holocaust could happen in the United States (survivors—79%; comparison—83.3%).

Mealtime behaviors were assessed in order to ascertain whether the prolonged starvation experienced by the survivors had a lasting effect on food consumption, practices and attitudes. However, the data on current mealtime practices showed no significant differences between the survivor and comparison groups. The parents of both groups reported usually finishing all of the food on their plates and encouraging their children to do so as well. Both parent groups indicated that more food was cooked for each meal than the family generally could finish. There were no group differences in the frequency of grocery shopping each week, or between meal snacking patterns. A number of food aversions were reported by the participants, such as eating pork and shellfish. However, the onset of these aversions was reported to have occurred prior to World War II, and most likely reflect religious proscriptions rather than any specific influences of the Holocaust.

The parents' attitudes about their children were also studied and compared. Both survivor and comparison group mothers reported that they worried a great deal about their children (survivors—86.2%; comparison—78.6%). On the other hand, a significantly greater proportion of the survivor fathers endorsed this item (88.9%) than did the comparison group fathers (50%).

Evaluating the offsprings' attitudes, we found that the majority of both the survivor and comparison group children reported feeling comfortable and secure in their daily lives (survivor offspring—74.5%; comparison offspring—73.2%). The majority also indicated that they would lead the same kind of life they were now leading even if they moved to a completely different place (survivor offspring—76.9%; comparison offspring—67.4%). A substantial number reported that they planned to raise their children in the same way they were raised (survivor offspring—34%; comparison offspring—30.9%). The children of both groups generally indicated that they felt a closeness to their parents, and an openness in communicating with them. They reported that they felt a concern for their parents, and they also felt that their parents were concerned about them. Both offspring groups indicated that their parents had sacrificed a great deal for them to have an education and be successful.

CONCLUSIONS

Our findings failed to support the belief that survivors as a group and their children as a group manifest significant psychological disturbance. This categorical belief about the current psychological status of survivors and their children clearly was not substantiated by our study. Our strategy of using a comparison group of similar age, religion, and European origin also allowed us to evaluate the attitudes and family processes that might be cultural in nature as opposed to being specifically related to being a survivor of the Holocaust. The overprotection and worry that has been viewed as specific to survivor parents was manifested by the parents and particularly the mothers of both groups. These concerns about their children therefore seem to be a cultural rather than a survivor process. Similarly, the concern by the parents and children of both groups about academic and vocational success most likely can be viewed as a first generation American phenomenon. Looking at mealtime and eating patterns, one again can find no group differences that might be related to starvation experiences, but a general attitude about eating well and not wasting food that was common to both groups. The specific food aversions, as already noted, fit in with a religious rather than a starvation explanation.

The findings of this investigation should not be interpreted to mean that Holocaust survivors did not undergo a horribly traumatic experience and were not influenced by this. Rather, our findings indicate that despite the fact that many survivors reported that they continue to be troubled by memories of their wartime experiences some 33 years after World War II, they have been able to overcome the often still present feelings of restlessness, nightmares, and memories of the past, and lead productive lives including the raising of children who are also productive and generally well adjusted.

Thus, what the parents transmitted to their children about their Holocaust experience might also include the modeling of how to cope with severe and prolonged stress, rather than necessarily the transmission of processes of psychopathology. While some individual families were less well adjusted than others, the same was true for the comparison group. The survivor families as a group were not significantly different in adjustment than the comparison group, and both functioned on the average within the normal range. A link between survivor status and self- or child psychopathology was not found. Therefore, our findings indicate that the transmission of pathology may be highly dependent on the psychological adequacy (or inadequacy) of the family of origin.

One of the issues examined in our study was the possible identification of mechanisms that seemed to have helped survivors overcome their traumatic experiences. The majority of survivors in our investigation married other survivors very soon after liberation, and a number had children while still in displaced persons camps awaiting resettlement in the United States. These persons can be viewed, therefore, as quickly reconstructing the family ties they lost during the Holocaust. For them, this process was apparently an adaptive one rather than maladaptive. Adaptive coping may also be reflected in the fact that many survivors quickly formed survivor clubs in the cities in which they were settled. Therefore, new social support networks were formed of persons who had undergone similar traumatic experiences. The survivors were able to relate to and gain the kind of understanding from each other that they could not obtain from others in the community.

From the perspective of this study, over three decades after the end of World War II, one can conclude that the family transmission of psychopathology in survivor families is not a universal phenomenon. On the contrary, empirical studies with appropriate comparison groups generally indicate a remarkable degree of strength and coping ability in many of the families assessed.[36] Perhaps in part the survivors were able to survive because of superior physical and psychological strength. If so, then the intergenerational effect of the Holocaust also might be one of conveying adaptive coping skills rather than maladaptive functioning. There are individual differences, however, that suggest that it is unjustified to make sweeping generalizations for all families either in the direction of adaptive coping or psychopathological functioning.

IMPLICATIONS FOR TREATMENT

Statistics on the utilization of mental health services suggest that many individuals at some point in their lives will seek help for emotional and interpersonal problems. Given the lore that seems to have arisen that most children of survivors are psychologically disturbed by virtue of their parents' Holocaust experiences, it is important for both the therapist and survivor offspring not to conclude uncritically that the problems of the client are directly related to concentration camp–induced parental psychopathology. On the other hand, the intergenerational transmission of maladapative functioning due to parental concentration camp–survival has been documented in some cases and may require extensive exploration where appropriate. One should also bear in mind that the experiences of the parents can have a significant although not necessarily psychopathological impact on family members, and adaptive versus maladaptive influences need to be assessed. For example, several children of survivors in our study with very normal MMPI profiles indicated that knowledge of their parents' experiences helped them to be more sensitive and caring for others, and became part of their motivation for pursuing medical careers.

At the present time, the children of survivors are likely to be adults and some will have children of their own. Family therapy with survivor parents participating in some way might be considered an option by some therapists. However, the resiliency of the intergenerational family system and the presence of adaptive as well as maladaptive coping patterns within this larger system needs to be assessed before deciding on a specific treatment for a troubled offspring.

Given the age of the parents and questions about their flexibility in changing longstanding patterns, it seems more beneficial to focus treatment on the offspring either alone or with his or her own spouse and children. Survivor parent influences and other problems can then be dealt with through the client. Examples of adaptive coping by survivor parents and their impact on family members need to be highlighted in therapy as well as the exploration of maladaptive processes. It seems therapeutic for the children to gain an appreciation where relevant of the resilience and competence of their parents as well as an understanding of maladaptive parental patterns that might be influencing the client's current adjustment. It is also important in therapy to help the client resolve or let go of past familial and other experiences and learn more effective interactional and coping skills for dealing with the present situation. In this way, psychopathology might not continue to be passed on from one generation to the next.

NOTES

1. Leo Eitinger, "Concentration Camp Survivors in Norway and Israel," *Israeli Journal of Medical Science* 1 (1965): 883–895; Otto Gronvik and Arve Lonnum, "Neurological Conditions in Former Concentration Camp Inmates," *Journal of Neuropsychiatry* 4 (1962): 50–54; P. Helweg-Larson, et al., "Famine Disease in German Concentration Camps: Complications and Sequels," *Acta Psychiatrica Scandinavica* (1952), Supplement 83; Henry Krystal, *Massive Psychic Trauma* (New York: International Universities Press, 1968).

2. Harvey A. Barocas and Carol B. Barocas, "Manifestations of Concentration Camp Effects on the Second Generation," *American Journal of Psychiatry* 130 (1973): 820–

821; Shamai Davidson, "The Clinical Effects of Massive Psychic Trauma in Families of Holocaust Survivors," *Journal of Marital and Family Therapy* 6 (1980): 11–21; Eva Fogelman and Bella Savran, "Brief Group Therapy with Offspring of Holocaust Survivors," *American Journal of Orthopsychiatry* 50 (1980): 96–108; Joan T. Freyberg, "Difficulties in Separation-Individuation as Experienced by Offspring of Nazi Holocaust Survivors," *American Journal of Orthopsychiatry* 50 (1980): 87–95; Axel Russell, "Late Psychosocial Consequences in Concentration Camp Survivor Families," *American Journal of Orthopsychiatry* 44 (1974): 611–619.

3. I. Boszormenyi-Nagy and J. L. Framo, *Intensive Family Therapy* (New York: Harper & Row, 1965); Murray Bowen, "The Use of Family Theory in Clinical Practice," *Comprehensive Psychiatry* 7 (1966): 345–374; G. Spark, "Grandparents and Intergenerational Family Process," *Family Process* 13 (1974): 225.

4. Salvador Minuchin, *Families and Family Therapy* (Cambridge, MA: Harvard University Press, 1974).

5. Murray Bowen, "The Use of Family Theory in Clinical Practice," pp. 345–374; ibid., "Theory in the Practice of Psychotherapy," in P. J. Guerin, Ed., *Family Therapy: Theory and Practice* (New York: Gardner, 1976).

6. Salvador Minuchin, *Families and Family Therapy*, p. 53.

7. Murray Bowen, "The Use of Family Theory in Clinical Practice," pp. 345–374; ibid., "Theory in the Practice of Psychotherapy."

8. Nathan W. Ackerman, "Interlocking Pathologies in Family Relationships," in S. Rado and G. E. Daniels, Eds., *Changing Concepts in Psychoanalytic Medicine* (New York: Grune & Stratton, 1956).

9. Karl Menninger, *Love Against Hate* (New York: Harcourt, Brace, & World, 1958).

10. Carl Whitaker, *Marital and Family Therapy* (Chicago: Instructional Dynamics, 1970).

11. I. Boszormenyi-Nagy and G. Spark, *Invisible Loyalties* (New York: Harper & Row, 1973).

12. Helen Epstein, *Children of the Holocaust* (New York: Putnam, 1979), p. 37.

13. N. Paul and G. Grosser, "Operational Mourning and Its Role in Conjoint Family Therapy," *Community Mental Health Journal* 1 (1965): 339–345.

14. William G. Niederland, "Clinical Observations on the 'Survivor Syndrome,' " *International Journal of Psychoanalysis* 49 (1968): 313–316.

15. Robert J. Lifton, *Death in Life: Survivors of Hiroshima* (New York: Random House, 1968).

16. Helen Epstein, *Children of the Holocaust*, p. 192.

17. Shamai Davidson, "The Clinical Effects of Massive Psychic Trauma in Families of Holocaust Survivors," pp. 11–21.

18. Judith Kestenberg, "Psychoanalytic Contribution to the Problem of Children Survivors from Nazi Persecution," *Israel Annals of Psychiatry and Related Disciplines* 4 (1972): 311–323; Dov Aleksandrowicz, "Children of Concentration Camp Survivors," In E. James Anthony and Cyrille Koupernik, Eds., *The Child in His Family* (New York: Wiley, 1973).

19. Harvey A. Barocas and Carol B. Barocas, "Manifestations of Concentration Camp Effects on the Second Generation," pp. 820–821; Axel Russell, "Late Psychosocial Consequences in Concentration Camp Survivor Families," pp. 611–619.

20. Ibid., pp. 611–619.

21. Shamai Davidson, "The Clinical Effects of Massive Psychic Trauma in Families

of Holocaust Survivors," pp. 11–21; Eva Fogelman and Bella Savran, "Brief Group Therapy with Offspring of Holocaust Survivors," pp. 96–108; Joan T. Freyberg, "Difficulties in Separation-Individuation as Experienced by Offspring of Nazi Holocaust Survivors," pp. 87–95.

22. Axel Russell, "Late Psychosocial Consequences in Concentration Camp Survivor Families," pp. 611–619.

23. Shamai Davidson, "The Clinical Effects of Massive Psychic Trauma in Families of Holocaust Survivors," pp. 11–21.

24. Murray Bowen, "Theory in the Practice of Psychotherapy."

25. Axel Russell, "Late Psychosocial Consequences in Concentration Camp Survivor Families," pp. 611–619; John J. Sigal, D. Silver, Vivian Rakoff, and B. Ellin, "Some Second-Generation Effects of Survival of the Nazi Persecution," *American Journal of Orthopsychiatry* 43 (1973): 320–327.

26. John J. Sigal, D. Silver, Vivian Rakoff, and B. Ellin, "Some Second-Generation Effects of Survival of the Nazi Persecution," pp. 320–327.

27. Harvey A. Barocas and Carol B. Barocas, "Manifestations of Concentration Camp Effects on the Second Generation," pp. 820–821.

28. Bernard Trossman, "Adolescent Children of Concentration Camp Survivors," *Canadian Psychiatric Association Journal* 13 (1968): 121–123.

29. Helen Epstein, *Children of the Holocaust*, pp. 41–42.

30. L. Steinitz and D. Szoni, Eds., *Living After the Holocaust: Reflections by the Post-War Generation in America* (New York: Bloch, 1975–1976).

31. Helen Epstein, *Children of the Holocaust*.

32. Murray Bowen, "Theory in the Practice of Psychotherapy."

33. Murray Bowen, "The Use of Family Theory in Clinical Practice," pp. 345–374; ibid., "Theory in the Practice of Psychotherapy."

34. Sarnoff A. Mednick and Fini Schulsinger, "Some Premorbid Characteristics Related to Breakdown in Children with Schizophrenic Mothers," in D. Rosenthal and S. S. Kety, Eds., *The Transmission of Schizophrenia* (Elmsford, NY: Pergamon Press, 1968).

35. Gloria R. Leon, James N. Butcher, Max Kleinman, Alan Goldberg, and Moshe Almagor, "Survivors of the Holocaust and Their Children: Current Status and Adjustment," *Journal of Personality and Social Psychology* 41 (1981): 503–516.

36. Norman Solkoff, "Children of Survivors of the Nazi Holocaust: A Critical Review of the Literature," *American Journal of Orthopsychiatry* 51 (1981): 29–42; Morton Weinfeld, John J. Sigal, and William W. Eaton, "Long-term Effects of the Holocaust on Selected Social Attitudes and Behaviors of Survivors: A Cautionary Note," *Social Forces* 60 (1981): 1–19; Arnold Wilson and Erika Fromm, "Aftermath of the Concentration Camp: The Second Generation," *Journal of the American Academy of Psychoanalysis* 10 (1982): 289–313.

12

Clinical and Gerontological Issues Facing Survivors of the Nazi Holocaust

BOAZ KAHANA, ZEV HAREL, AND EVA KAHANA

The traumatic events experienced by survivors of the Holocaust left an indelible mark on every aspect of their subsequent existence. Early and even longer-term impact of these events on well-being, personality, and peace of mind of survivors has been extensively documented by the clinical psychiatric literature[1] and more recently by more qualitative social science research.

As survivors of the Holocaust are confronting the stresses and challenges of aging that bring increasing frailty and vulnerability even to nontraumatized populations, questions arise whether survivors manifest special characteristics and needs at this final developmental stage of life. Our discussion in this chapter focuses on late life adaptation in the aftermath of the extreme trauma of the Holocaust. Findings of a recent study are presented based on interviews with 168 elderly Holocaust survivors in the United States. Our focus is on survival skills and coping strategies that enable such elderly individuals to handle successfully both cumulative stresses and recent life events. Responses of survivors about their coping resources, functioning and well-being, and their attitudes toward the aging process were also compared with those of 156 elderly Jewish immigrants to the United States who arrived from Europe during the period immediately preceding the Holocaust.

In an effort to place late life survivorship in its proper context, this chapter includes a discussion of methodological issues in interviewing elderly survivors of trauma followed by a substantive discussion of psychosocial functioning and well-being of elderly survivors, predictors of late life well-being in this group, responses to the aging process, and, finally, efforts to find meaning in survivorship. The trauma of the Holocaust is examined here from the theoretical vantage point of stress research.[2] Thus, we will focus on characteristics of the trauma as they influence psychosocial well-being on a long-term basis and the buffering roles of psychological and social resources in ameliorating the impact of stress. Our particular concern is with late life sequelae of the traumatic stress and the usefulness of understanding the developmental context for practitioners working with elderly survivors of extreme trauma. Our focus in this discussion is generally on the survivors with data on the comparison group presented when appropriate. Based on data from our in-depth, cross-sectional interview study of U.S. and Israeli survivors, this chapter is supplemented with findings of a separate survey of 275 older Holocaust survivors who attended the 1983 Washington Gathering of Holocaust Survivors.

The profound and wide-ranging impact of stress on psychosocial functioning has been well documented.[2] The framework of stress research is a particularly useful approach to understanding survivors of extreme trauma for several reasons. The approach allows for specifying elements of traumatic life situations and considering their short- and long-term effects on the physical and mental health of survivors. It also permits consideration of both personal and environmental/social resources as they may ameliorate adverse effects of stress. A conceptually useful aspect of this framework calls for separating the characteristics of coping strategies used to deal with stressful situations from outcomes of these coping efforts. Furthermore, characterological versus situation-specific elements of coping may be distinguished. The stress paradigm also permits the introduction of a temporal component and specification of ongoing and recent life events as well as earlier traumatic life experiences. Similarly, immediate post-traumatic outcomes as well as long-term consequences of trauma may be described.

Consideration of the impact of long-term stress on the elderly requires bringing together the methodological know-how of both general stress research and gerontological research. The elderly are confronted with cumulative stresses of a lifetime and must face new life events, role changes, even internal changes at a point in their lives when their adaptive capacities and social resources may be diminished.[3] For a long time, empirical research on the impact of stress has been largely limited to investigations of recent stressful life events and their sequelae.[4] With the increasing sophistication of stress research, it is now recognized that more comprehensive considerations of stress are necessary for understanding its impact on health and psychosocial well-being.

How applicable are conceptions developed in general stress research for the analysis and understanding of the impact of extremely stressful conditions such as the Holocaust? In arriving at an orientation to stress, our study follows generally accepted guidelines in the stress literature. Nevertheless, some important qualifications are also proposed in making conceptualizations applicable to extreme stress situations. Torrance[5] suggests that distinctive elements in extreme situations include the lack of conventional social structure, the loss of an anchor in reality, and the inability to predict or anticipate outcomes. This formulation also has its basis in the description of concentration camp conditions,[6] where individuals had little or no ability to anticipate and predict outcomes on a day-to-day basis.

Stress is considered in terms of its cumulative impact. Thus, survivors of the Holocaust 40 years after this extreme trauma are viewed as responding to cumulative effects of major life crises that they had experienced. These stresses encompass recent life events, life crises experienced during the post-Holocaust period (loss of family, loss of home, and relocation stress to a new country), the trauma of the Holocaust or even earlier pre-Holocaust crises, for example, the loss of a parent in childhood. It is anticipated that members of the comparison group who did not experience the Holocaust will have endured considerably less cumulative stress than did the survivors. Neverthless, this group will be by no means devoid of life stress, especially since they are immigrants to their respective new homelands of the United States and Israel. Furthermore, as Jews in prewar Europe, many had experienced discrimination or even persecution.

Traditional approaches to examine the sequelae of extreme psychic trauma have generally sought to uncover physical health problems and psychopathology among those who have endured extreme stress. In marked contrast, our research attempted to gain an understanding of the coping resources and adaptive strategies that enabled survivors to function and to find meaning in their lives subsequent to trauma and loss of parents, siblings, spouses, and children. Indications of the human potential for finding meaning in adversity may be found in the work of existential psychiatrists and psychologists as well as in qualitative stress research. Viktor Frankl[7] has provided poignant arguments regarding the integrative resources of survivors in seeking meaning amidst the tragedy of the Holocaust. Empirical studies of the physically ill and dying also suggest that great adversity may elicit great family cohesiveness and personal coping resources.[8]

Our approach here is to go beyond describing normative responses to adversity. Our study has provided confirmation in the often-documented negative psychological and physiological sequelae of traumatic life situations. Nevertheless we also find it useful to focus on understanding how and why older people can keep going, keep working, and smiling and help others, even in the face of extreme personal and social losses. We believe that an understanding of constructive personal meaning in response to extreme stress is a critical and as yet little emphasized prerequisite for developing clinical interventions with older persons who have undergone these extreme life crises.

Before turning to a consideration of substantive findings of our research we will discuss some critical methodological issues that bear on our understanding of posttraumatic adaptation of elderly survivors. We believe that in order to integrate clinical and gerontological perspectives in a meaningful manner, researchers and clinicians must reflect on any factors that play a role in obtaining data from survivors of the Holocaust. Special problems in obtaining representative samples of survivors and in interviewing elderly survivors about painful life experiences may impact on the substance of scientific information currently available about this group. While no study, including our own, has succeeded in overcoming these problems, awareness and sensitivity about limits of our understanding can place existing findings into a meaningful context.

METHODOLOGICAL ISSUES

The lack of systematic studies of survivors in the past is due to a considerable extent to methodological problems inherent in selecting a scientifically sound sample. In attempting to obtain a representative sample of survivors, we are confronted with the task of identifying the larger universe from which the sample is to be drawn. There has not been as of yet a comprehensive enumeration of survivors in the United States or in Israel (the two countries in which the vast majority of survivors reside).

One of the most prevelant (and potentially adaptive) defense mechanisms for coping with extreme stress is denial.[9] Victims of trauma may frequently choose to avoid remembering and talking about their experiences and hence fear participation in an interview. Furthermore, in the case of survivors there has long been a "conspiracy of silence"[10] where survivors were subtly and even overtly socialized to avoid dwelling on their past. As this curtain of socially and personally imposed silence is slowly lifting, researchers must be particularly careful to consider potential sample bias due to characteristics of those who are willing to volunteer and talk about their experiences. Potential biases may be better mental health, greater ethnic and religious identification, greater self-disclosure, a need for having a therapeutic experience through the interview process, greater assertiveness, and a self-perception as a representative spokesman for other survivors. Researchers must make every effort to maximize participation of respondents. Yet they must also respect the rights of respondents to privacy, anonymity, selective denial, and selective self-disclosure.

Regarding cooperation of individual survivors, several approaches have been successful. The importance of documenting and memorializing the legacy of survivorship helps in the recruitment process. Reluctant interviewees may receive reassurance from respondents who have been interviewed. Researchers should learn the variety of reasons for potential refusals and allay these underlying concerns. Some of the most commonly observed reasons for reluctance to be interviewed include: fear of reopening old wounds; fear of stigma; fear of self-disclosure; fear that outsiders won't understand; fear of trivializing the experience; and, finally, fear that information may be misused or get into the wrong hands. Some of these reasons have been responsible for the reluctance of survivors to seek counseling or utilize mental health services. Awareness by mental health professionals of the nature of such resistance in a research context provides useful clues for overcoming barriers to seeking mental health services as well.

Although discussing experiences associated with a traumatic period in their lives may be difficult for some survivors, our experiences in conducting interviews indicates that older persons are increasingly willing and even eager to discuss their experiences during the Holocaust. Recent media and public attention directed at the Holocaust has increased awareness by survivors about the importance of bearing witness to this episode in history so that future generations may remember lessons of the Holocaust.

PROBLEMS IN OBTAINING CONTROL OR COMPARISON GROUPS

In order to isolate the effects of extreme stress on survivors from ethnic/ cultural factors from immigration variables, suitable comparison groups must be found. If a comparison group of Jewish immigrants is used, they too have undergone the stresses of persecution prior to their escape or relocation to the United States. If a non-Jewish group of immigrants is used, the match of culture/ ethnicity is lost. The closest comparison groups of European immigrant Jews who have not experienced the Holocaust are German Jews who came to the United States within five years before World War II and Romanian Jews who lived in Europe during the war but experienced only limited persecution. These individuals, however, are also survivors in that they too were displaced or victimized by the Holocaust and often lost close relatives during this period.

The problems of obtaining adequate control comparison groups are at least in part generalizable to diverse studies of victims. One suggestion for optimizing the value of control groups is consideration of multiple comparison groups.

Challenges of Conducting Research with Survivors

Carrying out interviews with survivors about current life-styles and earlier trauma presents numerous challenges of its own. The interview must of necessity cover a broad time span ranging from early or postraumatic experiences to experiences during the period of extreme stress, postwar experiences covering the short-term posttraumatic adjustment of responses, and current life experiences. Issues of recall are compounded in such situations by the emotionally charged nature of the material being reported, the advanced age of respondents, and the long time period covered in the interview. Thus, differential short-term vs. long-term recall by the elderly and differential recall of traumatic vs. neutral subject matter may all come into play.

To minimize problems of recall and to facilitate accurate reporting of data, great care must be taken in designing and standardizing interviews.

An added problem has been found in following a structured interview format because of respondents' great need to recount in detail experiences of great personal salience. Furthermore, a wind-down period also appears necessary.

Our experiences have led us to modify interviewing procedures to fit with personal needs and preferences of respondents. In contrast to our past experience with gerontological interviews, where the elderly are found to experience fatigue after about one hour, Holocaust survivors typically wanted to continue talking for long time periods. For those experiencing positive catharsis by talking about past trauma and current mastery, three or even four hours appear too short a time period and frequently the interview is terminated by exhaustion of the interviewer rather than of the respondent. Thus, it appears that fatigue observed in elderly respondents by gerontological researchers may at least in part be a function of the lack of ego involvement on the part of respondents in the material covered.

Clinical and Ethical Issues in Conducting the Interview

In dealing with victims of extreme stress, clinical and ethical considerations assume special importance. Interviewers must portray empathy while remaining personally and emotionally uninvolved. Interviewers must have experience working with exceptional populations. Respondents depict a wide variety of responses to the interview ranging from lack of affective display to crying, cursing, and other extreme displays of feeling. In some instances, display of emotions did *not* occur in those segments of the interview which dealt specifically with traumatic Holocaust events. In other situations it appeared that psychic wounds that were apparently "healed by time" were reopened during the interview and given an opportunity to be worked through.

Only a small proportion of survivors had ever sought professional counseling or therapy for mental health problems created by the trauma of the Holocaust. At times respondents volunteer for the interview as a means of obtaining psychotherapeutic help. In this regard it is particularly helpful to establish a referral network of mental health professionals who have expertise in dealing with victims of extreme stress, particularly Holocaust stress. Such expertise needs to include a comprehensive understanding of the history and geography of the Holocaust, ethnicity factors, psychiatric and social science literature regarding survivors, and experience in treating survivors.

Additional issues are raised with regard to differential self-disclosure of respondents to interviews vis-à-vis to their own family. At times respondents state that the material discussed in the interview had never been shared with family members or even with their spouses. Some respondents are extremely concerned about anonymity and confidentiality while others have a strong need to bear witness and disseminate and publicize their experiences.

The sharing of strong emotional experiences during the interview has produced, in a number of instances, a strong bond between respondent and interviewer. In these cases we found it useful to conduct brief follow-up interviews and telephone calls. Respondents were told to feel free to contact the interviewer should they feel like conveying additional information or feelings regarding themselves and the Holocaust.

In presenting methodological issues confronted by studies of survivors of the Holocaust, we would like to acknowledge concern regarding trivialization of the Holocaust by setting it within the framework of the ordinary stress literature. Nevertheless, we are also acutely aware of the danger of avoiding scientific studies of the Holocaust and the consequent loss of documentation for both the social and behavioral sciences, and mankind in general, of any potential understanding of the characteristics, problems and abilities of the extraordinary minority of persons who survived the Holocaust and managed to reach old age in the aftermath of that experience. The present study aims to document the impact of severe stress, survival skills, and strength as well as problems of survivors.

An important and potentially dangerous implication of previous research conducted on survivors of the Holocaust thus far is the tendency to blame the victim in subtle and not so subtle ways. Thus, the focus has not been primarily on the nature of the extreme stress or the often valiant efforts by victims to cope with indescribably adverse circumstances. Instead, we are often confronted with a laundry list of negative adjectives focusing on psychopathology in these victims. The present study aims to bring both a more comprehensive and humanistic perspective to understanding adaptation of elderly survivors of the Holocaust. Ultimately, we feel there is an optimistic aspect of studying elderly survivors of extreme trauma. Their triumph in coping with physical, emotional and social stresses associated with aging superimposed on having survived the indescribable trauma of the Holocaust bear ultimate witness to the triumph of human endurance.

STUDY OBJECTIVES AND METHODS

Traditional approaches to research on Holocaust survivors have generally sought to identify physical health problems and psychopathology among those who have endured extreme stress. In contrast, our research attempted to gain an understanding of the coping resources and adaptive strategies that enable survivors to function and to find new meaning in their lives subsequent to trauma and loss of parents, siblings, spouses, and children. The present study considered mental health in addition to mental and physical illness focusing on strength, coping, outlook, and a positive philosophy of life.

A major goal of this research was to determine if older adults who had experienced extreme trauma early in life differed significantly in well-being and outlook from a reasonable comparison group.

Both the survivor and comparison sample were identified through the Jewish Federation records. This represents a good source for identifying participants, since 95 percent of Jewish immigrants are thought to be registered with the Federation. In addition, we worked with survivor organizations and also relied on snowball techniques to locate unaffiliated survivors.

Structured interviews with survivors and comparisons included measures of mental health,[11] affective states,[12] reported physical health, coping and cumulative life crises,[13] communication with family and friends, world outlook (the survivor's message to the world) and many questions regarding the details of their Holocaust experiences.

RESULTS

Differences were considered between survivors and the comparison group in terms of physical health, psychiatric symptomatology, and social functioning.

In terms of physical health and pathology, results from this study are consistent with earlier investigations. Survivors report significantly more physical symptoms than the comparison respondents for certain types of physical illnesses. Thus, significantly greater proportions of survivors reported symptoms that are likely to be psychogenic in nature. On the other hand, few significant differences emerged between the survivors and the controls for conditions which have not generally been documented to be stress-related disorders, such as arthritis, cancer, and Parkinson's disease.

Survivors' perception about the impact of the Holocaust on their well-being confirmed the experience of adverse effects. Accordingly, 89 percent reported that the Holocaust adversely affected their physical health, although only 31 percent said that major negative effects were extreme. Regarding emotional well-being, 92 percent reported that their Holocaust experiences adversely affected their emotional well-being. Survivors were also haunted by frequent and instructive memories of the trauma they experienced. In response to the question 'How often do you think of your Holocaust experiences?'', 61 percent stated that they think of the Holocaust daily or several times a week.

In terms of psychological distress, survivors' SCL–90-R primary symptom dimension profiles were elevated relative to both comparison participants and standardized norms. In terms of morale, respondents' responses to Lawton's 17-item Morale Scale indicated striking differences between the survivor and comparison groups on seven of the 17 items. Generally, survivors were more likely than comparisons to: feel lonely a lot (41% vs. 22%); have a lot to be sad about (67% vs. 27%); get upset easily (61% vs. 34%); feel life was hard most of the time (49% vs. 15%); be afraid of many things (34% vs. 12%); get mad more than used to (28% vs. 12%); sometimes worry so much that they could not sleep at night (56% vs. 26%). On the more optimistic side, on 10 out of 17 items of the Lawton Morale Scale, there were no significant differences between survivors and comparisons.

Our overall findings portray significantly greater symptomatology among survivors than controls. It should be noted however that there is considerable overlap between survivors and controls and that many survivors appear no different from controls. Indeed some survivors portray less symptomatology than some controls. Whereas such overlap in distributions are not surprising, they raise an important note of caution against stereotyping the "typical" survivor as being very different in mental health from "normal groups."

COPING WITH AGING

Regarding the influence of the Holocaust on coping with problems of getting older, 45 percent of the survivors stated that the Holocaust made it more difficult for them to cope with aging; 29 percent said it made no difference, and, interestingly, 26 percent said it made it easier for them to cope with aging (i.e., once you survived the Holocaust, you can survive normal aging).

Data indicate that the majority of survivors see themselves as different from those who have not experienced the Holocaust. When categorizing these differences, it appears that many survivors viewed themselves as negatively affected (46% of those who said they were different), whereas almost as many reported strengths and positive features (39%), which differentiated them from other people.

SOCIAL FUNCTIONING

In contrast to their physical health and well-being, survivors appeared remarkably intact in terms of social functioning. Relative to the comparison sample, although survivors had significantly less education, their income is significantly greater than the comparison group. Survivors had superior job histories and were more apt to be gainfully employed. Survivors demonstrated both significantly greater residential stability and lower divorce rates.

Survivors' children appeared to portray high levels of personal achievement. Parents appeared to be very close to their children and take great pride in their children's educational and occupational achievements as well as in their personal value systems.

Problems with survivors' children tend to center around overconcern of parents about their children's welfare and parents' inability to understand their children's personal problems, rather than concerning problems with obedience or substance abuse. Finally, survivors also felt significantly greater responsibility toward their community than the comparison group. This is demonstrated by their involvement in grass roots organizations and as volunteers.

While both the comparison group and survivors endorsed altruistic values, survivors portrayed significantly higher levels of altruism than did the comparison group.

Our data also provided some interesting insights into patterns of social interactions and, in particular, helping during the period of trauma based on in-depth interviews with survivors. These insights may help place findings about altruistic orientations into a broader context. In describing help received and help given to others during the Holocaust, 82 percent of U.S. survivors indicated that they were both providers of help to others and recipients of assistance from fellow victims. Forty percent of respondents reported that they were the major source of help to at least one other victim, while 16 percent attributed their own survival to assistance they received from a fellow sufferer. Thus it appears that helping others was a prevalent and almost normative pattern of behavior among victims of the Holocaust, even while living under the most inhuman circumstances. Acts of helping others reflect highly altruistic patterns where the helper assisted others often at a great cost to himself or in the face of great danger to him or herself. The data about the prevalence of receiving help from others also indicates that reports of helping others that are based on long-term recall are not based on the tendency to report socially desirable behaviors.

These findings indicate a divergence between symptomatology or distress and social functioning. Psychological symptomatology reported by survivors should perhaps be conceptualized as normal reactions to a very abnormal event earlier in their lives. The findings regarding survivors' social functioning attest to an amazing ability to adapt in the face of adversity. They attest to hardiness and resilience as significant coping resources among this group of older survivors.[14]

PREDICTORS OF POSITIVE AFFECT

Efforts were also aimed at identifying factors that mediate/moderate between early life trauma and well-being in later life.[15] Specifically, we considered concepts of positive and negative affective states based on the Bradburn Affect Balance Scale.[12]

Based on regression analysis, the following factors were identified as significant contributions to positive affective states.

1. Sharing wartime Holocaust experiences with family and friends.
2. Having an altruistic orientation toward the world.
3. Having an internal locus of control (i.e., feelings that one is in command of one's destiny and is not a victim of fate).
4. Having a spouse who is also a survivor.

All of these factors may be conceptualized as comprising personal coping resources. It is interesting to note that such late life personal orientations and resources were more clearly associated with positive affective states than was the specific nature of the stress experience endured by the respondents.

Accordingly, our findings indicate that being in concentration camps, as opposed to being in ghettos, did not distinguish survivors on the Affect Balance scale. Current likelihood of experiencing positive emotions was not essentially different for those who were incarcerated in concentration camps. It is possible that all survivors experienced such great stress that they crossed a "stress threshold." These findings suggest that once the level of stress has reached an extreme level, differential exposure to extremes in stress does not distinguish later life adjustment.

In contrast to current attitudes and adaptive styles which were found to be associated with positive affect, negative affect was found to have a distinctly different set of predictors. These included a perception that the Holocaust adversely affected their mental health and counseling received, and that the Holocaust made adjustment for aging more difficult.

Finding Meaning in Survivorship

In reviewing respondents' answers that indicated something positive resulting from their traumatic past, three typologies could be discerned. The first group may be termed the "Concerned Survivors." This group comprises 27 percent of those who find positive meaning in their survivorship. This group reflects greater idealism and concern for others. Their statements reflect humane, empathetic, and compassionate views toward others. A second group (36%) may be termed the "Appreciative Ones." This is exemplified by such statements as "I appreciate life more," "I appreciate the United States of America," "I appreciate everything I have." The third and largest group (46%) may be termed the "Resilient and Resourceful." This group reports with pride the sources of strength they found within themselves. Their strengths encompass physical stamina, strength of character, and better coping and resourcefulness.

Ongoing Efforts to Express Lessons from the Holocaust

Our research also explored survivors' attempts to confront and come to terms with their experiences during the Holocaust years. For this purpose two sets of questions were introduced which elicited responses concerning philosophy of life, and the message the survivor may have for others who have not experienced the Holocaust.

We asked survivors, "Is there any special message which survivors have for the rest of the world?" and received the following categories of replies (categories are not mutually exclusive):

1a. *Humanitarian treatment of one another.* Thirty-three percent responded to this category. The following statements are illustrative: "Humane treatment of one another," "People must help one another," "We cannot tolerate indoctrination of hate," "Love your neighbor," "Eliminate hate," "Never be cruel," "Care for one another," "Be helpful to others," and "The world must understand the horrors that people can inflict on one another."

1b. *Promotion of peace in the world.* The following responses are illustrative: "Nations and religions must love one another and not hate because of religion" and "We must respect each other's religion."

2. *Resist human rights violations.* Forty-three percent included these responses:

2a. "Never let it happen again to anybody, to any race" and "Keep the legacy of the Holocaust alive so that history will not repeat itself."

2b. "Be vigilant for anti-Semitism and anti-racism—don't take discrimination lightly," "Outlaw the Ku Klux Klan, Neo-Nazis," and "Fight totalitarianism, support organizations that fight racism."

3. *Be strong, speak-up, support a strong nation of Israel.* Nine percent included these responses: "Fight back as a people, since nobody else will speak up on your behalf," "Don't bend your head to anyone else," "Fight back," and "Don't go as lambs to the slaughter."

4. Concern over another Holocaust emerging in the future and affecting their children (3% included this response).

5. "The world has lost out by allowing this to happen" (8%). "Humanity is going downhill—very sorry that the world stood by idly." "It will be the end of the world if it happens again, because it can happen to other groups." "Fear over the world's negligence."

6. Don't know what to say (3%).

People who have experienced adversity cannot always articulate the meanings that they derive from these experiences. Indeed, some have a need to "forget" and go on with their lives. Nevertheless, we find it fascinating that a substantial proportion of older persons who have endured great psychic trauma, and who have a limited education, were able to find positive meaning in their adversity. For many, the need to bear witness and to save our society from such potential atrocities in the future becomes a major *raison d'être* in their old age. Thus many become activists of sorts in their later years. Some survivors lecture to high school and college students on the Holocaust as well as to church groups. Others become active in setting up Holocaust memorial centers in their cities or contribute to literature, music, and art of the Holocaust. Still others develop their own grass roots charities, such as visiting the ill in hospitals, becoming involved in consumer protection, lending wedding gowns to poor brides, and so on. While some may have done this for a good number of years, others have first started these activities after retirement.

In summary, the elderly have an often unheralded potential to find meaning in adversity and share this meaning with others.

Our results suggest the importance of acknowledging the pervasiveness and permanent imprint left by the trauma on survivors' physical and psychological well-being. The clinician needs to validate the salience of this past experience for present and future functioning of the survivor. It is only after trust is established through such validation that the patient may successfully focus on coping with negative affective states, anxieties, and other mental health problems.

Whereas our data confirm the salience of past experience through intrusive memories of the trauma, they also provide insights about positive coping strategies both during the Holocaust and in its long-term aftermath. Our findings about the prevalence of helping other victims, even during the most traumatic periods of incarceration,[16] can provide useful material for therapists to build self-esteem and reduce guilt feelings in patients. Thus, the therapist need not approach the patient with the presumption that the survivor must have been only a passive victim who cannot find any anchor of efficacy or self-pride during the darkest hours. The presumption of personal efforts to help others rather than the suspicions of callous disregard for needs of fellow sufferers may be therapeutic to the survivor in and of itself.

The diversity among survivors indicated by our data underscores the importance of individualized assessment and therapeutic approaches to survivors. Thus, therapists should not infer from the shared trauma a uniform psychological response. Instead, they should be vigilant to deal with a very wide spectrum of mental health outcomes in the aftermath of the Holocaust.

The importance of family to survivors that is reflected both in the findings of low divorce rates and strong attachment to children, points to the potential value of the family as an extremely important support and potential therapeutic ally to the survivor. At the same time, these attachments which are superimposed on the deep-rooted losses of family during the Holocaust may render survivors particularly vulnerable to recent life events involving losses of family members or problems experienced by family members. Therapists should be particularly alert to help survivors cope with family problems, which present an extreme threat to self and personal survival. The therapist should also exercise care in challenging survivors to confront family conflicts.

Our data provided some useful insights into the value and role of late life coping strategies in contributing to positive affective states among survivors. The utility of self-disclosure to friends and family has direct relevance for therapeutic interventions. Using cognitive as well as dynamic approaches, the therapist may facilitate and reinforce efforts of patients to be more disclosing about their wartime experiences. Such self-disclosure should not be limited to the therapeutic encounter but should be extended to interactions with trusted friends and family. Whereas the therapeutic context may serve as the best environment for cathartic functions of self-disclosure, less intense forms of disclosure to friends and family may benefit the person through enhanced and ongoing social support and understanding.

The useful effort to find meaning in survivorship by identifying with Holocaust organizations and with the social role of being a survivor (one of many dimensions of survivorship), may offer the potentially problematic by-product of keeping the survivor focused on the past and unable to escape it. The therapist may help the survivor accept this role but at the same time move in and out of it. Thus the survivor may find it acceptable to serve as a part-time guardian of the legacy rather than as a full-time one. The patient may learn to appreciate that allowing himself to abandon the role of survivor-guardian some of the time may re-energize him to refocus on this mission with greater efficiency later.

In an incisive essay on the meaning of life and old age, Moody[17] suggests that for modern man the quest for meaning in life is a highly individual preoccupation wherein each person must seek his own purpose in being, one that seldom transcends the individual life course. For the elderly survivor of the Holocaust who had to confront the great limitations inherent in an individual definition of the meaning of life, finding collective meaning in the sense of peoplehood presents a viable or even necessary alternative. It is noteworthy that most survivors seek some collective wisdom or lesson from the horrible miscarriage of humanity they witnessed and were the victims of during the Holocaust. In this sense, it is not surprising that instead of, or alongside, personal despair in late life many survivors experience a sense of purpose and meaning that allows for positive affect and a sense of satisfaction. It is perhaps for this reason that both negative and positive affects exist not as opposites but as orthogonal characteristics in the psyche of elderly survivors.

The task of the therapist, then, is to safeguard and build on this collective meaning or shared survivorship rather than to redirect the elderly survivor to a more individual or private sense of well-being. Ultimately, we agree with Moody (1986) that individual and collective levels of meaning must be connected in order for psychological well-being to occur in late life.

CONCLUSIONS

Our findings, based on the study of elderly survivors and a comparison group of immigrants who did not spend the war years in Europe, confirm to some extent earlier research regarding adverse effects and mental health sequelae of traumatic experiences. Nevertheless, a major finding that emerged from this investigation is the variability in how survivors responded to the trauma as well as significant overlaps in outcomes between survivors and the comparison group. Our findings indicate that Holocaust survivors are clearly not a homogeneous group. Their diversity may provide important clues about the complex nature of posttraumatic adaptation. Although there is evidence that some survivors have been adversely affected by the Holocaust, physically and/or psychologically, there are also indications that others have adjusted well as individuals and have furthermore made substantial contributions as productive citizens in their new environment.

Social functioning of survivors revealed many previously undocumented strengths. Furthermore, current attitudes and adaptations emerged as better predictors of positive affect in later life than did specific types of Holocaust experiences. Our results illustrate that examining mental health as well as mental illness among survivors of extreme trauma greatly expands our understanding of this group. The elderly survivors have an often unheralded potential to find meaning in adversity and to share this meaning with others. We have known for a long time that survivors have nightmares. It is now time to look at all of their contributions to our society when these survivors are awake from their nightmares and facing a new day.

NOTES

1. Henry Krystal and William G. Niederland, "Clinical Observations of the Survivor Syndrome," in Henry Krystal, Ed., *Massive Psychic Trauma* (New York: International Universities Press, 1968).

2. Leo Goldberger and Shlomo Breznitz, Eds., *The Handbook of Stress—Theoretical and Clinical Aspects* (New York: Free Press, 1982).

3. Irving Rosow, *Social Integration of Aged* (New York: Free Press, 1964).

4. Judith G. Rabkin and Elmir L. Streuning, "Social Change, Stress and Illness: A Selective Literature Review," *Psychoanalysis and Contemporary Science* 5 (1976): 573–

624; Thomas Holmes and Richard Rahe, "The Social Readjustment Rating Scale," *Journal of Psychosomatic Research* 11 (1967): 219–225.

5. Ellis Paul Torrance, *Constructive Behavior: Stress, Personality and Mental Health* (Belmont, CA: Wadsworth, 1965).

6. Bruno Bettelheim, *The Informed Heart* (New York: The Free Press, 1960).

7. Viktor Frankl, *Man's Search for Meaning* (New York: Washington Square Press, 1963).

8. Rudolph, H. Moos and Jeanny A. Schaefer, "Coping with Physical Illness," *Crisis of Physical Illness: An Overview and Conceptual Approach* (New York: 1984), pp. 3–25.

9. Norma Haan, *Coping and Defending: Processes of Self-Environment Organization* (New York: Academic Press, 1977); S. Breznitz, *The Denial of Stress* (New York: International Universities Press, 1983).

10. Henry Krystal, "Alexithymia and the Effectiveness of Psychoanalytic Treatment," *International Journal of Psychoanalytic Psychotherapy* 9 (1982): 353–378.

11. Leonard R. Derogatis, *SCL–90R: Administration, Scoring and Procedures Manual*, Vol. 1 (Baltimore, MD: Clinical Psychometric Research, 1983).

12. Norman M. Bradburn, *The Structure of Psychological Well-being* (Chicago: Aldine, 1969).

13. Aaron Antonovsky, *Health Stress and Coping* (San Francisco, CA: Jossey Bass, 1979).

14. Suzanne C. Kobasa, Salvatore R. Maddi, and Samuel Kahn, "Hardiness and Health: A Prospective Study," *Journal of Personality and Social Psychology* 42, no. 1 (1982): 168–177.

15. Eva Kahana, Boaz Kahana, and Zev Harel, "Coping with Extreme Trauma," in J. P. Wilson, Z. Harel, and B. Kahana, Eds., *Human Adaptation to Extreme Stress: From the Holocaust to Vietnam* (New York: Plenum Press, 1988).

16. Boaz Kahana, Eva Kahana, Zev Harel, Mary Segal, "The Victim as Helper—Prosocial Behavior During the Holocaust," *Humboldt Journal of Social Relations* 13, nos. 1 & 2 (1986): 357–373.

17. Harry R. Moody, "The Meaning of Life and the Meaning of Old Age," in Thomas R. Cole and Sally A. Gadow, Eds., *What Does It Mean to Grow Old?* (Durham: Duke University Press, 1986).

VII

Special Problems

13

Alternative Therapeutic Approaches to Holocaust Survivors

ROBERT KRELL

THE CONCEPT OF SURVIVORSHIP

With the passing years, survivors of the Shoah have survived other difficult and painful obstacles. Those who reflect on this passage of time and their perception of themselves offer information relevant to the understanding of the condition of survivorship. Particularly interesting to us who have worked with survivors in therapeutic situations are the comments pertaining to the psychological status. "We are damaged goods," states one. "It was not possible to emerge unscathed from that disaster, whether in camps, whether in hiding, no matter what the precise circumstances."

There is notable concensus with this self-assessment on the part of survivors. Several consequences follow the percept of being irreparably damaged in some way. One result is that, this being understood, no therapist need try to fix it. It is not fixable. Another is that since it is an accepted condition of survivorship, in itself it deserves no particular attention. What is deserving of attention is that in spite of the damage, there is a life to be lived and how that is done, given a background that defies one's imagination.

This knowledge of the irreparable has been with the survivor from the time of liberation. For those survivors in need of therapy, and I refer primarily to those who have presented as outpatients, their greatest need was not to express associations to the time of trauma, humiliation and grief cathartically. There was and perhaps remains a greater need, the need to impress upon the therapist that in an earlier time they were normal, came from loving families, possessed high aspirations, and had jobs and possessions.

They might have said to the therapist, "You've caught me at a bad time." Some wanted assistance in recapturing a good past in order to help deal with the present—not deny the trauma but skip it. They were aware of being "tainted with death" before Lifton's astute description.[1] This pervasive theme of survivorship was endowed with meaning by Wiesel who put this matter in perspective: "For the survivor death is not the problem. Death was an everyday occurrence. We learned to live with death. The problem is to adjust to life, to living. You must teach us about living."[2]

Another need existed as well, the need to be seen as competent if competent, strong if strong, successful if successful. The survivors' successes were diminished by the cavalier view of their accomplishments as a reaction to their misfortunes rather than as a continuity of their prewar past. There are countless examples of survivors negating the experiences in the concentration camps not by denial, but by consciously subtracting from their age the years that were taken from them. Those who have worked with survivors will have heard "I was for three years in labour camps, then Auschwitz and Buchenwald. I don't count those years as part of my life." Child survivors, who were deprived of schooling for years, made extraordinary efforts postwar to catch up to their nonsurvivor contemporaries. The need to recapture normalcy was paramount, as was the need to somehow erase the years of discontinuity.[3]

There exists a leaning toward negative assumptions that intersect with the concept of survivorship of the Holocaust survivor. These assumptions, as noted in the psychiatric literature, suggest that survivors exercise denial (in the negative sense), uniformly experience survivor guilt, and demonstrate a variety of identifications with the aggressor.

These assumptions are badly flawed. The failures of psychoanalytic language are quite evident in articles by otherwise knowledgeable people. Dr. Hoppe's descriptions reveal the difficulties inherent in describing survivors.[4] Eitinger's article on denial in concentration camps is probably a suitable response to much of what has been written.[5] Essentially he demonstrates that even such a well understood and acceptable psychologic concept as denial takes on new meaning in the shadow of the Nazi camps. He explains: "I have tried to show that the use of denial was rather complex, necessarily connected with other coping mechanisms, seemingly more contradictory than many others of the meaningless contradictions in the extermination camps. Denying death could be life-saving under certain circumstances, while denying the small seemingly unimportant fact of daily life and a struggle would result in certain and premature death." The denial attributed to the survivor perceived as unwilling or unable to talk is no less complex and often actually reflects the therapist's denial.[6] Here too, denial as a concept acquires new meaning.

Unfortunately, the notion of guilt has crept into the postwar life of the Holocaust survivor as if it were a universal condition. For one to feel guilty, one has to commit an offense, a crime, a wrong—or simply imagine the offences, crime, or wrong and feel responsible.

I am told by survivors who were assisted with emotional problems in the early years that it was common to have the therapist suggest "You must feel guilty for having survived when all around you died,'' in the existential sense of guilt that might hold as it would for the only survivor of a car crash where all others perish. However, survivor-patients heard more than that. They felt they were held personally accountable in some way for not having died. The statement about guilt, expressed in so many subtle and unsubtle ways, implied they must have done something awful to someone to have survived. The therapist, with no true understanding of the conditions, sat in judgment, and failed to distinguish between his own assumptions and what was related by the survivor.

THE FAILURE OF THERAPY (THERAPISTS) AND SURVIVOR RAGE

What was it that led mental health professionals to rely so heavily on their own assumptions, so often evading examination of the extraordinary problems facing the survivor? What led to the failure to understand that something had happened beyond ordinary understanding? Why did professionals seek refuge in the safety of familiar but largely inappropriate terminology?

The reasons are many, but I will mention two which are related: the therapeutic impotence of the therapist and the rage of the survivor.

Until the appearance of the survivor as patient, psychiatry and its practitioners had been enthusiastic in their expectations of being helpful. Even the dreaded illness of schizophrenia was being tamed with medication and attempts were made to explore it to its very core.

If words are the scalpel of the psychiatrist, it was discomfiting to use these words to open wounds, the magnitude of which had never before been encountered. Those who sensed the colossal grief and pain were probably aware that the incision would not stop with the individual patient.

A self-protective strategy evolved that avoided the pertinent questions or blamed the failure of treatment on the survivor-patient. This self-protection may not differ greatly from other painful subjects avoided by therapists for fear of revelations about experiences for which treatment responses are primitive or inadequate. In recent times, the dimensions of sexual abuse have become known because therapists began to pose the pertinent questions.

An even closer analogy may be the web of silence drawn for many years around the Vietnam veteran, as if his experience would not leave lifetime scars as well. It has taken nearly 20 years to recognize that the so-called Post-Traumatic Stress disorder symptomatology of the Vietnam veteran, has been described in the medical and psychiatric literature of the Holocaust since 1952 in hundreds of articles.[7] It stands to reason that, even now, preparations could be made to investigate the inevitable consequences for children of the Vietnam veterans who suffer psychologically. And yet, professional "unawareness" continues.

Even in the 1980s, well-meaning and well trained psychiatrists/psychoanalysts have asked me such questions as, "Do you routinely ask child patients who are second generation about their parents' Holocaust experiences?'' ''Do you get Holocaust survivors to describe their in-train and in-camp experiences?''

The questions demonstrate the reluctance to broach the topic, a reluctance well described in 1972 by Kestenberg[8], who found that a number of psychoanalysts whom she surveyed were either not aware that their patients were of Holocaust families, or did not link their patients' dynamics to the history of their parents' persecution when they were aware.

Since we have been taught to understand our patients in minute detail, how is it possible to entertain the notion of sidestepping direct or indirect Holocaust experiences of our patients?

Clearly there is considerable anxiety about what reactions questions may elicit, complicated by the therapist's feeling that when such questions are asked, the responses may require the therapist to do something.

And what can one possibly do about and for a survivor who has just told you of witnessing the death of his children? Which of us wants to step into the abyss with the survivor and into such depths of anguish and rage that one can do nothing but weep?

The problems with posing the questions is that the answers take the therapist to a dimension of experience where all language fails and emotions are scraped raw. It is no wonder that so many second generation children could not talk with their parents about the war. They were sensitive not only to their parents' grief but also to what lay beyond. The rage was not meant for the children— better to stay silent. The survivor's rage is so great, it rendered some speechless for years, others unable to cry. To my knowledge, none has taken a gun and gone out on a rampage of violence. The rage is too great even for vengeance. It is so enormous, survivors must settle for justice.

Perhaps this accounts for the fact that survivors may present for care following an injustice that taps this rage. One child survivor I saw had functioned superbly for 20 years in his marriage and work. He had survived in hiding and was orphaned. He pinpointed precisely his breakdown as the day a Nazi in his country of origin was released after serving only three years of a life sentence. He was unable to work and remained under psychiatric care for ten years. After immigration to Canada he continued in psychotherapy and only recently returned to work.

Another Holocaust survivor, doing fairly well with supportive psychotherapy for the past three years, experienced a major depressive episode. A terrorist who had killed Jews sought asylum, and lawyers were arguing that he had mended his ways and would be a good citizen now that he had renounced violence. My patient flew into a rage that left him sleepless for weeks. He said he had never harmed a soul and look what they did to him and his family. Where is justice? What is fair?

Rage is mentioned in the psychiatric literature of the Holocaust,[9] but seldom discussed as a focal point for survivor distress. Yet it is the dominant and understandable emotion of the survivor and hence of every child who has lived in the presence of that contained rage. It is likely that the survivor has in large measure adjusted to the rage within and that the child has begun to understand that it is not meant for him. Where this has not happened, the therapist can provide a useful forum for clarifying and directing rage.[10]

Krystal discusses rage as an impediment to healing.[11] He states, "It seems virtuous to 'feed' righteous indignation and treasonous to stop the rage." I would suggest that the recognition and expression of rage, properly directed, is itself healing. It might help also to reconceptualize survivor reactions, not within the framework of "identification with the aggressor" but "rage at the aggressor" and then re-explore the mechanisms by which this rage, so threatening to survivor and therapist, is released.

Martin Bergmann offers the explanation that the primitive wish is for revenge that might appease rage.[12] He suggests that sublimation can change that feeling to "the dead shall not have died in vain," accomplished through remembrance. It is this subtle maneuver that suggests that therapy can and must also focus on the awareness of remembrance and education as a constructive outlet for a rage beyond comprehension.

WORKING WITH SURVIVORS

There are two, perhaps more, assumptions I make about a survivor patient. I assume I am about to see a person with considerable personal strength that has sustained him or her for most of life. I also assume I am about to see a person who is not stupid.

Since the vast majority of survivors are indeed not stupid, far from it, it did not take long for them to sense that much psychologic therapy represented a series of accusations, a continuation of victimization. They were accused of denial if they resisted describing the concentration camp experience; of guilt or guilt feelings, perhaps having done something "shady" or worse in order to survive; of exhibiting Nazi-like behavior if aggressive and angry, under the generic terms "identification with the aggressor." Let me cite several typical survivor-patients' responses indicating their personal awareness of these psychodynamic themes.

Survivor #1

The patient was referred to me by a psychiatrist who stated that his patient was depressed, a survivor, and unable or unwilling to talk about his Holocaust experiences. He was therefore exercising denial. The referring physician hoped that I, as a survivor, and known in the community for involvement in Holocaust education, would have greater success.

The patient was indeed depressed. A survivor of Auschwitz, he stated that he told the nice doctor a bit of his story and noticed how he looked away, fidgeted, and constantly interrupted him with entirely unrelated questions. While in fact feeling quite positive about his psychiatrist and improving with respect to a depression which was precipitated by a business reversal, he stated: "I decided not to talk of the camps. Why cause him pain? He obviously couldn't handle it."

Survivor #2

Another patient talked about the problem of guilt, "I have read a lot. Like others I'm obsessed with what happened. I feel I shouldn't, but I see all the movies, find all the articles. How can I not be obsessed? I was in the first group of labourers forced to build the crematoria at Auschwitz? I've read I should feel guilt. For what? We were defenseless? Hands against machine guns. I made a point of not hurting anyone myself. Other than that, I tried to survive and I'm proud of it. All those like me, preoccupied with what they should have done, also had no options. The only real choice in camp was whether you wanted a quick death or slow."

Survivor #3

A woman patient struggling with a difficult adolescent boy expressed fear of her own anger and rage. Like so many others, she was aware of the connections between her personal aggressive feelings and their connections to the camps.

"When Adam drives me crazy and my anger rises, I think what is the worst that I can call him. I tell him he is my Hitler, that he is worse than Hitler."

"And of course he's not. Hitler killed my six brothers and sisters. But when I am like that I behave strange. It is as if I were in the camp and I fantasize having control over him. I think he wouldn't do this if I were his Kapo. What awful things I learned."

From the survivor's understanding emerges an important note of caution. If terminology so central to the constructs of psychoanalytic therapy as denial, guilt, and identification with the aggressor do not serve us well in the treatment approaches to the Holocaust survivor and family, what constructs can we turn to instead? Obviously, some facets of denial, guilt, and identification do play a role in the dynamics of the survivor, so far as these are understood at present. There are, however, serious limitations in understanding the survivor and these limitations derive from at least three fundamental problems.

1. The inability to truly fathom the experience of chronic persecution, torment, and extraordinary bereavement.

2. The failure of existing language and perceptions to describe and interpret the experience by the teller.

3. The absence of theoretical constructs to bridge the gaps of understanding so that a meaningful intervention is possible.

Given the limitations, it may help the therapist to approach the survivor from a perspective suggested by Gawalewicz[13] who responded to some philosophic questions posed about the human condition by a refined lady in postwar Sweden, "But let us theoretically make a small experiment; let us crowd a hundred people such as you or even better ones—if they exist at all—in a cattle wagon for eight days without giving them anything to eat and not even a drop to drink, I repeat, not a drop. On the ninth day we may organize with those who came out alive from those wagons the discussion of the subject of people who are naturally good. Those persons will already be at least partly prepared for such a discussion."

The therapist must be able to imagine himself there, in that train, with starved and thirst-ridden children, perhaps his own, for whom he can do nothing. It requires a vivid imagination, the necessary prerequisite to do therapy with survivors. If one can imagine the inside of that train it might free one of the temptation to use the language of the familiar. The train takes us into the universe of death where there are no choices. All who chose wrong are dead. Those who chose correctly did not know so at the time. The perpetrators constructed a universe with the objective of depriving persons of personhood, humans of humanity. The object of this deadly exercise can not be described as suffering "infantile regression" or having "narcissistic preoccupations." It is not correct to equate the consequences of overpowering degradation with a return to an earlier level of normal function in the infant or child. There is nothing normal to be found. We must recognize that entree into the survivor's world requires the temporary surrender of the normal scale of human experience, individual or collective.

In light of that reality, we must depart from the notions that traditional uncovering psychotherapy, with free association and a reliance on insight and dream interpretation, can help. They seldom can.

TREATMENT CONSIDERATIONS

One major factor contributing to the possible failures of therapy with survivors relates to the most fundamental of all therapeutic techniques—the science, the art of listening. One must be able to listen differently. One must devise different ways of listening.

The therapist who listens carefully to the survivor will hear the descriptions of ordinary aspirations based in a time when there was still order and hope. The survivor expects the listener to realize how normal they might have been, if not for the Holocaust. The catastrophe itself is not necessarily the only reason for wishing to be heard and understood. Despite its impact, remarkably, it is not necessarily *the* focus of postwar life. In pursuit of psychopathology, the therapist may miss crucial aspects of the survivor's normal life, normal successes and normal mistakes. To focus on the Holocaust experience as their essential life experience would be to overlook the survivor's personhood and often successful reclaiming of humanness. It is the latter that ought to captivate us, the fact that any survivor of this unfathomable tragedy has resisted this insult to body, mind, and heritage.

Ordinary listening has not worked. There are many reasons the listener cannot listen. The survivor's eyes have actually seen what is described. To look into eyes with that knowledge is not easy. If the listener's imagination is sufficiently vivid, he joins the teller on a journey preferably avoided. If the pain becomes too great, there are many ways to stop the teller; interrupt with nonsensical interventions, accuse the patient of denial, remain objective and cool.

Mr. A. complained to me of particularly vivid nightmares for the past three months. Eager to tell his story, he recounted a horrendous set of experiences. Nightmares had been a common experience since 1945 with only occasional periods of tranquility. The content of the dreams were memories of family and separations. Mr. A. asked if he could get rid of the nightmares. He quickly reversed himself when I suggested that perhaps they served in him the purpose of remembrance. He agreed. In fact, he added that the intensity of nightmares had coincided with a particularly momentous anniversary, the date back in 1946 when he discovered that his parents were both dead.

I suggest that to listen to the content of nightmares of some Holocaust survivors as commemorative may change the survivor's perspective on this painful and intrusive form of remembrance.

In this instance, rather than "traditional" therapy, the patient was offered the opportunity to tell his story to high school classes as part of our local Holocaust education program. Initially anxiety-ridden, the positive feedback from students, the notes of gratitude, the poetry written in his honor, the comments attesting to his courage in bearing witness, resulted in diminished intensity of the nightmares and other improvement.

Education as remembrance brought relief no sleeping pill or insightful analysis could match. Of all this survivor's many community meetings and his meetings in the business world, the only ones he "enjoys" are those to plan Holocaust education events.

Mr. B. was 61 years old when he came to see me. He had become depressed, and was referred by his general practitioner to a psychiatrist, who asked him to go into the hospital, which he dutifully did. He walked in one door and out another.

In tears he told me in quick succession that he lost eight brothers and sisters, lived through nine concentration camps, and that he wanted my assurance that he would not be hospitalized. If he grew more depressed, so be it, he would kill himself.

The account he related was extraordinarily evil in a world of extraordinary accounts. His worst trial was the murder of his brother after sharing three years of captivity. After a series of death marches, he was liberated from a ditch filled with corpses near Theresienstadt. Married to a survivor of Ravensbrück, they had one daughter who has intermarried.

In a series of interviews he told me of unsuccessful attempts to get compensation from Germany, his inability to tell his child of his experiences, and a vast array of rather typical symptoms including nightmares and a variety of ailments. One striking feature was his preoccupation with the month of February, when his depressions would grow worse. It was in February he was imprisoned with his brother; in February his brother was murdered; February was his birthday. After the war, it was February in which he packed up his family on five occasions, and moved back to Europe to live in the city of his birth. Faced with the reality that neither family or friends were alive, each time he returned to Canada and that depleted his savings.

What possible therapy was available to this fundamentally fine and decent man, devoted to caring for an ailing wife but so bitterly disappointed in life?

After several difficult, nonproductive visits I asked him to write his memoirs in his native language and suggested he begin with the day of his liberation, expecting that to be easier for him. With my help, he gradually filled in the years prior to that day when he was ready. He wrote an impressive and poignant account and this has become his legacy to his daughter. In fact he allowed her to read it and it was her first detailed knowledge of her father's experience. It resolved a number of outstanding issues between them.

We also reviewed his abortive attempts to seek compensation. He had been turned down summarily for failure to comply with some obscure regulations, and for missing a deadline. I, myself, could not understand the forms. I was wondering how any survivor could ever answer such questions without considerable help and the toll it exacts for a survivor to recite dates and facts on forms written in German. It seemed an exercise in the continuum of humiliation to have to prove the events really took place.[14]

Together we applied when a new opportunity for compensation presented itself. Over a period of two years, returning once a month (with occasional biweekly visits) we spent most of the time drafting letters, organizing materials, and persisting in the pursuit of compensation.

After three years of what might be called supportive psychotherapy in a nontraditional manner, what was accomplished? Mr. B. remains despondent but he is alive. His account has been read by his daughter. He has been awarded a small sum of money. He is a poor man, but the issue for him had little to do with the amount. Compensation to him was confirmation that he had in fact been the victim of an enormous injustice, and the award diminished his personal rage to the point of his experiencing a sense of ease.

I also put him in touch with another survivor, whose personal response to him was astonishing and inspiring. Having read Isabella Leitner's book[15] in which she calls for the abolishment of May, I asked my patient to write to her about what to do with February.

Who else but Isabella would truly understand?

We are all familiar with the importance of allowing patients to make discoveries about themselves and gather insights in order to effect change. One well-documented strategy to achieve these objectives recommends that the therapist must be relatively silent and reflective. The therapist must be cautious with patients who wish to be too intimate, too personal, and thereby win over the therapist in some way, which will ultimately not serve them well. Interestingly, in the therapy with Holocaust survivors and/or their children, the therapist may be sought out for precisely those reasons that make them feel that some degree of intimacy is possible. The reason I receive referrals is the hope of those who refer and those who are referred that I will understand them at a level that is not the normal starting point for the therapist and patient. In the situation of the survivor presenting as patient, the issue of trust is supreme. Whereas with most patients, trust is patiently won as the outcome of a process in which the therapist earns the patient's trust through his earnest commitment to the care of his patient, the survivor may not allow the elaboration of such a process.

In fact, the survivor seeks information of various kinds early in the initial assessment. A phrase in Yiddish is offered to see if I will understand it. The survivor will translate and my decision is whether or not to stop him (if indeed I understand). Connections are sought regarding degree of Jewish observance, community involvement, awareness of mutual friends and acquaintances. This is not to imply that one must be Jewish or understand Yiddish in order to treat a survivor. In larger communities, survivors will seek therapists far removed from their daily lives, beliefs, and origins.

No matter the choice of therapist, the survivor does considerable homework prior to the decision and a great deal more within the first few visits. I opt to offer much more of myself than I do with other patients.

At the mention of their place of birth, I ask them to show me on a map I keep in my office. If in the general proximity of Polish Galicia, I may mention my father was born near there. The usual response: "But you were born in Holland." I explain how many Polish Jews went to Holland even in the 1920s and early 1930s.

The power of a map! What a discovery it is when the survivor who has told his story to nonsurvivors, including his or her children, has never been asked to point out the location of his city or village. With the precise geographic locale come reminiscences of great Rabbis, important ancestors, pride in heritage and roots, distress, and despair over its destruction.

Few survivors are asked the route by which they made their way to North America, how they picked the city in which they have lived, and how they have kept themselves well enough not to seek help. Unless one asks, it will not be offered. Questions about personal commemoration are equally revealing. "How do you personally remember your loved ones?" One survivor patient repairs to the basement every day to light a candle for his parents. Another begins each day with a glance at well hidden photographs, weeps silently for a few minutes, and carries on with the day. Except for the occasional need for support, they are pillars of strength in their respective families and the community.

When the therapist becomes familiar with the origins of his patient, the secret ceremonies of commemoration, the intricate maneuvers employed to adopt and cope, a foundation of trust is established. And with most patients at some point, I must plead my failure to be helpful. What is their response? They never expected "treatment"; they ask for so little. During the times of despair, during a breakdown of their functioning, they demanded no answers. It was sufficient to join them in their search. Their need was for company while struggling to return to an acceptable level of functioning.

As a psychiatrist who has been involved with traditional individual analytic therapy, child and family therapy, audiovisual documentation of Holocaust survivors and Holocaust education, I feel we may have missed the boat with many of our treatment approaches.

For example, where a second generation child has suffered for lack of knowledge of the parental background, few therapists have been able to engage the family together, although some have tried.[16, 17] Occasionally, a second generation child in individual therapy is encouraged to seek information from the family. No infrequently, the discussion ends where it always ends, in tears and silence. For some, it simply remains impossible to explain the unexplainable to their child and to contain their personal rage. It should have been obvious long ago that few parents, silent for 30 years, could ever tell the chronological account of their tragedy and pain to the child they loved, protected, fought with, overvalued, prodded. By interviewing that same survivor parent in a two-hour audiovisual interview, during which the interviewer assisted them to relate a coherent account of prewar life, the Shoah, and postwar life, it is possible to provide a copy to the family. In this situation the survivor returns home, sits the family down, and they watch the account together. Survivors who normally break down in answering questions posed by members of their family, which abruptly ends the discussion, are frequently comfortable enough to actually comment during the viewing of the tape and answer questions. There are no tears or nonverbal hints to discontinue the account which would otherwise seldom be resumed. Once captured on tape, the account is captive as is the audience.

It appears that working therapeutically with survivors requires departures from the usual psychotherapeutic methods with which most of us feel comfortable. These departures may include active participation in the writing of memoirs, assistance with seeking compensation, producing audiovisual interviews, and involving survivors as teachers in educational programming related to the Holocaust.

The survivors of the worst imaginable experience take us into a realm where they define the parameters of understanding, not we. To quote once again Elie Wiesel,[18] when addressing an audience of physicians, one of whom asked how they should treat the Holocaust patient, his response was: "Listen to the survivors, listen to them very carefully. They have more to teach you than you them."

NOTES

1. Robert J. Lifton, *The Broken Connection* (New York: Simon and Schuster, 1979), pp. 92–93.

2. Elie Wiesel, "The Holocaust Patient," an address to Cedars-Sinai Medical Staff, Los Angeles, 1982.

3. Robert Krell, Special Section: Child Survivors of the Holocaust: 40 Years Later. *J. Amer. Academy of Child Psychiatry* 24, no. 4 (1985): 377–412.

4. Klaus Hoppe, "Severed Ties," in *Psychoanalystic Reflections on the Holocaust* S. A. Luel and P. Marcus, Eds. (New York: 1984), pp. 95–111.

5. Leo Eitinger, "Denial in Concentration Camps," *Nord. Psykiatr. Tidsskr.* (1981): 148–156.

6. Robert Krell, "Holocaust Survivors and Their Children: Comments on Psychiatric Consequences and Psychiatric Terminology," *Comprehensive Psychiatry* 25, no. 5 (1984): 521–528.

7. Leo Eitinger and Robert Krell, *The Psychological and Medical Effects of Concentration Camps and Related Persecutions on Survivors of the Holocaust—A Research Bibliography* (Vancouver: University of British Columbia Press, 1985).

8. Judith Kestenberg, "Psychoanalytic Contributions to the Problem of Children of Survivors from Nazi Persecution," *Israel Ann. of Psychiatry* (1972): 311–325.

9. Yael Danieli, "Families of Survivors of the Nazi Holocaust: Some Short and Long Term Effects," in *Stress and Anxiety* C. D. Spielberger, I. G. Sarason, N. A. Milgram, Eds. (Washington, DC: Hemisphere Publishing, 1982), pp. 405–421, 412.

10. Robert Krell, "Family Therapy with Children of Concentration Camp Survivors," *American J. of Psychotherapy* 36, no. 4 (1982): 513–522, Case 2.

11. Henry Krystal, "Integration and Self-Healing in Posttraumatic States," in *Psychoanalytic Reflections on the Holocaust*, S. A. Luel and P. Marcus, Eds. (New York: KTAV, 1984), pp. 113–133.

12. Martin Bergmann, "Reflections on the Psychological and Social Function of Remembering the Holocaust," *Psychoanalytic Inquiry* (1985): 9–20, 14.

13. Adolf Gawalewicz, "A Number Gets Back Its Name," *Auschwitz Anthology* 3, pt. 1 (Warsaw: International Auschwitz Comm., 1971), pp. 4–66.

14. Kurt Eissler, "Perverted Psychiatry," *Amer. J. Psychiatry* (1967): 1352–1358.

15. Isabella Leitner, *Fragments of Isabella* (New York: Thomas Y. Crowell, 1978).

16. Axel Russell, "Late Psychosocial Consequences of the Holocaust Experience on Survivor Families: The Second Generation," *Int. J. Fam. Psychiat.* (1982): 375–402.

17. Shamai Davidson, "The Clinical Effects of Massive Psychic Trauma in Families of Holocaust Survivors," *J. Mar. and Fam. Therapy* (1980): 11–21.

18. Elie Wiesel, "The Holocaust Patient," an address to Cedars-Sinai Medical Staff, Los Angeles, 1982.

14

The Religious Life of Holocaust Survivors and Its Significance for Psychotherapy

PAUL MARCUS AND ALAN ROSENBERG

In a secular age when most psychotherapists tend to diminish the religious dimension of their patients' lives, it is not surprising that the Holocaust survivor's religious experience both during and after the event has been underemphasized.[1] Despite the fact that the significance of the religious dimension has been repeatedly articulated in survivor diaries, testimonies, and contemporary literature, psychotherapists have not adequately appreciated the importance of this element in their work with survivors of the Holocaust.[2] In our readings and professional experience we have observed that many therapists are not sufficiently aware of the variety of conflicts and issues that are of concern, consciously or unconsciously, to the survivor with religious sensibilities and the survivor who came from a religious background but lost faith because of the Holocaust. Therefore, this chapter concerns itself mainly with the survivor's religious realm as it affects the psychotherapeutic process. It will also provide a conceptual framework for helping the therapist understand the significance of religion in the survivor's life.[3]

The process of exploring the varying effects the Holocaust has had on the survivor's faith and religious behavior, at least as it affects the psychotherapeutic experience, touches on some of the most profound questions that emanate from the cataclysm: How did faith in God and religious activity help concentration camp inmates cope with the physical and mental pain experienced during the incarceration? What kinds of Holocaust experiences and pre- and post-Holocaust factors influenced whether a survivor remained a believer or renounced a belief

An earlier version of this chapter has been published as "The Holocaust Survivor's Faith and Religious Behavior and Some Implications for Treatment" in *Holocaust and Genocide Studies*, Vol. 3, No. 4, 1988, 413–430.

in God after the Holocaust? Has the survivor who still believes in God significantly changed the nature of that belief? How can God be affirmed meaningfully
in a world where evil enjoys such power? And finally, what is the effect of a
renunciation of faith? These and other questions need to be clarified and elaborated in order for psychotherapists to be better able to help the survivor.

The importance of psychotherapists being sensitive to these issues goes beyond
the seemingly straightforward notion that therapists need to "know where their
patients are coming from." More to the point is the problem of how psychotherapists work with and conceptualize the impact of a severe trauma on the
symbolic world of an individual. In this case, it is the symbolic world of the
religious survivor, both the survivor from a religious background who may still
have a religious framework or sensibility, and the survivor who is faced with
the awesome task of replacing his religious world view with another perspective.
By symbolic world we are referring to a total system of beliefs, values, morals,
and knowledge—which for the person are often highly abstract and loom far
above everyday life, yet tangibly impose themselves upon everyday life in their
capacity to inspire or to give meaning to individual or collective activity, to
delegitimate other activity, and to bring to bear the force of social control.
Symbolic worlds provide an important ordering impulse to social affairs and to
collective views of the world.[4] The importance of these ideas about a symbolic
world to the religious survivor lies in the view that socially structured, taken-
for-granted meanings enjoy a "stability deriving from more powerful sources
than the historical efforts of human beings"[5] and contribute therefore to the
creation of ultimately powerful and meaningful notions of reality ("sacred cos-
moi"). A symbolic world thus provides a framework of ultimate meaning. It is
important to appreciate that a symbolic world refers to more than just a universe
of discourse, a going community of meanings and values that rationalize a given
way of behavior. The investigation of the symbolic world is centrally concerned
with that which makes such a world real, how it penetrates and shapes everyday
life. It must be made clear that this is our characterization of the believer's
world—the believer might simply view his world as the "real" world—this
perhaps is why the collapse of his world is so traumatic.

For many survivors, religion was (and still is) the symbolic world that formed
a reservoir of meaning that could be utilized in private—a psychological world
of significance that nourished them when the outside world was assaulting their
very physical existence and mental integrity. In some sense this "sacred
canopy"[6] offered the survivor a certain degree of understanding, predictability,
safety, and satisfaction. It was a religious framework of meaning that permitted
the survivor to develop and maintain a viable sense of self-esteem, the reflective
and intuitive sense that he or she is fulfilling a significant role in a meaningful
cosmic drama. In other words, these individuals felt themselves "to be a locus
of primary value in a world of meaning."[7]

Now what happens to such a person when this sense of ontological security
is radically challenged or breaks down, as was the case with many survivors?

What happens when something that the self identifies with so profoundly (i.e., God), and is viewed as necessary to one's well-being, is undermined or destroyed?

It is painfully clear that when the fundamental order in terms of which the individual can "make sense" of his life and recognize his own identity is undermined, the process of psychological disintegration and disorganization begins. It is this issue that draws the psychotherapist into the picture, for it is the task of therapists to help the patient recreate, as far as possible, a feeling of ontological security, to alleviate the pain, chaos, and anxiety associated with the loss of such security and to help the patient reconstruct a symbolic world so that he experiences his life as a more coherent narrative.[8]

RELIGIOUS LIFE BEFORE THE HOLOCAUST

In order to understand better the manner in which religion has an impact on the psychotherapeutic experience with survivors, it is necessary to appreciate the kind of community and social context they were part of prior to the war. Although there were many survivors who significantly altered their beliefs and practices, and others who completely gave up their religion, it is very important to be aware of their pre-Holocaust ways of thinking, feeling, and organizing the world, though their manifest life-style today and conscious frames of reference bear little resemblance to those of the past. These earlier patterns and especially theological upbringing may affect the survivor's present world view in a myriad of taken-for-granted and unconscious ways. For example, there are survivors who were raised to view God as all-seeing and all-knowing, a God who punishes individuals for their sins. In their post-Holocaust world, they may have given up their belief in God but retain a diffuse fear that they will be punished if they don't obey the law. There is a tendency to blame themselves for their problems in living. Moreover, it is the therapist's awareness of the continuities and discontinuities in the survivor's faith and religious behavior that will permit the therapist to appreciate maximally the survivor's experience, especially the manner in which his world was affected by the Holocaust. It is the discontinuities in particular which contribute to the survivor's internal conflict and disrupted sense of self-sameness (i.e., being a locus of primary value in a world of meaning). This impedes his attempt to recreate a meaningful world that incorporates the past in a manner that isn't jarring and debilitating.

As historian Jacob Robinson has estimated, about half of the 6 million Jews murdered during the Holocaust were Orthodox Jews, who strictly observed the *halakhah* (Jewish Law).[9] Brenner's survey of survivors now residing in Israel further supports the claim that the Jewish communities of Eastern Europe prior to World War II constituted a religiously observant community.[10] Moreover, as Dawidowicz has pointed out, even in those communities where secularism was most imposing, the Jewish community was still greatly influenced by traditional Jewish values and halakhah.[11]

Halakhah dealt with every aspect of a Jew's life, his relationship and responsibilities to God and man. His everyday ordinary existence was made intelligible
and was completely determined by this very tightly organized system of religious
prohibitions and commandments. More than formal law, halakhah was "the
way" in which the Jews walked, which reflected their ethos—the "tone, character, and quality of [their] inner life, its moral and aesthetic style and mood;
it is the underlying attitude towards themselves and their world that life reflects."[12] This devotion to the Law was rooted in the conviction that to love
God, one had to serve Him through cognition of the Torah, and hallowing life
by meticulously following His Law.[13] The halakhah man could not accomplish
his task in isolation, but viewed himself as part of a communal way of life lived
in the presence of God that served as a meaning matrix and powerful reference
point for all his endeavors. As Lichtenstein points out, halakhah thus makes the
service of God part of a total life that is infused with religious significance,
harmoniously organized into a divinely ordained whole and gives man a sense
of purpose and a sense of divine purpose.[14]

In the early stages of Nazism, religious Jews usually put their persecution into
the historical context of Jewish suffering. The Jews have been persecuted since
ancient times, and the Nazis were viewed as another variation on this theme of
Jewish suffering and victimization. In other words, Jews were putting their
suffering into the familiar category of Jewish scapegoating by the *Goy*. The
religious response was maximizing prayer, ritual, and good deeds. In this way
God would be more likely to deliver them from their suffering.

RELIGIOUS LIFE DURING THE HOLOCAUST

The variety of religious responses and problems after the Holocaust can be
adequately understood only within the context of the survivors' actual incarceration conditions and specific Holocaust experiences. The question of the ways
religion was used by inmates to help cope with the brutality and degradation
during their incarceration is a subject that warrants a book in itself. For our
purposes, given the scope of this chapter, some brief comments will suffice.[15]

The manner in which the psychotherapist understands the behavior of the
religious concentration camp inmate significantly affects the way he approaches
the survivor's current problems. For example, therapeutic technique with the
survivor stems, in part, from the assumption underlying the therapist's account
of how the presenting problem is linked to his Holocaust behavior, and this in
turn is related to the therapist's acceptance of a particular narrative of how the
survivor coped with his experience in the first place. As Ornstein points out, for
the therapist to empathize accurately with the survivor and protect himself from
giving meaning to the survivor's experience from his own idiosyncratic perspectives, it is necessary for the therapist to understand the mode of adaptation
to the conditions as they existed during the years of persecution. This, Ornstein

says, is "the missing link" that could meaningfully connect the survivor's pre-Holocaust past with her/his recovery and adaptation to a new life.[16]

For the survivor, continues Ornstein, establishing a sense of continuity, a connection between past and present is of central significance in psychological recovery. The understanding of the mode of adaptation to extreme conditions provides the therapist with an in-depth, longitudinal view of the survivor. For the survivor, the reconstruction of his adaptation facilitates the integration of the Holocaust experience into the totality of his life history. It is in relation to establishing a sense of continuity that recounting the circumstances and conditions to which adaptation had to take place has its significance.

Finally, the importance of the therapist being aware of the inmate's successful coping strategies used while incarcerated is that the therapist can more readily sense the manifest and latent strengths of the person—strengths that can possibly be tapped in the present in order to help the survivor more adequately cope with his current problems.

Even in the concentration camp, many inmates with religious convictions made a world for themselves. That is, to some extent they were able to imagine patterns of meaning that transcended the immediacy of the situations they had to endure. Through the capacity for symbolization the religious survivor was able to better cope with the environment and attain a degree of freedom relative to it. For the religious Jew, religion acted as a meaningful reality that comprehended him and all his experiences. This all-embracing fabric of meanings gave sense to his life, especially to the dissonant and painful aspects. By the individual having a plausible theodicy (a vindication of divine justice in allowing evil to exist) in particular, he was better able to integrate the painful experiences of life into a framework that makes him feel that his experience makes sense: "It is not happiness the theodicy primarily provides, but meaning."[17] As Berger points out, and Frankl[18] demonstrates, in situations of acute suffering, the need for meaning is as strong as, or even stronger than, the need for happiness. Being able to understand why one suffers, that is to have a convincing theodicy, is experienced as of equal or greater important than relief from one's oppressive situation. As Nietzsche stated, "any meaning is better than none at all."

Dreksler points out that in the ghettos, the concentration camps, and even in the extermination camps there was an ongoing religious life for particular Jews and for the community as a whole. In the underground in hidden bunkers, for example, there were *hederim* and *Talmudei Torah* (religious academies) where Yeshiva students learned. Dreksler further notes that there is ample evidence of the community's success in organizing public worship, kindling the Hanukah candles, wearing *zitzit* (fringes), even observing *kashrut* (dietary laws) in the concentration camps under great danger.[19]

The contributions of Eliach, Berkovitz, and Landes, primarily focusing on the Hasidic and Orthodox communities, indicate the powerful need on the part of incarcerated devout victims to maintain their humanity by reaffirming their boundless belief in God, the integrity of the Jewish people, and the goodness of mankind.[20] Rabbi Ephraim Oshry's extraordinary *Questions and Responses from Out of the Depths*, written on scraps of paper in the Kovno ghetto, is a seminal work of emergency rulings on both ritual law and Jewish ethics. His book describes his own religious activities and the efforts of his fellow inmates to observe their Judaism.[21] In this book and Kirschner's *Rabbinic Responsa of the Holocaust Era*, we see the religious community's attempt to apply traditional precepts to a catastrophe of unprecedented proportions.[22] One illustrative question put to a rabbi was about a man who smothered a child inadvertently, to avoid detection of a group of Jews hiding from the Nazis. The ruling was that the man had acted lawfully, even though a pious and holy course of action would have been to suffer death rather than take an innocent life.

These and other responsa written during the Holocaust reflect the struggle of religious Jews to preserve life and integrity under the most extreme conditions, that is, the need to affirm the self in thought and action—to give one's own personal stamp to self and world as well as the profound ontological need to be rooted in a self-transcending power source mediated by a significant other.

Thus, the Jews who were deeply involved in Judaism generated a meaningful order of existence for themselves, who without this sheltering cosmos would have experienced the horror and chaos even more sharply. It is furthermore clear that the religious factor is only one of the crucial elements that enhanced the inmates' probability of survival. Other circumstances, such as one's age at the time of incarceration, the particular conditions in the camp where one was imprisoned, one's pre-Holocaust personality, and whether one was lucky—are all important considerations when trying to understand the reasons for an inmate's survival. But we believe the religious dimension in some cases was also a very important element of survival.

It also seems important to emphasize that any person, religious or otherwise, who had a well organized symbolic world to which he strongly adhered was somewhat more likely to survive camp experience.[23] Pawelczyńska has pointed out that if an inmate had values and models that were deeply internalized, the strength derived from these values greatly contributed to resisting any alien system that denied those values.[24] Levi and Frankl point out that people with strong religious convictions, like the Jehovah's Witnesses and Orthodox Jews, coped better than most under the hardships of the concentration camps.[25] These people, says Lasch, found strength in the revealed word of an absolute, objective, and omnipotent creator, as they saw it, not in personal values meaningful only to themselves. Survival, says Lasch, must have some purpose external to ourselves that gives us a reason to live or to die.[26] Such deeply internalized convictions enhance psychological resilience in situations of extremity.

AFTER LIBERATION

Many survivors went into displaced person camps following the war, while others returned to their homes only to find death and destruction. Many survivors' religious beliefs seem to have gone through an initial period of disorganization and confusion after liberation.

The most basic physical and psychological needs were more pressing, and there was often a temporary pause in grappling with religious questions. In addition, when survivors found out about the deaths of loved ones and the destruction of their communities, a deep depression usually ensued, sometimes taking many years before it receded; at other times a significant residue lasted for a lifetime. Other survivors reacted quite differently; they too were often depressed but dealt with this by throwing themselves into the recreation of the Jewish community, helping establish synagogues, conducting religious services, and acquiring kosher food for religiously observant survivors. Still others tried to maintain their sense of continuity and Jewish life by becoming involved with Zionism and other Jewish self-help movements.

A very significant influence on whether a survivor remained religious immediately after the war was the response he received from the host community he went into.[27] For example, one survivor, who prior to the war was a cantorial student at a prominent academy in Germany recontacted the head rabbi of that academy, who had left Europe before the Holocaust and was now living in the United States, and requested help in continuing his training there.

The survivor was extremely angry when the first question the rabbi asked him was if he kept a kosher kitchen and if his wife went to the *mikvah* (ritual bath) regularly. But more to the point, and underlying this anger, was the survivor's pain at the realization that there was no longer any continuity between his pre-Holocaust world and his present one, with its very different needs, wishes, and sensibilities. Compounding this jarring realization was the painful and disappointing feeling of being misunderstood by a former role model and the further realization that the gap between his post-Holocaust world and the rabbi's was unbridgeable. The consequence of this interchange was that the survivor's wish to continue his cantorial studies and practice Judaism was irreversibly ruptured. He worked in the garment district for 30 years and died a bitter old man.

A further influence on the survivor's religious beliefs was his own internal need to have an extreme response to God. A choice that felt less than extreme appeared grossly inadequate and unworthy of what one had experienced. Hence, a total rejection of God or absolute piety were the two options most available to survivors.[28]

A plausible reason for this is suggested by a long tradition of theory in social psychology that argues that we are motivated to keep our attitudes and experiences in order.[29] Specifically, we are motivated to avoid contradictions and inconsistencies within our attitudes and between our attitudes and behavior. When inconsistency does occur we are often motivated to overcome it. Inconsistency or dissonance is a negative state (experienced as tension or discomfort) we may seek to avoid. For the survivor, his Holocaust experience was viewed as profoundly dissonant with much of what he believed, knew, and did prior to the war, and it was therefore necessary after the war either to change radically one's beliefs or to recommit oneself to the former beliefs—both being ways to bring a sense of order, coherence, and harmony to one's world. The survivor had a great need to maintain intact the logical structure of his symbolic meaning framework, and only an extreme reaction one way or the other could achieve this goal.

SURVIVORS WHO REMAINED RELIGIOUSLY COMMITTED

The Holocaust has been viewed as a transformational event by most survivors; nevertheless, there were those individuals whose faith and/or religious behavior remained largely unchanged (at least manifestly), although in many instances there were subtle ways in which their Holocaust experiences affected their religious world both positively and negatively. That there were as many survivors who remained more or less religiously committed after the Holocaust speaks to the fact that humans struggle against the loss of their world, the whole range of action and objects that they so laboriously and painfully fashioned during their lives. They fight against the subversion of themselves in the only world they know.[30]

Among those survivors who remained religious after the war there were a variety of responses to their suffering, and these different responses are as numerous as there are survivors. We therefore will draw from a few examples to show that survivors tried very hard to maintain and/or recreate their symbolic world, in order to preserve their own sense of being part of a meaningful order, with its consequent feeling of self-cohesion and continuity. That is, as Berger has shown, a theodicy legitimates the marginal and alienating experiences that constantly threaten a person's existence. Sickness, injury and death are interpreted as events in a larger cosmic history, and as such are given an ultimate significance. In the course of everyday life theodicy allows a person to carry on life after the death of a significant other and to anticipate his own demise without being paralyzed in his daily routines by the terror of it.[31] Thus, to the extent that a person is able to make sense of the pain of life, so is he able to feel that he is securely moored in the world, with a past worth remembering, a present worth living, and a future worth facing.

Among the survivors who remained committed to their religion, there were those who severely doubted the assumptions underlying their beliefs and behavior and who were generally less comfortable with themselves. There were also those who were less questioning and tended to make sense of their suffering in light of their belief in the traditional God of the Hebrew Bible. These people drew from the well-tried classical theodicies that Jews have used for thousands of years to account for national catastrophes and personal tragedies. The point to keep in mind is that all of the theodicies used by survivors are ways of maintaining their world.

One response by some survivors to the Holocaust was to view the event like any other tragedy, in that the cataclysm and their suffering during it put into sharp focus the problem of evil. However, it did not, they believe, profoundly change the problem or add anything new to it.[32] This attitude may also have been reinforced by the many personal tragedies that challenged their faith in God (e.g., loss of parent or a child, etc.) prior to the war. They thus had seriously struggled with their belief in a just, compassionate, omnipotent, and intelligible God. The Holocaust was fitted into this interpretive framework with the event viewed as a worst case example of the problem of evil without traumatic discomfort.

Other survivors interpreted their Holocaust experience as the extreme of human evil, the price humankind has to pay for human freedom. They believed that the Nazis were human, not gods, and that Auschwitz reflects shamefully on humans but does not touch God's existence or perfection.

This belief often manifests itself in the unwillingness of the believing survivor to contemplate the problem of God's seeming indifference in the first place. "I do not allow myself to think about it," said one survivor. The contemplation of God's role during the Holocaust is too painful, while the best way to deal with these feelings is to avoid the problem altogether. Often this attempt to deny the issue is accompanied by manic-like activity in another sphere, such as work, in order to strengthen the defenses against examining God's silence and lack of intervention in ending Jewish suffering. Furthermore, when doubts about God are evoked, the religious survivor can draw from traditional sources that demand ridding oneself of alien thoughts that could foster irreligious behavior or attitudes, since one has not acquired the wisdom to truly decipher the significance of the doubts. The unwillingness to judge God may be an aspect of pious resignation rooted in the rabbinic view that God in His perfect wisdom and goodness knows best.

In other words, writes Berger, the problem of theodicy becomes the problem of anthropodicy.[33] The question of God's injustice becomes a question of man's sinfulness. There is a submission to God's omnipotence—a submission to the totally other who can neither be seriously questioned nor challenged, and who, by his very nature, is sovereignly above any human ethical standards. The religious survivor, like all of us, fights against being uprooted and disorganized; he thus tenaciously clings to the cosmic perspective and unified vision which assures him a secure place in a universe of known dimensions and definite purposes. To refrain from aggressively challenging God's inaction during the Holocaust by focusing on human cruelty becomes a way for the survivor to maintain the self-transcending meanings for which he and all humans hunger.

A third response from devout survivors was to view the Holocaust as an unfathomable mystery. It is a modern *akedah* (sacrifice of Isaac), a test of one's faith. However, like all of God's ways, the Holocaust transcends human comprehension and requires faith and silence. These survivors felt that the Holocaust tested their faith as God has always tested His people, and although it is not always clear that one is being challenged or why, it is one's obligation to rise to the challenge in faith and devotion. This view, although seemingly dogmatic, actually reflects a philosophical acceptance of the lack of explanatory certainty one has in the face of God's behavior during the Holocaust. It is an attitude that in whole or in part underlies many of the diverse survivor theodicies and all religions, namely, the awareness that for a religious person the heart of the matter is always mystery, especially the riddles of suffering in an assumed ethically caring universe. Perhaps Spinoza best captured this sentiment when he said, "simple faith is the path to salvation."

Such a theodicy may be augmented by a fourth perspective: the belief that the Holocaust is an example of the temporary "Eclipse of God." That is, there are times when God is inexplicably absent from history or unaccountably chooses to turn His face away.[34]

These religious survivors often feel a compelling need to challenge God about His lack of presence during the Holocaust. For them it is a way of venting their anger at Him without being passive. And yet there is a need to preserve their God, despite the numerous questions and debates frequently raging in their minds:

It is all I think about. . . . My life is a running, nagging dialogue with God . . . He is always on my mind. Why? Why? I sometimes find I have been walking the lonely, crowded streets of Tel Aviv, wandering aimlessly, conducting a question and answer session with Him—with no satisfactory answers forthcoming. I believe in Him with the same certainty as ever. The Holocaust couldn't change that. But I find I want very much to keep after Him and try to the best of my ability to overcome the obscurity of His ways and I can't escape Him, however much He may have wished to escape us. I will do this to my last breath. I know it. More than this, I believe this is precisely what a Jew must do, to keep after Him for answers. And it brings me a measure of repose and comfort to conduct these conferences, to be God's interlocutor, to keep after Him by creating and inventing, like the traditional Jew of the past in history, new arguments against Him, and new justifications for Him. For me it is the entire Torah, the Etz Chayyim [Tree of Life]. Although I have no choice to the contrary, I am happy to hold fast to it.[35]

One significant aspect of this vignette is the fact that this debate with God provides the survivor with an existential drama, giving a post-Holocaust purpose to his existence. The survivor in this example never has peace, something always has to be questioned, something always has to be recapitulated; but in these repetitions there is embedded a structure with which he can organize his life. Thus, this man's religion serves to maintain the reality of that socially constructed world within which he exists. Moreover, this survivor feels that he is involved in a debate that is condoned by Jewish tradition and through this identification with the group he thereby feels that there is continuity with his personal and Jewish past.

Finally, in this illustration we see the survivor being capable of relaxing his individualistic self-assertion, and rooting himself in a secure self-transcending framework. That is, the survivor in this mode-of-being is able to sustain his self-esteem by fashioning a self-transcending mythic drama.

A fifth rather disturbing perspective on the meaning of the Holocaust was articulated by devout survivors. They viewed the Holocaust in terms of *mipenei hata'einu* ("because of our sins we were punished"). According to this view, the Jewish people were sinful and the Holocaust was its just punishment.

The tendency to blame oneself for one's problems is a characteristic defensive reaction to the passivity inherent in externally imposed suffering. Indeed there is such a line of thought in Jewish liturgy (e.g., Leviticus 26) that has probably helped condition religious Jews to interpret their suffering as a result of their sin and transgression to God. Said one survivor,

The Holocaust was saying that Jews who keep the mitzvot are doing the right thing and Jews who do not are doing the wrong thing, a terribly wrong thing, but we will all suffer and be punished alike. The innocent and guilty together until we all become religious and observant Jews.[36]

"The six million died because of their sins towards God and towards man"—a survivor.

This is a retributive God similar to a child's view of an angry father, who disciplines and punishes his children for not obeying his rules. This view also does something to one's view of the victims. In psychological terms it allows one to view the fate of the victims as their own fault. One does not have to feel so bad for them, a distancing can take place. Also, one's survival can be interpreted as due to one's greater piety, while God metes out strict justice, and each person is dealt with according to what he deserves.[37]

A very interesting sixth theodicy articulated by some survivors goes like this: The Holocaust is the ultimate in vicarious atonement. The Jewish people are the "suffering servant" of Isaiah—Israel suffers and atones for the sins of others. Some Jews die so that the Gentiles might be purified and live. Said one very observant Jewish woman, "The six million perished for the sins of the rest of the world. When they sin we suffer." A variation on this view is that sometimes survivors feel that the death of the 6 million resulted from the sins of less religious Jews around the world, something like a burnt offering. The good Jews suffered to save the sinful ones.

The belief in messianism is one important consideration here and warrants a brief diversion. According to this belief, there will be a resurrection of the dead upon the arrival of the Messiah. It follows, therefore, that the martyrs who died and those who survived honorably will be reborn and enjoy eternal bliss with the Messiah within God's kingdom.

As Berger points out, the belief in messianism permits one to relativize the suffering of the present in terms of it being overcome in a glorious future. "The anomic phenomena are legitimated by reference to a future nomization, thus reintegrating them within an over-all meaningful order." By articulating such a theodicy, the survivor feels the comfort of knowing that in the final analysis the sufferer will be comforted, the good man rewarded, and the evil punished. This perspective permits the survivor to maintain his messianic hopes, but at the same time, says Berger, transposes such beliefs to a mysterious, empirically inaccessible sphere safe from the vicissitudes and challenges of history.[38]

A seventh perspective on the Holocaust, although not technically a theodicy, was articulated by many survivors: Remain religious in order not to give Hitler a posthumous victory. In this view, the Holocaust is revelation, it issues a call for Jewish affirmation. As Fackenheim has written, from Auschwitz comes the command: Jews survive![39] Said one survivor:

> Before the Holocaust I was a simple observant Jew. Today I'm an observant Jew but very complex. . . . I have now a clear reason in my mind and very deep motives for practicing Judaism whereas before it was not as clear. Besides everything else, it's my revenge against Hitler and the Nazis . . . it is a spitting on their grave. My way of getting even is by practicing my religion with fervor and enthusiasm. Serving God and the Jewish people and carrying on my father's and my grandfather's and ancestors' traditions.[40]

In this example we see among other things a survivor's attempt to transform narcissistic rage into mature self-assertion rooted in the need for inner continuity with one's personal and traditional past. A by-product of viewing their suffering in this way is the feeling that through their survival, God was telling them that there was some higher purpose for their survival. This was usually interpreted as a mandate to reinforce their faith in Him and do His commandments.

We can also see how the Holocaust is interpreted in the survivor's religious frame of reference, and how a feeling is generated that one should be more committed to religion. It was construed that because of this commitment, one was saved, and thus greater loyalty to God was evoked.

Some survivors appear to have remained observant after the war, and indeed on a behavioral level this is so. However, the cracks in their symbolic world are deeper than implied in those survivor theodicies already mentioned. Sometimes it is the extensive need for disavowal that indicates the severe challenge that the survivor's Holocaust experiences have posed to his symbolic world. For example, another way that survivors maintained their religious faith and continued their religious behavior was to view their Holocaust experience as belonging to another long lost alienated period of their lives without any connection to their present concerns. These individuals view the Holocaust as a weird detour in their personal lives, without significance for the present. They pursue one of the ways to preserve one's world in the face of a deeply disturbing challenge by acting as if that challenging experience is completely unrelated to one's current world. Through exiling one's jarring experience to psychological and biographical irrelevance, one can preserve the integrity of one's world construction.

We have reviewed prevalent ways that survivors were able to maintain their world in the face of the great anomaly—the Holocaust. We have also seen that people have a tremendous need to consciously and/or unconsciously maintain their symbolic world in the face of overwhelming suffering. The reason for this, says Arendt (writing in another context), is that when one loses one's sheltering "sacred canopy," then one finds oneself without a guide in the wilderness of bare facts, "for when man is robbed of all means of interpreting events he is left with no sense whatsoever of reality."[41]

SURVIVORS WHOSE FAITH WAS LOST OR DIMINISHED AFTER THE HOLOCAUST

There were survivors who were not able to sustain their religious worldview during the Holocaust. Without God their world began to fall apart and lost its plausibility, its personal sense of reality. As Berger points out, for the religious person, "The subjective reality of the world hinges on the thin thread of conversation"[42] (i.e., maintaining an ongoing dialogue with God, significant others, and, more broadly, active involvement with the religious community and tradition). In the camps, religion filled the inmates' need to be rooted in a sustaining source of self-transcending power grounded in a divine person and/or divine world. Traumatic disruption, however, occurs when the dialogue ends or is interrupted as was the case for many religious inmates. For the survivor, when a religious framework no longer served as an all-embracing sacred order against the dread of physical and/or psychological annihilation, he was left alone against the threats of chaos, meaninglessness, and death. That is, his entire world began to lose credibility.

In the concentration camp the fear of death predominated. Perhaps nothing undermines human meanings, and threatens the very foundations upon which humans erect their self-esteem, more than the fear of death.[43] Furthermore, when a person observes the death of a significant other and anticipates his own death, he is strongly compelled to question the ad hoc cognitive and normative operating procedures of his "normal" life in society.[44]

For the religious survivor, then, the loss of religious perspective is experienced as becoming worldless. His orientation in experience becomes tenuous, and in extreme cases he loses his sense of reality and identity. When a person can no longer make sense of his life, he also loses his "moral and cognitive orientation" with debilitating psychological ramifications.[45] These consequences will be discussed later. In this section we want to describe the reasons why many survivors gave up their faith (in whole or in part), their religious beliefs, and/or religious behavior.

The relinquishing of faith in a just God by survivors in some ways is the most expected reaction after the Holocaust. Brenner reports that as a general rule faith declined as a consequence of the devastation, and during it as well. Moreover, belief in the major articles of faith never recovered to their pre-Holocaust level.[46] The survivors to be described in this group tended to view the Holocaust and their suffering during it as an anomaly that could not be easily assimilated into their interpretive world. For these survivors, none of the previously mentioned theodicies was satisfactory in making sense of the cataclysm; there was an absence of a synthesized, coherent worldview that adequately explained and/or justified the Holocaust.

Many survivors consciously view their lack of faith as based on a rationale that goes something like this: The Holocaust is proof that "God is dead." If there were a God, He would certainly have prevented Auschwitz; if He did not, then He does not exist. In *After Auschwitz*, Rubenstein argues that after the Holocaust the belief in a redeeming God, who is active in history and who will redeem mankind from its troubles, is no longer possible. Belief in such a God, and a loyalty to the rabbinic theodicy that attempted to justify Him, would imply that Hitler was part of a divine plan and that the Jewish people were being punished for their sins. This belief is not plausible in a post-Holocaust world, says Rubenstein.[47]

However, survivors had great difficulty speaking about a God who is dead. Rather they preferred to speak about God's total absence. The idea that "God was dead" and never to reappear in their lives was experienced with tremendous anxiety.

That God could have done something to prevent the Holocaust but chose not to is a more disturbing feeling for the survivor than the declaration that He does not exist. If God is the master of the universe and stood idly by while his chosen people were destroyed, then this would make Him what Rubenstein calls a "cosmic sadist." Most survivors prefer not to believe in God rather than to view Him in this satanic manner.

Survivors also find belief in God impossible because they view the victims as entirely innocent. What makes God's absence more distressing is that the victims were totally undeserving of their fate. They were a pious and decent group, and the death of so many innocent children made faith in a God that allows this to happen seem untenable. That is, when good people offer good prayers for good purposes and God remains silent amidst the horrific cruelty, there can be a loss of basic trust, and the relinquishing of faith is understandable.

For the religious survivor, perhaps the predominant internal reaction to the loss of their world was a terrible sense of abandonment by God. Nowhere is this agonizing sense of radical abandonment better described than by Elie Wiesel in the often-quoted passage from *Night*. In this powerful episode, the S.S. decided to publicly hang three camp inmates for sabotage, one of them being a young child with a refined and beautiful face like that of a "sad angel." Wiesel continues:

The three victims mounted together onto the chairs.

The three necks were placed at the same moment within the nooses.

"Long live Liberty!" cried the two adults. But the child was silent. "Where is God? Where is He?" someone behind me asked.

At a sign from the head of the camp, the three chairs tipped over.

Total silence throughout the camp. On the horizon, the sun was setting.

"Bare your heads!" yelled the head of the camp. His voice was raucous. We were weeping.

"Cover your heads!" Then the march past began. The two adults were no longer alive.

Their tongues hung swollen, blue-tinged. But the third rope was still moving; being so light, the child was still alive. . . .

For more than an hour he stayed there, struggling between life and death, dying in slow agony under our eyes. And we had to look him full in the face. He was still alive when I passed in front of him. His tongue was still red, his eyes not yet glazed. Behind me, I heard the same man asking:

"Where is God now?" And I heard a voice within me answer him: "Where is He? Here He is—He is hanging here on this gallows. . . . ' '

That night the soup tasted of corpses.[48]

What follows from such an experience of God's abandonment in the face of such brutality is rage, despair, and hopelessness, in short, the loss of trust in the plausibility of one's world. Says Wiesel, "Never shall I forget that nocturnal silence which deprived me, for all eternity, of the desire to live. Never shall I forget those moments which murdered my God and my soul and turned my dreams to dust."[49]

Rage at God in particular is centrally connected to feeling abandoned by Him in the most critical hour of need, especially because this abandonment led to such personal suffering and loss of loved ones. As Brenner points out,[50] it is important to emphasize that the survivor who blasphemes God, curses Him, denies Him, hates Him, menaces Him, and/or threatens to withhold faith in Him is doing so in part because of this terrible narcissistic hurt he experienced while incarcerated, when God was absent. "God, if you don't do something I'm going to stop believing in you . . . '' was the way many survivors confronted God during imprisonment. When there was no help given by Him, this feeling of abandonment *by* God was transposed and became abandonment *of* God. As Brenner further indicates, of those individuals who were seeking to punish God by shouting His nonexistence to His face, they were reacting as if they were a deserted lover crying out in pain, "I don't love you anymore; for me you no longer exist." In other words, for many survivors, God's nonexistence is often proclaimed as a way of punishing God for concealing Himself when He was desperately needed.

We have seen why it was that survivors lost their faith, as well as the significance of this for their ability to maintain themselves as a locus of primary value in a world of meaning. In the following section we will look at some of the psychological problems that this loss generates and its impact on the psychotherapeutic experience. We will also offer some suggestions as to how psychotherapists can best facilitate reconstruction of the survivor's symbolic world.

TREATMENT ISSUES WITH SURVIVORS

Regardless of theoretical orientation, most people agree that psychotherapy with the Holocaust survivor is an enormously difficult task. Psychoanalysts in particular have attempted perhaps more than any other professional group both to treat survivors and to theorize about the origin of their symptoms and their problems in living.[51] Regrettably, their success in treating survivors, as with most other approaches, has been rather limited. Thus, Eissler has serious doubts that survivors can be helped by psychoanalytic psychotherapy since the trauma of persecution remains incomparable and incomprehensible.[52] Kijak and Funtowicz stress the difficulties of treating survivors because their incarceration led to "irreversible deterioration of the ego."[53] Barocas despondently claims that hardly anyone could have emerged from the Nazi death camps without having been scarred, scars "which will never be removed by psychotherapy."[54] Krystal stresses the limitations of psychoanalytic psychotherapy with elderly survivors, primarily because their ability to grieve effectively has been impaired by the enormity of their suffering and losses.[55] He elsewhere grimly concludes that "the therapist has to be satisfied when the patient is restored to his chronic survivor syndrome state with its symptoms, handicaps and problems."[56]

We believe that one of the reasons survivors have been so difficult to treat is that the models being used to understand and conceptualize their problems have not adequately considered the awesome significance of the survivors' loss of their symbolic world: "When a man is so utterly stripped of life meaning [as was the concentration camp inmate] he has no furnishings for his inner life, he is as good as dead, even though his organism gropes blindly towards life."[57] Therapists need to understand that conceptualizing the survivor's symptoms solely in terms of classical psychoanalytic theory does not sufficiently account for the core of the survivor's experience nor illuminate the significance of this pain.[58] Viewing the survivor's symptoms primarily in terms of the product of conflict between a repressed impulse and the repressing agency (compromise formations) or in terms of Freud's theory of trauma or its variations[59] fails to grasp the significance of the survivor's symptoms for his overall functioning.

According to Becker, neurosis as a clinical problem can be seen in part as an existential failure to create a personal drama in a world of meaning that supports self-affirmation.[60] Man becomes neurotic when vital living bogs down. There must be the capacity and the confidence to thrust oneself into active participation in the world. Clinical neurosis testifies to a behavioral poverty, to the blocking of the forward momentum of action and the restriction of experience. For the survivor in particular, it is the experienced result of the failure to develop patterns of behavior that allow the individual to merge successfully with the demands of a sustaining cultural drama. Only such a merger allows for the development of an assured sense of self-respect, and gives a person the courage to open himself to a reality that is both inviting and terrifying.

Such a framework for psychopathology helps us better understand the often reported symptoms associated with survivorship embodied in the so-called "survivor syndrome." The survivor has been described as having chronic depressive states, a tendency to isolation and withdrawal, reappearing manifestations of anxiety, some disturbances of cognition and memory, guilt, and psychosomatic complaints.[61] Perhaps the underlying reason why survivors develop this way of being-in-the-world has to do with the trauma of the loss of loved ones and the inability to mourn them during and following the Holocaust. For the survivor who abandoned his faith, this trauma may be because it also meant the loss of identity as it was reflected in membership in the religious community, since the survivor's religious world was the world of meaning that provided the framework for a sense of self-value. The survivor who was once deeply religious and who no longer defines himself as God's rational partner has, perhaps more than any other kind of survivor, to come to terms with the painful and disorganizing consequences of losing his symbolic world.

It is not by chance that depression and isolation and withdrawal are repeatedly cited as key symptoms of the survivor who comes to therapy. Depression can be precipitated by the loss or removal of anything that the individual values. To the extent that one's sense of well-being, safety, and meaning is dependent on love, social position—or God—to that extent one will be threatened by its loss. When the reliance is preponderant, the person despairs of survival and gives up. It is this despair that we call depression, and this was a common reaction for many survivors.

Hopeless and helpless, the survivor may give up the struggle. It is this abandonment which makes depression different from other psychological conditions. The ego is paralyzed because it feels incapable of meeting life's demands.[62] Bibring's ego theory of depression which points to the importance of loss of self-esteem (as opposed to viewing depression as self-directed aggression) allows us to broaden our understanding of the religious survivor's depression to include the entire range of social phenomenon:

Since the ego is rooted in social reality, since self-esteem is composed of social symbols and social motives, depression becomes a direct function of a cognitively apprehended symbolic world.[63]

The religious survivor's depression is concerned with more than object loss, but fundamentally includes the loss of norms or rules for significant action that were embodied in religious observance and community. These "social rules and objects provide an individual with a staged drama of significance which is the theatre of his action."[64] To lose a loved one is to lose someone to whom one has made appeal for self-validation. To lose one's norms or rules for significant action is to lose a performance part in which identity is fabricated and sustained.[65] The survivor is thus unable to feel that he is an object of primary value in a world of meaning.

The survivor's depression has other dimensions that can be more deeply understood when viewed from a model that stresses man's need to be a center of personal significance in a meaningful world. As with other survivors, the survivor who has lost his religious world often has a restricted and closed life-style. Indeed, a depressed person builds himself firmly into his cultural world such that he is imprisoned in his own narrow behavioral mold. Becker, in his brilliant essay on the *Pawnbroker*, calls this fetishization "the organization of perception and action, by the personality, around a very striking and compelling—but narrow theme."[66] Becker points out that the reason a survivor would artificially inflate a small area of the world and overvalue it (in the pawnbroker's case it was money) is because it represents an area that he can firmly hold on to, can skillfully manipulate, use easily to justify himself—his actions, his sense of self, his option in the world. As Becker writes, "the fetish, in word, is an arbitrary focus for your derivation of self-value."[67]

The religious survivor who lost the sense of meaning, who views the richness of his past life as unrelated to his harrowing present, needs to reorient his personality around a narrow and compelling source of meaning, of self-sustenance. Without organizing his self-concept around such a theme the survivor feels that he has no justification for his entire life, no justification for going on.

The often-cited guilt of the survivor can also be conceptualized more broadly when using this new perspective. In the early theorizing survivor guilt was assumed to occur in relation to the feeling of not deserving to live when all or most relatives and friends were murdered during the Holocaust. Survivor guilt was classically viewed as a result of early hostility and death wishes to the lost love object.[68]

Ornstein, however, views survivor guilt rather differently. She believes it is related less to having survived while others had died than to survivors' difficulty in reconciling the alteration in their behavioral and moral conduct during the Holocaust with their conduct and behavior under civilized conditions.[69]

Developing Ornstein's conception somewhat differently, we suggest that survivor guilt reflects the survivor's difficulty in having lived in one symbolic world which is accepted for the purpose of survival, that is, "l'universe concentrationnaire," and then moving into another post-Holocaust symbolic world that is experienced as morally discontinuous with the previous one. An example of this is the inmate who survived in the camp by bribing a Kapo to remove his name from the list of those to be gassed and replacing it with someone else's name. Elie Wiesel offers another example, writing that when incarcerated he had the thought that he wished his father was dead so as not to be an additional burden to his own survival. The difficulty after the Holocaust in coming to terms with this behavior, behavior that made sense at the time within the camp context, is obviously awesome because it demands a way of integrating the survivor's Holocaust experience into the value structures that he now judges himself by. Since most of these values reside outside the reflective capacity of most people, the survivor's attempt at integration is extremely difficult and complex.

Likewise the survivor's psychosomatic complaints make more sense when we consider the degree to which bodily complaints focus one's mind and behavior around the ache or pain. The survivor who narrows his concerns to sorting out the vagaries of his physical condition actually has a project that anchors him in a "fetishized" world of meaning. Through such a creation of meaning the survivor does not have to face a sense of helplessness at piecing together a world of reciprocal relationships and a world that integrates the past and present.

The survivor's reappearing anxiety is a complicated matter and is tied in part to his symbolic difficulties. One often cited characteristic of survivors is alexithymia—the inability to identify, symbolize, and express feelings and fantasies.[70] As Becker points out (1966, p. 178), "For the symbolic animal, anxiety derives largely from lack of words—lack of conventional reasons for action."[71] That is, the symbol gives focus and reality to vague feelings of restlessness and tension. For the survivor, having abrogated a religious framework has meant the near discontinuity of existence on a symbolic level. This discontinuity of identity fosters a sense of anxiety about the future, anxiety about the task of redefining oneself anew in an unfamiliar context. Thus, when an individual loses his ability to symbolize and articulate his meaning in the world, the world begins to lose its credibility and one's everyday life feels pointless.

Survivors' situation is further complicated by their jarring memories, sometimes expressed in their difficulties in sleeping and nightmares. The task for the survivor is twofold: on the one hand, he has to come to terms with the brutal and painful memories associated with camp internment and suffering. On the other, and perhaps more agonizing than the memories of being physically tortured, are the rich, meaning-saturated, life-affirming pre-Holocaust memories that intrude into his life, disrupting it and rendering his current life valueless and meaningless by contrast.

Said one survivor when walking into a synagogue many years after liberation,

My eyes filled with tears but my lips wouldn't quiver with prayer. It was as if I have a paralysis of the mouth. My mind began racing toward past times of joy in the synagogue with my father and my grandfather and the other Jews of our town; happier times and happier places.[72]

When the past is experienced as so overwhelmingly painful, it is extremely difficult for the survivor to feel meaningful aliveness in the present. The past is not experienced as a positive resource but rather a negative influence pulling the survivor backward into the painful and debilitating memories.

We have tried to suggest another way of articulating and understanding some of the survivor's symptoms as described in the psychological literature. We hope it is clear that when a survivor's religious framework, his symbolic world, can no longer "make sense" of his life, and he can't recognize his own identity, his psychological world begins to crumble. The survivor's symptoms thus broadly signify the rupturing, if not loss, of his symbolic world. The specific symptoms, especially as they are compromise formations, are to be regarded as the person's attempt to preserve self-cohesion, self-continuity and self-esteem[73] in a tottering symbolic world. It is within this context that the survivor may seek out psychotherapy, and it is to this subject that we now turn.

PSYCHOTHERAPY WITH THE RELIGIOUS SURVIVOR

We have divided religious survivors who come to therapy into two different groups: those who have maintained their faith, although in a problematic way, and those who have lost their faith. The usefulness of this somewhat simplified categorization resides in the fact that these two groups of survivors present the therapist with different clinical problems.

In the former group are survivors who still consider themselves as God-focused and members of a religious community. They still observe the halakhah; however, their faith has weakened and most importantly the ontological security derived from the "sacred canopy" has lessened. Perhaps the most salient characteristic of a survivor from this group is his attitude towards the *mitzvot* (commandments) he performs. Said one survivor:

you could not tell from my religious behavior what I have undergone, what the Holocaust has done to me, but in my soul where my beliefs reside there has been a tremendous transformation. My faith has been crushed and I am nearly a non-believer . . . you may say I've been changed philosophically, and religiously in connection with beliefs about God, but not changed at all where for a Jew it counts most—in actions. In this respect I'm still a pious Jew.[74]

Such survivors may feel that they must perform mitzvot because they fear God—his retribution and power. But they are not able to serve Him in love like they once were. It is as if their symbolic world has lost its capacity to energize and propel them. Even with this loss of vigor there is still the understanding, familiarity, predictability and safety derived from being in their religious framework with its many behavioral obligations and so it is not abandoned even though one's faith has been severely undermined.

With the survivors from this group the fundamental viability of their religious framework still exists, yet there are modifications in their symbolic world, sometimes radical ones, that are necessary to maintain the plausibility of their world.

The second group of survivors alluded to earlier are those who have lost faith and no longer consider themselves as active relational partners with God; they no longer feel part of a faith community. These individuals require a replacement for their demolished religious symbolic world. Such survivors generally experience more anomie, anxiety, and meaninglessness than the group already described.

The basic focus of psychotherapy with religious survivors ought to be the rebuilding of viable human meaning formations in their lives. That is, the survivor needs help in constructing a revised or different plausible symbolic world. Following Atwood and Stolorow we believe "that the need to maintain the organization of experience is a central motive in the patterning of human action."[75] When that organization of experience loses its narrative coherence, as was the case of survivors who lost their religious world, there is a subjective sense of "self-dissolution" and "self-loss." That is, the survivor no longer feels himself to be a "locus of primary value in a world of meaning." The aim of psychotherapy with the survivor becomes the resurrection and/or creation anew of world structures which generate a feeling of meaning, continuity, self-cohesion and overall narrative coherence. This is accomplished, say Atwood and Stolorow,[76] by having the therapist focus on the illumination of meaning in the survivor's personal experience and conduct. The goal of psychoanalytic therapy with the survivor thus becomes the unfolding, clarification and transformation of personal subjective worlds. The above goals of psychotherapy are not easy for the religiously inclined survivor to achieve, in part because the loss (or near loss) of basic trust that came about due to the Holocaust makes faith and trust in the benevolence of an omnipotent God seem implausible.[77] Therapists need to be aware that for survivors the rupturing in the dialogue with God is experienced as traumatic. One of the ways to strengthen the survivor's religious framework, especially when the survivor wants a God-focused life, is to help him broaden the conception of God from a somewhat narrow notion of Him.

This can be achieved by helping the survivor to create a replacement attitude. Indeed, survivors have accomplished this when the personal conventional God of the Bible is replaced by an impersonal God who is not actively involved in their lives. This modified view of God often stresses the idea that there is some kind of order and design in the universe, but avoids assigning to God the capacity to intervene in history. Other survivors revised their conception of God somewhat differently—God is still all-good but He is no longer all-powerful. By the therapist's helping the survivor (who is so inclined) to reconstruct a viable post-Holocaust God, the survivor is given the opportunity to feel linked, albeit with modifications, to his religious community.

The loss of basic trust in God, in the orderly and ethically caring nature of the universe, is a major problem for the survivor, and it manifests itself quite dramatically sometimes in the transference—or rather more accurately, in the survivor's difficulty in developing a transference. The profound anger and sense of abandonment and loss (of loved ones and of God) that the survivor may harbor due to his Holocaust experience makes the emergence of an intense, intimate relationship very anxiety provoking if not impossible. The idea of trusting another human being, a member of the species that did him so much harm, is terrifying for the survivor, as is the loss of control and the associated regression implied in a transference.

Likewise, the capacity of the survivor to build himself back into a world of significance is seriously truncated by this impairment in his human relationships. The capacity to recreate new relationships of personal meaning and/or the capacity to deepen previous ones is perhaps the main way a survivor can recenter himself in the world.

The survivor's difficulties in basic trust also have bearing on the therapist's potential counter-transference. The fact that the survivor may seem to have a truncated capacity for intimacy must not be interpreted by the therapist as an indication that the survivor is too damaged for in-depth psychotherapy. Rather the therapist needs to empathize with the fact that the survivor's Holocaust experience, with its loss of loved ones and loss of God, also involved the rupturing of the taken-for-granted ways of being-in-the-world, that is, the survivor's modes of perception, expression, and participation with other human beings have been changed, fostering a new order of consciousness. Thus, therapy with survivors involves quiet listening and patience on the part of the therapist until some sort of trusting relationship can evolve, until the survivor can construct a hopeful image of a human person.

The issue of continuity for the survivor is of considerable importance primarily because it highlights the felt disharmony between life before, during, and after incarceration. Without the feeling that there is an essential sameness about him—even though he was in *l'universe concentrationnaire*—there is only a small possibility that recovery can take place. For the therapist, the survivor needs to be encouraged to focus on his mode of adaptation during incarceration with all its implied strengths and resources.[78] Only in this way will he be able to understand that indeed something did endure amidst the horror, qualities of strength, and courage or whatever, which existed before the Holocaust, which were expressed in the camps and can now be used to create a new world of meaning. Many survivors, for example, who come for treatment, have married or remarried and have had children. Sometimes these families are viewed almost completely in terms of the past. Wives and husbands and especially the children are seen as replacements for lost loved ones to such an extent that the present and past merge. The survivor lives in a kind of strange double-world heavily colored by Holocaust imagery and themes. Indeed the focus of therapy has to be on helping the survivor separate these images, to ascribe a contemporary meaning to his new family, such that he appreciates them on their own terms. Only in this way will he feel himself anchored in a world of present significance.

Last, survivors have also replaced their religious symbolic world with other perspectives, often secular commitments such as Zionism, Jewish survival, Jewish culture, fighting anti-Semitism, Holocaust scholarship, and/or commemoration. Such a focus gives the survivor a feeling of active mastery of his environment, especially in light of a possible feeling of victimization during the Holocaust. Also, survivors who are involved with such replacement activities often feel that there is a powerful truth in what they are doing which is similar to the religious person's sense of overriding truth and validity to his faith in God and his religion.

CLOSING REMARKS

As the religious survivor reaches old age, many of the psychological problems already described are experienced more sharply. Most importantly, however, the survivor has to evaluate his life within the broader context of the vicissitudes of senescence, with the inevitable awareness that one is getting closer to the end. This coming of age has all the problems usually associated with this phase of the life cycle; however, the goals of integrity[79] and integration[80] in old age are especially problematic for the Holocaust survivor. Psychotherapists are by and large working with survivors who are now in old age. An awareness on the part of therapists of some of the special difficulties that Holocaust survivors have to struggle with as they reach the last phase of the life cycle seems to be an appropriate coda to our chapter. This subject is especially relevant to psychotherapy with the survivor, since as Des Pres has pointed out,

One of the principal discoveries to come out of follow-up studies of Jewish and Armenian catastrophes is that the impact of historical trauma does not lessen but rather *grows* with time, both in the memory of aging survivors and in the passions of subsequent generations, if, that is, no way to reconciliation presents itself.[81]

In addition, in a recent survey of 275 survivors, it was found that a very high percentage of them at a later age were suffering from nervousness, fear, chronic tiredness, feelings of loneliness, inability to concentrate, depression, insomnia, and psychosomatic complaints, problems often related to a fall back on the memories of the past.[82]

In our view the problems of the aging survivor can best be conceptualized by using Erikson's life cycle framework. Erikson[83] has called the last stage of the epigenetic process of development "integrity." It can be described as a state one arrives at after having taken care of things and people, products and ideas, and having adjusted to the successes and failures of one's life. This is accomplished, says Erikson, when the individual is able to accept his life cycle "as something that had to be and that, by necessity, permitted no substitutions. . . . For he knows that an individual life is the accidental coincidence of but one life cycle with but one segment of history. . . . "[84] Through such accomplishments individuals may reap the benefits of the previous stages of life, and perceive that their life has some coherence and meaning within a larger order. When one has achieved integrity, one maintains with dignity his own life-style and defends it from potential threats.

Erikson further says that when the individual is unable to accept his life cycle as the ultimate and one and only meaning that living embodies, he feels despair. Despair of what has been implies that what has been, has been meaningless. Despair is the protest of a person who is not yet satisfied with a life that has fundamentally been unsatisfying. Despair indicates an unwillingness, paradoxical as it may be, to end a life that has failed to achieve fulfillment and that now culminates in the sum of a thousand little miseries.

For the aging Holocaust survivor, achieving integrity and its corresponding ego attainment—wisdom ("detached concern with life itself, in the face of death itself"[85])—is a complex and difficult problem requiring lengthy analysis. We, however, will only mention a few of the difficulties for the aging survivor to achieve integrity.

The process of the survivor's reviewing his life is often terrifying and anxiety producing, primarily because so much energy has been devoted to fending off intrusive painful and disorganizing memories. This avoidance of one's history makes psychotherapy quite difficult, since facing the past is such an important factor in psychotherapeutic experience. Klein has commented on why so many aging survivors avoid their past. The "sensitivity to cleavage and dissonance" which "reaches its crest . . . in the twilight years when irreversible finitude is finally to be faced and the effort to bring together past, present and the shrinking future into a self-justifying meaning is especially poignant and difficult."[86]

For the survivor, acceptance of the Holocaust "as something that had to be" part of his life cycle is painfully paradoxical. As Krystal points out, acceptance on the part of survivors that what happened to them was justified by its causes implies an acceptance that Nazism was also justified by its causes. This acceptance, says Krystal, is too closely reminiscent of the submission to persecution:

The process of making peace with oneself becomes impossible when it brings back the helplessness and shame of the past. Many survivors would experience the self-healing as "granting Hitler a posthumous victory," and therefore angrily reject it. To them, self-integration appears antithetical to the only justification for their survival: to be angry witnesses against the outrage of the Holocaust.[87]

According to Krystal, a final obstacle that prevents survivors from reaching integrity and self-acceptance is their incomplete mourning. Many survivors have had to grapple with the premature, absurd, and grotesque deaths of parents, spouses, and children. This is especially difficult because of the awareness that their loved ones were murdered simply because they were Jews who were living in the wrong place at the wrong time, while the world stood idly by. The capacity to sustain such multiple losses within such a bizarre context—without surrender to despair and hopelessness—requires great inner strength. This is poignantly true when we remember that the human capacity to endure psychic pain and guilt is limited.

Religious survivors must grapple with many of the same issues that nonreligious survivors struggle with. They too have to wrestle with integrity and despair. Indeed, the religious survivors who come to psychotherapy may have great difficulty coming to terms with the overall quality of their lives and with their God. The survivor may find that the previously useful theodicies no longer make sense as he reaches old age. A strong feeling of God's injustice begins to stir uncomfortably in his mind. Many of the related painful existential questions that were in sharp focus during and after the war return to haunt the survivor. He begins to feel that he was cheated by God, he feels rage and sadness and doesn't understand why he was chosen to suffer, why his life was mercilessly derailed.

Sometimes religious survivors come to therapy because of a sudden onset of problems rooted to old age (e.g., loss of a spouse, illness), whereas in other situations the circumstances relate to a more chronic sense of unhappiness. Regardless of the reason for coming to therapy, the aging religious survivor usually directly or indirectly links these current problems with his Holocaust past, and it is this constellation which poses a profound threat to the plausibility of his symbolic world.

Psychotherapists who work with aging religious survivors need to focus on helping them find a way to integrate this threat into their religious world. The therapist needs to help the survivor shake up his protective "sacred canopy," since there is not enough time left for the survivor to create a new world of meaning.

For the therapist to aid the religious survivor in the above task, always within the context of the survivor's coming to terms with his life, with integrity, means, among other things, supporting the survivor's need to assess his accomplishments and failures from the perspective of an ideal of total commitment, unconditional and unqualified, to the service of God. To the extent that he was able to live life, bear pain with spiritual self-awareness, self-assertion, and self-creation— all within the context of the demands of tradition and community—then can the religious survivor review life and say to himself that it was dedicated to the sacred; that it had meaning worthy of God's benign judgment.

For the aging religious survivor in psychotherapy to achieve this kind of life-affirming self-evaluation requires that the therapist help expand the survivor's religious worldview. Religious survivors at their best, perhaps more than any other religious personality, recognize that the key to religious self-acceptance and the acceptance of God is the awareness:

That faith is a life response of the whole person to the presence in life and history. Like life, this response ebbs and flows. The difference between the sceptic and the believer is frequency of faith and not certitude of position.[88]

Ernest Becker has amplified the significance of the above notion in a way that points to the ultimate aim of psychotherapy with the religious survivor, namely, that meaning and conviction ought to be grounded in "a sense of intimacy with the cosmic process" which would provide a perfect closure of human striving. Becker continues:

Genuine heroism for man is still the power to support contradictions, no matter how glaring or hopeless they may seem. The ideal critique of a faith must always be whether it embodies within itself the fundamental contradictions of the human paradox and yet is able to support them without fanaticism, sadism, and narcissism, but with openness and trust. Religion itself is an ideal of strength and of potential for growth, of what man might become by assuming the burden of his life, as well as by being partly relieved by it.[89]

For the survivor, as with us all, strength for creation of liberatory meaning is most firm when rooted in a personal dialogue that calls forth one's spontaneous powers and encourages their development in terms of a shared ideal of human potential. Ultimately, this ideal for the religious survivor must be grounded in a religious community oriented toward an open and nondogmatic God-personal-experience, usually, but not always, within a traditional context.

Finally, as the religious survivor begins to move toward achieving some modicum of integrity, it is important for the therapist to appreciate the survivor's evolving attitude towards what is generally regarded as a person's greatest fear—his own death.

For the religious survivor, the deepening of his faith in God, which is often the consequence of the therapist working effectively within the survivor's frame of reference, allows him to view his own death as a return to his beloved Maker. Life is a borrowed treasure and it must be reclaimed by its Owner. In this way, he links his existence back into a higher ground of meaning, which allows him to view his suffering and his achievements in terms of God's purpose for creation,[90] in terms of religious group continuity, and in terms of ultimate judgment. As a result of this, death loses some of its terror, as there is the hope and comfort in final redemption. At this point the religious survivor can surrender his life not in fear and trembling but in love, trust, and fellowship with God.

As for the secular psychotherapist who may view death very differently, often with extreme anxiety, the genuinely religious survivor may seem like a naive anomaly. However, if he is to be able to empathize with and ultimately help the religious survivor, there must be the recognition, acceptance, and support of the integrity of the survivor's symbolic world.

NOTES

1. For example, the *Chicago Psychoanalytic Literature Index*, as well as the most recent and comprehensive research bibliography on the psychological effects of Nazi persecution on survivors, does not have any entries that deal with the religious dimension of survivorship. See Leon Eitinger, Robert Krell, and Miriam Rieck, *The Psychological and Medical Effects of Concentration Camps on Related Persecutions on Survivors of the Holocaust* (Vancouver: University of British Columbia Press, 1985).

2. This point is illustrated in remarks made by Henry Krystal, perhaps the seminal thinker in the field: "Desperate attempts are made by survivors to restore and maintain their faith in God. However, since problems of aggression and the destruction of basic trust that resulted from the events of the Holocaust make true faith and trust in the benevolence of an omnipotent God impossible, the yearning for the comfort of religion only results in a piling up of rituals." "Integration and Self-healing in Post-traumatic States," in Steven Luel and Paul Marcus, Eds., *Psychoanalytic Reflections on the Holocaust: Selected Essays* (New York: KTAV and University of Denver, 1984), p. 129. Krystal's generalization does not seem to take account of the large theological literature and survivor testimony which sharply challenges his conclusion. Also see Paul Marcus, "Jewish Consciousness after the Holocaust," in *Psychoanalytic Reflections on the Holocaust: Selected Essays*, pp. 179–196; Paul Marcus and Irene Wineman, "Psychoanalysis Encountering the Holocaust," *Psychoanalytic Inquiry* 5 (1985): 85–98.

3. This essay is based on three data sources: first, 30 focused interviews with Jewish concentration camp survivors from Orthodox Eastern European families. Their ages and educational and socioeconomic levels varied. Second, Paul Marcus's work in psychoan-

alytic psychotherapy with survivors for a number of years. Third, secondary sources including diaries, novels, and the very helpful raw data from Reeve R. Brenner's *The Faith and Doubt of Holocaust Survivors* (New York: The Free Press, 1980), which contains a survey of 780 survivors.

4. Robert Wuthnow, James Davidson Hunter, Albert Bergesen, and Edith Kurzweil, *Cultural Analysis* (Boston: Routledge and Kegan Paul, 1984), pp. 37, 75.

5. Peter Berger, *The Sacred Canopy* (Garden City: Doubleday, 1967).

6. Ibid.

7. Ernest Becker, *The Revolution in Psychiatry* (New York: The Free Press, 1964), p. 44.

8. Roy Shaefer, *A New Language for Psychoanalysis* (New Haven: Yale University Press, 1976); also Anna Ornstein, "Survival and Recovery," *Psychoanalytic Inquiry* 5 (1985): 99–130.

9. Jacob Robinson, "Holocaust," *Encyclopedia Judaica*, VIII (1972): 827–906.

10. Brenner, *Faith and Doubt*, p. 37.

11. Lucy Dawidowicz, *The War Against the Jews 1933–45* (New York: Holt, Rinehart and Winston, 1975), p. 248.

12. Daniel Landes, "Spiritual Responses in the Camps." In *Genocide: Critical Issues of the Holocaust*, Alexander Grobman and Daniel Landes, Eds. (Chappaqua: Roseel Books, 1983), p. 272.

13. Joseph B. Soloveitchik, *Halakhic Man* (Philadelphia: The Jewish Publication Society, 1983).

14. Aharon Lichtenstein, "Joseph Soloveitchik," in Simon Noveck, Ed. *Great Jewish Thinkers of the Twentieth Century* (Washington, DC: B'nai B'rith Books, 1985).

15. Paul Marcus and Alan Rosenberg, *Faith During the Holocaust: A Psychological Inquiry* (New York: Praeger, forthcoming).

16. Ornstein, "Survival and Recovery."

17. Berger, *The Sacred Canopy*, pp. 54, 58.

18. Our position is similar to Viktor Frankl's (*Man's Search for Meaning*. New York: Pocket Books, 1963) insofar as we believe that meaning constitutes the major problematic for understanding the human condition. We fundamentally disagree with Frankl in that he believes that meaning is "given," that it is something that one "finds." We, however, believe that meaning is a social construction, that human beings collectively create and develop their "locus of primary value in a world of meaning."

19. Adina Dreksler, "Holocaust, Spiritual Resistance in the Ghettos and Camps," *Encyclopedia Judaica*, 17, Supplement (1982): 311–313.

20. Yaffa Eliach, *Hasidic Tales of the Holocaust* (New York: Avon Books, 1982); Eliezer Berkovitz, *With God in Hell* (New York: Sandhedrin Press, 1979); Daniel Landes, "Spiritual Responses in the Camps."

21. Ephraim Oshry, *Questions and Responses from Out of the Depths* (New York: Judaica Press, 1983).

22. Robert Kirschner, *Rabbinic Responsa of the Holocaust Era* (New York: Schocken Books, 1976).

23. Viktor E. Frankl, *Man's Search for Meaning*; Hillel Klein, "The Survivor's Search for Meaning and Identity," *The Nazi Concentration Camps: Proceedings of the Fourth Yad Vashem International Historical Conference* (1984): 543–554; Terence Des Pres, *The Survivor* (New York: Pocket Books, 1976); Primo Levi, *The Drowned and the Saved* (New York: Summit, 1986). Jean Améry, in *At the Mind's Limits: Contemplations by a*

Survivor on Auschwitz and its Realities (New York: Schocken, 1986), makes the subtle point that in Auschwitz an intellectual background and/or basic disposition was of little help in survival primarily because the intellectual was alone with his intellect and no social reality that could confirm or support it. Moreover, if the intellect was not centered around a religious or political belief, it was more or less useless. The religious and political prisoners, says Améry, survived better or died with more dignity than their irreligious or unpolitical intellectual comrades.

24. Anna Pawelczyńska, *Values and Violence in Auschwitz* (Berkeley: University of California Press, 1979).

25. Levi, *The Drowned and the Saved*; Frankl, *Man's Search for Meaning*.

26. Christopher Lasch, *The Minimal Self* (New York: W. W. Norton and Company, 1984).

27. Paul Marcus and Alan Rosenberg, "A Philosophical Critique of the 'Survivor Syndrome' and Some Implications for Treatment," in Randolph Braham, Ed., *Psychological Perspectives of the Holocaust and of its Aftermath* (Boulder: Social Science Monographs, 1988). Distributed by Columbia University Press.

28. Brenner, *Faith and Doubt*, p. 122.

29. Leon Festinger, *A Theory of Cognitive Dissonance* (Stanford: Stanford University Press, 1957).

30. Ernest Becker, *The Revolution in Psychiatry* (New York: The Free Press, 1964).

31. Berger, *The Sacred Canopy*: Wuthrow et al, *Cultural Analysis*.

32. We have generously drawn from the very useful book by Steven T. Katz, *Post-Holocaust Dialogues* (New York: New York University Press, 1983), in our enumeration of the basic strategies and models used by survivors and theologians to account for God's "behavior" during the Holocaust. Furthermore, it should be clear that survivors usually use these explanatory frameworks in a variety of interrelated and complementary ways.

33. Berger, *The Sacred Canopy*, p. 74.

34. See Martin Buber, *Eclipse of God: Studies in the Relation Between Religion and Philosophy* (New York: Harper Torchbooks, 1957).

35. Brenner, *Faith and Doubt*, p. 98.

36. Ibid., p. 58.

37. It should be pointed out, however, that 72 percent of the 780 survivors contacted in Brenner's study thought that the 6 million were destroyed not because of sin, but only because of man's relationship to man, with no connection whatsoever to God, *Faith and Doubt*, p. 225.

38. Berger, *The Sacred Canopy*, pp. 69, 71.

39. Emil Fackenheim, *God's Presence in History* (New York: New York University Press, 1970).

40. Brenner, *Faith and Doubt*, p. 59.

41. Hannah Arendt, *Hannah Arendt: The Jew as Pariah*, Ron H. Feldman, Ed. (New York: Grove Press, 1978), p. 24.

42. Berger, *The Sacred Canopy*, p. 12.

43. Becker, *The Revolution in Psychiatry*.

44. Berger, *The Sacred Canopy*.

45. Ibid., p. 22.

46. Brenner, *Faith and Doubt*, pp. 162, 201–202.

47. Richard L. Rubenstein, *After Auschwitz: Radical Theology and Contemporary Judaism* (Indianapolis: Bobbs-Merrill, 1966). Other scholars agree with the theological

dilemma that Rubenstein has sharply raised, however, they do not share his conclusion that "God is Dead." See Katz, *Post-Holocaust Dialogues*, for an overview of the varying responses to the problem of belief in God after the Holocaust.

48. Elie Wiesel, *Night* (New York: Avon Books, 1958), p. 76.

49. Ibid., p. 44.

50. Brenner, *Faith and Doubt*, p. 100.

51. Martin S. Bergmann and Milton E. Jucovy, *Generations of the Holocaust* (New York: Basic Books, 1982).

52. Kurt Eissler, "Die Ermordung von wievielen seiner Kinder musi ein Mensch syndrom fre, ertragen koernen, um eine normale Kunstitution zu haben?" *Psyche* 1 (1963–64): 197–241.

53. Moises Kijak and Silvio Funtowicz, "The Syndrome of the Survivor of Extreme Situations," *International Review of Psycho-Analysis* 9 (1982): 25–33.

54. Harvey Barocas, "Children of Purgatory: Reflections on the Concentration Camp Survival Syndrome," *International Journal of Social Psychiatry* 21 (1975): 87–92.

55. Henry Krystal, "Integration and Self-Healing in Post-traumatic States," in Luel and Marcus, Eds., *Psychoanalytic Reflections on the Holocaust: Selected Essays*, pp. 113–134.

56. Henry Krystal, Ed., *Massive Psychic Trauma* (New York: International Universities Press, 1968). There are a few psychoanalysts who have reported more favorable results in their work with survivors. See, for example, Ornstein, "Survival and Recovery"; Klein, "The Survivor's Search"; Emmanuel Dewind, "Persecution, Aggression and Therapy," *International Journal of Psychoanalysis* 53 (1972): 173–178; Edith Gyomroi, "The Analysis of a Young Concentration Camp Victim," *Psychoanalytic Study of the Child* 18 (1963): 484–510.

57. Ernest Becker, *Angel in Armor: A Post-Freudian Perspective on the Nature of Man* (New York: Braziller, 1969), p. 80.

58. Ornstein, "Survival and Recovery"; also Frankl, *Man's Search*.

59. Henry Krystal, "Trauma and Effects," *Psychoanalytic Study of the Child* 33 (1978); Krystal, *Integration and Self-Healing: Affect Trauma and Alexithymia* (Hillsdale: The Analytic Press, 1988).

60. Becker, *Revolution in Psychiatry*.

61. William G. Niederland, "The Survivor Syndrome: Further Observations and Dimensions," *Journal of the Psychoanalytic Association* 29 (1981): 413–426.

62. Edward Bibring, "The Mechanism of Depression," in Phyllis Greenacre, Ed., *Affective Disorders* (New York: International Universities Press, 1953).

63. Becker, *Revolution*, p. 111.

64. Ibid., p. 112.

65. Ibid., p. 113.

66. Becker, *Angel*, p. 85.

67. Ibid., p. 85.

68. Henry Krystal and William G. Niederland, Eds., *Psychic Traumatization* (Boston: Little Brown and Company, 1971).

69. Ornstein, "Survival and Recovery," p. 128.

70. Krystal, "Integration and Self-healing."

71. Becker, *Revolution*, p. 178.

72. Brenner, *Faith and Doubt*.

73. Ornstein, "Survival and Recovery."

74. Brenner, *Faith and Doubt*, p. 49.

75. George Atwood and Robert Stolorow, *Structures of Subjectivity: Explorations in Psychoanalytic Phenomenology* (Hillside: Analytic Press, 1984).

76. Ibid.

77. Jean Amery, in a powerful essay, comments on the effect of torture on the Holocaust survivor. What I lost in torture, Améry contends, is trust in the world. "At the first blow . . . this trust . . . breaks down. The other person, *opposite* . . . whom I can exist only as long as he does not touch my skin surface as border, forces his own corporeality on me with his first blow. He is on me and thereby destroys me." *At the Mind's Limits: Contemplations by a Survivor on Auschwitz and its Realities*, p. 28.

78. Ornstein, "Survival and Recovery."

79. Erik E. Erikson, *Childhood and Society* (New York: W. W. Norton and Company, 1963).

80. Krystal, "Integration and Self-Healing."

81. Terence Des Pres, "Preface," in Richard G. Hovannisian, Ed., *The Armenian Genocide in Perspective* (New Brunswick: Transaction Books, 1986), p. 17.

82. *Internet on the Holocaust and Genocide* (Jerusalem, 1987), p. 5.

83. Erikson, *Childhood and Society*.

84. Ibid., p. 268.

85. Erik E. Erikson, *Insight and Responsibility* (New York: W. W. Norton and Company, 1964), p. 133.

86. George S. Klein, *Theory of Psychoanalysis* (New York: International Universities Press, 1976), p. 231. Quoted in Krystal, "Integration and Healing," p. 122.

87. Ibid., p. 123.

88. Irving Greenberg, "Judaism and Christianity After the Holocaust," *Journal of Ecumenical Studies* 18 (1963): 534.

89. Ernest Becker, *The Birth and Death of Meaning* (New York: The Free Press, 1971), p. 198.

90. Becker, *Angel in Armor*.

15

Mourning the Yiddish Language and Some Implications for Treatment

JANET HADDA

Of all life experiences, separation and loss are the ultimate universals. *Feelings* of grief and associated *behaviors* of mourning come naturally and inevitably in response to this unavoidable reality. Our cultures prescribe attitudes, and our religious rituals, to help cope with the suffering caused by bereavement. Ethologists report that other creatures mourn their loved ones as well. Yet the process of mourning, and its underlying psychological function, are still matters of disagreement. Moreover, the very nature of what may be mourned remains insufficiently investigated.

The issue of mourning is particularly pressing in the case of Holocaust survivors. Whereas most people may expect to suffer the loss of several beloved family members and friends in a lifetime, survivors of Hitler's murderous regime were often forced to endure the loss of an entire network of family, friends, and community. Moreover, these deaths were not the natural ones, due to old age or sickness, that are the lot of "ordinary" individuals. Rather, they were the result of savage and meaningless cruelty. Clearly, then, the magnitude of survivor mourning may be greater than is usually the case.

It is not only a matter of degree, however, that separates the mourning of Holocaust survivors from that of others. For the work of coming to terms with the loss of loved ones often had to be accomplished with the remains of the victims gone forever and without the support of a familiar context: without their families, their homes, and frequently without their villages or towns, for these had been destroyed as well.

An earlier version of this chapter has been published as "Yankev Glatshteyn Mourning the Yiddish Language" in *American Imago*, Vol. 45, No. 3, Fall 1988, 271–286.

Perhaps most importantly, for many survivors the very means of self-expression and communication—the Yiddish language itself—was all but annihilated. Yiddish had been born out of the European Jewish experience, had developed along with the culture of those who spoke it, was on the lips of many who were victims of the Nazis in Eastern Europe. Who would speak Yiddish now and who would understand it and the thoughts that were expressed through its particular character? Traditional-minded inhabitants of *shtetlekh* and villages, city-bred socialists, future poets and novelists—all had spoken Yiddish and all were gone.

In this chapter, I intend to show that Yiddish, the language of many Holocaust victims, could be as deeply and powerfully mourned by a survivor as a parent, spouse, or child. I use as a case study the works of a Yiddish poet—Yankev Glatshteyn—who observed the events of World War II from the safety of the United States. I chronicle the changing subjective reactions to the loss of an important means of self-identification and processing of meaning. Finally, I present some clinical implications for therapists working with Holocaust survivors and their families.

CASE STUDY

The American Yiddish poet Yankev Glatshteyn (1896–1971) experienced his native language in much the same way as he did human beings. Yiddish was far more to him than a vehicle of expression or even a set of vital symbols. The language was alive and independent in him, capable of change and response. It was not merely *mame-loshn*, his mother tongue, but also *tate-mame* and *bobe-loshn*—mother-father and a grandmother language. It functioned as a nurturing parent in his life, and, later, as a loyal, patient lover as well.

This relationship might not have come to light except for the tragedy of Hitler's Holocaust. One result of Glatshteyn's perception that his people had been decimated and his culture annihilated was his sense that Yiddish, too, had perished. Specifically, he grieved for it and displayed typical mourning behavior.

The unusual aspect of Glatshteyn's loss stems from the fact that languages do not commonly die suddenly: It takes genocide to effect such a situation. As a result of this catastrophic event, Glatshteyn was forced to grapple with a momentous change in his own identity. Although he had not been personally silenced, he knew that his poetic voice would be without resonance. Deprived of his sophisticated audience, he had, as well, been robbed of his connection to future generations of Yiddish speakers. An alternative might have been to seek comfort in translation, but, for Glatshteyn, this was nothing short of betrayal. Thus, there was no choice but to see Yiddish as lost to him and to respond accordingly.

The notion that mourning need not occur only in response to a living being is not new. In fact, Freud, at the outset of his seminal paper "Mourning and Melancholia" (1917), states unequivocally: "Mourning is regularly the reaction to the loss of a loved person, or to the loss of some abstraction which has taken the place of one, such as one's country, liberty, an ideal, and so on."[1]

The British psychoanalyst John Bowlby came to his ideas about mourning from his work with infants and their responses to separation from the mothering figure. His observations, with the help of information gleaned from animal behavior studies, led him to generalize about the larger subject of separation and subsequent mourning in adults. Perhaps the most important characteristic of Bowlby's formulation is that it arises out of the notion that the behavior of mourning is adaptive, that is, it has evolved to have a biological function.

Bowlby divides the mourning process into three stages: (1) attempted recovery of the lost object, (2) disorganization and despair, (3) reorganization. In the first phase of mourning, the individual is still focused on the missing object. Repeated efforts are made to achieve reunion, and the bereaved person frequently employs fantasy to deny the failure of such attempts. This stage is often accompanied by anger, weeping, protest, and accusations. These natural responses of the infant to a sudden separation are designed to bring back the absent mother and also to dramatize the infant's distress so that the separation is not repeated. As maneuvers, they are generally effective when the separation has not been caused by death. In the relatively unusual event of permanent loss, the initial reaction is the one that has, in the past, succeeded in achieving reunion.[2] This first phase is most fully represented in Glatshteyn's poetry.

The second phase of mourning begins when weeping and protest have clearly failed to accomplish the desired end of reunion. At this point, the healthy individual gradually gives up the search and, simultaneously, withdraws from the lost object. As yet, however, there is no replacement for the missing loved one, and this stage of mourning is thus characterized by personality disorganization, a sense of aimlessness and lack of purpose in life, often accompanied by a reduced feeling of self-worth. The bereft person typically experiences pain and despair.

The third stage of mourning is marked by a reorganization of the personality, associated in part with the image of the lost object and in part with new connections. That is, reorganization implies both a move toward substitutions for the beloved and the maintenance of certain values and behaviors that keep the old bond alive even in the face of permanent separation.

From the beginning of his career, Yankev Glatshteyn manifested a relationship to the Yiddish language that was both loving and concrete. How else can one describe one of his very first poems, "*Tirtl-toybn*" [Turtle Doves] (1919)?[3] This work about free association focuses on a single word recalled from childhood. The adult narrator finds himself thrown back to the time when, as a tiny child, he had first heard and absorbed the word *tirtl-toybn: Un s'lozt nit op,/Mit dem veykhn kneytsh fun tirtl,/Mit dem lastshendikn kneytsh* [And it (the word) doesn't let go,/With the soft fold of turtle/With the cuddly fold]. This early poem could, of course, be seen as an example of Glatshteyn's playful joy in creating, or as a way of trying to chart the child's acquisition of abstract concepts, without particular reference to the special role of language per se in his life. However, when Glatshteyn's response to the Holocaust is viewed through the prism of his ruminations about Yiddish, there can be no doubt about the latter's role in his life. Yiddish was as real to him, as vibrant, as flesh and blood.

At the earliest point of mourning, the irreparable loss is only partially conceivable. Therefore, grief alternates with disbelief and an optimistic fantasy that the wished-for reunion will occur. Glatshteyn's 1943 volume, *Gedenklider* [Memorial Poems] both begins and ends with a poem about the Yiddish language. Each represents an aspect of denial, where grief is countered by the idea that all is not lost. (In Glatshteyn's case at this juncture, as in the situation of an infant whose mother has disappeared, matters are complicated by the uncertainty of not yet knowing whether the object is truly gone forever.)

The first poem of the volume, "S'yidishe vort" [The Yiddish Word][4] opens hopefully, and, with its allusion to the rod of Aaron, hints at the miraculous: *S'yidishe vort blit af a mandlshtekn* [The Yiddish word blooms on an almond staff]. Since the words for Yiddish and Jewish are the same in Yiddish, at first it seems that the poem's reference could be to Hebrew rather than Yiddish. Yet, as the lines unfold, it is evident that Glatshteyn means to evoke thoughts of Eastern European Yiddishkeit: *Un yeder vort iz bazaft/Mit bobeshaft* [And every word is juicy/With grandma-ness]. The scene becomes increasingly dramatic: A desert wanderer approaches the rod, drawn as by some mysterious force; even the herbs that surround the blossoming rod possess magical properties. Specifically, they enable anyone who eats of them to perceive meaning and significance where there was none before. Above all, they cause everything to be . . . *ongetrunken mit freyd/Fun bobeshaft* [. . . watered with the joy/Of grandma-ness].

The positive tone of "S'yidishe vort" breaks down, however, by the conclusion of the poem, as the wanderer realizes that the blossoming Jewish word is not Yiddish at all, but Hebrew. In alarm, he shouts out: *Hoy-veygeshrign,/In der midber blit a mandlshtekn* [Lo, cry out a lament,/An almond staff blooms in the desert]. The poem, read without contextual consideration, suggests that the Yiddish language—even if it manages to achieve rebirth or resuscitation—will still be treated with hostility and condescension in the linguistic competition with Hebrew. As an expression of denial, it betrays the extent to which disbelief occurs within a framework of inchoate understanding, even at the earliest point of loss.

Gedenklider's final poem emphasizes the predominant characteristic of initial mourning, namely the effort at reunion. "*Undzer tsikhtik loshn*" [Our Tidy Language][5] is important in that it makes concrete, and not merely metaphorical, reference to Yiddish as an object. As such, it not only provides a contrast to "S'yidishe vort" but underscores Glatshteyn's experience of language as equivalent to a human loved one. Here, in another biblical allusion, Yiddish appears as a fiddle hanging mutely from a willow tree. Unlike the lyre of Psalm 137, however, which symbolized the *psychological* impossibility of joy at a time of dispersion, the fiddle is a victim of *physical* persecution. Jews are suffering by the tens of thousands:

> And the warm fiddle Yiddish,
> Understanding and clever,
> Is mute,
> And hangs from a willow,
> Amongst brother-graves.

The narrator of "*Undzer tsikhtik loshn*" unleashes his rage and anguish at the German people and their language. He angrily asserts that Yiddish is much too pure to be besmirched by describing Nazi crimes. People and language merge as the narrator exclaims:

> How can we, in our tidy language,
> Tell all that you have perpetrated,
> How you have extinguished our world?
> Our words are fainting, fainting,
> Our language is shamed, shamed. . . .

The narrator's rage at the German language and its speakers is, of course, understandable as a moral stance. It also fits closely with the searching typical in the initial mourning phase. The bereaved person, striving to relocate the absent loved one, experiences an upsurge of aggressive feelings, often against the object itself. Irrational on the surface, this behavior is in fact a primitive attempt at tyranny, designed to ensure that the separation will never occur again. Similarly, reproaches against the self or, as in the case of "*Undzer tsikhtik loshn*," against a third party, are indications of a magical formulation that, if someone is to blame, the loss can be annulled.

Glatshteyn's sentiments in "*S'yidishe vort*" and "*Undzer tsikhtik loshn*" were prophetic, and they emerged even more strongly some years later, when he knew for certain the awful fate of his people, his culture, and his language. Significantly, his 1946 volume, *Shtralndike yidn*, does not touch the subject of the lost tongue. Perhaps Glatshteyn was too stunned by the irrefutability of the truth to comment on it immediately. Then, too, he was absorbed in directly commemorating his murdered people. The more subtle realization may have needed time to fully emerge. Whatever the reason for his silence, when he resumed the struggle openly, his expression had gained clarity and energy.

The poem "*An os*" [A Letter of the Alphabet] appears in Glatshteyn's 1953 volume, *Dem tatns shotn* [*My Father's Shadow*][6]; it was not reprinted in *Fun mayn gantser mi*, Glatshteyn's 1956 volume of selected poems. While this is not a unique omission, I think its absence is significant. "An os," unlike "Undzer tsikhtik loshn," constitutes a complaint against Yiddish. I believe Glatshteyn wished to disavow this direct rebuke after he had reached a state of greater calm.

Part of Glatshteyn's grief concerned the extent to which his playfulness with Yiddish—an essential part of his relationship to the language—would have to be curtailed, now that Yiddish represented the voice of a decimated people. His entire identity as a poet was called into question by this simple yet profound ramification.

In "*An os*," the narrator, who has accepted his responsibility as a chronicler in grave times, finds himself confronted with a recalcitrant letter. Ruefully, he berates this rebellious member of his beloved alphabet: *Host gornisht gemeynt, nor gebrent* [You meant nothing, you merely burned]. The letter, much as the memory of a loved one may cause rage that the cherished person has disappeared, inspires indignation in the narrator as he tries to force it into the new position he has, of necessity, created for it. But he proves incapable of controlling the letter, and this is intolerable. It is finally preferable, he decides, to eliminate the offensive presence entirely, rather than be reminded of the past and its satisfactions:

> All night I heard your voice,
> Insisting on remaining a symbol,
> A meaningless scary letter.
> I rubbed you out.

Buried in this poem may be an acknowledgement that a Yiddish letter, even a so-called meaningless one, can be awe inspiring, indeed holy, like the tetragrammaton, the four Hebrew letters that stand for God's name. More prominently, the letter's evocative power emerges as a central concern. Unnerved, the narrator turns his impotent frustration onto the very thing that causes his unhappiness. It is as if he were saying: Because you remind me of the joy you once provided, and because you persist in denying yourself to me, I blame you and hate you.

In the final line of "*An os*," the narrator obliterates his irritating adversary, that is, the letter that would remain meaningless. He thus allows himself a liberty denied the mourner of a living object. His motive, however, is familiar, an attempt at undoing his loss; if the power to erase is there, so is the capacity to recreate. As a peculiarly literary form of denial, the narrator echoes the sufferer's general wish not to be helpless. Reasoned anger against the one who has left suggests, furthermore, that there is a point to the desertion, that the world is still a comprehensible place.

During the initial phase of mourning, memories and fantasies that stave off the brunt of sorrow need not, of course, be negative. Rather, they can grant a welcome respite, even as they prolong the realization of loss. In "*Tirtl-toybn*," Glatshteyn had used a word association to recall his childhood and the strange excitement of learning about language. Now, in contrast, he laid aside his playful attitude and, like a grateful son, paid homage to Yiddish. In words of bittersweet warmth, he placed Yiddish at the heart of his world, coupling this devotion with a commemoration of his lost parents.

"*A vort*" [A Word][7] concerns itself, not with a particular word, as had been the case with "*Tirtl-toybn*," but rather with the concept that any word can resonate with personal meaning. The narrator emphasizes explicitly that he is not concerned with identifying the word; what counts for him is the link between the word and the security of his childhood, when his father had stood over him in *kheyder* and his mother had greeted him with cheerful responsiveness. What is more, the narrator assumes that the connection is obvious:

> You will recognize it
> And you will sit down to warm yourselves
> Around the bright word,
> Which glows with the first, concerned joy of father
> With the barely cried-out
> Warmth of mother.

Once more language has taken on a life of its own, independent of its users. Here, however, it plays a salutory role, allowing Glatshteyn to revivify, not only the word itself but, through it, his parents as well. He thus manages, temporarily, to block out not only the demise of Yiddish, but, simultaneously, the reason behind this tragedy: the murder of its speakers. Additionally, through his connection of the word with manna, he implies that it is capable of nourishing a generation that must wander in the desert. Given the actual fate of Eastern European Jewry, the image acquires an ironic undercurrent, again revealing that all attempts to deny loss must ultimately, in the healthy individual, yield to unhappy recognition.

The line between language as representative of something else and language as representative of itself is certainly thin and often elusive. Yet, if Glatshteyn's discussion of Yiddish in "*A vort*" allows for an interplay between the word and those who hear and speak it, "*Mayn tate-mame shprakh*" [My Parent Language][8] focuses distinctly on the language itself, forming its speakers into vehicles, albeit beloved ones. The narrator explains that, for him, the workaday, weekly flavor of Yiddish is holy, unifying, and sanctifying everything around him. He needs it in order to accomplish his work of memory:

> You are not only a mother tongue to me,
> A language of my cradle days,
> But rather the seal of all my recollections.

What the narrator remembers is the lively and beautiful world of his irretrievable past. Without Yiddish, he is incapable of describing his treasure. This would be enough to certify its significance. Yet the narrator of "*Mayn tate-mame shprakh*" wants to say more. Playing on the term *mame-loshn* [mother tongue], he firmly equates the language with his parents. The narrator addresses Yiddish, much as he had done in "*An os*." For him, Yiddish is not an abstraction, but rather a definite being, possessing an existence quite apart from its articulation, even though this existence may be intangible:

> The whole kingdom of Hasidism
> That was you, my father-mother Yiddish.
> You spoke yourself so simply with the Baal Shem,
> You were the refined friend
> Of the yearning Bratslaver.

Here, then, as in "*A vort*," the narrator finds himself renewing his beloved Yiddish by remembering how it lived in the mouths of people who themselves have died. At the same time, "*Mayn tate-mame shprakh*" introduces a paradox because of the directness of its reference. Although Glatshteyn was clearly experiencing grief over the fate of Yiddish and exhibiting mourning responses, he was at the same time keeping the language alive through his use of it. Thus, when the narrator must, as always, admit that his good spirits are a protection against misery, he reveals that his mother's prayer, recited at the conclusion of every Sabbath, had provided him with the solace of Yiddish. Here, Glatshteyn does the impossible: He uses Yiddish to describe how the language comforts him even as he is suffering from its loss.

Although the strangeness of Glatshteyn's position does not precisely parallel what happens in human bereavement, it is similar to the phenomenon that Colin Murray Parkes describes as *finding*: "That 'searching' and 'finding' go together is not surprising. A 'sense of the continued presence of the deceased,' 'a clear visual memory of him,' and 'preoccupation with thoughts of him' . . . which have been referred to as components of searching, are also components of finding."[9] That is, a part of the first phase of mourning consists of a wish fulfillment that the lost object has been found. To the extent that Yiddish, lacking corporeal mortality, could "live" on, Glatshteyn's form of finding was more real. Yet, despite the objective continued existence of the Yiddish language, Glatshteyn was unable to elude the knowledge that his subjective Yiddish was gone, never to return.

As anyone who has observed or experienced bereavement will know, Bowlby's three phases must be seen as a continuum of responses, occurring at times almost simultaneously and subject to the forces of regression. Thus, the depression and despair that characterize the second phase of mourning may be glimpsed even in Glatshteyn's most powerful attempts at cheer. Nonetheless, there is an obvious distinction between the undercurrent of gloom in a poem such as "*A vort*," and the sheer anguish of a work like "*Etlekhe shures*" [A Few Lines].

The depression of which Bowlby speaks occurs when the mourner has finally begun to realize that the separation is permanent and hence slowly abandons the search for reconnection. The abject unhappiness of this phase is often exacerbated

by restlessness, agitation, and sometimes a feeling of worthlessness as the bereaved person hangs suspended, consciously bereft at the coveted lost object,
but as yet without a substitute. This is Glatshteyn's mood in *"Etlekhe shures,"*
which appeared in the 1961 volume intriguingly entitled *Di freyd fun yidishn
vort* [The Joy of the Yiddish Word].[10] The narrator is anything but joyful as he
describes the loss of his own poetry:

> A few trembling lines in my palm.
> I held them long
> And let them run through my fingers—
> Word by word.

Two aspects of this poem stand out. First is the striking concreteness of the
imagery. The narrator is not addressing the language this time, yet the sense of
independence and physicality remains evident. Nowhere has the experience of
loss been so clearly articulated. That is, despite all efforts to maintain his language—his *poetic* language in this case—the narrator has failed and the lines,
word by word, have dissipated. The second important new aspect of this poem
is the somber hopelessness of the narrative voice. There is no anger, no manic
defense against depression; in place of these is simple resignation. And, as the
poem continues, it becomes unambiguously clear that this loss has cost the
narrator his self-esteem. He admits to isolation, recognizing his position of
weakness. He begs not to be cast away as wretched. This plea is repeated twice,
thereby intensifying the terror implicit in the words themselves. The poem ends
on that plaintive request:

> Loneliness fits me like an old-fashioned nightshirt.
> Don't throw me away,
> In my bewildered fear.

Now the anxiety hinted at earlier in *"An os"* has become clear: The loss of
language threatens not only the narrator's equilibrium but his very existence. If
he has been cut off from the source of his sense of self, then who and what
good is he? Gone is the luxury of choosing sober meaning over youthful frivolity.
All is lost. As the narrator of *"Shoyn bald"* [Soon Now] laments,

> . . . in the dark we compose
> Lightning speech which is extinguished.
> And its meaning turns to ashes.
> Its meaning turns to ashes.[11]

It would seem ironic that these sad statements occur side by side with a five-
part poem entitled *"Di freyd fun yidishn vort"* [The Joy of the Yiddish Word],[12]
for which the entire volume is named. Closer inspection, however, betrays the
irony of the title itself, for the work actually concerns the unhappy fate of Yiddish.

The pressure to reach the broadest possible audience through his writing, an issue that clearly troubled and offended Glatshteyn, once again attains prominence here. The narrator fears that even if Yiddish could be resurrected in a linguistic Valley of the Dry Bones, even if its old essence of joyous meaninglessness were somehow molded anew, the outcome would be hopeless because the surrounding milieu would be as demanding of easy comprehensibility as before. Therefore, his unique capacity to approach the core of Yiddish would remain unappreciated, unwanted.

The theme of a changed, unrecognizable Yiddish goes hand in hand with Glatshteyn's perception of the language as dead. The personal linguistic possession that had sustained and gratified him as long as he could recall had disappeared. What remained in its place may have resembled Yiddish to the unpracticed or uninterested ear and mind, but it was merely a shadow of the original treasure.

In addition to familiar ideas, however, "*Di freyd fun yidishn vort*" raises a new and poignant worry: What if the beloved be forgotten? In a kind of dream vision, the narrator begs to be granted access to the joy of the Yiddish word. He doesn't care how much he suffers materially, just as long as he has full and uninterrupted time with a Yiddish that here, more than ever, resembles a person, indeed a lover; the narrator begs: *Lozt mikh nisht dos yidishe vort/Af a rege fargesn* [Don't let me forget the Yiddish word/For a moment]. He reminds himself that he has neglected his love.

Directly after this, the narrative voice shifts, and the narrator addresses himself as *du* [you], using the familiar form in Yiddish, rather than the less intimate *ir*. It is almost as if he had shocked himself by the possibility that he might forget. In his feverish dream, he reviews his lover's faithfulness:

> The Yiddish word waits for you, loyal and mute.
> And you sigh in your ignited dream:
> I'm on my way, I'm on my way.

At the conclusion of the poem, the narrator has awakened from his dream and resumed daily life. Yet the experience of the night does not leave him. He ponders his adored language with mixed emotions and says, perhaps to himself as well as to it: *O, zay gezunt, zay gezunt./Nit farlir mikh, zukh mikh op* [Oh, be well, be well./Don't lose me, search me out]. The wish to recover Yiddish, to be reunited with it, has a new purpose. Previously, it had signified the struggle to overcome separation, to fill excruciating emptiness. "*Di freyd fun yidishn vort*" accepts the loss as permanent and inevitable. Now the concern is how to keep the love alive while new possibilities for attachment intrude. At stake is Glatshteyn's ability to work through the third stage of mourning.

After the despair and disorganization that accompany the gradual relinquishing of any hopes for reunion, the individual who mourns confronts a dual challenge.

Those connections to the lost object that no longer bear fruit must be surrendered; others may safely be maintained internally, including goals and values, the confidence of having been loved and well-regarded. Such psychological equipment facilitates the building of a new bond, one that emerges from the prior relationship yet allows the individual to face present and future realities. In the instance of Glatshteyn and his tie to Yiddish, the effort involved reestablishing his original energetic and playful interaction with the language even while recognizing that he might be doing so only for himself. In other words, he had to come to grips with the fact that his personal Yiddish could flourish within him even if the outside world no longer perceived it.

Glatshteyn's final volume of poetry, *Gezangen fun rekhts tsu links* [*Songs from Right to Left*], published shortly before his death in 1971, reveals a man who was attempting with all his might to achieve resolution and peace. While he did not succeed entirely in this aim, he was able to reconcile himself with respect to his cherished Yiddish. The poem "*Gebentsht zol zayn*" [Be blessed][13] harks back to some of Glatshteyn's earlier work, but at the same time it delineates a fresh perspective.

The narrator begins with a familiar complaint: the perversion of languages as their speakers fall into moral decline. In the modern world, there is no room for honest words. Unlike other works, however, where the emotional content had expressed anger, despair, or the fear of annihilation, the tone of this poem is calm, celebratory, secure:

> So may our grandmother Yiddish be blessed.
> Unspoken, unread,
> In a rescued geniza
> Uncontaminated.

Gone is the lament for a dying Yiddish; gone, too, the almost desperate need to prove that the aged and ageless "grandma" quality of Yiddish both should and will survive. In its place is the placid acceptance of an inviolable tongue—earthy, warm, rich and pure in tradition, free of intellectual pretension.

The narrator elucidates his relationship with the unspoken, unread language:

> We, the refugees of our descendents
> Carry a memory like a predestined burden.
> No lips can defile
> Our Yiddish speech. . . .

Clearly, the language is internal, its roots in recollection. Still, the narrator feels that his general experience is understood by others, even if they cannot know the specific nature of his bond. Much like someone remembering a beloved person in the company of friends, he takes comfort in the shared acquaintance; the fact that each person remembers different things, and remembers them differently, is a given that enhances, rather than diminishes, the sense of individual memory.

The narrator speaks of a predestined burden. In creating this image, he acknowledges both the difficulty of maintaining an unchanging, internalized connection and his willingness to renounce his protest, to accept his loss as natural.

The most convincing evidence that Glatshteyn had achieved a point where Yiddish, once perceived as lost, could live anew within him is found, not in something he wrote, but rather in something he did: At the end of this, his final volume of poetry, he reprinted the first three poems of his career, including "*Tirtl-toybn.*"[14] Thus he reasserted the vitality and wit of his original bond with Yiddish. I used to feel that his inclusion of these poems was a rather sad admission by Glatshteyn that he would have no literary heirs, that he would have to look back upon his work himself, alone and defeated. There is ample evidence for that interpretation. Now, however, I suggest a second, perhaps contradictory thought. Glatshteyn understood that the language as he had known and reveled in it, was gone forever. Yet he had absorbed its existence within and, flying in the face of external reality, he presented the world once again with his beloved Yiddish. The paradox is that, like anyone who has learned to know a person through the memories of others, we feel Glatshteyn's living language and are enriched.

CLINICAL IMPLICATIONS

The therapist who embarks on work with a Yiddish-speaking Holocaust survivor or with a child of survivors can benefit from understanding that the patient's relationship with the language may be a source of meaning to be explored and a source of mourning to be effected. The actual mourning of the language in which they communicated and which was part of their self-identity may be essential for even those not as intimately connected to language as the poet Glatshteyn.

Anna Ornstein[15] has eloquently demonstrated the importance of helping survivors to recognize a continuity between the self that existed before the Holocaust and the one alive today, a sense of self that incorporates and accepts the behaviors that had been necessary for survival:

One of the traumatic aspects of the Holocaust was the total disruption of the emotional network in which the survivors had lived. . . . It is not surprising that 'relative sanity' could be preserved only if the survivor was able to reinforce his threatened sense of *inner continuity*. (p. 128; emphasis Ornstein's)

It is reasonable to assume that one aspect of inner continuity involves the ways in which the patient was wont to express him/herself before the Holocaust, as well as through the connections that were maintained by dint of a particular manner of speech.

There are many reasons why psychotherapy has frequently failed the survivor. However, one aspect may be the very nature of the "talking cure." The feelings of not being heard or of being misunderstood may stem in part from the survivor's sense of having lost an entire world that was internally described and made intelligible in Yiddish. The attempt to translate this world to the therapist may be experienced as hopeless, hence feelings of disruption and lack of continuity will pervade the survivor's sense of self in the present. It is not necessary for the therapist to speak Yiddish, no more than it is necessary for him or her to have come from the same cultural context as any other patient. However, special acknowledgement, attention, and understanding should be given to the survivor's unique relationship to a language which may be experienced as annihilated or at the very least may no longer exist for the patient as a vital, growing expression.

As with any other language, the attuned therapist will have to observe carefully the contexts in which a Yiddish term or phrase is used. He or she will also have to try to discover whether there is special meaning to a patient's sudden—or, for that matter, repetitive—use of Yiddish during a session: Did it occur at a moment of anxiety or the expression of conflict? Was Yiddish employed to describe a tender moment from childhood? Is it reserved for the description of life in Eastern Europe before the Holocaust? Did the patient dream in Yiddish? The meaning the usages may have will vary according to the subjective reality of the patient. What functions as a means of conveying an early, satisfying, mirroring experience for one patient may prove to be the vehicle for relating moments of humiliation and rejection for another. This is true of survivors and of children of survivors who may have a distinct reaction to the Yiddish language even though they themselves do not speak it.

We have advanced considerably since the days when trauma of the proportions that Holocaust survivors endured were all but ignored in psychoanalysis and psychoanalytically oriented therapy. Then, treatment sought to force these experiences into a framework of repressed aggression, identification with the oppressor, instinctual satisfactions, and the like. Now, with the tools that help the therapist probe ever deeper into the subjective experience of the Holocaust survivor's family, we are in the position to explore the very special aspect of "the talking cure" as it affects the Yiddish speaker.

NOTES

1. Sigmund Freud, "Mourning and Melancholia," Standard Edition, Vol. XIV, p. 243.

2. See John Bowlby, "Processes of Mourning," The International Journal of Psycho-Analysis 42, parts 4–5 (1961): 317–340.

3. This poem first appeared in the Yiddish literary journal Poezye (June, 1919), pp. 5–6.

4. Yankev Glatshteyn, Gedenklider (New York: Farlag Yidisher Kemfer, 1943), pp. 5–6. Hereafter cited as Gedenklider.

5. Gedenklider, pp. 82–84.

6. Yankev Glatshteyn, Dem tatns shotn (New York: Farlag Matones, 1953), p. 172. Hereafter cited as Shotn.

7. *Shotn*, pp. 20–21.

8. *Shotn*, pp. 150–151.

9. Colin Murray Parkes, *Bereavement: Studies of Grief in Adult Life* (New York: International Universities Press, 1972), p. 59.

10. Yankev Glatshteyn, *Di freyd fun yidishn vort* (New York: Marstin Press, 1961), p. 169. Hereafter cited as *Freyd*.

11. *Freyd*, p. 156.

12. *Freyd*, pp. 203–206.

13. Yankev Glatshteyn, *Gezangen fun rekhts tsu links* (New York: Farlag CYCO, 1971), p. 109. Hereafter cited as *Gezangen*.

14. *Gezangen*, pp. 140–142.

15. Anna Ornstein, "Survival and Recovery," *Psychoanalytic Inquiry* 5 (1985): 99–130.

16

From Jew to Catholic—and Back: Psychodynamics of Child Survivors

MARGRIT WRESCHNER RUSTOW

The right to sanctuary was an ancient right, established at the beginning of Judeo-Christian civilization, when the Lord told Moses to set aside six "cities of refuge" (*arei miklot*), where those who had "killed without intent may find refuge from the revenger" (Numbers, 35:9–15). But there was no safe haven for innocent Jews or their children in the countries under Nazi occupation. The mere fact that they were Jews marked them for persecution and annihilation. If they were hiding and caught, they would be sent to their deaths, along with those who had been hiding them.

Exceptionally, Jewish children in hiding did survive those dangers. I studied the impact of cumulative trauma on three Jewish children of different ages who during the Holocaust were separated from their mothers and found sanctuary in Catholic institutions; and who, after their hiding, returned to Judaism. The study is based on original interviews and published autobiographies of seven such survivors, and the results described and analyzed in a more extensive, recently completed, unpublished study of identity problems of children who experienced severe and cumulative trauma during the Holocaust.[1]

In this chapter, I illustrate the problems of these survivors by summarizing the experiences of three of those seven survivors and discuss in some detail how the children's experience of trauma during that period affected their identity in later life as adults. I shall conclude with a number of observations on psychodynamic patterns and appropriate forms of psychotherapeutic treatment of survivors, having undergone this particular form of traumatic experience.

The basic psychodynamic pattern may be summarized as follows: The central and major trauma of each child, around which later experiences were organized, was the separation from, or loss of, the mother (or both parents); and the quest for physical safety, protection, and stability while hiding was of primary importance.

The separation from parents, the new names that the children were given, and the new rituals in which they had to participate threatened their psychological sense of continuity and identity. Hence the children, initially, tended to cling to transitional objects and memories, including songs from the past or final parental words, in order to preserve a feeling of connectedness and coherence of self. But subsequently, as contact with parents subsided and images of the past began to fade, they needed to blend into the new Catholic community and develop a sense of belonging, of continuity into the future in case parents would not return. The role of religion as a substitute for parental love and protection became gradually more important, a substitute that came to seem more powerful and less vulnerable than their parents. Thus there came a sense of increased closeness to the new religion in their lives isolated from the outside world.

Following the period of hiding, a decisive factor for psychological development was an understanding and supportive postwar environment. For it was during this postwar period of adjustment and reintegration that trauma and losses had to be absorbed, mourning facilitated, delayed maturation (including suppressed sexuality and aggression) compensated for, and conflicts of identity and loyalty resolved.

The children of whom I will speak in more detail and their ages when separating from their mothers were: Eve, age 13, from France; Pavel, age 10, born in Czechoslovakia, who fled with his parents to France when the Nazis occupied his country of birth; and Frida, age seven, also from France.

Eve

Born in 1929 in Paris, where her parents, nonpracticing Jews (originally from Poland), owned and operated a lingerie store while the maternal grandmother ran the household, Eve's sister, five years younger, was mother's favorite, while Eve herself felt special to her father. The mother was attractive, vivacious, and fun loving, while the father is described as quiet and profound. In spite of the parents' poor relationship, Eve experienced her home as "sunny."

At the outbreak of World War II, Eve's father was drafted into the French Army. When the German Army marched into France, the women of the family filled their little car with all their belongings and joined the masses of refugees who fled southward. "We never had a normal day in our lives after that," Eve recalls. "Everything was chaos, we were running. . . . " After wandering around for a long time, they settled in southern France, where the father found them after his discharge from the army.

As the Nazis' intent to destroy the French Jews became clearer, the parents decided to have Eve, then aged 13, and her sister, then eight, enter a convent, while they themselves hid in a nearby village. In the convent, the girls were baptized and their names changed. The mother continued to visit them regularly, and the children stayed with the parents during their vacations. After about a year, when the children were home on a short vacation, the parents, having been denounced and discovered, were arrested. Indeed, the children watched them being loaded into trucks by the Nazis in the village square together with other Jews destined for deportation in the East; yet, miraculously, the children were chased away by the German guard. Then the grandmother, too, went into hiding and the children, after returning to the convent, were transferred to the orphans' wing.

In identification with her mother, Eve tried as best she could to make up for some of the physical and emotional deprivations in the convent and fill her mother's place in taking care of "mother's special baby." She knitted a new undershirt so that the sister would not have to wear the coarse institutional underwear. She also tried to save her sister's beautiful curls from the nuns' scissors, combing her sister's hair every evening to remove lice and nits, while praying to her newfound God: "Please, if You love us as they say You do, please make sure that my sister's head is clear of lice." And after the curls were lost Eve felt "That's what it was like to lose your identity . . . it gradually happened, the last pair of shoes from home; until you really melted into all the anonymity."[2]

One day, Eve's little sister was to be sent to a summer camp together with the rest of her younger groups, and the sister's request that Eve join that group was denied. As Eve sadly watched the children's departure, her little sister suddenly jumped off the moving truck, obviously unable to tolerate this separation, in a close replication of the scene when their parents had been loaded on a truck that would take them to a concentration camp.

After the war ended, Eve's grandmother, who had survived on a farm, showed up one day unexpectedly at the convent and took the girls to a Jewish orphanage. There, they were told to forget the convent and all their Catholic experience and to prepare for life in Palestine. They were now thrown into a world of confusion and chaos, in complete contrast to the structured, orderly, and sheltered life in the convent.

One day at the orphanage—suddenly and miraculously—her father returned from a concentration camp. "We saw a ghostly human being, no hair, not an ounce of flesh on his body, looking like a skeleton; but two tremendous, wonderful black eyes looking at us. When he grabbed me and said 'Eve,' I recognized his gestures and knew it was my father."[3] He prepared the girls for the fact that their mother, who had been in Auschwitz in Mengele's experimental block, would not return. Yet many months later, a message came that their mother, too, had survived and would return.

At that time Eve, now 16, found it difficult to reconcile her delayed but strong adolescent sexual stirrings and the Catholicism, which she had internalized by now and which had become a part of her psychic structure. She continued to attend church contrary to her parents' wishes, but within a few years married a Jewish man, who helped settle the family in the United States. Her daughter was born a year after her marriage, and later a son. Discontented in her marriage and unfulfilled in her life, Eve completed her schooling and professional training as a teacher; much later, she divorced her husband, and remarried a Christian, a much older and fatherly man. Her daughter from her first marriage is raising her children as traditional Jews, but Eve's son from that marriage married a Christian. For many years now, Eve, known by her husband's Scottish family name, has been teaching nursery school in a temple, introducing the children to Jewish holidays and culture.

Pavel

Born in Prague in 1932, Pavel was the only child of an upper-middle-class nonpracticing Jewish family. The father was an insurance lawyer, a lover of music and literature, stiff and emotionally distant. Once, for Pavel's birthday, he ordered "10 kilograms of toys suitable for a five-year old."[4] Only later did Pavel experience his father as being closer to him. Pavel's mother, down-to-earth, with a radiant smile and energetic manner, was the practical member of the family. During his first seven years, Pavel was taken care of by a governess to whom he was very attached.

When the Germans occupied Czechoslovakia in 1939, the family left for Paris, and the father, in a sentimental mood, gave Pavel a ring to remember Czechoslovakia by. In France, the mother supported the family as a beautician, while the ailing father failed to find work as an electrician. Pavel was twice placed in a Jewish children's home. The first was an ultra-orthodox one, where the children rejected him as a "goy" without earlocks, yarmulka, or knowledge of prayers. Holding him responsible for anti-Semitism, they tied him to a tree to beat him savagely. Pavel severely regressed and started to wet his bed. After six months at this children's home, his parents took him back. Later, in another children's home, he narrowly escaped from the German police.

Desperate, his mother arranged for Pavel to be accepted into a Catholic boarding school, where the ladies were going to save the soul of a Jewish child, not without risk to their own lives. Pavel, very unhappy, ran away to the hospital where his father was being treated for ulcers, but was returned to school, almost by force. Here his name was changed to a French Catholic one, Paul-Henri Ferland, to which Marie was added at the time of his baptism, "maybe to invoke the protection of the Virgin, the heavenly mother . . . less vulnerable than the earthly one, whom . . . the whirlwind was already sweeping away."[5] His father had signed a letter authorizing his baptism. Later, Pavel's parents attempted to cross the border to Switzerland, but were caught and soon deported to a German concentration camp. A short note thrown out of the departing train implored the woman who had helped place Pavel in the Catholic school: "Don't abandon the little one."[6]

Pavel, 10 years old when he entered the strict life of the boarding school, missed his parents, started to sleepwalk, and sank even deeper into withdrawal and depression. He got very sick from the croup and almost died. He wondered whether this sick child was really he. When mail was being distributed, he found out again and again that, for him, there was no letter from home; nor was there any place to go on vacations. He felt that "he was already an orphan."[7] The memory of his parents began to fade.

In contrast to these deprivations, the strict Catholicism at the school meant to Pavel calm and certainty: a cohesive world totally clear about good and evil, with time allocated by the minute to studies, prayers, and meals. This world seemed completely reassuring—except for his intermittent, sudden fits of undefinable terror. "[N]othing disappears, yet everything is transformed: the new identity then changes one's former existence into a prefiguration or a preparation." Yet he then adds: "The first ten years of my life, the memories of my childhood, were to disappear, for there was no possible synthesis between the person I had been and the one I was to become." Later he said, "I had passed over to Catholicism body and soul. The fact that the misdeeds of the Jews were mentioned during Holy Week did not trouble me in the slightest."[8]

Pavel threw himself fully into the religion that dominated his life. He began to assist at mass and wanted to become a Jesuit priest. "Worshipping Mary was the very essence of our religious universe. . . . Kneeling before the plaster statue with the sweet face . . . , her head crowned with tin stars, I rediscovered something of the presence of a mother." Soon Pavel felt altogether transformed: "Pavel had disappeared, Paul-Henri Ferland was someone else." He remained conscious of his Jewish origin; yet he readily joined in expressions of scorn for the Jews.[9]

When the war ended, Pavel was 12 ½ years old. He was given to understand that his parents would not return and was secretly pressured by Jewish organizations to leave the Catholic school. He felt utterly alone, and he developed seizures of rapid breathing and heart beat, a dry mouth, chills, and cold sweat. Above all, he felt an intolerable fear that ultimately became like a fear of death, with no place to hide, as though the executioner was on his way. Once this anxiety seized him while officiating at mass, and he felt as if he had a multiple personality. "There were three of us at that moment: the one who was afraid, the one who was watching him, and the one who was serving the Mass like a machine. Was I going crazy?"[10]

Slowly Pavel grasped that his parents were dead and he had to make his own choices in life. The school at this time confirmed him ahead of his age group, so as to protect his faith; but also sent him to talk to a Jesuit teacher who had liked Pavel. By recognizing "my right to judge for myself," Father L. was "helping me to renew the contact with my past." Yet Pavel also asked himself, "Wasn't it madness to identify with my Jewishness when Paul-Henri Ferland had no remaining link to the Jews? . . . Hadn't my ties with the past disappeared forever?" He was convinced of his clerical vocation and dreamt endlessly about his future as a priest; but he also was convinced of his need to return to the decimated, miserable group he had come from. Back in school, he asked not to be called Paul-Henri Ferland but Paul, the French equivalent of his original

name. A few months later, Pavel left the Catholic school for good to join a
Jewish religious family, small tradespeople who became his legal guardians. Yet
"in my heart of hearts I still feel a strange attraction, mingled with a profound
repulsion, for this place of my childhood."[11]

Pavel now entered a third, totally different world. Instead of the assimilated
refinement of his parental home, this was a rough-and-ready world of primitive
vitality, and Jewish customs and mannerisms. At his first Passover seder, he felt
as if he had rediscovered his freedom, but when meat was served, he excused
himself from eating it, since his Catholic conscience forbade him to eat meat
on Good Friday.

His new guardian spoke to Pavel about Eretz Israel, and, at age 15, Pavel
decided to go to Palestine in order to join the fight against the Arabs. Once in
Eretz Israel, he changed his name from Paul to Saul (or Shaul in Hebrew), in
effect reversing the name change the Apostle Paul underwent at the time of his
conversion to Christianity. He now lives in Jerusalem, is married, and has three
children. He is an internationally known professor of history, and teaches in
Israel, Geneva, and the United States.

Frida

An only child, Frida was born in 1934 in Paris, into a nonpracticing Jewish
family. Her father, a chemical engineer and Zionist, originally came from Russia
and her mother from Poland. When Frida was four years old, her father left the
family for Palestine, and later, in the convent, Frida could not remember him.
The mother, a one-time entertainer, supported herself and Frida by selling herring
and pickles in the marketplace. Frida had a close but ambivalent relationship
with her mother. She wanted to be "a real French girl" and felt embarrassed
about her mother's appearance and Jewish accent. When Frida was six, Germany
occupied parts of France, and Frida and her mother went into hiding in another
town, but returned home shortly thereafter.

Then, when their lives became more unbearable, Frida's mother decided to
send Frida, then seven, to a convent. When the train which took Frida to the
convent had arrived at the station, Frida took her doll out of the shoe box, "and
with one blow, without looking, sent the box, string and all, flying to the rails
. . . I felt as though I was falling with it. . . . I shut my eyes a minute; the shoebox
is going to be crushed by the train."[12]

Frida's adjustment to life in the convent was confusing: everything was so different. She came to admire the statues in the chapel and the beautiful songs that
the nuns and the children sang. "A hymn is a sweet and holy prayer. Even if you
don't understand all the words, you feel the music . . . you lower your voice because of the sad melody. Then I feel in my heart I would truly like to become
a saint. . . . We poor sinners need God's mercy, His grace and the help of Mary,
His Mother." And then, before going to bed, she would kneel in front of the
most beautiful holy picture which stood next to her bed on the table and say:

"I love you, little Jesus. I adore you . . . you suffer little children to come unto you, your paradise is open only to them. See, I am a little Christian girl now."[13]

Frida wanted to be baptized, and receive communion to become a daughter of the Church like all the others; but she was not allowed to, since her mother refused to give her permission. Now "I cannot confess, . . . and my sins will stay in my soul." This made Frida very unhappy, and she thought: "It is not my mother's business—it's *my* soul. But she is no longer my mother: I want to be the daughter of the Church." And in church that day she softly sang along "I am a Christian"—but suddenly her windpipe started to hurt and she felt a tugging at her throat. Yet she wanted God to hear her voice over all the others: "it is urgent—because I am denied the most important grace of all on account of my origins."[14] At dinnertime, all those newly baptized got two pieces of melon in addition to a cream puff, the dessert for special feast days; and Frida exchanged her cream puff for two pieces of melon, so that she could be like all the other girls. Then, suddenly, she had to throw up.

After a few months, the mail and packages Frida had received from her mother suddenly stopped. Frida wondered where her mother was, but pushed the thought out of her mind: "She had promised me a package and she never sent it . . . I don't want to think about it any more because letters from my mother are not something important in religion."[15]

The children cherished their few remaining items from home. Frida was afraid that an outgrown skirt would be given to a younger girl. Her mother had knitted it for her, and Frida kept it in a special place in her locker—until a nun found it. She pleaded to keep it, promising to knit an additional hem. When she could not produce the wool, the skirt was given to a girl whom it would fit. Frida now followed the girl around, to make sure that she took good care of it. At night, Frida would sneak to the girl's bed, find the skirt on the chair next to it, stroke it gently, and fold it correctly.[16]

Later Frida started to doubt her religion. She withdrew and regressed, and started to wet her bed. When she was scolded and ridiculed, she ran in her clammy nightgown up the ladder to hide in the attic. Suddenly she smelled the scent of herring and pickles from the market where her mother worked mixed with the smell of pee. "I hear voices speaking Yiddish. My mother calls me; I see her, then she disappears . . . It smells like home in Paris. . . . " It was an "aroma of memory."[17] Her mother, as it turned out, attempted to cross the Swiss border, was arrested, and deported to a concentration camp.

When the war ended, Frida, at age 11, was briefly sent to another convent, but lost her belief in religion. She found out that her mother had perished. She first joined an aunt in Paris, then her father and stepmother in Palestine. Her adjustment was difficult: a new family, a new language and school, and later the Israeli Army. Nevertheless, for the first time Frida felt proud of being Jewish and of her new country.

Now Frida is a writer and lives in the United States. She is married to a Jewish physician and they have no children.

PSYCHODYNAMICS

Some Common Elements During Hiding

Different as were the individual experiences of Eve, Pavel, and Frida, the story of their survival bears certain common features. Before going into hiding, all three were exposed to humiliation and harassment. Their parents lost their livelihoods and community positions. The children had to leave school, friends, and home, and later to separate from their parents to be placed in Catholic institutions. Two of the three children were baptized and given new names (as were most of the ones hidden in convents), and all of them had to pray to a God they had never known before.

The quality of care in the Catholic convents or orphanages was generally satisfactory. The nuns, often lacking food and other necessities, shared what little they had with the children. The Catholic institution with its strict ritual provided a closely regulated structure, which meant safety and security, stability and continuity—opening a possibility of new meaning to the children's lives. It also gave them an opportunity to recreate their own families: new, spiritual, and reliable. In their songs and prayers to Mary, God, and Jesus—the spiritual mother, father, and son—all were together, all were loved. Everything "bad"— sexual, ugly, or aggressive—was rejected as sinful and banned from the mind. Only loveliness and beauty prevailed: the statues, the faces, the music, the hymns. The weekly confessions cleared the conscience. All this created an utterly hypnotic and emotionally very attractive, pre-ambivalent atmosphere, where only beauty, love, and goodness were permitted, and aggression, anger, and hatred had to be suppressed.

The importance of religion was expressed by all three children. Eve, who had never been exposed to religion at home, felt excited about entering the religious community. "It was endearing to me you could talk to God, which I had never done before. You could go to the chapel and there He was . . . you could unload your problems . . . and walk out of there feeling very good about yourself."[18] To Pavel, too, religion was providing a structure within which he found order, safety, clarity, and continuity.

Confession served an important function, first reenforcing and then alleviating a sense of guilt, which plagued most of the children: guilt for wanting to live, guilt that resulted from anger toward parents for abandoning their children for whom they chose life, while they themselves went into their deaths. The spirituality and the religious figures lent themselves to be invested with magical powers to protect, love, tolerate, understand, and forgive.[19] Mary, the spiritual mother, wept over the fate of her son—and would understand their sorrow. Christ, too, had suffered injustice and cruelty, just as the children did now. The omnipotent God, with his power to perform miracles, could protect them—and, surely could bring back the parents. After saying 200 Ave Marias, Eve "knew" that her prayer had been heard and her parents would return from the concentration camp. Merging with the omnipotent good father (God) gave the children a sense of safety and strength, a father able to protect them from external and internal destructive forces, unlike their own vulnerable and weak one.

With the passing of time, the hypnotic influence of life in the convent became increasingly effective, but this in turn created more guilt and conflict. Each child had his or her own way of dealing with the profound stresses of the new situation. Those who had experienced more ambivalence in their relationship with their parents had more difficulty separating from them (because of hostility) and thus felt greater guilt, as for instance Frida who had had a strongly conflict-ridden relationship with her mother previous to separating from her.

While becoming increasingly more part of the Catholic environment, it was also necessary to maintain a link with the past in order to avoid the feeling of total parental abandonment: a safeguard against total forgetting and to confirm one's continuity, one's existence, and one's person. This was done through memories, contact with people from the past, material objects; Frida's doll, skirt, pictures, letters from parents, poetry, melodies, or any other symbolic replacement, most of them having a transitional character and sometimes a magic quality.[20] The parting words became the child's companions, the living remnants of the parents' love and their desire for the child to survive, "which were incorporated in the superego."[21]

The fear of loss of self and of the children's personal identity was described by both Eve and Pavel. Eve became frightened that she would forget who she was, and in the middle of the night she would say to herself: "Will I remember when it's over, if it is really ever over, that once upon a time I had a name that was not Marie-Catherine, that I was not a person who went to church, that I had parents and a life that used to be very sunny?"[22] The loss of the parental presence and the demeaning of the group to which their parents belonged—and now the strong, protecting influence of the new environment—all contributed to the internalization of the strict Catholic dogma and the identification with it, and provided an avenue for gaining a new and different sense of self.

After the War

The end of the war was a crucial phase in the lives of the children. It was a moment which had been anticipated with hopes, expectation, and fantasies; which as time passed became like a vanishing dream, one that would never come true. Neither the children nor the adults, who for the last three years had made most decisions in their lives, knew what to anticipate or prepare for: They waited with anguish for what was to come. It was a prelude to yet another transition in the children's lives: from a completely structured and closed community, which had saved their lives, in a setting where everything was closely administered, to an individual existence where they were frequently left to their own devices—one of uncertainty and confusion, with little help in finding their place in an often chaotic postwar world.

After leaving the institution, and sometimes after temporary placement else-where, the children joined returning family members whom they barely recog-nized, and who themselves were severely traumatized because of the terrible ordeals they had gone through. They themselves had no home to come back to, no work, and no money. Their world, too, had been totally destroyed, and now they had to help the children with their physical and psychological needs, and indeed their losses. Thus the children were again thrown into situations of con-fusion, uncertainty, and often chaos. They now were deprived of their recently found refuge, and the old childhood environment—physical and emotional—which they had longed for over the years, did not exist any longer. They also had to grope to define new goals, ideas, ideals, and values that the adults, too, had often lost.

How did the children deal with problems of their identity after the war? The postwar experiences of the children here studied share several crucial features: (1) having survived the war in Catholic institutions, they did not know whether their parents were still alive or would return; (2) they did not know what would happen in their own future; (3) each of them had to resolve issues of identity confusion in their own way. Whether parents survived whom the children ulti-mately joined was no doubt a decisive factor in resolving this identity issue; moreover, some married non-Jews with whom they did or did not stay together.[23] While all three children continued to pray and attend church for some time after the war, later they came to consider themselves as Jewish.

One other child included in my larger study, however, did decide to retain his Catholic religion. This boy, 10 years old when his father returned from a concentration camp (while his mother did not survive), had been hidden with an upper-class devout Catholic family whom he greatly admired and where he lived comfortably with the family's other six boys close to his age, without physical deprivation. (His one-year-younger brother, however, hidden with a similar type family, returned to Judaism after the war.) It seems that this adaptable latency boy was able to transfer object libido to members of his new family, from whom he received sufficient libidinal gratification. (He did, however, de-velop anxiety attacks and allergic reactions during his hiding period.)[24]

The identity conflict of the postwar period is vividly expressed by Pavel. Since both his parents had perished, he had to decide what to do with his future. His reaction to his own decision to leave the institution and his religious ambivalence are well described by him (see above). He felt himself "to be Jewish—no longer despite myself or secretly but through a sensation of absolute loyalty. . . . I knew nothing about Jews, and was still a Catholic. But something had changed. A tie had been reestablished. An identity was emerging, a confused one certainly, contradictory perhaps, but from that day forward linked to a central axis of which there could be no doubt: in some manner or other I was Jewish—whatever this term meant in my mind."[25] At the same time he endlessly dreamed of his future as a priest.

It seems that, for each child, there was a strong relationship between their conflicts around identity and loyalty, but that the older ones were better able to conceptualize their identity struggle than the younger ones. The more their home and their parents receded from memory, the more they wished to give their lives to the church, to become a nun or priest, self-sacrificing and devoted to God. Yet all this increased their feelings of guilt toward their parents, and hence their loyalty conflict.

Older children, such as Eve, were better prepared to care for themselves. This group had more fully developed superegos, having absorbed and internalized their parents' standards, and were able to remember and to live by those values. They had achieved more mature ego development, and thus had a larger variety of defenses at their disposal which facilitated their adaptation to the new environment, so that (except in cases of severe previous pathology) the older children, hidden in the convents, had reached a higher level of individuation and were further along in their psychic developmental maturation.

By contrast, the younger children undergoing this type of traumatic experience had a much more difficult time of it. They still depended more on the adults in their environment for their care. Their superegos were still harsher and more critical and their object relationships more sexualized. Their egos were still more brittle and less integrated, and they had fewer defenses for adaptive maneuvering at their disposal; as a result, they tended to regress more easily.[26] Their traumatization, guilt feelings, and loyalty conflict often caused psychosomatic symptoms or other severe character-neurotic problems, including development of a depressive core, particularly if they had not been able to mourn lost parents whom they often hardly remembered.

The dynamic pattern just described agrees with earlier findings of both Keilson and Ostow. Keilson, in his study of Dutch World War II orphans, concludes that children who were separated from their mothers at a younger age were more severely affected than those who were separated at an older age—except for the very young ones whose caretakers were so excellent that parental care continued without too much interruption.[27] Ostow, elaborating the theory originally developed by Erikson, says that the unconscious core of identity is established in childhood, whereas manifest identity results from the consolidation of personality during adolescence and is profoundly influenced by current cultural and political pressures.[28] The early home environment shapes the core identity of the child, whereas subsequent experience contributes additional content to this manifest identity.

CLINICAL IMPLICATIONS

What are the implications of the psychodynamic factors for any later psychotherapeutic treatment of survivors who lived through the type of experience just described?

The effect of multiple trauma on later adjustment of the children whose histories I described above depends on a variety of factors, including age and stage of development, severity of trauma, and the circumstances of readjustment.

Among the more specific determinants that affected the child's later development and became decisive factors in later adjustment are his prewar personality; capacity for adaptation at the time that life was interrupted; capacity for fantasy, internalization, and memory; and his capacity to live a dual existence. The quality of care during hiding, continuity or change in caretakers, and the degree of physical and emotional deprivation, of course, were crucial. Of similar, and possibly even greater, importance were actual experiences and losses discovered after hiding, and the quality of the available support at that time.

The child's age is a crucial factor, because the effect of the trauma on the child is closely related to the phase of development the child was in when the trauma occurred. For instance, there is a difference when a child's symbiosis with his mother is interrupted, or when separation from the parent takes place during the anal or Oedipal phases, when the separation—individuation process is in progress. The effect on Frida of leaving her mother during the latency period after her father had left her when she was four was a different one than on Eve who was then in the beginning of her adolescence. As Furst has indicated, "The phase-specific developmental task associated with each period of the life cycle constitutes the background or framework on which the challenge of trauma is imposed. As such they will determine certain vulnerabilities and responses which are characteristic for each phase."[29]

The Catholic environment was totally foreign to these children. There they lived as different people—with a different name, different history, identity, and religion—an environment where emphasis was on, and emotional satisfaction grew out of, their spiritual lives. In order to avoid regression, they had to fall back on ego defenses, such as blocking emotions and constricting cognition. For instance, after entering the institution, Pavel first became severely depressed and withdrawn and then fell critically ill. After recovering, he immersed himself in the new religion. He felt that Pavel no longer existed and Paul-Henri Ferland was someone else.

The strict Roman Catholic structure provided guidance, regulation, and clearly spelled-out expectations, and all these helped to overcome the helplessness, to repress and control impulses, and to reconstitute a relatively cohesive self with which adaptation to the new environment was possible.

The three children found themselves deprived of their previous sources of libidinal and narcissistic supplies; yet, in the new environment spiritual resources substituted for some of these. Accumulated guilt was to some extent relieved through confession, prayer, and song; and spiritual love obtained through self-sacrifice and disavowal. In this environment, where aggression and sexuality were considered sinful, and where a pre-ambivalent atmosphere of total beauty prevailed, the children could not normally proceed through regular developmental phases, such as adolescence and separation—individuation. (Eve, then 16, is an example of making up for missed maturation. She fantasized while being in the convent that the "beautiful priest" who performed Sunday mass looked at her intensely. Soon after the war, when living in a coeducational home, she fell in love with a young man, and later got herself pregnant three times.)

Leaving the convent at the end of the war unprepared; going once again to an unknown place; joining strangers or parents who had become estranged, uprooted, and traumatized themselves: all these added up to another trauma for the children. Keilson in this context speaks about "cumulative trauma" suffered by these children. Having given up hope, at least consciously, for their parents' return, most of the children had begun to see their future as nuns or priests, serving God in the stable and secure but constricted and rigidly controlled environment to which they had adapted and of which they had become part—the environment which had saved their lives, and where they had lived for the last three to four years. Leaving this environment meant once again destruction of the newly developed network, and an interruption of the more limited connectedness and relative self-cohesion. (Pavel describes his sensation of emotional disintegration when pressured to leave the Catholic institution.)[30]

After the war the nature, sensitivity, and help of the environment in which the children ultimately landed after leaving the convent was crucial. It was during that period that the children needed support and understanding in dealing with their losses and mourning; in finding themselves and defining their identity, while groping for meaning, new goals, ideas, and values. After years of leading a routinized existence, isolated and removed from the world, they now had to find a place for themselves in a world that had become totally different, confused, and chaotic. In this new situation, they often acted impulsively to prove that they were alive and to experience their newly found autonomy. This was also a way to avoid realization of losses and to defend against depression and feelings of emptiness.

Thus, during the postwar period, either the healing process could begin and the effect of the trauma be mitigated and at least partially integrated—or else the imprint of earlier trauma on the personality would be reenforced or solidified. Keilson felt that this postwar period was more important for the child's future development than the hiding period proper.

For younger children it was crucial that survivor parents allowed them their own feelings and reactions. They had to express rage for having been left, abandoned and unprotected by their parents, and for having had to live as Christians, while repudiating their earlier identity. For these and older age groups, parental idealization processes were often interrupted when separation from parents occurred.

Survivor parents, having been severely traumatized themselves, sometimes used the child as an instrument for their own needs; projected onto him images of lost family members, and expected the child to substitute for the lost ones in order to hold on to them. Similarly, when losses of family members were denied either by the children or the parents, mourning did not properly take place, nor did gradual decathexis of the lost object and subsequent internalization. Separation processes could not properly proceed (and sometimes they occurred with others rather than with their own parents), since separation meant death and basic trust could not be easily (re)established. Then boundaries between surviving children and their parents became blurred and the children's psychological development was impeded—a process that could produce such effects as passivity, ego weakness, poor self-esteem, superego impairment, confused identity, difficulties in developing intimacy, and lack of trust in the outside world.

For all these reasons, in subsequent psychoanalytic treatment of survivors, such as those described above, it is often difficult to gain their trust and to establish a therapeutic alliance. During the hiding period and postwar adaptation, the capacity for chameleon-like and quick adaptation to different environments and the capacity to blend in and behave according to environmental expectations and demands could turn out to be lifesaving devices.[31] According to Marion Oliner, for survivors such as these, "identity becomes like a garment that one can change at will: the more garments one has the more likely one is to survive."[32] However, this could become a handicap and even detrimental for later development of trust and intimacy and identity formation, as described by Saul Friedlander:" He now saw himself as a spectator, destined to wander among several worlds, knowing them, understanding them . . . but nonetheless incapable of feeling an identification without any reticence, incapable of seeing, understanding, and belonging. . . . "[33]

When treating these people, therapists need to discover islands of helplessness, which are due to interrupted maturation and therefore must be considered real lacks rather than resistance in treatment. In addition, the survivor needs permission frequently, help, or active encouragement from the therapist to speak about the trauma that he experienced, since it is emotionally loaded and totally or partially repressed. Such help may indeed be crucial to successful therapy; otherwise "those who have not lived through the experience will never know; those who have will never tell; not really, not completely. . . . "[34] In order to reconstruct the trauma experienced during the Holocaust it is necessary for the therapist to help the survivor patient fill in memories that are often incomplete and faded.[35] Various analysts who treated children who lived through these traumata emphasize the importance of helping them to express and deal with their aggression, so as ultimately to diminish depression and help to complete mourning processes. Emphasis in therapy should be on self-expression and communication which were curtailed in the earlier traumatic situation. The child-survivor may need help in distinguishing the world of the traumatic past and the present one. As James Herzog puts it, "we believe that the nightmare can be dispelled; that, through words, analysis can penetrate the shadowy inner world [of the Holocaust survivor] . . . and, by illuminating it, diminish pain, and heal."[36]

NOTES

1. Margrit Wreschner Rustow, *Identity and Trauma: Jewish Children Saved by Christians During the Holocaust*, unpublished doctoral dissertation, The Union for Experi-

menting Colleges and Universities, Cincinnati, 1988. (The names of those children in the study where material is taken only from personal interviews have been changed for the sake of confidentiality.)

2. "Eve," ibid., pp. 30–45.

3. Ibid., p. 42.

4. Saul Friedlander, *When Memory Comes* (New York: Farrar, Straus & Giroux, 1979), p. 37.

5. Ibid., p. 79.

6. Ibid., p. 90.

7. Ibid., p. 119.

8. Ibid., pp. 79f., 120.

9. Ibid., pp. 121f.

10. Ibid., p. 133.

11. Ibid., pp. 138–139.

12. Frida Scheps Weinstein, *A Hidden Childhood 1942–1945* B. L. Kennedy, trans. (New York: Hill & Wang, 1985), p. 16.

13. Ibid., p. 38.

14. Ibid., pp. 50–52.

15. Ibid., p. 103.

16. Ibid., pp. 126f.

17. Ibid., pp. 126f.

18. "Eve," in Rustow, *Identity and Trauma*, p. 32.

19. Ana-Maria Rizzuto, *The Birth of the Living God* (Chicago: University of Chicago Press, 1979), and personal communication from the author.

20. Judith S. Kestenberg, "Coping with Losses and Survival," unpublished paper (1985), p. 11.

21. Ibid., referring to Samuel P. Oliner, *Restless Memories: Recollection of the Holocaust Years* (Berkeley, CA: Judah I. Magnus Museum, 1979), pp. 9–11.

22. Rustow, *Identity and Trauma*, p. 35.

23. "Marcia," in Rustow, *Identity and Trauma*, pp. 23–30.

24. "Charles," in ibid., pp. 90–99.

25. Friedlander, *Memory*, p. 138.

26. This psychological mechanism is described by Adele E. Scharl, "Regression and Restitution in Object Loss," in *Psychoanalytic Study of the Child*, Vol. 16 (New York: International Press, 1961), p. 479.

27. Hans Keilson and Herman R. Sarphatie, *Sequentielle Traumatisierung bei Kindern* (Stuttgart: Enke, 1979), p. 269.

28. Mortimer Ostow, "The Psychological Determinants of Jewish Identity," in *Judaism and Psychoanalysis*, Mortimer Ostow, ed. (New York: KTAV Publishing, 1982), p. 159; cf. Erik H. Erikson, "The Problem of Ego Identity," *Journal of the American Psychoanalytic Association* 4 (1956): 56–121.

29. Sidney S. Furst, "Psychic Trauma with Particular Reference to Postchildhood Trauma," in *The Reconstruction of Trauma: Its Significance in Clinical Work*, Arnold Rothstein, Ed. (New York: International Universities Press, 1986), p. 37.

30. Friedlander, *Memory*, p. 133.

31. See Eddie De Wind, "The Confrontation with Death," *International Journal of Psycho-Analysis* 49 (1968): 302–305.

32. Marion M. Oliner, "Hysterical Features Among Children of Survivors," in *Gen-*

erations of the Holocaust, Martin S. Bergmann and Milton E. Jucovy, Eds. (New York: Basic Books, 1982): 279.

33. Friedlander, *Memory*, pp. 155f.

34. Elie Wiesel, "Some Measure of Humility," in *Sh'ma* (October 31, 1975): 2.

35. Flora Hogman, "The Role of Memories in Lives of World War II Orphans," *Journal of the American Academy of Child Psychiatry* 24 (1985): 390–396.

36. James Herzog, "World Beyond Metaphor: Thoughts on the Transmission of Trauma," in *Generations of the Holocaust*, Bergmann and Jocovy, Eds., p. 119.

Selected Bibliography

Améry, J. *At the Mind's Limits, Contemplations by a Survivor on Auschwitz and its Realities.* (S. Rosenfeld & S. P. Rosenfeld, trans.). Bloomington: Indiana University Press, 1980.

Aurehahan, N. C., & Laub, D. Annihilation and restoration: Post-traumatic memory as pathway and obstacle to recovery. *International Review of Psychoanalysis*, 1984, *11*, 327–344.

Barocas, H. A., & Barocas, C. B. Wounds of the fathers: The next generation of Holocaust victims. *International Review of Psychoanalysis*, 1979, *6*, 331–341.

Becker, E. The pawnbroker: A study in basic psychology. In *Angel in Armor*. New York: Free Press, 1969.

Bergmann, M. S. Recurrent problems in the treatment of survivors and their children. In M. Bergmann & M. Jucovy, *Generations of the Holocaust*, 247–266.

———, & Jucovy, M. E. (Eds.). *Generations of the Holocaust.* New York: Basic Books, 1982.

Bettelheim, B. *The Informed Heart: Autonomy in a Mass Age.* New York: Avon Books, 1971.

———. *Surviving and Other Essays.* New York: Alfred A. Knopf, 1979.

Chodoff, P. Psychotherapy of the survivor. In J. Dimsdale (Ed.). *Survivors, Victims and Perpetrators.* Washington: Hemisphere Publishing, 1980.

Cohen, E. *Human Behavior in the Concentration Camp.* New York: Universal Library, 1953.

Danieli, Y. The treatment and prevention of long term effects and intergenerational transmission of victimization: A lesson from Holocaust survivors and their children. In C. R. Figley (Ed.). *Trauma and Its Wake.* New York: Brunner Mazel, 1985.

Davidson, S. The clinical effects of massive psychic trauma in families of Holocaust survivors. *Journal of Marital and Family Therapy*, 1980, *6* (1), 11–24.

de Wind, E. Psychotherapy after traumatization caused by persecution. *Bulletin of the Philadelphia Association of Psychoanalysis*, 1971, *21* (3), 204–211.

Des Pres, T. *The Survivor: An Anatomy of the Life in the Death Camps*. New York: Oxford University Press, 1976.

Epstein, H. *Children of the Holocaust: Conversations with Sons and Daughters of Survivors*. New York: G. P. Putnam's Sons, 1979.

Faimberg, H. The telescoping of generations. *Contemporary Psychoanalysis*, 1988, *24* (1), 99–118.

Fogelman, E., & Savran, B. Therapeutic groups for children of Holocaust survivors. *International Journal of Group Psychotherapy*, 1979, *29* (2), 211–235.

Frankl, V. *Man's Search for Meaning, An Introduction to Logotherapy*. Boston: Beacon Press, 1962.

Freyberg, J. T. Difficulties in separation-individuation as experienced by offspring of Nazi Holocaust survivors. *American Journal of Orthopsychiatry*, 1980, *50* (1), 87–95.

Gyomroi, E. L. The analysis of a young concentration camp victim. *Psychoanalytic Study of the Child*, 1963, *18*, 484–510.

Hoppe, K. Psychotherapy with concentration camp survivors. In N. Krystal (Ed.), *Massive Psychic Trauma*. New York: International Universities Press, 1968.

Kestenberg, J. S. (Ed.). *Child Survivors of the Holocaust, A Special Issue of Psychoanalysis Review*, Winter 1988, *75* (4).

Klein, H. Children of the Holocaust: Mourning and bereavement. In E. J. Anthony & C. Koupernik (Eds.), *The Child in His Family: The Impact of Disease and Death*. New York: Wiley, 1973.

———. The meaning of the Holocaust. *Israel Journal of Psychiatry and Related Sciences*, 1983, *20* (1–2), 119–128.

Krell, R. Family therapy with children of concentration camp survivors. *American Journal of Psychotherapy*, 1982, *36*, 513–522.

Krystal, H. *Integration and Self-Healing. Affect, Trauma and Alexithymia*. Hillsdale: The Analytic Press, 1988.

———. (Ed.). *Massive Psychic Trauma*. New York: International Universities Press, 1968.

———, and Niederland, W. G. (Eds.), *Psychic Traumatization: After Effects in Individuals and Communities*. Boston: Little, Brown, 1970.

Laub, D. & Auerhahan, N. *Knowing and Not Knowing the Holocaust. A Special Issue of Psychoanalytic Inquiry*, 1985, *5*, (1).

Levi, P. *Survival in Auschwitz: The Nazi Assault on Humanity* (S. Woolf, trans.). New York: Collier Books, 1958.

Lifton, R. J. *Death in Life: Survivors of Hiroshima*. New York: Random House, 1967.

———. The concept of survivor. In J. Dimsdale (Ed.), *Survivors, Victims and Perpetrators*. New York: Hemisphere Publishing Corporation, 1980.

Luel, S. A., & Marcus, P. (Eds.). *Psychoanalytic Reflections on the Holocaust: Selected Essays*. New York: Holocaust Awareness Institute, Center for Judaic Studies, University of Denver and Ktav Publishers, 1984.

Marcus, P. & Rosenberg, A. A philosophical critique of the "survivor syndrome" and some implications for treatment. In R. L. Braham (Ed.), *The Psychological Perspectives of the Holocaust and of Its Aftermath*. Boulder, CO: Social Science Monographs and the Csengeri Institute for Holocaust Studies of the Graduate

School of The University Center of the City University of New York. Distributed
   by Columbia University Press, New York, 1988.
Moskovitz, S. *Love Despite Hate. Child Survivors of the Holocaust and Their Adult
   Lives.* New York: Schocken Books, 1982.
Niederland, W. G. The problem of the survivor. *Journal of the Hillside Hospital,* 1961,
   10, 233–247. Also reprinted in Krystal, *Massive Psychic Trauma,* 8–22.
———. The survivor syndrome: Further observations and dimensions. *Journal of the
   American Psychoanalytic Association,* 1981, *29,* 413–425.
Ornstein, A. The aging survivor of the Holocaust. The effects of the Holocaust on life-
   cycle experiences: The creation and recreation of families. *Journal of Geriatric
   Psychiatry,* 1981, *14* (2), 135–154.
———. Survival and recovery. *Psychoanalytic Inquiry,* 1981, *5,* (1), 99–130.
Quaytman, W. *Holocaust Survivors: Psychological and Social Sequelae. A Special Issue
   of Journal of Contemporary Psychotherapy,* Spring/Summer 1980, *11* (1).
Solkoff, N. Children of survivors of the Nazi Holocaust: A critical review of the literature.
   American Journal of Orthopsychiatry, 1981, *51,* 29.
———. Survivors of the Holocaust: A critical review of the literature. Catalog of selected
   documents in psychology. (1982) 12(4):47. Ms. 2507.
Wiesel, E. *Night.* New York: Avon, 1958.

Index

About the Editors and Contributors

Paul Marcus is a clinical psychologist in private practice and Secretary of the Group for the Psychoanalytic Study of the Effect of the Holocaust on the Second Generation. He has written a number of scholarly articles and has co-edited (with Steven A. Luel) *Psychoanalytic Reflections on the Holocaust: Selected Essays (1984)*. He is currently under contract to write a book with Alan Rosenberg entitled *The Faith of Holocaust Survivors: A Psychological Inquiry* (Praeger).

Alan Rosenberg is Lecturer in the Department of Philosophy at Queens College, the City University of New York. He is the author and co-author of a number of articles and reviews that have appeared in a variety of journals and books, including *Modern Judaism, Journal for the Theory of Social Behavior* and the *Simon Wiesenthal Center Annual*. He is co-editor (with Gerald E. Myers) of E*choes from the Holocaust: Philosophical Reflections on a Dark Time (1988)* and is contracted with Paul Marcus to write a book entitled *Faith After the Holocaust: A Psychological Inquiry* (Praeger).

Moshe Almagor is a faculty member in the Department of Psychology at the University of Haifa. His areas of interest are family therapy, and mood and personality. He is one of the founders of a family therapy clinic in Haifa and consults widely in Israel on family therapy problems.

Martin S. Bergmann, a psychoanalyst in private practice, is co-chairperson of the Group for the Psychoanalytic Study of the Effect of the Holocaust on the Second Generation. He serves on the faculty of the New York Freudian Society and the National Psychological Association for Psychoanalysis and is co-editor (with Frank R. Hartman) of *The Evolution of Psychoanalytic Technique* (1976) and *Generations of the Holocaust* (with Milton E. Jucovy, 1982).

Martin S. Cohen is currently rabbi of the Beth Tikvah Congregation and is on the faculty in the Department of Religion at the University of British Columbia. He holds a Ph.D. in Ancient Judaism from the Jewish Theological Seminary and is a former Lady Davis Fellow in Jewish Thought at the Hebrew University of Jerusalem. He has taught on various aspects of Jewish Studies at the Hochschule für Jüdische Studien in Heidelberg, West Germany.

Eva Fogelman is a psychotherapist in private practice. She is the co-director of the training program for Counseling with Holocaust Survivors and Second Generation at the Training Institute for Mental Health. She also directs the Foundation to Sustain Christian Rescuers at the Anti-Defamation League of B'nai B'rith and was the writer and co-producer of the award-winning documentary, *Breaking the Silence: The Generation After the Holocaust*.

Joan T. Freyberg is a psychologist-psychoanalyst in private practice. She is a faculty member and superviser at the Postgraduate Center for Mental Health and is the deputy secretary general of the International Federation of Psychoanalytic Societies. She has written a number of scholarly articles on the second generation, fantasy, and the treatment of narcissism.

Janet Hadda is Professor of Yiddish at the University of California, Los Angeles, and is a member of the Southern California Psychoanalytic Institute. Her most recent book is *Passionate Women, Passive Men: Suicide in Yiddish Literature (1987)*. She also maintains a private practice in psychoanalysis.

Zev Harel is Professor of Social Sciences at Cleveland State University. He is a fellow of the Gerontological Society of America and chairs the Fellowship Committee. He is co-editor of several books on aging, including the *Vulnerable Aged* (1974) and the *Black Elderly* (1983). He has also served as chairperson of the Study Section in Aging of the American Orthopsychiatric Association.

Milton E. Jucovy is a member of the Faculty and Training and Supervising Analyst at the New York Psychoanalytic Institute and former President of the New York Psychoanalytic Society. He is Supervising Psychiatrist at both Long Island Jewish–Hillside Medical Center and North Shore University Hospital and is co-editor (with Martin S. Bergmann) of *Generations of the Holocaust* (1982).

Boaz Kahana is Professor of Psychology at Cleveland State University and Director of its Center on Applied Gerontological Research. He is Fellow of the Gerontological Society of America and past Chairman of the Study Section on Aging of the American Orthopsychiatric Association. He has published extensively in the area of clinical psychology and aging and has served on study sections of the National Institutes of Mental Health.

Eva Kahana is Professor and Chairperson of the Department of Sociology of Case Western Reserve University. She also directs the Elderly Care Research Center and is a fellow of the Gerontological Society of America. She has served as Chair of the latter's section on Behavioral and Social Sciences and is a recipient of their Distinguished Membership Award. Her publications have focused on environmental influences on aging individuals.

Judith S. Kestenberg is co-Chairperson of the Group for the Psychoanalytic Study of the Effect of the Holocaust on the Second Generation and founder of the Jerome Riker International Study of Organized Persecution of Children. She is Clinical Professor of Psychiatry, Division of Psychoanalytic Education, New York University, and author of numerous professional articles on Holocaust survivors and their offspring. She is author of *Children and Parents* (1975).

Robert Krell was born in Holland and survived the war in hiding. He is the Clinical Director of the Child and Family Psychiatry Outpatient Department at the Health Sciences Centre Hospital at the University of British Columbia. He has been Visiting Professor of Psychiatry at the Hebrew University and at the U.C.L.A. Neuropsychiatric Institute. He has published a number of articles in professional journals and is co-editor (with Leon Eitinger) of the bibliography *The Psychological and Medical Effects of Concentration Camps and Related Persecutions on Survivors of the Holocaust* (1985).

George M. Kren is Professor of History at Kansas State University. He is the author of many articles on psychohistory and the Holocaust. He is the co-author (with Leon Rappoport) of the *The Holocaust and the Crisis of Human Behavior* (1980) and co-editor of *Varieties of Psychohistory* (1986).

Gloria R. Leon is a Professor, and Director of Clinical Psychology at the University of Minnesota. Her areas of research are stress and coping, personality stability, and change in dealing with severe trauma, and eating disorders. She has conducted research on Vietnam veterans and Holocaust survivors which has been published in a number of journals.

Anna Ornstein is a psychoanalyst in private practice. She is Professor of Child Psychiatry at the University of Cincinnati Medical Center and the Co-Director of the International Center for the Study of Psychoanalytic Self-Psychology. She has published a number of articles and studies on trauma and treatment issues with survivors.

Esther Perel is a family therapist in private practice. She is a consultant to both the Center on Ethnicity, Behavior and Communication of the American Jewish

Committee and the Jewish Board of Family and Children's Services in New York City.

Margrit Wreschner Rustow, a survivor, is a psychoanalyst in private practice. She is a supervisor and faculty member at the Metropolitan Institute for Psychotherapy and has taught at the Institute of the New York Counseling and Guidance Service. She has published articles on the treatment of Holocaust survivors and related subjects in the *Israel Journal of Psychiatry and Related Disciplines* and the *American Journal of Psychiatry*.

Jack Saul is a psychologist in private practice and the Director, Child and Family Treatment, Pace Health Services, in New York City. He is a former research associate, Jerusalem Center for the Study of Psychosocial Trauma and the Holocaust.

Gerald L. Skolnik was ordained at the Jewish Theological Seminary of America. He is currently the rabbi at the Forest Hills Jewish Center and serves as President of the Commission on Synagogue Relations of United Jewish Appeal–Federation of Greater New York and as a member of the Board of Governors of the New York Board of Rabbis.

Arlene Steinberg is a psychologist in private practice and staff psychologist at Gouverneur Hospital. Her major professional interest involves the Holocaust, with particular emphasis on its impact on survivors and their children. She has presented numerous papers at various professional meetings including the American Psychological Association.